THE THRILL
OF IT ALL

For Chris Andrews

THE THRILL
OF IT ALL

THE STORY OF BRYAN FERRY &
ROXY MUSIC

David Buckley

André Deutsch

First published in Great Britain in 2004 by

André Deutsch
an imprint of the
Carlton Publishing Group
20 Mortimer Street
London W1T 3JW

The publishers would like to thank the following sources for their kind permission
to reproduce the pictures in this book.

Plate Section 1
Page 1: Audrey Fletcher (middle)/Private collection (top, bottom);
Page 2: Getty Images/Tony McGrath; Page 3: Redferns/Harry Goodwin; Page 4:
Corbis Images/Neal Preston; Page 5: Getty Images/The Observer; Page 6: Redferns/
Glenn A. Baker; Page 7: Redferns/Henrietta Butler; Page 8: Denis O'Reagan

Plate Section 2
Page 1: Retna Pictures Ltd/Michael Putland (top)/Redferns/Dave Ellis (bottom); Page
2: Retna Pictures Ltd/Michael Putland (top)/Rex Features/Brian Moody (bottom);
Page 3: Rex Features/Dezo Hoffman (top)/Rex Features/Brian McCreeth (bottom);
Page 4: Retna Pictures Ltd/Michael Putland; Page 6: Retna Pictures Ltd/Michael
Putland; Page 7: Rex Features; Page 8: Rex Features/Sipa Press

Plate Section 3
Page 1: Rex Features/Sheila Rock; Page 2: PA (top)/Redferns/
Peter Still (bottom); Page 3: Rex Features/Perfect Picture (top)/Rex Features/Sheila
Rock (bottom); Page 4: Rex Features/Richard Young (top)/Rex Features/Richard Young
(bottom); Page 5: Rex Features/Brian Rasic/Rex Features/Brian Rasic (bottom); Page
6: Retna Pictures Ltd/Kelly A. Swift/Rex Features/Richard Young (bottom);
Page 7: Rex Features/Bernadete Lou; Page 8: Rex Features/Ismo Henttonen (top)/
Rex Features/Nigel R. Barklie (bottom)

All lyrical quotations are for the purpose of study or critical analysis only.

Every effort has been made to acknowledge correctly and contact the source and/
or copyright holder of each picture and Carlton Books Limited apologises for any
unintentional errors or omissions that will be corrected in future editions of this book.

Typeset by E-Type, Liverpool
Printed and bound in Great Britain by Mackays

CONTENTS

So many people helped me during the eighteen months I spent researching and writing this book. I would like to thank the following people. To anyone I have left out: my heartfelt apologies:

Ann Henrickson – my wife, in-house editor and the woman who, on Valentines Day 2000, preferred to give her red roses to Bryan Ferry.

Louise and Elsa Buckley (not forgetting the cats, Hoggle and Ziggy Buckley), for looking after the author at home.

Harold and Mabel Buckley.

John Buckley, for that magical moment under the Christmas tree lights, when I was still young enough to believe that Santa himself had dropped off the first Roxy Music album.

Harry Buckley, for his Mike Proctor impersonations.

Ros Edwards, Helenka Fuglewicz, Julia Forrest and all at Edwards Fuglewicz Literary Agency.

Ian Gittins, my editor, for daring to re-form the old *Strange Fascination* double-act, and for so much help during the project.

Lorna Russell, my point of contact at Carlton Books.

Bryan Ferry, for being so gracious and polite on the times we have met.

John O'Brien, curator of the virtual museum that is vivaroxymusic.com and compiler of the excellent discography and videography featured in this book.

John Wetton, for a fun interview and dozens of friendly e-mails.

Grant Coles, for tracking down the originals of almost all of Bryan's cover versions – and listening to them all.

Peter Sinfield, for a fantastic interview (see Peter's website for the text www.songsouponsea.com) and numerous beautifully written e-mails.

I would also like to thank the following people, all of whom were kind enough to answer my questions, either in person or via e-mail:

Paula Brown, Michael Brick, Roger Bunn, Ian Burden, Kevin Cann, Paul Carrack, Chris Charlesworth, Paul Du Noyer, Audrey Fletcher, Guy Fletcher, John Gustafson, Peter Ingvarsson, Eddie Jobson, Zev Katz,

Richard Mills, Philip Oakey, David O'List, Mark Paytress, Mark Radcliffe, Colette Robertson, Mick Rock, Jon Savage, Peter Seely, Steve Severin, Sylvie Simmons, Mat Snow, Garry Tibbs, Robin Trower, Martyn Ware, Richard Williams, Geoff Ward, John Watson, Ashley Wright.

My thanks also go to the following for their practical help and/or moral support:

Angi Andrews, David Beevers, David Blackshaw, Steve Brickle, Beth Buckley, Gill Buckley, Jenny Bulley, Mark Cailes, Chris Difford, Sarah Edwards, Colin Fallows, Klaus Federa, Simon Galloway, Graham Johnstone, Juliet Mann, Mark Paytress, Nigel Reeve, Marc Riley, Steve Thornewill, Chris Turner, Sarah Watson, Alex Weston.

Finally, thanks to Roxy Music – Ta-ra!

THERE'S A NEW
SENSATION ...

"... A fabulous creation ..."
(Roxy Music, "Do The Strand", 1973)

This is a very English story; a tale of against-the-odds success set to the urban drumbeat of post-war popular music. Bryan Ferry, a working-class boy from Washington in the un-trendy north-east of England, had a head full of music and a heart full of sorrow. He became one of Britain's biggest pop stars, before fading year by year from the public view, working so quietly, so preciously, and with such an innate sense of insecurity, that some of us though he'd vanished for good, obscured by a cumulonimbus of self-doubt.

This book attempts to burn off that cloud and reveal the bright, burning star of a genuine pop avatar. For people of a certain vintage (those born between the mid-fifties and the mid-sixties) and a certain intellectual trajectory, Bryan Ferry was, along with David Bowie, Britain's most brilliant pop performer. With an overlapping fanbase, and an ongoing and thorough commitment to style, conjoined with a piercing irony, they appeared to be two sides of the same glam rock coin.

With hindsight, though, there is something altogether different about the Bryan Ferry version of the English pop dream, something so un-rock-star-like that it renders his story unique. While Jagger, Lennon, Bowie, Elton, Bolan and Rod are brash self-publicists who could work the room at parties, make opportunistic gestures, stage grand rock spec-tacles and, at times, border on the degenerate in their private lives, Ferry is a very different animal, with a more personal and reflective approach. Both Ferry himself and some of his closest supporters and advisers regarded Roxy Music as apart from the cruder elements of the seventies' quest for superstardom. Ferry has always been something for the connoisseur.

Fashion designer and close friend Antony Price has spoken of him as a man trapped in "het hell", a gay man in every sense other than his sexuality – the perfect description of this uncommonly fussy and obsessively stylish *artiste*. Roxy Music was Ferry's baby, his vision: others could contribute the odd line, even the occasional near-show-stealing scene, but he, Ferry, was the stage director, editor and producer rolled into one. Good at talent-spotting and brave in surrounding himself with a circle of like-minded creative talent, he was very much the *auteur*, or at least thought himself to be.

Many musicians, however, consider Ferry to be uncommonly dependent on his support network. He might be the still-beating heart, but the connective tissue, the exoskeleton of sound has ultimately seldom been his, constructed as it is by an ever-growing roster of hired hands and collaborators. Never a great musician in performance terms, and as a singer at times sometimes lacking in confidence in the studio, he needs the back-up of experienced musicians. Despite this fundamental weakness at the heart of his creative process, Ferry nevertheless has the central vision. Desperate to retain command over the final product, happy to collaborate, he is often unhappy to delegate. The quest for perfection would lead him, delude him, and come close to destroying him as an artist: "It's like a gift, you don't know where the hell it comes from, creating things," says Ferry. "So you feel responsible to' yourself to make everything as good as you can."

Nowadays, pop is entertainment; in the seventies, it was culture. The music made by the rockers in the quake/wake of the Beatles' demise was not a lazy reaction to then-recent events; it was genuinely pioneering and agenda-setting, an almost implausible concept given today's rock scene. Yet Ferry remained wracked with self-doubt, a poor self-publicist. While Bowie and Lennon gave journalists superb copy and were fleet of foot when pressed in interviews, Ferry has seldom warmed to the press, giving the impression of disdain for the whole wretched process of media promotion, as if it were beneath him: "I always feel vaguely embarrassed talking about myself," he said in 1982. "There's something not quite right about it. Plus, I like to think that the work speaks for itself and doesn't need footnotes."

Ferry's relative media-shyness has, of course, served to obfuscate the story of his life and work. *The Thrill of It All* is the first step towards a clearer and more complete picture of a man who, it might reasonably be claimed, is uncommonly preoccupied by issues of privacy to the point where even the most harmless and mundane of biographical details are worried over before given up for public consumption. "There is a common element in the creation of a star," said rock archivist and historian Victor Fader in 1975. "By keeping details of your genesis shrouded in mist you create mystery. The few facts that do emerge are enlarged upon, deified, become mythic in their import."

On one level, the Bryan Ferry story is simply one more tale of a hunted creature trying to put us all off the scent, frightened of the media kill but thrilled by the chase. Despite his uniqueness, he is also, simultaneously, very much part of the pop world and the star-making machinery. Like almost all the great pop icons, Ferry has deliberately sought to mystify his origins, to keep a vacuum seal on his personal life and to cover his tracks, often with backfiring results. Checking into hotels under assumed names (Mr Bagley is apparently a favourite), dressing down to go out, for years avoiding all contact with the media: it's a manifestation of an outward disdain for the press, and at the same time a very real fear of rejection. Yet despite his obvious need to retain a tight hold over what information is on the record and what isn't, Ferry's high-society, model-dating lifestyle makes him easy prey for the tabloids. Unlike his contemporary, David Bowie, a much bigger star who is able to lead a private life of virtual anonymity, Ferry just keeps being eaten up by tabloid speculation. As every love affair is publicly dissected, Ferry is eviscerated in newsprint.

One journalist commented that Ferry was the only person she had ever seen visibly shrink back in his chair when she entered the room to interview him. Seldom has someone so unsuited to a life in the media sought out that life so brazenly, while at the same time, like all other rock stars, reserving the right to anonymity and reaping the financial rewards celebrity brings. By 2003, his personal estate was valued at £30m, yet Ferry was still reportedly discontented with his lot, a handful of similar-vintage rockers having amassed a fortune five or ten times that of Ferry's.

Bryan Ferry became a star despite avoiding so many of the routes into self-publicity open to the rock singer. A short-lived dalliance in the mid-seventies excepted, he's rarely appeared on TV chat shows and the like. The result is that the public perception of Ferry is that of a rather cold, patrician, aloof *artiste*. This perception is only partly correct: easily embarrassed, shy, and sensitive, he is nevertheless witty, charming and unfailingly courteous to fans. But there's still something odd about a man who often avoids eye contact, who is wont to pace around the room, suddenly lurching to one side before quickly turning around as if snapping to, in an attempt to regain concentration and control through gestures of a conversation which he might be in danger of losing through words.

Whilst he has never been a total stranger to the unholy trinity of sex, drugs and rock 'n' roll, there has never been any street-savvy or edge to Ferry. Although not beyond throwing the occasional luvvie tantrum, in the main he is the perfect gentleman, generous to fans, although sometimes dealing with his workmates with a single-mindedness bordering on, if not ruthlessness, then often a certain slightly pious disregard. Empathy feeling has never been one of Ferry's stronger attributes, as a few disaffected *hors de combat* ex-collaborators will later attest

Having a fastidiousness, an attention to detail and a sense of quiet style completely at odds with the sense of youthful rebellion of the rock world, Ferry possesses a filmic cool, and a more painterly approach to making music. In the eighties and nineties he would self-finance endless recording sessions, quite prepared to suffer for his art and to pay for the privilege of doing so. His songs were like canvasses: he had so many works in progress that he would fiddle and tinker with them for years before deeming them fit for public approval, or leaving them half-finished and abandoned for ever. He sank into depression and into a mid-life crisis which was to cost him dearly, both financially, as the endless dithering over *Mamouna*, the 1994 album that would eventually be released to a lukewarm critical reception having involved 111 musicians at a reported cost of £800,000 to the Ferry coffers, as well as artistically, as Ferry lost his relevance and the public's patience.

"We all makes mistakes," Ferry told me in 1999. "It would be so boring if life were all one straight line, but, I'm afraid, it's all ups and downs and severe turbulence most of the time in my life." "He's such a painter with his words and such a mournful, sad guy beneath his suave exterior," is how his first producer, Peter Sinfield, puts it. "I don't know if you've ever seen his paintings, but they are huge canvasses of black and dark green, quite doomy ... very Rothkoesque."

This was all a far cry from the time when Bryan Ferry was arguably the best songwriter of his day, a young and, generally speaking, happy man. His early lyrics were either situationist slogans to be read out to shock the bourgeoisie, or the sort of mini-manifestos so beloved by the Dadaists in the 1910s: "There's a new sensation!", "Make me a deal, and make it straight", "Stay cool is still the main rule" or "Throwaway lines often ring true". He tested the limits of the absurd: "Badgers couldn't compensate at twice the price", "Too much cheesecake too soon" and "Just like flamingos look the same", whilst peppering his songs with punning masterstrokes: ("and the bridge, it sighs!", "Turn up the music, hi as fi can go"). Most of his lyrics were written and rewritten, revised and re-evaluated, and some were left on the cutting-room floor for decades before being redeployed. The words for Ferry's 2002 song "San Simeon", for example, were unused originals written for the classic "In Every Dream Home A Heartache" almost two decades before.

For two or three years in the seventies, Ferry mined a rich, unbroken seam of creativity. Observant of the powerful new strains of irony and postmodernism bubbling under the surface of British culture at the time, his songs made sly references to the process of becoming a rock star ("We've been around a long time/to try, to try to try to make the big time"), poked fun at old, worn-out sixties pop, and alluded across generic divides to film and art, whilst retaining an alien, trash aesthetic and a poppy beat. But always, always, Ferry's songs were things of genuine beauty. Never has mainstream pop been so romantic as "A Song For Europe"; never has there been so complete a pop art statement as "In Every Dream Home A Heartache".

Reflected in his art, Ferry's private life has seldom been a happy one. Often downbeat and gloomy as a person, one suspects he seeks out more vibrant, upbeat people for companionship and love; very often such companions have been much younger than him. Ferry having always been attracted to glamour and beauty; the cover girls adorning the Roxy albums and stage shows are now legendary, if not downright infamous. He has also, one suspects, always seen himself in the role of father figure. His relationship with teenage model Jerry Hall, his marriage to Lucy Helmore and his brief, and highly public, tryst with a backing singer and dancer thirty-five years his junior all reveal an attraction for much younger partners. One of Ferry's most recent (and best) songs is "Goddess Of Love", a story of unrequited love for that most perfect of icons of sexuality: Marilyn Monroe. His love unrequited, the object of his desires doomed, the song is the leitmotif in the tragic melodramas of his own life.

Ferry has so often written about love gained and lost that it might be tempting to dismiss him as a pedlar of clichés and hackneyed old themes. Yet this would be wrong, for, whilst his least successful songs may seem trite or sentimental, his best have a sense of nostalgia and history that make them unique. What is so striking about Ferry's whole approach to pop is that it is dialogical, a two-way conversation between the past and the present. Ferry's music (particularly his solo work) isn't merely interested in the recent past either. He was the first of the new pop stars to make us appreciate that there had been a pop music scene before the Beatles, before Elvis Presley. Ferry loves the balladeers, the songwriting craftsmen of the thirties, and the jazz and bluesmen and women of the forties, and throughout his career (and borrowing from one of his favourite artists Duchamp) he has produced what he calls "ready-mades", covers of the long-forgotten hits of his father's youth.

And the same sense of ordered decorum of the more polite and genteel world of the pre-rock 'n' roll era has always been part of the Ferry musical genetic code. It's given him an aloof and precious air in the rock world of degradation and excess, but it's also meant that, in a way, he hasn't aged. The white-tuxedoed super-cool Bogart-inspired image of the 28-year-old man that graced his second solo album, *Another Time, Another Place*, might have reduced Ferry in the eyes of some to a cartoon or cliché of smug music-biz wealth and high manners, but it's also the sort of filmic look that sits just as easily on the 58-year-old of today. As Ferry approaches his sixtieth year on the planet, he's never looked ungraceful or foolish, but remained resolute in his attempts at pop perfection. Not interested in style-hopping, he's almost never attempted to entrap the latest pop trend; his musical world remaining peculiarly untouched by the music generated outside of it. This has meant that his music has remained self-consciously detached from the pop world for over twenty years, in a dreamy melancholy that is both conservative and solipsistic.

Whichever way you look at it, though, there is no getting away from the fact that Ferry's impact on rock culture was made with Roxy Music. The worst of Roxy's eight albums is still better than the very best Bryan Ferry solo album. And it was Roxy Music that inspired young musicians at the time. David Bowie is a long-standing admirer. Early punks such as Siouxsie Sioux saw behind the suave carapace of sly sophistication and discovered the dark soul of a pop pioneer; Siouxsie and the Banshees formed after meeting at a Roxy gig. Kevin Rowland, Elvis

Costello and Midge Ure were all Ferry fanatics. Even journalist Julie Burchill fell for his charms, along with that most acute observer of London's style wars, Peter York. Spandau Ballet's Tony Hadley, Japan's David Sylvian and teen idols Duran Duran all made early-eighties music in the image of their master, and took out Ferry's haircut on permanent loan. Morrissey's camp witticisms are also cut from the same cloth as those of Ferry. "I believe that sort of sad chap, Morrissey, is a progeny of mine," said Ferry, "though I don't think he is nearly as virile. I'm fairly certain that Robert Smith, of the Cure, is a descendant somewhere down the line ..." Jim Moir, aka comedian Vic Reeves, has always had a touch of the Bryan Ferry about him; ditto Jonathan Ross and his dandyisms.

Yet, as writer Ian Gittins so aptly says, whilst Ferry was a "tremendous inspiration" he was also a "terrible influence". At least initially, Ferry appeared to lampoon the fashion world, seeming to play the glamour game rather than actually living it. A new breed of singers took it all too literally; their attempt at cool sophistication was all too often bland and insipid. Dreadful wine-bar music, wobbly crooning, young men in bad suits; it was all there in the mid-eighties. Even the smugness of "quintessentially English" Hugh Grant from the world of film could be a distant echo of the Ferry legacy. Ferry himself has always cultivated the mainstream market too. For every classic slice of demon art rock there has been a clunky chunk of middlebrow, safe, inoffensive schlock for the wider audience. Too often Ferry has allowed himself to be filed under mainstream, and mainstream of the worst kind.

No, it's Ferry's Roxy years which will be largely regarded as the music that matters, and it is the Roxy story, not Ferry's solo career or those of his fellow Roxy bedfellows, that rightly dominates the pages of *The Thrill of It All*. Ferry's astonishing, ululating voice, like Brian Eno's spacey synths and Andy Mackay's squealing-pig saxophone, might have possessed a very personal relationship to pitch, but it was this very sense of the untutored that fired their music and made it unique. They were uninterested in making music that sounded like any of the touchstones of modern recorded music of their day: they didn't want to sound like the Beatles, they didn't want to be virtuosos, they didn't want to play the blues. Their rejection of their era made them great. The music of Roxy Music was nothing if not eccentric, with its strange musical contours and unexpected twists and turns; thirty years on, it is music which, at its best, is as mystical and radical as any being made today.

Roxy Music and Bryan Ferry also pulled off something comparatively rare within pop: they appealed to both sexes. Women found Ferry sex-on-a-stick attractive. With none of Jagger's almost goat-like carnality (as Angie Bowie once famously commented) or Bowie's air of gamine otherness, Ferry has nevertheless always attracted a healthy mainstream heterosexual lust and a huge gay following to boot. Whilst both sexes love the sense of play, the irony, and the sheer depth of the music, sexiness combined with high literacy and intelligence is the perfect cultural cocktail for many an aspirant intellectual.

For those of us lucky enough to have witnessed Roxy Music's first push for stardom (my own first encounter with the band came in December 1973 when, just short of my ninth birthday, I watched them perform the classic "Street Life" on *Top of The Pops*) will recall a thrilling collision of signs and musical motifs, coupled with garish, unforgettable looks. I'd just missed out on Captain Eno, Roxy Music's astonishing avant-garde soul, removed from the band in June of that year. But the Roxy I grew up with and loved still made some of the best pop music of the times, from "Love Is The Drug" through to the late-period classics like "Dance Away", "Same Old Scene" and "More Than This". There was never a bad Roxy single.

Counterfactual history may be pointless but it's also good fun. With Eno, Roxy Music was a force for change. Without Eno, they gained a hitherto unattained professionalism and musicianship at the expense of their sense of cool and danger. What if Eno had stayed? In many ways, Ferry's career never really recovered from the blow of Eno's departure. Some will always judge Ferry's career, and that of Roxy Music in general, as the great missed opportunity. Seldom has one band contained two such leaders, creative geniuses and cultural icons, and the fact that Ferry and Eno couldn't find a way of accommodating each other's outré whims and astonishing creativity is surely one of rock's most glaring examples of "what might have been", their severed alliance in 1973 just as significant as the dissolution of the Morrissey/Marr partnership in the Smiths in 1987. It's an important thread in this new history of Roxy Music, because missed opportunities and errors of judgement mark the career path of Ferry. His is a story of great triumphs, but also of dead-ends, distractions, turmoil and tears.

The Thrill of It All contains direct input from former band members, friends, producers, ex-managers, fans and writers, and indeed new testimony from Bryan Ferry himself: I had the pleasure of speaking to him in 1999 and meeting him on two subsequent occasions. It's a loving tribute to an old-style gentleman, and a great talent more deserving of our attention and of a place in rock history than hitherto acknowledged. There have been no inductions to halls of fame, no *Q* awards, and no honours' lists for Bryan Ferry or Roxy Music. Nebulous and diffuse, they appear to this day unknowable and ineffable, part of a quiet revolution within pop. Too mainstream to be cult, too precious and plain weird to ever be globally successful, they've been dismissed in the annals of rock history, reduced to a few paragraphs, whilst others take centre stage. That is, until now....

David Buckley
Munich

DIDN'T YOU USED TO BE BRYAN FERRY?

It's a well-known scenario. After years of taking to the streets in false beards, wigs, woolly scarves and scruffy duffle coats – in fact, anything that reinforces the image of the rock star in mufti – there comes a time when the disguises are no longer necessary. The burnt-out red dwarves of the third-division rock game, former pop celebrities are left to pick through the cosmic debris of a once glowing, brilliant career, perhaps to appear on a retro package of half-remembered acts, the odd game show, or to pen an autobiography for an uninterested public long after their fan base has disappeared. The very British love of the underdog is seldom extended to the vicissitudes of tarnished idolatry within the pop world. Because, when you're down, the public and, particularly, the journalists love to count you out.

So, spare a thought for Bryan Ferry, sitting in the back of a taxi in the late nineties. Certainly no third division rock star, but not a Premiership act either. A handsome man in his early fifties, slightly stooped, his dark brown hair, once dyed raven black, now beginning to grey: a star from the seventies and eighties who had been largely hitless for over a decade. In the seventies he was to be seen in exclusive nightclubs with beautiful models, or earnestly interrogating the canvasses at trendy vernissages; his band, Roxy Music, was one of the most influential of its time. In the eighties he had played on the global jukebox that was Live Aid, singing to an audience of scores of millions. Now he's wealthy, and still sporadically writing and performing, but his cultural cachet has long been diminished by a dozen years of uneven work. Perhaps jealous of his contemporaries, the Bowies, the Rods and the Eltons who broke onto the scene in the glam wars of a quarter of a century ago, all now multimillionaires, he pleads poverty. He's still recognised, of course, still working, but not quite the superstar his early career had promised.

On the day in question, this shy, rather self-effacing man is chatting to the driver as they negotiate the evening rush hour on the way back to his home stuio in west London, his daily place of work. Ferry might be out of the limelight but he's not idle. For month after month he's been recording, singing, honing his craft in an endless search for the perfect pop song. "What do you do nowadays, then? Didn't you used to be Bryan Ferry?" enquires the driver. "Yeah, I did," replies the man in the back wryly, seeing the lighter side.

This was *still* Bryan Ferry of course, but the previous decade had been none too kind to him. In that time he had managed to release just one album of original songs, and one album of cover versions. His record company had been so unhappy with his latest product that they had decided not to release it, an astonishing, and depressing turnaround in fortune for a man with gold discs on his walls. The years of superstardom had gone. Ferry had always claimed not to be a pop star, and had spoken – with good reason – of his music as art, but now even the filmic grandeur of his superstardom appeared wan and faded.

What went before, and what happened next, is the story of *The Thrill Of It All*. It's the tale of how one of the biggest pop draws of the seventies resurrected his career with a duo of new solo albums and a remade-remodelled nostalgia trip. It's the story of one of the most influential bands of the seventies: Roxy Music, the band that fused irony, electronica, fashion and pop into a seamless entity that inspired a whole generation of musicians. And it's the story of one of Britain's most influential artists of the pop era.

The sassiness, the sexiness, the lasciviousness, and the glamour chase of the seventies that made Bryan Ferry the huge star he is had rather humble origins. Unlike those rock stars who claim working-class heritage when in fact they were brought up very comfortably in a suburb such as, oh, I don't know, Burnage or Woolton, Bryan Ferry, despite the tuxedos, the air of the suave old toff and the high-art trappings, is in fact a *true* working-class hero. It all began nearly sixty years ago in an era of tin bathtubs, outside lavs, ration books, and the quest to be other. Got to search for something new …

PART ONE

1945-1973

WASHINGTON BLUES: 1945–1968

"We're all totally alone anyway and we never will understand"
Bryan Ferry, 1973

Alone atop an Alpine scree, the wanderer stands and contemplates the futility of existence, a swirl of mist and a seemingly endless vista of mountain upon mountain before him. It's perhaps one of the most resonant images of the Romantic period in pictorial art in continental Europe, portraying the idea of humankind as forever wandering, spirited away to another level of consciousness through communion with a higher being, bewitched by a rarefied concept of beauty. The torture of existence and, at the same time, the consolations of solitude – these are the inspirations behind the true doomed romantic spirit. This is the sort of image associated with many so-called tortured geniuses throughout the next 200 years; *male* artists, garret-bound and driven to near madness by their creativity, the quest for the divine spirit always somehow just beyond their grasp. And it is this image, the image of the artist in rapture but also in torture, which we associate with Bryan Ferry. More accurately, it's the image Ferry created for himself at a very young age.

In adulthood most of us cast off our nascent and unrealisable dreams and enter the real world of harsh reality rather than the dream world of the artist or bohemian. But Bryan Ferry simply never grew up. Like so many celebrities, his fame arrived just in time to confirm and preserve him in his idiosyncrasies. Stardom is a way of keeping infantile dreams alive: dreams of being popular, special, different, noticed. It's little wonder that the world of celebrity is one of emotional constipation. The rest of us mostly learn to throw off most of our adolescent imaginings, but in rock people pay you, and protect you, to be as odd as you like.

3

And the quest for perfection! Bryan Ferry took it to rarefied and, at times, ridiculous extremes.

Despite the wealth and fame, the impression Ferry gives is that he never truly enjoys his artistry. The pain of creation is always too much: ask Bryan Ferry how he is, and the reply won't be a polite "fine, thank you" but a mumbled "so so". His dialogue will be littered with non-vocalised evasions, despairing murmurs of, "Oh, I don't know", and mildly inquisitive retorts of, "Oh, really?" This is a man whose art has a worry ulcer.

So, as in Caspar David Friedrich's 1818 painting, *The Wanderer*, the enduring image of Bryan Ferry is that of the tortured, lovelorn romantic. The tuxedoed, bequiffed rock star with the cinematic cool of a Bogart-like film star of the forties, drawing on a St. Moritz, submerged in sound, turning his back on the crowd as the piano figure of "A Song For Europe" echoes round the hall. Yet if this is the undying image of Ferry the rock star, the life of Ferry the man is, perhaps, rather different. In place of the unending Alpine panorama, the beautifully coiffured blue-black hair (initially dyed, by the way), and the elegantly groomed glamour, there first of all lay the grime and grit of post-war north-east England and the cold reality of the ration book.

The man famously dubbed by the critics the "coolest man in Britain" and the "Sultan of Suave" arrived on September 26, 1945 in Washington, County Durham: "an orchid born on a coal-tip," as he would later say. David Bowie shares his birthday with Elvis Presley, and, perhaps equally appropriately, Ferry shares his birthday with both George Gershwin and T.S. Eliot, a fact which did not go unnoticed by Ferry himself: "It's weird, when I started reading Eliot, I really felt incredibly close to some of the things I read. I could feel this. It's fabulous when you do that, when you discover somebody who you like, when you kind of feel those feelings, even though he articulates them better. He would probably be my favourite poet. Some of it is really beautiful and sad, haunting. Words can be very powerful. I find them very difficult."

The domestic circumstances were straitened, but not truly impoverished. Ferry, the only boy in the family, had two sisters, one elder, Ann, and one younger, Enid. Father Frederick Charles Ferry (1908-84), a former farm-worker turned pony-handler in the Glebe Pit during the Depression, was a humble, unassuming, hard-working man, and always supportive of his son. "He was much liked: very special; very quiet. He was a Thomas Hardy figure," recalls his son. "I loved him more than anybody really." He courted Ferry's mum wearing spats and riding a carthorse with a sprig of lavender in his buttonhole. "He was a bit of throwback, which was why I loved him so much," Ferry has reminisced. "My father used to win prizes for his ploughing but during the Depression the farm failed and he had to work underground, tending pit ponies. He courted my mother for ten years before they got married. It brings a tear to my eye every time I think about it."

"My parents thought my childhood was incredibly well off compared with theirs," Ferry told the *Mail On Sunday* in 2001:

> They lived in houses without electricity or running water, breaking the ice before breakfast. I loved hearing those stories. When my dad was courting my mother, he lived in the country and she lived in the town. Dad used to ride to see her on a plough horse, wearing a bowler hat and spats. That embarrassed her terribly. They courted for ten years, because he didn't have enough money to marry her. Eventually they did marry and lived in a little farm cottage. He was a farm labourer and used to win medals for ploughing. Then it was the Depression. Things got so bad that my father had to go to work down the mine, looking after the pit ponies. It was a country job, but underground. It must have been awful for him. He earned a pittance of a wage – much less than a regular miner. He gave it all to my mother, and she'd give him tobacco money for his pipe. We could only get more well off after that.

Unsurprisingly, Fred Ferry maintained a life-long dislike of being underground and away from the sunlight, and, as a result, loved hard work in the open air and in the garden. After his stint down the mines, he worked as a gardener at Cook's Hall, a local manor house about half-a-mile away from where Bryan lived during his school days. Much later, when Bryan asked his elderly dad to live with him, he would work tirelessly in the expansive Ferry grounds at his Sussex home without much auxiliary help. Ferry senior would maintain the gardens and, according to Antony Price, "ride around on a lawnmower wearing a mad hat, having a whale of a time." Bryan would urge his father to get a taxi to a local pub for a break, but no: Fred walked. In a world full of nannies, minders, bodyguards, PA's and other retainers to the courtly rock star, Fred Ferry's down-to-earth nature must have been an important reminder of more humble origins and unglamorous roots. "He had this story about this man who was mistreating ponies," says Ferry. "And he had to punch him. He got hauled up by the boss of the pit, and thought he was going to get the sack. But the boss said, 'Well done, Fred. Somebody had to do that; we all wanted to.' Because he was a very good boxer, my dad."

As a child, Ferry remembers his father waking up well before sunrise to milk the cows. "He was the most humble, unassuming man I've ever known, and he and my mother gave me a really lasting set of values," said Ferry in 2000. "There was no car, no phone, and, until 1953, no television set. Newcastle United reaching the FA Cup final, not the Coronation, was the reason for the installation of a rented set." Now, there is a danger that the middle-aged Ferry, sipping a lightly-chilled Sauvignon at the Savoy Grill, might be mistaken for one of the characters out of Monty Python's biting "Four Yorkshiremen" sketch, the self-made man looking back at the horrors of a bleak, northern, working-class upbringing: "Of course, we had it tough." However, unlike many of the rockers of his vintage who could count on the financial support of well-off middle-class parents, or who felt comfortable in a bookish environment, Ferry grew up in the culture of the labouring classes.

Ferry's strikingly good-looking mother, Mary Ann Ferry (1909-91), who was also frequently known as Polly, idolised her only son and instilled in him the importance of good manners. "The family would have high tea with knives and forks and napkins when others would have a bit of bread and jam and a quick wipe round the mouth with a cloth," remembers a neighbour, Fry Betley. "Bryan was always well-turned out, even as a nipper." But there was coldness too: "We never talked intimately at all – [we were] very working class in that sense," said Ferry a few years after his mother's death. "We were as quiet as mice, eating high tea in front of the television."

Audrey Fletcher, who attended school with Bryan, also remembers the Ferry family:

> Bryan and his mum were very close. She and husband Fred started their family late in life, but were nevertheless blessed with three children: Ann, Bryan and Enid. They were warm and caring parents who always had their children's interests at heart, and who always took pride in their children's achievements.
>
> Ann was a teacher for many years at the Washington Village Primary School but I believe she has now retired. Well, she would be in her early sixties. My niece was in her class, oh, it must be thirty

years ago now. Ann used to live on the John F. Kennedy Estate, and she would often come into the Village Green Library when I worked there in the mid-sixties. My mum was friends with Bryan's mum. Bryan's younger sister is Enid. She would be about five years younger, I reckon. Because she is younger than me, I actually know very little about her. However, she also went to the Washington Grammar School. Bryan has always been close to his Aunt Clara. I think she is his mum's sister, but I'm not sure. My husband's aunt used to live next door to Bryan's uncle, so twenty or so years ago we used to get all the news just about first-hand.

[Bryan's parents] spent their early years of marriage in the war years in a downstairs, two-bedroom flat in a street named Model Dwellings, directly opposite the Glebe School. Today the Glebe School is renamed the John F. Kennedy School in remembrance of the assassinated President of the United States. When the new council houses were built about a quarter of a mile away, around 1950, Bryan's parents were offered an up and downstairs house in Gainsborough Avenue, which had all mod cons, including a fitted kitchen and a bathroom. There was also a big back garden, which suited Bryan's dad down to the ground.

Bryan's grandma, Mrs. Meynell, lived directly across the main road, at 16 The Terraces. Built in 1921, these were large three-bedroom houses with a scullery, a huge kitchen with big black range, a front room used only for weddings and funerals, and a downstairs bathroom. The toilet was in the backyard, for hygiene reasons. Mrs. Meynell didn't like the idea of electricity and even as late as the mid-fifties, she still had her house all gas. We lived next door in number 15.

Bryan spent his toddler years in Model Dwellings, where the tin bath hung in the back yard, alongside the toilet. Toilet paper wasn't in vogue then: no one could have afforded it anyway. Instead, newspaper torn into squares hung on a nail behind the door. During the winter months it was a real adventure going to the toilet, shielding the candle from going out then watching the shadows dancing on the toilet wall. If the cistern was frozen over, a bucket of water was used to flush the toilet.

There always seemed to be a lot of snow back then, but to us youngsters it spelt the excitement of snowmen, snowball fights, sledges and slides. We loved the fresh air and would gather under the glow of the street lamps until called in for bed. On the long summer nights the whole street would be outside, the women in their pinnies, the men having a smoke, and the children playing a game of rounders or footy.

My dad always said that church was for those who had money and wore kid gloves, while the chapels were for the working classes. Consequently most children in mining villages attended chapel, and Bryan was no exception. Like the rest of us he attended the Methodist Chapel in Station Road and the Mission Hall in Brady Square where Dora Richardson was his Sunday School teacher.

Music was vitally important. Bryan's earliest memory is a musical one: his first piano lesson, which he had when he was five years old. "I remember coming home with my little music case and sitting down and playing this scale. My sister, who was a great pianist, then came in and started teasing me, saying, 'No, you don't do it like that, you do it like this!' She then sat down and started playing Beethoven's *Moonlight Sonata* very well. I got angry and started punching her and I never took another piano lesson." Ferry's mum, Polly, a sentimentalist, loved the ballads of the thirties and forties. However it would be Aunty Enid who introduced Bryan at a very early age to the popular music of the day: "She used to baby-sit and play 78s of Nat 'King' Cole, the Inkspots and Billy Eckstine; the first real music I ever heard."

As a child, Ferry received a good education and was a diligent and able schoolboy, recalls Audrey Fletcher:

> There were two schools in the local vicinity: the Glebe and the Biddick. In the fifties, most parents hoped that their children would be accepted at the Glebe because the pass rate there for the Washington Grammar School was extraordinarily high. Being a mining community they didn't want their children to end up down the mines; they wanted something better for them. Bryan's parents thought no differently, and they were pleased when all three of their children attended first the Glebe and then the grammar school.

The reason for this grammar school entry success rate was Miss Swaddle, who was the teacher of the final year students at the Glebe School, preparing them for the Eleven Plus exam. She instilled in her students, including Bryan, a love of learning, literature and art. Concerning art, at which Bryan excelled, Friday afternoons were spent on planning, preparing then painting a huge frieze, which eventually covered the whole of the back classroom wall. Every student was involved and the frieze, which was usually based upon some aspect of literature, would be several months in the making. Miss Swaddle was so well liked and appreciated by her students that every year they would each pitch in a sixpence and present her with an end of school year thank-you present.

Ferry has spoken of feeling "out of place" in his junior school years, yet has very fond memories of Miss Swaddle:

> She was incredible. Very tall. She always wore spotless white plimsolls and long skirts to mid-calf. Very glamorous; looked like one of those fifties models. Eyes in the back of her head. She'd be writing on the board, then get the duster and whack you with it, a dead shot ... This is in the days when they used to clip children ... I'm personally all for it. Anyway, Miss Swaddle got us writing essays. I was a bit sad, used to write these really sad stories, and there was one in particular. She knelt by my desk and said, "Where did that come from? You have such an imagination." And I really did just look at her then [widens eyes boyishly] like my heroine ... I didn't feel I fitted in at all, otherwise. And it was pretty much the same at grammar school.

Football would bind the community together, and Bryan was a keen sportsman, despite his shyness. Audrey Fletcher continues:

> Football was an important aspect of life in Washington. The miners and chemical workers usually followed Newcastle United; in the first half of the week they would discuss the previous Saturday's match, and in the second half of the week they would discuss the up-and-coming game. Like Fred and Polly Ferry, my parents also got a television set in 1953 and for the same reason: to watch the FA Cup Final and the Queen's Coronation. Our house was full to capacity with neighbours on both occasions, as I am sure Bryan's house was as well.
>
> A love of football was encouraged almost from the cradle, or in some cases, dressing-table drawer. At every opportunity the lads were out in the streets playing footy, especially for a couple of hours after Sunday dinner. Bryan was no different, he loved his game of football, and this was further encouraged when Mr. Morrow joined the staff of the Glebe School. He became the football coach and set up a team,

which included Bryan as the goalie. A fellow member of the team, Alan Cutts, who lived at 11 The Terraces just along from Bryan's grandma, later played for Newcastle. Another member of the team, Raymond Lumsdon of 14 The Terraces, was offered the opportunity to train with a team up Glasgow way, but his mum said it was too far from home. One wonders how successful Bryan may have been had he pursued a career in football.

And, as a youngster, Ferry wasn't a mixer: "I had friends, a couple of boys I played tennis with, then a couple of boys I went cycling with, but I always felt on the outside of the gang. I was a bit precious, never one of the boys." But his successful schooldays continued, as Audrey Fletcher recalls:

Following in the tracks of his older sister Ann, Bryan started at the Washington Grammar School in 1957. Like the rest of us he was proud to wear the green and gold uniform with the Washington Coat of Arms on the blazer pocket. However even at grammar school, he was never far away from his cultural heritage as there was a lovely view of the pit heap from the classroom windows.

While at grammar school, Bryan took on a job at Anderson's shop, down Brady Square, as a paper lad. The delivery aspect wasn't so bad, even in bad weather; it was the collection of the money that took up the time. My husband, Edwin, also worked there as a paper lad and he remembers that the pressure was always on. Even if he or Bryan were sick the newspapers, weeklies and comics still had to be delivered. With the staggering amount of homework they had, it is a miracle that they found time to take on a part-time job for what was even then a pittance of a wage.

Washington Village has been well known during the past 800 years as the ancient seat of the Washington family. Washington Old Hall was the ancestral home of George Washington – the first president of the United States. William de Wessington the First, from whom George Washington was descended, settled there with his royal Scottish bride in 1183. The Old Hall is built on the southern slope of a Celtic hill, which is today topped by the Holy Trinity Church. On the other side of the hill lies the village smithy, which dates back to at least the 1500s. At that time there was a village pond next to the smithy, and it was in this pond that Jane Atkinson was tried and condemned as

"The Washington Witch". Bryan passed these important historical sites every day on his way to the grammar school. A long time ago the pond was filled in and the area became known as the village green. It was here that US President Jimmy Carter planted a tree in 1978. It subsequently died and had to be replaced.

Showing an early predilection for the stage, Bryan played Malvolio in the grammar school Christmas play *Twelfth Night* in December 1963. "Bryan spent countless additional hours learning his role as Malvolio," remembers Audrey Fletcher. "Even in his formative years he displayed a flair for showmanship, as well as the stamina and determination to fulfil his obligations and to achieve his goals and his dreams."

Another classmate, John Watson, says, "I remember that Bryan Ferry was a gifted artist and won a painting competition for the school which was sponsored by Fry's or Cadbury's Confectioners. The theme of the competition was circus/fairground and his submission was a fairground scene. The Arts Master at the time was a Mr Howard and this was probably first or second year, when we were twelve and thirteen. Also, I believe, he played in the school football team at some stage. Other than this the old memory lets me down. I think Brian's closest friends included Michael Purvis, Alan Barber, David Gale and Brian Mack."

Ferry would gain 9 'O' levels before going on to study for his 'A' levels. He was a hard-working and talented pupil. Amongst the luminaries to attend Washington Grammar and Technical School over the years were the arch Republican and Labour MP, the late Willie Hamilton, and Fraser Kemp MP. A certain Howard Kendall, later to become one of the most successful Everton FC players and managers of all time, was in the school football team. Other famous Washington lads and lasses include singer Martin Stephenson and Heather McCartney-Mills. Looking back at his hometown, Ferry once told *GQ* that it was a "lovely place; tranquil, and then it was developed and completely spoilt. I remember going to visit my parents, years after I'd left home, and couldn't find my way to their house; I came off the motorway and there were signs to Sector B – it was like *Brave New World*. There were no corner shops. People like my parents, pensioners who didn't have cars, would have to wait hours for a bus to be taken to a shopping mall. It was so sad, I brought them down to live with me straight after that."

"I still am a working-class hero as far as I'm concerned," Ferry told journalist Sylvie Simmons in 1995. "My working-class roots are very strong and very much part of me and certainly nothing I've been ashamed of, but I try not to wave them around too much because they can be very boring." Keen, perhaps, to counter the snooty image with which he is so readily identified, Ferry has also frequently referred to earlier childhood experiences in order to stress his working-class roots. "We went to Blackpool once when I was a child," he told *The Guardian*'s Dave Simpson in 2002. "The pavements were boiling hot. It seemed incredibly exotic." As a youngster, Ferry was a sporty adventurer, albeit one with a distracted air. At 15 he was "really mad" about cycling and racing: "I was really into it. I just thought it was so glamorous. I suppose young people think football is glamorous – soccer ... when I was that age, cycling just seemed so glamorous, European and continental." In 1985 he told James Truman of *The Face*:

> Adventure was the thing that appealed to me, all those *Boys Own* things. I loved anything heroic. I was very interested in cycling, so at one point I was dreaming of being a professional racing cyclist and winning the Tour de France. Then I wanted to be a great explorer or mountain climber. I started a mountaineering society at school, with some friends in the Lower Sixth. I loved the whole idea of nineteenth-century mountain climbing, because the style used to be perfect – the baggy corduroy trousers, and clay pipes, reading poetry on the slopes, sleeping in those tiny mountaineering tents. Everything always had to be *just so* for the magic to be there for me ... it was just the importance of doing something properly, perfectly.

"Properly, perfectly." This could be Ferry's very own axiom, for the search for beauty in art would be his greatest asset and also his biggest handicap. The excessive tidiness of mind and attention to minutiae was simultaneously a help and a hindrance. By middle age Ferry was clearly a victim of this early character trait, kept in abeyance at first by the enthusiasms of youth but ultimately too powerful a tendency to resist.

From the very outset, Ferry appeared to be distanced from the parent culture, as if he were a tourist within the scene, not a product of it. His willingness to portray a quite run-of-the mill experience as somehow exceptional simply makes Ferry sound as if he's trying too hard to be "one of us". So begins, perhaps, the central theme of the Ferry story – a desire to escape out of his own class whilst simultaneously attempting to "atone" for this by stressing his working-class roots.

In the seventies, when Ferry became a star, a mover and shaker in the best discos, a tasteful art connoisseur, and a lover of the mores of the English gentry, he entered a society that he had not been born into but to which he had always aspired. Never particularly easy-going as a person in any case, this sense of social dislocation gave his awkwardness endless ways in which to manifest itself.

The baby-boom years into which Ferry was born witnessed astonishing social, political and cultural change. The ending of the Empire and the concomitant blow to national esteem; the beginnings of a pluralistic society and the first tentative steps towards racial integration and sexual liberation for women and gays; profound changes to the social fabric of society with the creation of the welfare state; the nationalisation of many industries; the decline of the working classes; and the empowerment of the middle classes in the new consumer-driven age irrevocably changed the UK in the two-and-a-half decades that followed the war. Although still a more class-ridden society than most in Europe, Britain in 1970 was undeniably a more modern and liberal one, albeit at the cost of its previous position of global hegemony.

One of the features of this "long revolution" was the decline of the traditional aristocracy. During the war, there was public outcry at the fact that the upper classes had suffered and sacrificed less for the common good than was deemed acceptable. "There was also noticeable hostility, depicted and promoted in such populist newspapers as the *Daily Mirror*, to those in authority," writes David Cannadine in his book *Class In Britain*. "[They were] described and demonised in a Cobbett-like idiom as ... consisting of Colonel Blimp, the old school tie, and vested interests."

Paradoxically, it was exactly this elite that Ferry seemed inexorably drawn towards. In the early eighties, he would marry into a moneyed family with high-societal connections, educate his sons at Eton and feel comfortable as a small *nouveau riche* cog in the wheel of low-level aristocratic society. So Ferry would, like so many of us, outgrow his roots. But the manner of this rebellion against the stiffness of post-War society was totally atypical. Although he was certainly no archetypal Thatcherite, nor a harridan anti-intellectual seeking to abolish class, he did share with many of Thatcher's breed a disaffection towards some of the forms of behaviour that gave the sixties their flavour. Eschewing the outright rebelliousness, delinquency or adoption of alternative ways of living and loving that marked the counterculture of the sixties, Ferry's rebellion, like, one suspects, so many of his generation, was a much quieter one.

Soon it was clear that Ferry had very different concerns and expectations: "I was always attracted to the glamorous side of art, glamorous lifestyles, and I don't just mean posh lifestyles," Ferry told James Truman in 1985:

Just things that were more interesting than where I came from ... I was always a natural oddball, not fitting in to what was around me. I felt I had to do something fairly unusual to become me, as it were ... I'd always had very refined tastes, considering the income bracket I came from. I've always been drawn in some sense to the finer things of life. Perhaps to some people that makes me a snooty person, but that was just what attracted me. Any success I might have had, as an artist, tennis player, whatever, seemed to offer a nicer lifestyle than I would ordinarily have achieved.... having seen the inside of a thousand billiard halls it was very intriguing to me to see the other side of the coin.

Ferry was so removed from his working-class roots that he appeared to be mildly voyeuristic in his fleeting attachments to various social scenes. In later interviews, he spoke of his time in the billiard halls with the Teds, or the nights wiled away at the Regal, the Ritz and the Washington, wide-eyed before the golden age of glamour that was fifties Hollywood. But it was as if Ferry was sampling experience through expediency, rather than feeling part of the culture himself.

"I created myself," Ferry told me in 1999. Roxy Music's Eddie Jobson agrees: "He's the only person I've ever known who became someone else." It certainly seems that during his teenage years, Ferry identified that his class, status, and ethnicity were a disadvantage (he was arguably a prototype for white musicians who would have preferred to be born black), and so began the long, and ultimately successful, programme of self-stylisation. Unlike the would-be pop stars of today, and even those of his own times, Bryan Ferry needed no external makeover. He was quite skilful enough to change from within.

Ferry never really possessed much of a Geordie accent, and any lurking in the dark recesses of the Ferry voice were presumably eradicated early on. "You can't really read Shakespeare in a Geordie accent," Ferry would later explain. According to Roxy's drummer, Jarrow-born

Paul Thompson, he only lapses into his native dialect "when he's angry". And so it went on: the sense of style, the suits, the immaculate tonsure, the identification with Americana. Ferry changed himself completely before he became a pop star. Unlike some of his musical contemporaries, whose transformations in style and image were made from within the music business, Ferry's re-make/re-model came first, in his teens and early twenties, as a schoolboy and a student.

Of course, the transition from adolescence to adulthood is seldom made smoothly or without changes in one's sexual orientation or personality. However, that said, Ferry's attitudinal transformation appears to be unusually complete and unusually premeditated. Ferry would later admit: "I thought, well, I'm not going to just be this, or that, and stay in the north-east all my life. There was this attitude which said you can't do *this* because you're born like *that*. There's a lot of that up there." In 1993, Ferry also told *Times* journalist Alice Thomson: "It's very sad for someone like me, because I feel pulled in different directions by it, being aware of my roots and at the same time being one of the so-called classless people who through a measure of success has been able to transcend that ... I thought of excellence as a way of getting out." "*Don't go down the pits, lad!*" According to Bryan Ferry, that was the best piece of advice he ever got. Yet he denies that his humble origins are an embarrassment to him: "My background was incredibly simple, really humble, which I'm thankful for. It's not as if I don't like my origins. I feel very strongly about them."

"I'm from Sheffield, and he's from Washington. From your childhood, part of the reason why I liked show business and glamour is that it was the exact opposite of what I grew up with," is how musician and Roxy Music fan Martyn Ware, of Heaven 17, describes it. "As far as I'm concerned, it's fulfilling a very deep-seated brief that I had from very young that I wanted to see the world and basically improve myself. And I think this love of high society is Bryan Ferry's version of it. He's obviously, from his early fame, sought that world."

Class is an issue that has ignited the Ferry ire for decades. Writers and journalists mention it at their peril, and are guaranteed a wearied and defensive response from Ferry himself. It's obvious that, after thirty years of what some would see as social climbing, he has yet to fully come to terms with who he is now, and how the new version relates, if at all, to the young working-class model. Class is such a big issue for someone like Ferry, because, unlike most upwardly mobile people, he's skipped not just one class but two, going from pauper to prince and leaving burgher well alone. In 1982, he told the *Observer* that he was "the first rock star to join the English aristocracy."

Ferry keeps on being asked about class because it's obvious that the trappings of upper-class society are so important to him:

> I'm so far removed from where I was born that it's ridiculous. But I don't think it's a false position to be in, you see? I've worked on a building site and in a factory. So, if people ever accuse me of being spoilt, I can say, hey – shut up! I have a grounding in life; I know all about working-class stuff; I've been there. And people might say, come on Bryan, bonny lad – back you go. But no, to me, you can become whatever you want to be; do not allow anybody to drag you down.

Ferry's defence is that, as an artist, he is drawn inexorably towards beauty, wherever and whenever it is. Writer Chris Salewicz, who spent many months with Ferry in 1987, puts it like this: "Bryan Ferry's supposed fondness for the arcane world of high society doesn't appear to stem from a desire to be a social climber. Rather that he is genuinely attracted, as he says, to things and situations that are out of the ordinary, to which the surrealist in him is drawn."

Ferry's route to self-betterment was initially through education and, like so many born to disadvantaged families in the baby boom, he was one of the first in British history to benefit from the progressive socialist policies of grant-aided tertiary education. However, Ferry was never a collectivist, always an individualist. When asked about his politics, Ferry would say that his broad sympathies were more often with the Right. Writer Paul Du Noyer's assessment of how Ferry saw his progress is spot on:

> Ferry, almost uniquely for a man of his generation, saw his advance not in class or social or socialist terms but in individualistic terms, and saw the answer not in the abolition of class, or the replacement of one class with another, but with one's individual adoption by the upper class. Whether you like it or not, it's a very unusual strategy, certainly in the post-war period. I'm sure that in days gone by, that was what people generally did; if they were trying to get out of one class, they individually entered the one above by adopting its mannerisms. But in our lifetimes, since the sixties any way, that is not how

people have gone about it, is it? Outside of the lives of those Victorian rogues who would award themselves fake military titles and go and charm wealthy widows and that sort of thing, it's just not the sort of thing people do now – utterly abolishing their accents and previous lives to become seemingly "to the manor born". It seems to me that Ferry is attracted to the old-fashioned upper class, not to capitalism as such: the aristocracy rather than capitalism.

In a way, one of the things I've found appealing about Bryan Ferry is what I imagine is the vulnerability of somebody who has moved outside of his class and has not found complete security in the new one. He's never become sure of himself. I think his immaculate poise is probably some sort of compensation for his basic insecurity.

Writing as long ago as 1975, *Melody Maker*'s Caroline Coon noticed very much the same thing about the rampant Ferry insecurities and the liminality that makes the persona:

There are basically two breeds of rock musician. Some are working class and have exploited their inarticulate but expressive origin to the full with uncompromising punk image and sound, like Family, Status Quo and Ian Hunter. And there are the educated middle-class musicians like the early Soft Machine, Pink Floyd, Yes and Mick Jagger, who, while using the medium of rock 'n' roll, have always had the freedom to augment the music with references from their highly articulate heritage. Ferry falls between the two. He's not middle-class, but he is educated. His music speaks to that sensitive raw nerve of insecurity in anyone who is trying to move out of one class, which is a betrayal, and into another, which is to risk being an outcast. A new generation of upwardly mobile, educated working-class fans can easily identify with his torments and aspirations.

Ferry would be between classes, Bowie between genders – the two most important pop icons of the early seventies reflected society's new open values and blurry world-view, as the counter-cultural values of a progressive elite in the sixties filtered down into the lives of ordinary working men and women.

As a teenager, Ferry harboured airy notions of being artistic in some way, maybe as an artist or as a painter. With so many of his friends being left with little choice but to earn their living in the local mining community, or in manual work of other sorts, Ferry was determined to avoid the deadening anonymity of working-class toil. His tastes were already high-cultural: he saw a touring production of *La Boheme* at the Theatre Royal in Newcastle, and later told journalist James Truman: "It had quite a strong effect on me, the whole thing of the bohemian life, the romantic life, the sacrifice for art." He also became fascinated by style in general, and by classy clothes and great tailored suits, seeing perfection and beauty as ends in themselves. Whilst still at school, he worked weekends in a tailor's shop. His first car, an American Studebaker Champion, bought for £60, was chosen not for its performance but for its design: "It had a beautiful shark-like quality … in those days looks were everything as far as cars were concerned. I never bought a car for its performance or anything, I was just interested in style." The Studebaker would, of course, make its way into the lyrics of what is perhaps the defining pop song of the early seventies, "Virginia Plain".

In Fred Astaire and Cary Grant, Ferry found two Hollywood stars who provided a template for his self-invention; two style gods, both from humble beginnings. Rather than being defined by rock iconography, Ferry's image has always been the product of an enduring fascination with Hollywood glamour, intertwined with a serious interest in high fashion:

> At a certain age, I became interested in how I looked. I was keen on art at school when I was 13. Before that, from the age of 11, I was a music fan. At that time, there were no video games to distract me: I could lose myself in music – jazz, blues, that kind of thing. Then I worked in a tailor's shop on Saturdays, whiling away the hours looking through books with wonderful illustrations of gents getting out of Rolls-Royces in fabulous suits.

But music also mattered to Bryan – and lots of it too. Like so many of his generation, he loved the blues. At an early age his sister Ann would play him jazz, and so began a lifelong fascination with the then hippest of music:

> Yeah, I was into all the different kinds of black music. There was a big earthy part in the music that influenced me. Some of the early blues singers I was really into, like Leadbelly and Big Bill Broonzy and people like that. And jazz, too; you see, when I was young, I mean

precociously young, I was a jazz fan. At about eleven years old I was going to concerts, and I was really into that before I ever got into the r&b music. So there was really a big background there for me – Charlie Parker, and all those kinds of people. I obviously never saw him, but I collected records by him and other bebop people, and just the whole range of jazz – Coltrane and Ornette Coleman – appealed to me. I was very into that, plus the fact that later I had this art school thing, and admired the art music people like John Cage and so on. It was interesting reading John Cale's autobiography [*What's Welsh for Zen?*, 1998] because it's quite interesting to see that he came from a mining community as I did, although his was in Wales. He was also into this art music, as I was. The difference was that he was a real accomplished musician, which I wasn't. But luckily, I had a voice.

The first EP Ferry ever bought was by Charlie Parker. "I played it so much that I can remember every solo on it to this day," he recalls. He loved the way the jazz musicians seemed to sing through their instruments. He listened in awe to the brilliant extemporisations of the bebop musicians and later, when he began making his own music, he would be enamoured of the consummate professional, the intricate solo, the weave and the texture of sound: "I was a little bit snooty about … Elvis, the kind of white, more pop things, because I really got into my kind of jazz thing and it was my own precious world."

But of all the early influences, the biggest was probably Leadbelly, "the first person I heard on the radio who made me want to make music," remembers Ferry. "I was about ten, a bit melancholy, just waiting to be saved. And it was like, 'Wow, what's he … why is that man singing like that?' And so I got the blues, then jazz, then r&b. I used to deliver the *Melody Maker* when I was ten or eleven. I would walk down the street with a big bag of papers reading about jazz and blues singers, and I became hooked. But they were all old people; music wasn't by teenagers then … it wasn't in my consciousness that music had to be youthful."

As a teenager, Ferry would be a regular concert-goer. He had the Nabob Of Sob Johnny Ray's autograph. He won a competition on Radio Luxembourg for tickets to see the latest rock 'n' roll sensation from across the pond, Bill Haley and the Comets, at the Sunderland Empire in 1956: "When they read out, 'And the winner is Bryan Ferry,' the whole street came banging on my door." Ferry's first concert would be Chris Barber's Jazz Men and, as a youngster, he would watch enthralled as the Modern Jazz Quartet, Ella Fitzgerald and Count Basie played the City Hall in Newcastle. It would be the black artists with whom Ferry most strongly identified. Initially, it was their presentational skills that made the biggest impact – the sharp suits, black ties, and wonderful choreography – and the emotional veracity that made the performance so strong: stylish, yet heartfelt. These were attributes that would later be Ferry's trademarks.

But on a more emotional level, Ferry identified with black music because it expressed the sense of estrangement he so keenly felt at the time. In 1994, Ferry drew attention to his perceived disadvantages and problems:

It was not so much the working-class thing; it was coming from the north in particular. I suppose that it's doubled if you come from the north, put it that way, because there is in England a great north/south divide. The north is the industrial region and all the rest of it, and you're made to feel from an early age that you're in this ghetto – one develops a ghetto mentality. And on hearing black soulful music, I felt very much at home with it, because it was very tough, although I was actually very lucky because I had wonderful parents. But I think there was a toughness about the music that wasn't in some of the southern English bands or artists. I suppose I reinvented myself from teenage onwards, saying, "I've only got one life, and I'm going to be the person that I want to be."

The writer Jon Savage called Ferry a "great (British) soul singer" in 1994, and it's certainly true that black music has always exerted a powerful hold. The early years of Roxy Music aside, Ferry has always worked with black Afro-American styles and idioms, and later with top black producers and session musicians in search of an authentic black style. More importantly, it's Ferry's take on the blues that has made his utterly unique vocal what it is.

And what a voice it is – a peculiarly stiff version of the sensuality and directness of black music. In the same way that Ferry is an extraordinarily gauche mover on stage, so his vocal is nothing if not unique. "It's certainly not a classic singing voice," says Paul Du Noyer in a spectacular piece of understatement, "but I guess it's always appealed to me because it embodies fragility. He's put the weakness of his voice to very effective use, I think. Ferry's almost fashioning a white response to black music. You can't claim objectively that you're oppressed, down-trodden and poor because clearly in global terms you're not, and so what he's expressing is not the raw anger and sensuality of the black tradition, but instead, existential angst. His voice is a good medium for conveying that."

Seldom has a rock star been quite so obviously handicapped by his insecurities. In an era of raging, rampant egos, Ferry just seemed so vulnerable, and this vulnerability and lack of confidence was nowhere more blatantly revealed than in his private life. A sucker for model-style good looks and for the manners and mien of the refined society gal, Ferry seemed utterly incapable of finding anyone who even came close to satisfying his rarefied needs. Surprisingly, given his striking good looks, his smart mod-inspired dress style, and his immaculate quiff, he was a late, hesitant starter with the girls. He was 17 when he had his first love affair: "I seem to remember it ended in tears," Ferry would airily say in 1993. Later he would write of love, and love lost, of unobtainable, immortalising love for a long-dead screen idol, love for a blow-up doll, courtly love, love as a drug, and in this way breathe new life into the hackneyed melodrama of the boy-girl relationship that constituted so much of the thematic material of the idiom. But there's seldom happiness or joy here. Writer Mat Snow takes the point further: "My guess is that Ferry was not very successful with girls for a long time and, in the classic way, his music career was his way of trying to attract girls."

But, for all of his teenage years, and for the first half of his twenties, all thoughts of becoming a musician were part-time at best. Not for him the obsessive drive of his contemporaries Marc Bolan and David Bowie, who appeared from a very early age to be secure in their utter self-belief that they would be successful pop stars. Not for him the teenage recording contract, the long history of gigging and "paying his dues." No, Ferry became a musician almost by default, and became successful in his late-twenties, an almost implausibly old age for a new pop icon, seventies-style.

It all started when, in his late teens, a friend from his local cycling club asked him to front a combo called the Banshees, and they spent the summer doing the clubs and covering Chuck Berry and Bo Diddley songs. But Ferry's real passion lay elsewhere. He wanted "to be an artist, very much so. That quickly narrowed down to being a painter, and then, in my usual dreamy, roundabout kind of way, it took several years to channel that into becoming a musician."

Ferry left school in 1964 and began a degree at the Department of Fine Arts at Newcastle University. His parents didn't understand. "My parents' attitude was. 'What are you studying for? There's no future in it ...' We weren't the sort of family to have intellectual discussions, but I think that helped me an awful lot, because it gave me a real earthing ... it made me want to go away beyond that into something really weird. So surrealism, Dada, Jack Kerouac ... it was all waiting for me. Anything bohemian or different from the attitude of, 'We have no money, but we're honest people ...' After that, everything was exciting." Ferry continues:

In the sixth form I was getting into my art – my creative, bohemian phase – and I thought, "Oh no, I'm not of you lot." I was ... I can't think of a word other than ashamed, which sounds so awful. I remember being very cross with my dad and saying, "Oh, what do you know? You're just a miner." And he was so hurt. He hated being called a miner, not because of a snob thing, because he wasn't that, but he never was like those guys – they were much rougher ... I was studying these great writers and artists ... I felt so much at home with the people I was suddenly discovering, and so it took me well away from the aesthetics of my environment, and I rejected my parents in my mind. I felt like a cuckoo.

But schoolmate Audrey Fletcher has a different memory – that Bryan Ferry had doting parents who were full of pride:

No one was more pleased than Bryan's parents when he gained entry to Newcastle University to study for his degree in Fine Arts. It was his passport to a future away from the pits. His mum did used to worry, though, when he neglected his studies in favour of his music. I remember her chatting with my mum, Blanche Hall, one day. Bryan's mum's words were something like this: "Eeh, Blanche, I do get that worried about our Bryan. He's got his chance at university and it's like he's throwing it away. It's his music: he's letting it interfere with everything. He puts his music first and everything else comes next."

At the time, the city of Newcastle mirrored to some extent, if less successfully, its north-western counterpart, Liverpool, as Ferry's first biographer, publicist Simon Puxley (writing under the name Rex

Balfour) observed: "Like Liverpool on the opposite coast, it breeds a fierce sense of identity and independence, evident in the broad local accent and proud lack of interest in London and the south." Newcastle's Cavern was the Downbeat Club: their Beatles, the far more bluesy Animals.

Ferry was fortunate in that he had, for one year only, the celebrated British pop artist Richard Hamilton as one of his lecturers. Along with Eduardo Paolozzi, Lawrence Alloway and Peter and Allison Smithson, Hamilton had formed the Independent Group, which based itself at the Institute of Contemporary Art (ICA) in London. His small collage made for their 1956 exhibition, *This Is Tomorrow*, has gained almost mythic status given its prescience. Entitled *What Is It About Today's Homes That Makes Them So Different, So Appealing?*, it stands as a snapshot of contemporary consumer culture of the late-fifties whilst simultaneously predicting its next stage. A male body-builder and a semi-naked woman are collaged amongst the signs of consumer society – a television, a reel-to-reel tape-recorder, a vacuum cleaner. A cartoon hangs framed on the wall, whilst the entire collage is canopied by a lunar landscape. The collage, as the writer J G Ballard so aptly says, is "a theatre of possibilities": the body beautiful, lunar exploration, consumerist choice, the rise of technology, the portable sound recording unit, even the work of Roy Lichtenstein, are all predicted. As we will see later, one of Ferry's greatest lyrics, "In Every Dream Home A Heartache", would be inspired by such imagery. Hamilton himself said that the collage was designed from a list of categories: "man, woman, humanity, history, food, newspapers, cinema, television, telephone, comics (picture information), cars, domestic appliances, space." The pop art manifesto Hamilton wrote for the exhibition could easily be thought of as the framework for early pop *music* too: "Pop art is: Popular (designed for a mass audience), Transient (short-term solution), Expendable (easily forgotten), Low Cost, Mass Produced, Young (aimed at youth), Witty, Sexy, Gimmicky, Glamorous, Big Business."

Along with other artists at the Department of Fine Art at the time, including Mark Lancaster, Hamilton was fascinated, for example, by the annual travelling fair that came to the town moor. They were particularly intrigued by the trucks used to transport the fairground show, and specifically the lettering used on the paintwork to announce the various acts which, although authentic folk art, read like slogans. "Some of those words – 'flea circus', for example – and the way the words were written were so poetic, and yet so banal," remembers Richard Hamilton. "So poetic, so banal" – as we shall see, this collision of seriousness and frivolity would prove endlessly fascinating for the later version of Bryan Ferry. Not without good cause did Hamilton later say: "Bryan Ferry, my greatest creation!" Hamilton's work provided something of a blueprint for seventies pop irony. Immediate yet disposable; all surface, yet deep; playful, yet serious – it mapped out the entire trajectory of Roxy Music, and many other British pop artists. Bryan Ferry recalls:

> When you think of Richard, you think of him in an intellectual way, because he always seemed incredibly clever and one was rather daunted by that as a student. You always felt that you had to push your idea a little bit further than you perhaps wanted to. And that was a very good thing to have somebody there who was quite austere, at least from the outside. He seemed very much his own man, had his own style. He always wore the same clothes – this kind of Levi's suit, and the very cool kind of Cuban cigar. One was slightly intimidated and thought, this is a cool guy! At the time, he was working on a reconstruction of Duchamp's *The Large Glass, or The Bride Stripped Bare By Her Bachelors, Even* for the Tate Gallery. Duchamp was a friend of his. So he was a remarkable man, and I was very fortunate to have his last year of teaching there. And all the other people who were there, the other students, made you question things all the time. It was far enough away from London to be its own place.

"If you ask me whether Bryan was a great painter, I would have to say no," Hamilton told *GQ* in 1991. "I always thought his interest in music was greater than in painting. Newcastle has a great social life, and he was always the life and soul of the party. So in a sense I was more conscious of him in a social way than as assiduous artist. His paintings suffered as a result of his music, but then general development had become one of the functions of the art school by then – exploring an individual way of life. We were very conscious of style at Newcastle, and Bryan was a great exponent of style – he had a very good understanding of what were the current social mannerisms."

Under Hamilton, life would be lived in a knowing, ironic manner; the world framed by inverted commas. "What I was trying to instil was the principle that anything you did in the way of art you should think about," said Hamilton, "which was going against the trend at the time, which was very much towards the art-from-the-gut style of abstract expressionism. I took the opposite view – that you had to think about things, like Duchamp." This seems to define Ferry as a pop artist perfectly; never let it be said that he ever did anything "from the gut". For better or worse, Ferry would show a cool perfectionism in everything he did.

"Richard Hamilton was an enormous influence, though he left at the end of our second year," recalls a university classmate of Ferry's, Michael Brick:

The nature of that influence is rather hard to put your finger on. He only taught in the first year, but his presence was felt throughout the school, and both Bryan and myself continued to have contact with him during our second year. Richard placed great emphasis on a rigorous analysis of imagery, also that there should be no hierarchies of images. Anything could be used to make art, from advertisements to scientific charts and graphs. It was a department that was fascinated with America, rather than a purely pop art department. Indeed, practically all of Richard's best students turned into late modernist/minimalist artists rather than pop artists. Duchamp, of course, was a huge influence. The prevailing art in the department was distanced, highly intellectual and almost dandified.

Bryan Ferry spent much of his student life in digs in Eslington Terrace in Jesmond, within walking distance of his university department. Ferry's friends Nick De Ville and Tim Head, later to become important artists in their own right, lived in the same street. The artist Stephen Buckley was a contemporary. Mark Lancaster, a former resident of Eslington Terrace, spent a year working at the Factory with Andy Warhol. Each Newcastle student was given use of a spacious studio.

Ferry's first art exhibition was scheduled to take place at neighbouring Durham University, as Michael Brick recalls: "Bryan was an artist of great potential. His degree show is the only one that I remember from that year and that should tell you something. The work was elegant and minimalist. I have tried to get him to take it up again via printmaking. He has expressed mild interest." Tim Head recalls the first stirrings of the Roxy-esque: "Bryan had a show of paintings in this tiny gallery. And for the show he got a friend of ours, Nick De Ville, to take this photograph of him leaning against this American car that he had rusting outside the door, with a background of trees. Even though it was a railway line, it looked like this wonderful boulevard in California. So, there was the first Roxy Music cover – for Bryan's painting show."

The image of Ferry, with short hair and in a sharp mohair suit and a shirt with a button-down collar, leaning against his beloved stream-lined, shark-like Studebaker, does indeed look like a Roxy Music prototype album cover. Substitute a trashy model for Bryan Ferry, and the image is textbook Roxy. Discussing the photograph with *Melody Maker* in 1974, Ferry wryly commented, "I was much more flash then than I am now."

Ferry already possessed a very forceful personal style, but was never brash or macho. Michael Brick recalls the quiet, understated intelligence of a special talent:

We were both in the same year and lived together in the same house in our second year. Over the four years of the degree I got to know him reasonably well and liked him enormously. He was very cool and slightly shy, though not as much as I was, and very intelligent, both visually and in the normal academic sense. He was also very funny in a wry, rather sardonic sort of way. He was highly articulate in the sense that he chose words with great care and used them tellingly. He was, even then, hugely attractive to women, though he was never a womaniser. I would be shyly talking to some girl, Bryan would walk past in the background, and they would walk through me to get to him. And that was before he was "Bryan Ferry".

Despite all this, music remained an abiding love, and Ferry was a DJ at Newcastle's happening joint, the Club A Go Go. Whitley Bay was ten miles down the road from Newcastle and Ferry would stroll round the great fairground there, Spanish City, listening to the latest Everly Brothers song blurting out over the loudspeakers. "The sort of music my fellow students listened to was nearly all Beach Boys and stuff like that, or Martha and the Vandellas," recalls Ferry. "It was all American, dance-y kind of stuff. Light music; not dark." Ferry would later list "Telstar" by the Tornados in his all-time Top 10 ("it reminds me of fair-grounds"), along with classics from Billie Holiday, Smokey Robinson, Ike and Tina Turner, Percy Sledge, and Bob Dylan.

Apart from the Beatles and the Stones, Ferry was little enamoured by British popular music. "Will You Still Love Me Tomorrow?" by the Shirelles was his all-time favourite record. Just about the only psychedelic artist to fry Ferry's onions was Jimi Hendrix. So for Ferry and his circle, American music was in, and Ferry himself, at direct odds with the prevailing trend, wore his hair short and immaculately groomed. Sharply dressed and clean-cut, Bryan Ferry was light years away from the psychedelic or hippy look: "[We wore] pink shirts, white jeans and sneakers ... any surfing music was considered the hippest thing around. It was the American Dream for us ... as you can imagine, being stuck up in Newcastle."

Sartorially, the mod look, mixed in with elements of hip Americana, would dominate Ferry's years in Newcastle. While the rest of the world began to go hippy, "three-inch suit-vents, three-button jackets, narrow lapels and tab-collar shirts, kind of like William Burroughs wore," would be the basis of cool style, said Ferry, reminiscing in 1991. "I suppose I was a sort of 'intellectual Mod': I used to go to this great clothes shop in Newcastle called Marcus Pryce. I knew Marcus, the owner; he was one of the founders of the whole mod movement. It was always untrue that mod was just in London. There was another great shop as well, called City Style – really cheap, a bit more tacky."

In 1967, Ferry hitchhiked to London to see the Stax Revue on tour. It would be a defining moment in his life: "I think that was like my sort of vision on the road to Damascus or something. I saw Otis Redding, Sam and Dave, Steve Cropper, all those people on stage in their splendid stage suits and it was just the best thing I've ever seen, you know. It was just what I wanted to see and hear."

Whilst at university, Ferry began singing with his band, the Gas Board, playing gigs on the local Newcastle circuit. As an eight-piece, including four brass players, the sound was big and honking, the repertoire Bobby Bland and Freddie King; they were heavily influenced by American soul and r&b. It was good-time music, in the main tradition of the hugely successful blues acts such as the Animals, who had broken out of the Geordie scene two years earlier. Gordon Sumner, later better known as Sting, remembers seeing the Gas Board in concert: "They were very good. Ferry was just the same as he is now, really." The band included Mike Figgis, now a successful film-maker based in America, with *Leaving Las Vegas* on his CV. Included in their repertoire was the Wilbert Harrison standard, "Let's Stick Together", later a hit for Canned Heat in the rewritten form "Let's Work Together", and to be covered by Ferry a decade down the line. From the very outset, though, for Ferry the presentation was always equally as important as the music. "I've always thought that if you're going to present yourself on stage, you should dress up," he told journalist Steve Turner in 1972. "Even with my college band, Gas Board, we wore bobby-sox suits with our initials on our pockets!"

In a move so characteristic of Ferry, Nick De Ville would become part of the Ferry/Roxy nexus, a valued and trusted friend used as a designer and photographer on a succession of projects. And two members of the Gas Board, bassist Graham Simpson and guitarist John Porter, would also be sought out in future projects. As if instinctively aware that it would be strategically important to have the best around him, Ferry began a five-year process of building a musical and visual team. It might be said that Ferry was never a confident enough song-writer, singer or stylist to make it on his own, but all potential superstars need their support networks, and few constructed it so meticulously and so effectively as Ferry. He wanted good people around him, and he made sure he got them.

There are two versions of what happened next in circulation. The Ferry version is that when the Gas Board decided to turn professional, he declined the gig: "I stayed on to get my degree. I wasn't really sure what I wanted to do. We would play nights and go into college rather bleary-eyed the next day. I was living this dual life for a while, torn between the two things [music and art], because for me, at the time, they were quite separate. And it wasn't until a few years later that I managed to pull them together." Art school certainly gave the likes of Ferry credibility as he moved into the music business in the early seventies, the era of bubble-gum and glitter rock. As the author of his own script, not a product of the pop sausage-machine, people would take him seriously.

Version two says that Ferry was sacked from his own band, a version corroborated by Roxy Music guitarist Phil Manzanera in 1974: "I think it was something to do with him not wanting to rehearse," he told *NME*'s Nick Kent in 1974. "He'd just turn up to a gig with two girls on his arm. He was always a smoothie, so to speak. He had that style even then ..." Mike Figgis claims that Ferry was fired "because he wasn't a very good soul singer; he had that tremble." "How dare he say that of me!" said Ferry to journalist Mat Snow in 1993. "It's fucking rude, isn't it? I think he was jealous of me."

Art school has left an indelible mark on the history of British popular music. Members of the Beatles, the Stones, the Animals, the Kinks, the Who, the Bonzo Dog Doo-Dah Band, Ian Dury, the Clash, Pulp, and Blur have all attended art school programmes, but Roxy Music would be the most visible and obvious manifestation of the art school intellect. Art school provided the ideal environment in which to experiment with mixed media. Academic and expert on the history of art schools Colin Fallows points out how the basis of learning at art school provided the perfect grounding for the new breed of rockers: "A number of the teaching and learning methodologies traditionally employed in art schools are transferable and mirrored in the process of pop – for example, practical studio-based, project-centred work and experimental approaches to media and exploration of self, presented for critique by the peer group."

Of course, in the second half of the sixties, showmanship and theatricality was coming to the fore of British music, from the Stones' gender-bending, through the Who's auto-destructive stage show and mock-operatic music, to the Bonzo Dog Doo-Dah band's *Python*-predicting English surrealism. But, despite the excellence of all three, they could never fairly be considered as pop art experimentalists. The sense of kitsch, irony and glamour was sorely lacking. "I tried, but I could not find a way," Ferry would sing in 1972. And back in 1968, the grand experiment that was carried off with such panache in 1972 seemed nothing more than a ridiculous pipe dream.

Indeed, the very idea that pop music could be serious was then a very new and not wholly acceptable concept. The very term "popular", shortened in the mid-twentieth century to "pop", had always carried with it carried with it pejorative connotations: "pop music", "pop culture", "pop art" were all phrases initially used by critics to describe the more trashy, discredited, "low" forms of culture: music, cartoons, films and novels that were designed for the mass market. Up until the mid-fifties, intellectuals certainly seemed uninterested in analysing these low forms of culture. They were distinct not only from the high culture of serious literature, arts, opera etc, but also from authentic folk art and music, which was deemed superior as it was made by the people, for the people. Popular music and popular art were regarded by their very nature as being compromised by capitalism. They were not built with excellence in mind, nor as an expression of the values of the people, but to make money. Moreover, practitioners of popular cultural forms, whether they were actors, singers or involved in advertising or fashion, were regarded as being dupes of the capitalist system, devoting their time and energies to service consumer society and manipulated by big business to do so.

In the mid-sixties the cultural climate slowly began to change. Singers such as Bob Dylan, who, as we have seen, were originally protest singers indebted to the folk tradition, and who made faithful cover versions of folk songs with deep traditions, began writing more personal songs about relationships, love, and altogether more intimate themes. They also eschewed the traditional instrumentation connected with serious and authentic folk music and started using amplification. They became both artists and showmen.

Pop art was caught up in this complicated nexus of ideas. Largely serious, intellectually-minded men and women, very often connected to academia, made it, but it took as its subject matter icons of the new consumer society. Those very forms of "low" culture that the elite regarded as mere trash – advertising, cinema, popular music, cartoons and so on – fascinated this new breed of artist, and they took these themes seriously. Furthermore, they found the symbols interesting in their very banality. It was because these images were so immediate, and so lacking in the depth of the traditional novel, play, or portrait, that they found them so beguiling. They were the first people to respond to, and to turn into art; the new symbols of post-World War II capitalist societies. "Pop art has many meanings," cautions Michael Brick, "from the nihilism of Warhol to the celebrations of Rosenquist. If you take Richard Hamilton's famous definition – sexy, glamorous, ephemeral, etc – then, yes, Ferry imported these values into pop. An obsessive interest in the surface of things is another attribute. All of these, at one time or another, apply to Bryan and Roxy Music."

If Bryan Ferry was looking for a way to combine pop music and pop art, then there really was only one meaningful template: that provided by the Velvet Underground. In 1967, the Velvet Underground released an astonishing debut album. It was bought by almost nobody at the time, but apocryphally it is said that all those who heard it went on to form a band. It's no surprise, therefore, that the future members of Roxy Music, and their original media supporters, saw Roxy Music very much as a British version of the Velvets. In Lou Reed they possessed, like Ferry, a brilliant tunesmith. And in the classically trained and avant-garde-minded John Cale they had someone whose viola playing gave them an astonishingly *outré* sound. Although initially no virtuoso, Eno would later perform such a function in Roxy Music. And the Velvets' Richard Hamilton, of course, was Andy Warhol. Warhol managed the band for a short period, designed their first album cover, and made them a part of the scene at the Factory in New York in the mid-to-late sixties. Their touring mixed-media show, the Exploding Plastic Inevitable (EPI), combined fun, sadomasochistic dancing, strobe lights and blasts of atonal music to such a devastating effect that it has a good claim to be the inspiration for all subsequent art-rock experiments in the seventies.

In their brazen theatricality and slams of outrageously incongruous sound, Roxy Music's would be the EPI English-style – more stylish, more studied, more ironic, and less street-wise, but arguably just as excessive. Eno was a huge fan of the Velvet Underground, particularly their third album. Ferry was less so, initially at least: "They must have been an influence, but not so much as one might imagine. I was aware of them from the first album, although I like them much more now than I did then. No musicians that I knew liked them." However, the early Roxy sound, slightly sonically flat and no instruments really leading, and with bright, naïve tunes, would update the original Cale-Reed blueprint.

Ferry left university in 1968. Plans for him to study in New York on a scholarship at the Royal College of Art fell through, so the chance for him to enter the fine art world collapsed. A passable, if untrained, singer, with no compositional skills but with a headful of Hamilton and a lower second-class degree in Fine Art, at 23 he was already older than most of the new pop stars who found their first taste of fame in the late sixties. However, Ferry was ambitious and alert to new opportunities. In the next three years, the jigsaw of Roxy Music would slowly form itself into a complete picture. And Ferry would find a way.

SO DIFFERENT, SO APPEALING: 1968-1971

In order to become a pop star, Bryan Ferry became a Londoner. In the sixties, the local scene meant clubs and cabaret and minimal exposure, whilst London, the sharpest city in the world, brought national and international attention. These were the days before Northern outposts such as Newcastle, Liverpool, Sheffield and Manchester had developed much of a scene of their own, with few record labels and little active promotion. To make it big, would-be stars had to relocate to where the press, publicity, and recording studios were. So, in 1968, Ferry left Newcastle to further whatever artistic designs he had. He became a metropolitan creature, gradually assembling over the next three years the band that would become Roxy Music. Or rather, allowing the band to gradually assemble itself as if by some weird kismet all of its own.

His parents, of course, being sensible, thought young Bryan was quite mad. Mind you, they also thought it was odd that their son had eschewed normal routes into clever-boy middle-class respectability back in 1964 when he opted for art above banking or teaching. But a life in music? "They really thought I was crackers," said Ferry many years later, "but they never tried to stand in the way of anything I did."

Graham Simpson, the bassist with the Gas Board, would be a regular visitor to Ferry's new Kensington flat, even lending him an upright piano on which to practise. At 25, Simpson was two years older than Ferry. He'd grown up in Manchester, Bristol and Edinburgh, and was proficient on violin, cello and guitar. After studying English at Newcastle University he had moved to London on a similar mission to make it in the music business. With Simpson's help, Ferry began learning the piano and tried his hand at writing songs. He added a £5 harmonium for chord work, but there would be no gigging and no serious attempts to form a band. Ferry had taken one piano lesson as a boy, and now had around ten more, but still he couldn't call himself a musician. In fact, it appears that Ferry went out of his way to avoid contact with fellow aspirant musicians. By day, he had a number of jobs – as a van driver, antiques restorer and, finally, as a ceramics teacher at Mary Boon Secondary, an all-girl school on Earby Street in Hammersmith. As if still unsure where his future lay, he also exhibited his ceramics at the Thomas Gibson Fine Art Gallery and the Piccadilly Gallery. Ferry's attitude to "proper" work appeared laissez-faire to say the least. "If they wanted to talk about their boyfriends, we talked about their boyfriends," Ferry admitted in the *NME* in 1975. "If they brought records in, I'd play them." By the end of 1970, his contract had been terminated.

Finally, Ferry resolved to throw his lot in with the music scene. "I moved to London to seek my fortune, and myself," as he eloquently put it:

After I'd been there for about a year or so, I began to think that while I was in my early to mid-twenties, if I didn't give myself an opportunity to do something in music I'd always regret it later in life. It wasn't particularly the case that I was going to give up art completely and that I'd become fed up with it; such is the fact that it's a more reflective activity, which I could do later in life anyway. I thought that if I were to do anything in music then it had to be now whilst there was still hot blood surging through my veins!

Applying chaos theory – in which a seemingly insignificant or incidental event leads ultimately to a cultural tsunami of history-changing proportions – to rock history, we have Pete Sinfield and Robert Fripp to thank for there ever being a Roxy Music in the first place. The reason? In their search for a replacement for the then recently-departed Greg Lake, they decided to pass on a budding but completely unknown vocalist. Although a seemingly completely unimportant event at the time, that vocalist would go on to front the early seventies' most important band. "Yes, I auditioned for King Crimson before I put Roxy together," says Ferry:

That's how I found the company EG who managed us. I thought King Crimson's first album was really interesting, and I saw this advert for an audition. It was in the basement of some sort of shop, and Peter

Sinfield and Fripp were there. I sang a couple of their songs, but they said what they really wanted was a bass player who could sing, which is what they eventually got – a guy called Boz, I think – to replace Greg Lake. So, sadly, that didn't happen, but it meant that I met Sinfield, who produced the first Roxy album, and Fripp, who had the same management company. He's a wonderful character Fripp, a very good musician. A bit mad, but then, aren't we all?

Peter Sinfield has only the dimmest of recollections of the audition: "No … in all honesty I can't remember it well. However, I'm sure I would have had reservations about Bryan singing 'Epitaph' and voted no!"

However, it was around the winter of 1970 that Ferry suddenly discovered a gift for composition. Like David Bowie, he played "composer's piano"; not the most graceful, and certainly not the most *correct* way of playing, but it did the job. Ferry developed an odd approach to playing chords, often missing out the third completely: musicians would later comment that he only played the black notes. But like so many musicians who don't have the first clue how a chord might resolve, or what harmonic pattern will fit, he began writing dozens of songs from a decentred angle, with a visionary clutter of jarring cadences and beautiful piano fills sliding up next to dissonance and impenetrability.

The basics of Roxy Music's first record took shape that winter as Ferry made his first concerted attempts at composition. His art school training meant that, for the 25-year-old Bryan Ferry, there were no boundaries. Thinking of himself more as an inspired amateur than a musician *per se*, he was firmly of the belief that the tools learnt in one area of artistic endeavour could be applied to another. "Any form of self-expression I think of as one sort of field," he told broadcaster Paul Gambaccini in 1975:

I wasn't sure if I had any ability as a musician at that point. I couldn't play any instruments, except, I suppose, harmonica, which was always kind of a joke-type instrument. Whereas, I knew I could paint pictures and write about art. Originally, I wanted to be an art historian when I was at school. Just as I kind of taught myself how to paint pictures, how to draw and so on, so at a later stage I began to teach myself piano and as a fairly emotional-type person could project myself into singing which is very much sort of physical/mental activity – it's very all-embracing really.

In the winter of 1970, Ferry advertised in *Melody Maker* for more recruits, in particular a keyboard player. One of the respondents was 24-year-old Andy Mackay, a trained saxophonist and oboe player rather than pianist, but the possessor of a VCS3 synthesiser, then the top of the range. The VCS3 was made by Electronic Music Studios in Putney, London and was actually called "the Putney". The separate keyboard was known enticingly as "the Cricklewood". "It was a very strange instrument, the VCS3," recalls Mackay:

> The only previous [electronic] stuff had been done in university physics and music departments, with synthesisers the size of rooms. Then came this little device that the BBC Radiophonic Workshop used. It was a sort of putting-together of all these noise-making twiddly things. And you could treat things through it, which we liked. You could treat the voice or the sax, or the oboe. It was expensive: I think it was about £350, but I thought it would be my passport to something. It worked out rather well.

Like Simpson, Mackay had read English at university, in his case at Reading, and, like Ferry, he had performed in a student soul and R&B band, his version of the Gas Board being the rather more coolly entitled Nova Express, the name taken from a novel by William S. Burroughs.

Mackay was born on July 23, 1946, in Lostwithiel, Cornwall. In stark contrast to the slagheaps and pits of Ferry's Washington, Mackay's birthplace is one of the prettiest parts of England. Founded by Normans on the banks of the River Fowey, Lostwithiel was known in the Middle Ages as the "fairest of small cities" and the "lily of the valley" and is now a tourist trap. Andy grew up, however, in Pimlico in central London, where he attended St James The Less School. He fell in love with music at a tender age. While the BBC Light Programme and Radio Luxembourg gave him an early taste of pop, as a performer he developed into a talented classical musician. Unlike Ferry, Mackay had an able tutor in the form of his father, a talented amateur pianist, and he quickly developed an appreciation for both classical and popular music. At Westminster Grammar School he concentrated on the oboe and won a weekly scholarship to Guildhall School Of Music, where he studied under James McGillivray. He was also head chorister. He later played oboe with the London Schools Symphony Orchestra, and at the age of 18 took up saxophone.

After a brief spell as a librarian, Mackay read Music and English Literature at Reading University. His influences were a mix of art, music and pop – Beethoven, Chopin, Wagner, Smokey Robinson, John Lennon, Elvis Presley. It was at university that he played soul with Nova Express, but he was also drawn to the avant-garde world of John Cage and Karlheinz Stockhausen, becoming an avid concert-goer and supporter of new music. It was at one such avant-garde event at Winchester College of Art that Mackay would make the acquaintance of a certain Brian Eno. "We did sort of nihilistic happenings," remembers Mackay, "very strange spontaneous theatre events and avant-garde, John Cage-type music pieces. We would sit in silence for a long time, and someone would climb up a stepladder; we would make some funny electronic noises with a tape recorder, that sort of thing. Eno turned up at the one we did at Winchester Art School and we became friends at that point." The two discovered a shared love of pop music, and actually considered forming a group themselves, two years before Roxy Music started. "We discussed names," continues Mackay. "The only one I can remember was Brian Iron and the Crowbars, but we never did anything – [it was] total fantasy."

After, by all accounts, just scraping through a BA Honours degree, Mackay decided to try and make it as a professional musician. In an ad in *Melody Maker*, the musicians' rock magazine, he offered his services as that most rare of beasts, the rock 'n' roll oboist, but to no avail. Disheartened, Mackay left London for the Far East, "which was the obligatory thing to do that year". He came back, took casual work, and then left for the continent and an extended sojourn in Rome to take stock. On returning to the UK, he found a job teaching music at Holland Park Comprehensive School in west London. Close to a musical breakthrough he was not.

One suspects that, as with Ferry, time was also running out for Mackay. Already in his mid-twenties, he might be a proficient musician, but he was a country mile from making the big time. "He was rather like an old schoolteacher," Ferry remembers. "He was a bit fogeyish. I mean, several of us were teaching at the time, including Andy, because if you had a degree you actually got paid quite well." "I knew I had to be a musician, and I wanted to be a rock musician," says Mackay. "I suppose I could have been a classical oboist, but it didn't seem free enough. I couldn't have supported myself by playing electronic music – the audience is very limited; the only way I could be a musician was in rock, but with people who had a lot of ideas." Ferry and Simpson were interested in him, and the three began playing and writing together, occasionally with the help of John Porter, another alumnus of the Gas Board. It was a chance meeting, however, which would swing Ferry and co. around on their axis to point at a decidedly more eccentric, alternative universe.

Mackay happened to bump into Brian Eno again on the tube one day, and got him interested in the new band he was putting together. Here at last was someone who was interested in the synthesiser, leaving Mackay to develop the rock oboe and sax within an increasingly bizarre musical landscape. Eno, who was working as a second-hand-electronics dealer at the time, remembers the fluke meet-up that arguably made Roxy Music: "I was getting on a train, on the Northern Line, and there was a choice between one carriage and the next. I got in and bumped into Andy Mackay. If I'd got into the other one, I wouldn't have joined Roxy Music, and I probably would have had a completely different life."

The Llanfairpwllgwyngyllgogerychwyrndrobwllllantysiliogogogoch of the rock world, Brian Peter George St John le Baptiste de la Salle Eno was born in Woodbridge, Suffolk on May 15, 1948. An educationalist, St John Baptiste de la Salle (1651-1710) was one of the leading lights behind the development of modern pedagogy, and the founder of the Institute of Christian Schools. Whether the astonishing name was some sort of homage on the part of Eno's mum and dad is unclear, but one thing is for sure: Eno was certainly an educator.

Rather than stake a claim for himself as musician, Eno would, despite all his fierce intellect and musical talent, later become rock's most famous back-seat driver. The noise architect behind Roxy Music, the essential ingredient of weirdness with Bowie and Talking Heads and, quite frankly, the saving grace of pomp rockers U2 and James, he did whatever he did brilliantly. He cast a spell on the music, he made sure that the creative environment was as pure as it could be, and he quite simply had an inexhaustible supply of lateral ideas to aid the recording process. An amateur theorist, an original thinker, and, in the early nineties, rock's most important producer, he became one of those people who are perpetually busy. In demand by the media, by musicians, by seemingly everyone, he gives the impression, through his extreme industry and networking with many like-minded thinkers and theorists of the everyday, of being terribly important. He has an innate sense of cool: bands and singers look up to this bald, slightly tubby, shortish middle-aged man as some sort of icon of left-field weirdness. The fact that he looks more like a history lecturer than a rock god matters not one jot: whatever it is, Eno has it.

While Ferry was impeccably stylish, enjoying increasing clarity as a songwriter, and Mackay a more than adequate musician, Eno was a very different type altogether: intellectual, cerebral and distinctly eccentric, he had an edge, decadence, and flamboyance. Acutely aware of avant-garde music, he was almost obsessed by the possibilities afforded by the new tape and recording technologies. He had no real formal musical training, and couldn't actually play a note, but, at the forefront of a new breed of non-playing musicians, in a world of prog-rock virtuosity, it made him new, different, in fact rather punk in attitude – a musical illiterate with better musical ideas than almost any other trained musician. In the mid-to-late seventies, he became an icon for the new wave of electronic groups, new musicians who followed in the footsteps of Captain Eno: big on ideas, crap on technique. Eno was the first person to show that it wasn't *how* you did it, but *what* you did that mattered.

Brian was the second of the four children of William Eno, a postman, and Maria, a Belgian immigrant. As he would later joke, he came from "a long line of people in the communications field" as his uncle, grandfather and great-grandfather had also been postmen. Tati-esque images of generations of Enos cycling around the interminably flat Suffolk countryside would only make up so much of the Eno ancestry however, as all his immediate forebears appear to have possessed creative talents too. Brian's grandfather was reputedly the only bassoon player in Suffolk, his uncle mended porcelain, and his father was a passionate clock and watch-repairer.

The nuns and thereafter the brothers of the De La Salle Order educated the boy Eno. He claims that this initial dose of Roman Catholicism left a stain on his nature: "It certainly creates unbalanced personalities," he told Caroline Coon in 1977. "Catholicism instils a tremendous amount of guilt. One of the maxims is that you dedicate everything to Christ. Now, if you think that your every action carries that kind of weight and relevance, it really does instil guilt. It takes the fun out of things."

"Even in childhood, Brian was always looking for something different," his mother, Maria, told a journalist, Arthur Lubow. He loved as a small boy to visit an eccentric grandfather, who lived in a deconsecrated chapel crammed with stuffed animal heads, African spears, Japanese armour and a dozen cats. Brian spent most of his most enjoyable hours alone, hunting for fossils in nearby woods. "My great debt to my parents is that they showed little interest in what I was doing," he says. "So many middle-class parents, when the kid comes home with a little painting, they put it up on the fridge. If your parents don't pay attention, you're not tempted to repeat the same drawing six times to get the same buzz."

As a child, Eno was bitten by the bug of fifties American pop music. In the same way that youngsters in Liverpool got a jump-start on the rest by being able to listen to the latest rock 'n' roll being shipped into the docks from America, so Eno, who lived five miles away from two US air bases, had a constant source of exotic fun. The local jukeboxes were stocked with the latest American hits, and Eno's sister, Rita, used to acquire the latest happening singles: "She used to bring home these incredible southern doo-wop records, R&B, stuff that you never heard on the radio. So she was a huge musical influence on me. What we were listening to at the time was so bloody pathetic – Craig Douglas, Cliff Richard. And when you heard the originals that they copied from, it was so alive. I didn't realise for years it was done by black people." Rita Eno would eventually marry one of the 17,000 American servicemen stationed in the UK.

From the outset, Eno was interested not so much in the tunes or the lyrics, but in the *sound* of music. Doo-wop, for example, struck him as odd and fascinating because British singers simply didn't make sounds like that. And, on cold winter mornings before school, he would play his uncle's Ray Conniff records. "What was interesting about Ray Conniff was it was music as environment," Eno told *Q*'s Andy Gill in 1993. "It was an attempt to say, 'What's important here isn't the tune, it isn't the beat, all those sorts of things; it's this beautiful sound.'" Linked to his admiration of the music, on which he would later base his own ambient experiments, was the thrill he, like so many aspirant musicians of his generation, felt at the spectacle of Little Richard. Whether on Hendrix in the sixties or Prince in the eighties, Richard has been a model of black, gender-bending outrage. "Just the way of singing," said Eno of Little Richard, "the uses of the voice, were so original and unrestrained." Eno looked at the mainstream music of his day, and saw the strange beauty of the sound. And that is what he's done, as a musician and a producer, ever since.

Reportedly unable to afford musical instruments, the teenage Brian Eno formed his own *a capella* group singing American gospel music. However, he was less interested in creating sounds than in playing with those that already existed. The teenage Eno soon developed an interest in how sounds could be recorded. Eric Tamm's excellent book, *Brian Eno: His Music And The Vertical Colour Of Sound,* unpicks Eno's aesthetic in painstaking detail, arguing convincingly that his basic musical aesthetic is rooted in his foregrounding of the very element of modern music that makes it so distinctive, yet is almost impossible to articulate. What appears to be the prime motivation behind Eno's musicality is his overriding interest in tone colour or timbre, that magical quality that differentiates the sound of a piano playing middle C from that of a violin playing the same note. They're the same note but in terms of timbre they are very different. "This aspect of musical sound can be thought of as 'vertical' since it depends to a large extent on the harmonics, or barely audible frequencies, that are stacked 'vertically' on the primary heard note itself," writes Tamm. Of course, traditional musicology has tended to ignore timbre because it's impossible to annotate, yet it is precisely these almost intangible elements, from the dirty blues notes of Muddy Waters to the crystalline timbres of Kraftwerk, that mean so much within pop music.

Armed with a tape recorder, Eno's first experiments in sound engineering in the early sixties involved the sound of a pen striking a tin lampshade, which he then slowed down. At the same time, the BBC's Radiophonic Workshop was experimenting with similar techniques for fantasy programmes such as *Doctor Who*. In his home recording studio in 304 Holloway Road, London N7, Joe Meek was also busy creating an astonishing parallel universe of sound on such classics as "Johnny Remember Me" and "Telstar." Indeed, during the mid-to-late-sixties, experiments in tape looping, effects and distortion were common enough to be thought of as mainstream. Yet Eno was to give these ideas a twist. Not for him the curlicues of trippy sound associated with psychedelia, but something more basic, more simple, and, to coin a favourite pop art adjective which connoted both a sense of irony and distance, as well as something hip and happening, more *cool*.

He had already dabbled in music making. In 1964 he had formed a group called the Black Aces. Later he put together Maxwell Demon with guitarist Anthony Grafton. They recorded only once – a song called "Ellis B. Compton Blues", on 4-track, on Christmas Day, 1968. "I used to just wave this thing around all the time that generated very pure, very loud soundwaves,' Eno has recalled. Merchant Taylor's Simultaneous Cabinet, reportedly playing free-form avant-garde, was another early Eno project, then in 1970 he joined the Portsmouth Sinfonia as a clarinettist. The Sinfonia would take a non-improvisatory form – classical music – and improvise, with little or no musical talent, over the top. They actually saw some low-end chart action in 1981 with "Classical Muddly", playing just the "best" bits from dozens of famous overtures and operettas. Eno, of course, couldn't play a note.

Brian Eno attended Ipswich and Winchester Art Colleges, where he thrived in the new atmosphere of fluid creativity: "There wasn't any perception of high and low art; there was just a strong sense that it's not what you can do with your hands that matters, it's what you do with your head." Eno's interest in tape recorders became an obsession; at one stage he owned no less than thirty-two. The fact that a non-musician could make music as credibly as a concert pianist taught him a lesson that would be the prime motivation in his career: ideas matter more than technique. He would emerge, even more so than Bryan Ferry, with markedly resonant ideas about popular music as culture.

By the time the middle of the decade arrived, Eno had already armed himself with his famous black notebooks full of ideas, lists, theories and suggestions, the writing, for some reason, always running across the lines. In March 1967, aged 18, he married Sarah Grenville, and their daughter, Hannah, was born in the July of that year. Round about this time, he began inventing himself as the Eddie Izzard of his day, a straight man, if not embracing transvestism wholesale, then certainly playing around with traditional gender roles. Velvet bodices, feather boas and make-up were in, but not skirts. According to Tim De Lisle, "his explanation was that he was dressing from jumble sales, 'where they don't tend to sort clothes by gender.'" The writer Jon Savage argues that, "straight men can adore gay culture without having to do the actual sex acts. Indeed pop culture is a place where sensitive or divergent straights can play around with male id." Eno certainly did his fair share of "playing around". At school he had been "experimenting with androgynous clothing and make-up and wearing cross-gender clothes. For me there was no sexual aspect to it – I was not gay or anything, and never have been – but I just wanted to look great. And looking great meant dressing as a woman! Or at least as some kind of weird new hybrid."

Although Eno was later to become perhaps the most extreme dresser of the early glam-rock period, when Ferry first clapped eyes on him in seventies, "he was more like a mad boffin": "With Eno, there were always wires everywhere and bits of old speakers all over the place." The Ferry/Mackay team originally hired Eno in January 1971, not as a musician but as a technical adviser or "sound doctor". The new band would be highly unusual in that, in effect, it contained not one but two non-musicians. Eno offered up his small bedsit in Camberwell for rehearsals: "There were six of us in there with all the gear and the noise was fucking staggering." Eventually Eno's role would grow; as the synth player and tape operator, he became an actual performing member of the band.

Roxy took time to coalesce into the line-up that would make their debut album in March 1972. "Most of the songs on the album were played for about a year-and-a-half before we ever played live," reveals Eno. "There was a long, long period of time rehearsing these things and going over and over them, which actually I think was rather unusual." Throughout 1971, Roxy were a group waiting to happen; in fact, for many months, they were also a group with no name.

"I made a list with Andy Mackay, I think, a great list of names of cinemas: *Odeon, Gaumont, Essoldo* – all those names that had a nice ring to them, but they didn't really mean anything except that they were a place you went to escape everyday life. And *Roxy* seemed to be the nicest one," says Ferry. Like the pop art Ferry admired so much, the name "Roxy" was both deeply mundane and powerfully evocative. It spoke of the decadent glamour of the movie house, of bright lights and adolescent escapism in grimy northern towns, whilst also punning "rock", the musical style. And it was always written in inverted commas, implying an irony and sense of distance carefully designed to fit the new image. To this day, those connected with the band tend to call it "Roxy", not "Roxy Music". The expanded band name came about later in 1971, when it was found that an American band had released an album under the name of Roxy the year before. But the forced name change was fortuitous: "Roxy Music" spoke of a whole new way of viewing the pop scene, a completely fresh musical start, and a completely new kind of music.

The least secure gig in rock would be that of the Roxy Music bassist. Throughout the various reincarnations of the band, Ferry would use an astonishing fourteen different musicians in this position. However,

American Dexter Lloyd was in place on drums. A classically trained timpanist, he had played with the Cleveland Symphony Orchestra. "He was the only drummer we tried who could play anything creative on the slow numbers," said Ferry in 1971. Additionally, the band would have two different lead guitarists before Phil Manzanera. Every band worth its salt seems to suffer at one stage or other from the Pete Best syndrome, according to which those if-only musicians who were members before the big-time bail out or are dumped before the stardom is achieved. The Darwinism of the rock world, with its sackings and fall-outs, its coups and *coups de grace*, makes it a very messy business indeed. Roxy Music would be no exception: a series of musicians joined and departed, and later, a series of acrimonious business and personal fallings-out and divorces were to make the Bryan Ferry story something of an ongoing near-crisis.

Roxy's original lead guitarist was Roger Bunn. Born in Norwich in 1942, Bunn was at the Star Club with the Beatles, jammed with Jimi Hendrix, and played with Stevie Winwood and Traffic before making a 1971 solo record, *Piece Of Mind*, with the Dutch National Orchestra. Active in the anti-apartheid movement in the eighties, today he runs the Music Industry Human Rights Association, whose job is to "to activate the roots of the music industry to educate themselves on what needs to be changed and centralize protest to advance better working conditions within the industry." In short, he is a very different sort of chap to Bryan Ferry, who, today, is more likely to be targeted by hunt saboteurs then be seen supporting a liberal cause.

Bunn played with Roxy from around the early spring to the late summer of 1971. "I saw an ad in a paper and gave them a call," says Bunn:

I got there and they could see I had a pro attitude. My first meeting was at Bryan's place at Olympia. I just walked over and took my guitar and an amp and jammed with them for a while. Pretty soon after that we moved out to Eno's gaff in south London, which had a larger back room. Eno had a tape recorder, and his computer with his *[makes electronic whooshing noise]* and we used to squeeze into this little room with space for little drums. The guitar sound I had on those early recordings was awful; it sounded like a fuckin' banjo. It was definitely not a modern guitar sound, and that was probably down to the fact that I wasn't terribly interested in the gig at the time. One of the arrangements they later released was very close to an arrangement I had put together, which I found a little disconcerting. It was an arrangement that was pretty avant-garde and had a lot of chaos musically, but there was a theme running through it. It was released on some Roxy Music thing, but I never heard back from them.

Bunn was unimpressed by Ferry as a vocalist:

I think Ferry called me a "proper musician" in *Mojo* magazine. Little did he know how little I knew! I was obviously more experienced than he was, because I was dying to ask him if he could try and sing in tune. There are some people who talk a song, some who act a song, and some who sing a song. There are some people who can't do anything else but belt a song. I'm not sure which of these categories Bryan Ferry comes into. He was very nervous, probably the most nervous singer I've ever worked with. Bryan was extremely white, extremely English and extremely nervous.

Bunn was also highly suspicious of Ferry's ultimate motives: "I was quoted in the early days of saying that, when I first met Bryan Ferry, I looked into his eyes and I saw dollar signs. That's what happened to me. I went along with his requests. He told me that he was looking for a guy called Davy O'List eventually, so I wasn't that enthusiastic about taking the gig on, because it was obvious that I was just a fill-in for him. Nobody else mentioned that of course; they were quite happy about having me in the band."

In fact, 1971 was the crucial year in the development of Roxy Music. All the songs that would go into making the first Roxy Music album, plus tracks such as "Grey Lagoons" and "For Your Pleasure", which would be used for the follow-up, were worked on during the months of rehearsals. No gigs were played, and none were sought. Roxy were honing their craft behind closed doors, not on the road. Whilst the band's repertoire took shape, Bryan Ferry attempted to establish some sort of media interest that might lead to a management deal and a recording contract. Since all the rest of the band had day jobs at the time, the onus was on Ferry to interest record companies. Without exception, each one rejected him in turn. He then decided to switch tactics; rather than impress a record company, he thought it would be equally helpful to impress a management company. But he needed an ally in the media. He fell lucky.

In a series of articles which broke what he saw as an important new band, Richard Williams, then a broadcaster and rock writer at *Melody Maker*, was the first major British print journalist to champion Roxy Music. Assistant editor to Ray Coleman, Williams was also about to begin as the first presenter of BBC's new flagship rock music programme, *The Old Grey Whistle Test*. He was an incredibly assiduous journalist, bashing out 25,000 words a week, always willing to listen to new bands and new ideas. At the time, *Melody Maker* was the most important weekly British music paper. A *Melody Maker* front cover could single-handedly launch a new group, or push an established one onto a new level of critical acceptance.

Williams interviewed Ferry at his home in Shepherds Bush, west London. The first article, published on August 7, 1971 in the magazine's "Horizon – New Names That Could Break The Sound Barrier" section, was headed "Roxy In The Rock Stakes". In it, Williams raved about, "one of the most exciting demo tapes ever to come my way. Although it was recorded on a small home tape machine in what sounds like a Dutch barn it carries enough innovatory excitement to suggest that Roxy [as they were then still called] may well be ahead of the field in the avant-rock stakes." "I thought that if there was anyone who was going to like the stuff I was doing it was going to be Richard Williams," is how Ferry remembers it. "I just identified with his taste a lot of the time in his writing. And he called me up and said the tape was one of the best things he had ever heard. I was just overwhelmed." Richard Williams continues the story:

> I lived in Shepherds Bush at the time. I don't know quite how this happened, but Bryan came round with a tape. I wasn't in, but the person who was took it and said, I'll give it to him when he comes in. And he said, this nice bloke called Bryan Ferry has just popped round and given you this tape. People used to send tapes quite a lot but they didn't bring them round to the flat by hand! I used to listen to everything because sometimes there would be interesting stuff. *Horizon* was a spotlight for completely unknown people, people with no record deal or anything. In many ways I used to like writing about odd things more than I liked writing about more established people. I put the tape on, and it sounded really interesting and weird. I'll never know to this day whether I played it at the right speed, or whether it was a quarter-track tape I was playing on a half-track

machine or vice versa, or whether indeed I played it backwards, but it sounded really odd and interesting, like a culmination of lots of things I was interested in: a bit of Velvet Underground, a bit of free jazz, a bit of doo-wop, but not as crude as that. It was as if somebody had listened to lots of different things and had tried to blend them all into some form of experimental rock music, which there wasn't very much of in the era of embroidered denim shirts.

So, I think I must have rung him up, because there was a telephone number on the tape box. It had interesting stickers on it as well, which they'd done themselves. At that time they were called Roxy and the stickers were of little aeroplanes flying over skyscrapers, making a sort of skywriting thing with the name: "Roxy". That was touching; they'd obviously gone to a bit of trouble. Nice handwriting, that's what I remember on the cover of the tape, with the titles and the telephone number and his name. You can tell a lot about a person from his handwriting. So I rang him up and I think we had a drink in – what were those terrible places that used to do fry-ups on Fleet Street – the Golden Egg on Fleet Street, and I suppose I interviewed him. He had his picture taken in Lincoln's Inn Fields, I think by Barrie Wentzell, our photographer.

It was clear from their first major piece of media coverage that Roxy Music were not going to follow the normal dues-paying route of gigging and hard slogging in the provinces. Theirs would be a new tactic, and, like most things new, it immediately ruffled the feathers of the pop Establishment. Bryan Ferry told Williams: "We've got a lot of confidence in what we're doing, and we're determined to make it in as civilised a way as possible. The average age of the band is about 27, and we're not interested in scuffling. If someone will invest some time and money in us, we'll be very good indeed."

In September 1971, Roger Bunn left Roxy Music, and once again an advert was placed in *Melody Maker*, this time reading: "Wanted: Tricky Dick lead guitarist." Ferry got his man in the shape of David O'List. Formerly of the Nice, O'List was very much a "proper" musician, and securing him for the band was a very real coup on Ferry's part. O'List would play the first Roxy gigs, remaining with the band until just before they were signed. However, he vehemently disputes the claim that he answered Roxy's siren call and was hired by the band. According to him, it was the other way round:

During the late summer of 1971, I ran an advertisement in *Melody Maker* for an image-conscious, progressive rock group with a recording contract and agency (contrary to press statements that I answered an advertisement from Roxy Music, which is not true). Bryan Ferry replied to my advertisement. When I told him who I was, he said he had been looking for me for months to complete the line-up of Roxy Music When I asked if the group had a record deal, Bryan hesitated then said no, all the record companies had turned them down. This put me off somewhat. However, when Bryan said that he was an avid fan and had watched me play at the Newcastle City Hall with the Nice in 1968, I asked him about the line-up of his group. He told me about the avant-garde percussionist, the VSC 3 synth player, the oboe and sax player, and himself on electric piano and vocals. It began to sound interesting, especially for a group in 1971, so I said to Bryan that I would try out the group, with an intention of producing and writing for it, but there would have to be an agreement that Bryan Ferry/Roxy Music will ensure payment for my writing, performance and production work with royalties once it had a record contract. Bryan guaranteed he would. I also said that with my press, agency and record company contacts I could obtain a recording deal for Roxy Music if they were good enough and I liked them. Bryan was over-joyed to hear this.

O'List agreed to meet the current members of Roxy Music and play some loose arrangements of songs. His assessment of the musical merits of Roxy Music was that a lot needed doing: "It was below standard, but I thought the unusual combination of instruments could be commercial if my guitar was added and I produced it. The songs needed to be arranged appropriately with new chord additions, melody, structure/mood, etc." Having received assurances that he would be a full member of the group, with full composing and performing rights, O'List joined Roxy as their new guitarist.

Rehearsals went on apace during the autumn of 1971 in a large photographic studio in Hampstead, lent to the band for one or two evenings a week by a photographer friend of Ferry's at *Time Out* magazine. Ferry and Mackay took out a loan to buy a proper PA, which was stored in the loft of the studio. O'List introduced material of his own, including "Green Willow Tree" and "White Indian Butterfly", which O'List and Ferry sang as a duet, and "O'List's Waltz". He also suggested that a change of drummer would be necessary if the band were to beef up their sound and make it more commercial. O'List's version of events runs as follows:

> The avant-garde percussion was great fun. Eno was experimenting with treating the various percussion instruments through his VCS3, but I knew the group needed a commercial rock drummer if they were to reach the required level. I discussed this with the group and the following week an advertisement appeared in *Melody Maker* for a rock drummer. Several people applied, including a woman called Sue. She would have been an interesting image inclusion if she had been a more experienced drummer. One of the other applicants, Paul Thompson, rang back to ask if he could be auditioned the following week as his kit was stuck in a Tin Pan Alley studio. At his audition my opinion was that he was the most experienced so far but I was not sure if his personality would gel. With hindsight, it turned out I was right. If we had gone on auditioning further drummers and been choosier, the split might not have happened at all. The various personalities within Roxy Music did not always gel, especially Paul and Eno. Eno did not consider himself a musician. Eno was after pop stardom and how I could obtain this for him.

It was the crucial addition of Paul Thompson on drums in 1971, after the departure of Dexter Lloyd, which turned an interesting avant-garde rock group into a tour de force, O'List's reservations and later personality clashes notwithstanding. Thompson brought a much-needed professionalism to the Roxy rhythm section, and he was a permanent fixture until 1980, when his rumoured sacking by Ferry outraged Roxy fans. Unpretentious and hard-working, he's never been trendy or sought out publicity, yet the epithet "The Great Paul Thompson" sums up the fans' feelings perfectly about arguably the most popular member of Roxy Music.

Thompson, the youngest member of the original line-up, was born in Newcastle on May 13, 1951, and so was just 20 when he joined the band. When he was six months old, his family moved to Jarrow, where Paul would attend West Simonside Infants and Junior School. "I remember the music lessons in the infants," says Thompson. "There were drums, triangles, bells and tambourines. I always wanted to try the drum, but never got picked, so one day I waited until everyone left the classroom, then slung the drum over my shoulder and rattled out a tune. That's when I knew I could play." His first drum kit was made out of his Meccano set: "I hadn't yet developed enough mechanical skill to make a bass drum pedal, so I used to stamp on the floor!"

Still without a proper kit, he persuaded his mother to buy an Olympic drum kit on hire purchase. "It was about £70, about four pounds a week," remembers Thompson. "I could tell they were worried about making the payments, but I convinced them that I could contribute by the money I would get by playing gigs at the local youth club. They nervously signed the agreement – they knew how badly I wanted those drums, bless them. We used to carry our equipment to the club in the guitarist's dad's wheelbarrow; people used to laugh, but we didn't care. We just wanted to play." Throughout his early teens, Thompson played in various bands, including Johnny Blue and the Blue Boys and the Thyme, then left school at 15 to start an apprentice-ship as a metalworker in Palmer's Shipyard in Hebburn. He left the Thyme to join the Urge, working with the singer who later became known as John Miles (he of "Music" fame), and Vic Malcolm, later of Geordie. "They were playing seven nights a week," continues Thompson. "I was earning about £35 per week with the band playing in night clubs, pubs and working men's clubs, and about £3 per week in the shipyard. I used to come in from a gig at about 3am and have to get up for work at 7am. Eventually I got fired for falling asleep at work, so at the age of 17 I became a pro musician. I carried on playing the club scene with various bands, including Billy Fury's backing band."

So, unlike most of the rest of Roxy Music – a slightly strange mix of electronics boffins, established stars, and reluctant schoolteachers – Thompson was an undiscovered musical talent with an apprenticeship in rock. However, he was still far from being a successful musician. The progressive rock he now enjoyed didn't go down well in the clubs and, soon enough, Thompson had left music again. For a while he found employment with Ted "the Tatie Man" Hooper, "who paid me a pound a day for humping bags of spuds. I decided this was the time to head down south to find my fortune." Thompson continues:

I bought a copy of *Melody Maker*. The ad said, "wonder drummer wanted for avant-rock group." I rang the number and a bloke with a bit of a posh accent with a slight Geordie tinge answered. It was Bryan Ferry – he seemed happy to hear my own Jarrow twang. We arranged an audition for a few days later; when that day arrived I was in a state of panic as my drum kit was locked in a studio in Denmark St where I had been doing a session a few days before! Luckily I was staying with Matthews' Southern Comfort's roadie, who lent me their kit. I made the audition and landed the job. There were no wages at that time with the band, so I got a job on a building site in Fulham (me and 200 Irishmen), to keep the wolf away from the door. I remember turning up at our first John Peel session in my work gear. The band was growing bigger every day. Eventually we signed a deal and were getting a small wage. Goodbye cement dust, goodbye Irishmen, hello the road to stardom! The rest is history.

In late 1971, although there were now the beginnings of serious interest in them, the band were still without either management or a label. Not only was the future Great Paul Thompson working as a brickie, but both Andy and Bryan were still cobbling together some money teaching. Roxy might easily have remained an "avant" rock group, unsigned and unsuccessful. All the while, though, Ferry was building a coterie of the like-minded to mastermind the first rush towards super-stardom. This aspect particularly impressed Richard Williams; Ferry was already assembling a team of like-minded people to work with him:

> I got to know Bryan a little bit, had dinner with him a few times, and with Andy. I was very impressed by him. He was someone who had a very clear idea of how he wanted to present himself. I thought he was a nice bloke too. I liked the way in which he deployed his ambition. He was ambitious but he wanted to use his ambition creatively, and to draw other creative people into his world and to make use of them, for example Nick De Ville [artwork], Eric Boman [photography], Antony Price [fashion], and Simon Puxley [publicity], as well as the musicians. It was obvious that, from very early on, he was creating a world.

These were the days before style magazines such as *i-D* or *The Face* existed to give pointers to would-be pop aesthetes. Ferry simply had impeccable taste and knew the most interesting people on the scene. Nick De Ville he knew from university. Central to the Ferry story would be Antony Price, whom he had first met at a party in 1971 when Price was working at Stirling Cooper, a designer on Wigmore Street in London. "That was really the 'in' place, with new weird clothes and designs. Tight trousers, big shoulders ... a very sexy sort of look," recalls Ferry. "When I actually talked to Antony a few weeks later, it was at the bar of the Speakeasy of all places, just around the corner from Air Studios. See, there were very few places to go at the time. Antony always kids me about calling him from a call-box in the Kings Road to come and talk to him about doing the cover, because I was always, like, very shy and hesitant and he was so, 'Come on, let's get on with it!' in a very blunt Yorkshire way."

"We just hit it off," says Antony Price. "Bryan invited me to his place and played me some tracks he'd been working on. We were both working-class northern boys trying to make it in London, but we were both art students. We had this idea to fuse music and fashion, which was outrageous at the time but it worked."

Ferry was no dilettante either. As a teenager he had worked at a tailor's shop at weekends, and this had given him knowledge of the business and a feel for the right cut. Looking good would become essential for Ferry. In interviews he would claim that he only looked good from certain angles, or that his clothes were not that expensive, or even that he had been known to slob around in a pair of jeans, but, be this as it may, ninety-nine percent of the time he dresses excellently, classically, if, it has to be said, predictably. "I was into sculptured clothes rather than the chiffon-y sixties look," is how Ferry puts it. "There was a harder edge to it, working in elements of American gangsters and so on. It had more cross-referencing for me: you could get bits of Raymond Chandler or even Fred Astaire coming in." Thirty years later, when he almost lost his life on board a British Airways flight assailed by a deranged man with a death wish, one of his main comments to the press was that he had been disturbed by the design of the man's socks.

At the end of 1971 and the beginning of 1972, the infant Roxy took their first eccentric steps. They played a gig at the Friends Of The Tate Gallery Christmas Party in 1971, followed by a private party at the Fine Art department at Reading University, where Andy Mackay had studied. O'List remembers the gigs, not altogether fondly: "Our first gig was in a big reception hall above a large pub opposite Olympia, in aid of an American girls' college. I remember it well, as I was the only member suitably dressed for Roxy Music. I wore a fashionable pink satin jacket. My mother, a stage actress, came to the gig, and she said afterwards that we ought to get another singer. It's true, Bryan just did not have the power, but I believed it would come with more experience. It was only our first gig, after all!"

O'List is keen to counter claims that he was unwilling to "muck in" with the other band members and do his share of the fetching and carrying because of his "star" status: "I have always chipped in with the lifting and transportation ever since my first band Little Boy Blues." Yet others remember different: "He had already been in an enormous band and the prospect of starting from scratch did not appeal," is how O'List's eventual successor in Roxy, Phil Manzanera put it. "They were humping all their own gear then. I remember a gig for Friends Of The Tate, with Bryan staggering in with this huge stack on his back while David O'List was sitting there playing to himself."

One of the next gigs was at the 100 Club in Oxford Street in December 1971. This was a period, however, when the audience were dressed more extremely than the band. According to biographer Johnny Rogan, "Ferry restricted himself to wearing a baseball jacket and jeans." "I was a schoolteacher at the time, teaching music at Holland Park in the day and driving the van and humping the gear at night," Andy Mackay recalled in 1983. "I would be picked up from school and we would change into the flashest clothes we had and go on stage." Richard Williams was the only journo at the gig:

> I went and saw them at the 100 Club. That was much more impressive than the tape, partly because you could see that they had already got a little audience of their own. There might have been about two-dozen followers there, but they were interesting-looking people, wearing what I'm sure now were Antony Price creations: leopard-skin pillbox hats and that sort of thing. The other interesting thing, apart from the fact that the songs were stronger and more distinctive, was that Brian Eno stood at the back with his VCS3 adding noise elements and sound modifications to what they were doing. The 100 Club is very shallow. It's narrow, but length-wise narrow, so that the stage is quite long, and the audience goes out quite a way to the left and right, but it's not very deep. Brian Eno situated himself where the sound mixer would be today, which was highly unusual to say the least! O'List was in the group then. I had seen him with the Nice three or four years earlier, and I thought he was a great guitarist, really good. I was really surprised to find him in Roxy Music, as I'd always regarded him as a hippy musician in a way, and they definitely weren't a hippy group. I do remember Brian and Bryan, and I remember the audience, and how good the songs sounded. It all made a considerable impression.

According to O'List, the show was arranged entirely for Williams' benefit:

> It was specially put on so that Richard Williams could view the group before writing his article for *Melody Maker*. He became interested in the group because he knew me and had written before about me with the Nice. The article was needed to put Roxy Music in the limelight for the record companies. Communications on stage were non-existent; nobody looked at each other, and I could not catch anyone's attention. They all looked bemused, especially Paul and Eno. Eno had put himself out of sight so we could not see him, and they were all unaware of me trying to surge something special up for Richard Williams.

Perhaps O'List's critique of the band – a bunch of disconnected musicians, lacking in traditional stagecraft and musical expertise – is accurate. But perhaps, also, it was simply the fact that Roxy Music were part of a *new* breed of rock acts that flummoxed him. A success with the Nice in the sixties, O'List was a musician who had been schooled in a different era. Despite their naivety and manifest rough edges, Roxy were something else again.

By the end of 1971, the pop world was beginning to come to life after what seemed to have been a three-year coma. T. Rex, much loved for their sense of cheeky chaos married with great pop tunes, had began mining the basic structures of early rock 'n' roll, blues, and acoustic folk in a string of huge singles ("Hot Love", "Jeepster") and brilliant album cuts ("Life's A Gas", "Cosmic Dancer"). They were the biggest group of 1971. Elsewhere, though, the pop/rock divide was as rigid as ever. Serious artists like Led Zeppelin, Genesis, Pink Floyd, Yes, Jethro Tull and King Crimson concentrated full-square on serious music, song-suites, brilliant playing, astonishingly fiddly time-signatures and musical excellence, building up huge fan-bases of hairies with value-for-money and, at times, wildly theatrical stage presentations.

The sleeping giant was, of course, David Bowie, who had spent the whole of 1971 writing and recording two complete albums, *Hunky Dory* and *The Rise And Fall Of Ziggy Stardust And The Spiders From Mars*. The former, released just before Christmas 1971, had been a complete flop, and Bowie remained a cult waiting to happen. In 1971, few could have predicted that it would be Bowie, off the radar since what was beginning to look like a novelty hit three years earlier with "Space Oddity", who would be the face of 1972, quickly eclipsing Bolan as the biggest British rock star since the Beatles.

The intervention of Bowie, and his success, pre-dated that of Roxy Music by just a couple of months. Yet this too would be crucial to the Roxy Music breakthrough. Their music, more extreme than Bowie's, needed someone to pave the way for what would turn out to be their almost instant success. In the pop world of 1972, cool irony eventually replaced journeyman authenticity. The sixties were finally over.

THE SIXTIES END
TODAY: 1972

Roxy Music were Britain's first punk band. This is an astonishing claim, perhaps, if to you punk means burning down the house of convention with rough, untutored playing. However, if you think punk was more about the triumph of the absurd over the boring and the mainstream, and, more particularly, if it means the do-it-yourself ethic of musicianship and promotion, then Roxy Music were as punk as they come. The line-up of the Roxy Music that hit the record racks in the summer of 1972 contained only one *bona fide* professional musician. The astonishing music on their eponymous debut album had all the devil-may-care sonic disruption of many of punk's artier sections. But what rooted them firmly in the broad intellectual and musical tradition of punk was their promotion. Roxy Music had simply bypassed many of the normal avenues completely, arriving, as if through some Dadaist scam, fully formed for the rock world.

Roxy Music dealt a mortal blow to the sixties, four years before the last of the flower children were dead-headed at the behest of Malcolm McLaren and the Pistols. Bowie, of course, was Roxy's androgyne accomplice and, between them, they altered the face of British pop culture. Earnest rock, played by scruffs for scruffs, continued after 1972, but it would be obvious from then on that people who liked "that sort of thing" were dinosaurs; there was simply something wrong with them. And although progressive rock continued, destined to endlessly repeat, and hoary old rock carried on too with Deep Purple, Bad Company and Status Quo, it was neither cool nor right. Even aficionados of Genesis, the most progressive of the progressive rock bands thanks to Peter Gabriel, knew that what they were experiencing was something of a guilty pleasure.

Pop history has never been driven solely by what is *pop*ular. The acts that have really made a difference, whether they be Radiohead in the nineties, the Smiths in the eighties or Roxy Music in the seventies, were almost instinctively adopted by a cult of forward-thinking record-buyers who might not be all-powerful numerically speaking but, as tastemakers, were crucial: they made pop culture. In those terms, from 1972 to 1975, Roxy Music were Britain's most influential band.

What Roxy and Bowie did was to declare that they were putting on a performance, for both artistic *and* commercial gain. Dressing up, playing at playing, playing at being a woman, playing around with musical styles – it was as far removed from the earnestness of the Woodstock generation as could be imagined. However artily framed, this was *show business*. It was important to be seen to have references from outside of rock: from high and low art, literature, film, in fact from a broad base of culture. It was equally important to flaunt this learning, to appear brazen and self-confident, whilst at the same time aloof, sexy and exotic. Folk idealism was out; witty, sly irony was in.

By the early seventies, it was also clear that popular music was still at the centre of youth culture, but that its power was being harnessed for very different purposes than those of the heady days of sixties' optimism. At its very best, music is a more accurate indicator than any other popular art form; more immediate and true than cinema, drama or literature, at its most potent it both comments on and creates its own agenda, articulating the immediacy of our emotions so completely that, a pop song can be more meaningful than any other cultural artefact. In early-seventies Britain, when Bowie wrote (and Ian Hunter sang), "Is that concrete all around, or is it in my head?", the atmosphere was one of retreat, uncertainty and dread.

The "modernisation" of the sixties was now revealed as the ersatz culture it had always been, an urban sprawl and architectural Armageddon visited upon many a city and town. The woozy optimism of the counterculture was gone, and what was to replace it had not quite formed. In all their perfectly weird mix of future nostalgia and gender-bending arrogance, Roxy Music revealed early-seventies Britain to be (in) a confused state. With racism, bigotry, xenophobia and sexism so rooted in the British psyche, the arrival of glam, then punk, on the British youth culture scene outraged the status quo and loosened Britain's culture of deference from its moorings, proving that British pop music was more significant culturally than ever before.

Roxy Music marked the end of rock-as-rebellion, and the true beginning of rock-as-art. Soon, Roxy fans would be walking, talking works of art themselves, glam look-alikes willing to test their nerve – and the nerves of parents up and down the land – as they dared themselves towards a future of dyed hair, outrageous costuming and, for some, in-between sexualities. The Roxy Revolution would entice a new generation of fans who were bored by the tedium of the music scene in 1972. But they had their vocal detractors too.

For that sizeable part of the record-buying community (plus almost all the rock and pop journalists, at least initially) who saw rock as a means of projecting the voice of protest, or embodying the youthful articulation of more simple emotions, Roxy were a colossal nuisance. Those who didn't get the joke deemed the importation of witty asides, cool ironic glances and brazenly decadent showmanship to be tacky. In fact, the joke was on them. With Roxy, there would be no rumours of crazy drummers whammed on monkey tranquillisers, or fishy tales of women and lobsters in hotel rooms. Roxy brought style into pop, along with a certain contrived elegance. "Other bands wanted to wreck hotel rooms," said Ferry. "Roxy Music wanted to redecorate them."

Roxy's rapid (and, some said, vapid) ascent, almost unprecedented in its speed and completeness, came about because crucial gatekeepers spotted their potential almost immediately. We've already seen how Richard Williams, one of the most influential music journalists of his day, had championed the band. They were soon able to count on another media heavyweight too, in the form of John Peel:

> They were terrific because they were a proper band. I went to see them at a place called, unbelievably, the Hobbit's Garden in Wimbledon, with Genesis. They were about the only band that came along at the time that didn't contain at least one member from a previously successful band, which was how the record industry would work then. Band A would break up and the constituent parts would go on to form bands B, C, D and E, with varying degrees of success. That was the only way you would get signed to a record label. Roxy Music were about the only completely new band to appear in the first half of the seventies.

In the year leading up to their first album, Ferry had acted as both booking agent and promoter and, despite his bashful nature, had succeeded in assiduously pressing the flesh of the media and the record business. Guitarist Davy O'List claims that, as a high-profile musician, it was his involvement with the group that ultimately secured Roxy's success. But Ferry's considerable personal charm, his secure vision for the future of the band and the sheer excellence of his songwriting were not inconsiderable selling points either. People who met Ferry liked him and were impressed by his drive and intellect. And the music, for those with ears, was something remarkable.

Appearing one day at John Peel's BBC Radio One office, equipped with the Roxy demo tape, Ferry recognised Peel's sidekick and producer John Walters, who had played in a jazz band in Newcastle. Having handed over the tape, Ferry came back a week later for the verdict. "I didn't know what Bryan did, you see," remembered Walters in 1999. "I said, 'The vocalist with that kind of atonal "aieeeeeeoooooeiioo" strange Larry The Lamb kind of thing, leaping about. That was really interesting and made it stand out.' 'Oh good,' said Ferry, 'well, actually, I'm the vocalist.'"

Peel arranged for the band to appear on the highly influential *Top Gear* BBC TV show. Recorded on January 4, 1972, and broadcast on January 21, the session comprised five tracks earmarked for inclusion on the band's debut album: "The Bob (Medley)", "Would You Believe?", "Re-Make/Re-Model", "If There Is Something" and "Sea Breezes". It was far from slick, but the sound was unique; with his heavy licks and guitar runs, O'List brought dynamism to the sound. In fact, the entire middle section of "If There Is Something" was given over to an extended solo. O'List is adamant that his role in reshaping the material was crucial: "During the rehearsals I restructured/refashioned Bryan's songs, adding new beginnings, new middles and new endings and generally beefing up the sound. You can hear on the first album evidence of all my work, they kept it all in because without it they would not have had a deal. Phil Manzanera copied me, note for note, buying the same guitar to obtain the same sound."

The band was still without either a manager or, crucially, a record label. However, the situation was about to undergo a rapid change. After several months, and several rejections, EG management were the ones to bite the bullet and take on the band. EG's clients already included T Rex, Emerson, Lake and Palmer and, of course, King Crimson, headed by Pete Sinfield and Robert Fripp. "The original EG Management, that is to say David Enthoven and John Gaydon, were absolute darling people," enthuses Sinfield.

I believed they actually re-mortgaged their house to pay the bills so that we could finish the first King Crimson album. More than that you can't really ask of your management! And they were charming: ex-Harrovian, wonderful people. John Gaydon now works in films, and David's doing pretty well as the manager of Robbie Williams. Round about that time, they had these other partners who came into it, Sam Alder and Mark Fenwick.

"I remember David Enthoven was the first man I ever saw who shaved his head, as did his girlfriend," recalls former *Melody Maker* journalist Chris Charlesworth. "They rode motorbikes together with shaved heads, in 1971." "It was kind of gentlemen at play," is how Bryan Ferry remembers the Gaydon/Enthoven axis. "They had their Harley Davidsons and they were like public schoolboy Hell's Angels with their leather jackets and cowboy boots." "Bryan came in with the tape – it completely blew me away," recalls Enthoven. "This has only happened for me twice. Once, when I first saw King Crimson, and the second time when I heard this Roxy tape. It was unlike anything else that was going on, but I just knew I had to have it." In actual fact, Enthoven was somewhat undecided. The story is that EG offered Ferry a contract as a solo artist first, and only when this was turned down did they discuss giving the band a chance to impress.

Roxy were asked to audition for EG in a disused cinema, the Granada in Wandsworth Road, London. As Roxy biographer Johnny Rogan notes, "The setting could hardly have been more appropriate." The venue was being used most nights for bingo. "Fruit machines line the foyer and there's a big sign with lots of numbers on it hanging over the stage," wrote *Melody Maker*'s Richard Williams, who was present at the audition. "It's a cold Tuesday afternoon and the ladies who throng in for 'eyes down' later on are still at the laundromat. Stroll through the door marked 'No Entry' and up the concrete steps into the disused balcony, where the seats are heavy with dust. Suddenly a burst of machine-gun guitar scatters the cobwebs, to be followed by the sound of a rock 'n' roll band gunning their motor through the changes of a song which sounds like the product of a weird meeting between the Marcels [an early sixties doo-wop group] and one of the heavier German bands."

It was the most important gig of the band's life and it did not run swimmingly. According to reports, the audition degenerated into farce as drummer Paul Thompson and guitarist O'List were involved in a heated exchange of views that, some say, boiled over into a full-blown fistfight. Thompson denies that they came to blows, but admits that O'List "never wanted me in the band anyway." O'List recalls a sour atmosphere all round, and makes it plain that Eno, in particular, wanted him out of the group:

> There was tension between Bryan Ferry and Brian Eno over who was the focal point in the group. On the way to the performance for EG I knew something was wrong because of the tension in the car. It was not relaxed, fun and jovial as usual. Communication within the group was at a low level, especially when we got onto the stage. Eno had decided not to play much and just stood there watching at the back of the hall, pretending to mix with another person, Phil Manzanera, who was masquerading as Roxy Music's road manager by then. It just did not look right. It became obvious to me that Eno had made a move to get a replacement for me.

Richard Williams says Roxy had asked his advice before agreeing to attend the audition:

> After I went to the 100 Club gig, and got to know them a bit, we were relatively friendly. I knew Phil Manzanera because I think he sent me a Quiet Sun tape for that same column, "New Horizons", and I had done a piece on them, completely coincidentally with no connection to Bryan or Roxy Music at all. Then Bryan rang up and he asked me if I knew anything about EG. He probably rang a lot of people up; it wasn't just me. I knew them through the publicist BP Fallon. He was Marc Bolan's publicist, and King Crimson's for a bit. I said I thought they were very good, which they were. And then Bryan said, well, we're playing an audition for them in Wandsworth, in a cinema. I got a lift down with David Enthoven in his Aston Martin. Anyway, they were really good, and David was clearly interested but puzzled, because he'd never seen anything like it; nobody had really. But it was obvious that they weren't the kind of band that had been on the road. They didn't have the kind of polish that three years in clubs and colleges would have given them, but they were, of course, very interesting. David asked me

what I thought of them, and I said, great, and then the next thing I knew they had made a deal.

Having gained a management deal, they then proceeded to lose a guitarist. Listening again to the very earliest Roxy Music recordings, its true that David O'List sticks out a mile. He was already a superb technician, and his guitar work was intricate and fitted the Roxy sound. Up to a point. Whether Ferry was so keen on allowing space in the music to showcase O'List's guitar solos is a moot question. Ferry's later work would, of course, fall foul of the muso tendency to allow session men to ruin a perfectly good tune with a dullsville solo but, back in 1972, Roxy simply weren't the sort of band to let an individual member take centre stage. There were also reports of O'List living a more rock 'n' roll lifestyle. The producer of the John Peel session, John Muir, reveals: "When the band came into the control room to listen back to the mix, I asked, 'Where's Dave?' 'In the studio', they said, and there he was, lying flat on his back."

For O'List, however, it was plain that he was being manoeuvred out of the band: "Bryan once said that the group must have seemed pedestrian to David O'List, which is why he probably left. This is not true. He wanted me out of the limelight as I was catching all the attention, and if this went on I would become the favorite in the group. Brian Eno and Bryan Ferry did not want this to happen. They both wanted to be the focus of attention." O'List would be the first big-name casualty of the power struggle at the heart of the band. As the decade progressed, Ferry's grasp on Roxy would turn the group from a democracy into a dictatorship, benign or otherwise.

Step forward 21-year-old Phil Targett-Adams. "I joined Roxy Music in 1972," remembers Phil. "It was doubly exciting because my 21st birthday was on January 21, and then on February 14 we signed our first recording contract with EG Management." His first act on joining the band was to adopt a new surname: that of his mother, Manzanera. Vaguely exotic, it was a better fit than the preppy original.

Manzanera was born Philip Geoffrey Targett-Adams in London on January 31, 1951, to a Columbian mother and an English father. His early years were spent in Hawaii, Venezuela, Colombia and Cuba. He began playing the Spanish guitar at the age of six, and learned Cuban folksongs at the time of the Cuban Revolution. At the age of eight he began experimenting with the electric guitar (since the demise of Roxy, his diverse work as producer and solo musician has shown him to be something of a pioneer in the marrying of Latin rhythms and rock).

Manzanera's first group was Wing Commander Nixon and His Wheat-Eating Bees, followed shortly afterwards by the equally unpromisingly monikered Pooh And The Ostrich Feather. Still a teenager, in the early seventies, he worked with the progressive rock act Quiet Sun, but the band folded having won little acclaim. Charles Hayward went on to play in Mal Dean's Amazing Band and Gong, and bass player Bill MacCormick joined Robert Wyatt's Matching Mole, and also stood for Parliament for the Liberal Party in Beckenham.

Manzanera, though, was still a long way from either technical excellence or, for that matter, commercial professional breakthrough. Quiet Sun had, however, been featured in *Melody Maker's* "New Horizon" section, "along with this new guy Bryan Ferry and a group called the Roxy," Manzanera told *NME's* Nick Kent in 1974. "It eventually ended up with me going round to listen to the group, mainly because they'd been given more of a rave review."

As a lead guitarist, Manzanera was neither strong nor dominant. Rather, his slightly fey and undeniably eccentric guitar parts seemed to interweave themselves with the general pattern of the group sound. This was a lead guitarist who simply didn't lead – perfect for a band that already had two musicians who could hardly play. He had originally auditioned for the gig when Roger Bunn left Roxy Music six months earlier, but, passed over for O'List, he kept his day job at Clarkson's Travel Agency. Then, in late 1971, a vacancy came up for a sound mixer and Manzanera jumped at the chance, despite the fact that he didn't know how to mix sound. In the months leading up to the big breakthrough he was part of the Roxy Music extended family. As in so many families, money was a recurring issue. By this stage, Ferry was living at Andy Mackay's gaff in Battersea, while Paul Thompson, fresh from the north-east, crashed out at Eno's. Manzanera, intrigued by the band, was offered the chance to roadie for them in late 1971.

Ferry and co put Manzanera through a gruelling two-day audition before finally admitting him into Roxy. There is some evidence to suggest that Manzanera was not the only guitarist considered for the band. Musician Spencer Mallinson has claimed:

I joined the group, it seems, just after David O'List: if I remember correctly, around 1971-72. I had gotten into the group via Brian Eno, who lived at Leith Mansions, Grantully Road, London W9. I've had this address in an old address book I kept. His flat was around the corner from Jilly's, the restaurant I ran in Kilburn Square. Eno used to often come in for food, and had seen and heard me practicing my guitar behind the counter. We became friends and he asked me over to Bryan Ferry's flat to become Roxy's guitarist. He used to process my guitar with his Putney VC3 synth. We rehearsed a lot, but the group didn't seem to be going anywhere. I was sure wrong.

Although the chronology appears wrong (Mallinson must surely have been considered for Roxy after Roger Bunn and before O'List), it does now seem that there was yet another could-have-been musician connected with the long Roxy guitarist saga. But for his part, a relieved Manzanera felt as if he was joining a very special musical family: "I knew it was going to be incredibly successful. I knew and I wanted to be in it, absolutely," he says:

> I mean, all the guys except Paul were four years older, so they'd all been to university. The same week I got the opportunity on Roxy, I turned down going to university, but they'd already been to university and art schools and so they were much more sophisticated. They had bank accounts ... I mean, it was really like having elder brothers. I really sort of looked up to them and I felt very secure in the scenario as well ... It was very much the inspired amateurs thing that was the idea behind Roxy because technically none of us were that good, but the combination of little bits together and the ideas behind it made it what it was. That subsequently was the basis of punk and is the basis of people working now – anyone can do it if they've got a good idea.

The band played a series of warm-up gigs in preparation for the recording of the debut album in late winter 1972. On Friday February 18 they were at the Hand And Flower, Hammersmith, then at Leicester University the following night and Bristol University on Friday March 3. Ferry, who had been loaned a grand piano for the BBC John Peel session, was still playing his old Hohner Pianet on stage, whilst Eno was enticing the oddest sounds out of the band. Often, when Manzanera would solo, the sounds the audience heard bore no relationship to the actual notes played, as if he were the puppet to Eno's sonic ventriloquism. Eno was also delighting in just making noises, bleeps, sonic squiggles, and wave sounds; it was the sound of extraterrestrial infantilism, making sandcastles out of sound: "Actually, we were doing that before King Crimson – it's the first thing anyone does when they get a synthesiser, make the sound of waves. After I heard them do it, I thought we'd carry on with it, and treat it as a kind of pun." Roxy's post-modernism was taking shape: the send-up, the quotation, the hollow gesture, the copy of a copy. It would delight the intellectuals.

The next step was to find a producer for the crucial first recording sessions. The task would be an onerous one for, technically speaking, the band was not even half-good. Also, the pop world had seldom seen such an eclectic collective before, such a wide range of potential solos (guitar, drum, oboe, sax), and such utterly strange lyrical matter and vocal delivery. Brian Eno:

> Roxy Music were a rock band with a rather peculiar perspective. It was all about creating a collage of popular cultural elements: unknowable colours, leopard-skins, quiffs, pastiches of rock 'n' roll. And it was a group based on a complete confusion of musical personalities. I came to them from a background of fiddling with tape recorders. I was trying to use Roxy as a platform for the sort of sound experiments I'd done at college. Bryan was continuing his art school background of trying to get in his extension of the classical tradition. Phil had a South American style and was interested in jazz, which no one else was keen on. And Paul wanted to be John Bonham. He really held it together. Without Paul, Roxy would have been art rock at its worst.

In the end, by chance, an enthusiastic producer was found quite quickly: Pete Sinfield. Towards the end of completing a cycle of four albums under the aegis of King Crimson, Sinfield had found himself increasingly at odds with his partner in the group, Robert Fripp. Just before Christmas 1971, weary but with few regrets, he resigned from the band. Within weeks the first offer of work came from his management company, EG: would he care to produce the Roxy debut album? Eager to move on to bold, though hopefully less petulant, music, Peter Sinfield was ready to work on this new and distinctly odd project:

I think Johnny Gaydon had just left EG, because Greg Lake had decided that he didn't like him, and they were becoming Emerson, Lake and Palmer and huge and famous and moving on to other things. Greg had decided that he was not the right person to manage him (another story). Anyway, EG said, "We've found this band," and I went down to their rehearsals. I thought they were very, very interesting, not very advanced musically but very intelligent, with brilliant ideas. They made up for their lack of technical ability with imagination. I wasn't doing anything else particularly at the time. I had recovered from my split with King Crimson. They said, "Would you produce their album?", and I said, "Yeah", and then it all got very rushed. They said, "We'll give you a one-and-a-half percent royalty." It should have been three percent, really any producer would have got three percent, allowing for the fact that I had already done four albums and I knew my way round a knob or two, to coin a phrase.

The budget for the album was a mere £5,000 and the schedule almost implausibly tight. Sinfield continues:

It was all very rushed. We rehearsed quite a lot, two or three weeks, then we went straight into the studio. They had a few gigs in-between, and it was really when we got into the studio that the lack of technical ability made life difficult, given the standards that I was used to in King Crimson, with lots of very fine musicians. We didn't have the toys we use now. You couldn't put things back in time or pitch like you can now. You had to do another take or cut up large pieces of tape.

Also, the bass player, Graham [Simpson], was having personal problems at the time. He kept bursting into tears, which didn't help very much. The one stalwart person was the drummer, Paul [Thompson], who was solid, just like a rock. There is an old expression: "a band's only as good as its drummer". Well, thank God for him, man, because every time we did another take, he'd be right there, right on the clock, holding it together, which was a Godsend. If they had all been as good as that, it would have been much easier. He was always there, so at least I knew I would always get a drum track, and then I could drop a bass in and build it up from there.

Other people had to do the bass lines, and we struggled through. It was difficult to get anything inspirational or wild from Phil Manzanera. He wasn't Jimi Hendrix and he wasn't laid-back Eric

Clapton. He wasn't anything really, just a rather basic guitarist. It was hard doing the vocals, too, especially the softer ones, because Bryan didn't have the control or professional ability. So he developed this strange vibrato. I always say, if you can't sing well, then sing peculiar. Take Bob Dylan and Leonard Cohen. If you can't be the best, be original, is one of my mottos. He had that style and I brought it on a bit.

In Eno, Sinfield found a man whose musical philosophy was not dissimilar to his own. It has to be admitted, the parallels are quite startling. Sinfield was quoted afterwards as saying that Eno was doing *his* act. "I actually did say that," admits Sinfield:

But I added that he did it better. Which was sort of a joke, and sort of true, in so far as I was the "other member" of King Crimson but never appeared on stage, although I had all of the lights, and all of the sound, and the synthesisers in the audience. Now, he had the same synthesiser, the VCS3, and he had the peacock feathers. And I thought, if I were sitting at Sheffield City Hall or wherever it was, it was not the best idea to be sitting in the audience wearing peacock feathers. But we did more or less the same thing – we did the same tricks with the sound and the environment. Though he did it on stage and I did it off. Because he's this post-modern non-musician, which means that you can't play anything very well, but you have fantastic ideas, I relate very much to him. I can't play anything very well either. He puts dots on his piano keys. Well, I've been known to resort to similar techniques. He really took looping tapes and things to huge degrees, so we had a sort of affinity.

Despite the constraints on creativity, Roxy's eponymous first album is still arguably their most extreme and inventive. For his part, Pete Sinfield was able to stamp his trademark collagist ideas on the unique Roxy sound:

I was working sixteen hours per day with this engineer, Andy Hendricksen, who really should get a mention. He's an unsung hero is Andy; he later did my solo album. He had patience beyond Job. The album's quite King Crimson-y in a way. It has my style stamped all over it – the little band sitting in one corner, drum kits in another, bombs going off and all that stuff. There are lots of pictures in it, which I used particularly because they weren't as funky and as groovy and as clean as they later became. They just couldn't play well enough really, and it was *verboten* to get any session guys.

Although some critics have slated the production as being a tad sterile, and Bryan Ferry himself has admitted to having been unhappy with the shrillness of his vocal and the overall sound, listening with hindsight, Roxy Music's debut album is nevertheless full of production surprises, says Sinfield:

It was done very quickly; it was actually done, ironically, very live. It might be that I'm a messy producer; I'm more Shadow Morton [famed producer for the Shangri-Las, Janis Ian and the New York Dolls]. It was hard enough to get what we got. In fact it was incredibly hard to get what we got, and, the next album they took three times longer over, and they had the right sort of producer to take them on another step. I had the child really, and it was very difficult. I made lots of pretty colours, and made it expressionistic. Marc Bolan made messy records with a lot of humour and colour and warmth and texture to them, and I think it [Roxy's first] has that too. If they think it's a bit flat, well, I tried, what else can I tell you?

The record was made at Command Studios in Piccadilly, London, a studio Sinfield knew well:

One of the reasons the album sounds as it does is because we made it in Command Studios in Piccadilly, which used to be a BBC studio. It had a real echo chamber with tiles on the walls. They used to do programmes there, and it had a real old atmosphere and things which more modern studios didn't have – the echo chamber in particular, which you could hear on the King Crimson albums, and on the flute, and on my solo albums. It had a particular vibe, the way the sound came out with the old valve microphones. It gave an atmosphere, a warmth to records, which is now lost in the digital delights of these days.

Ferry doesn't overly care for the first Roxy album. To him, the singing is too strained, the production not quite the ticket. Yet Eno is surely more on the money when with his assertion that it offered a dozen different futures for rock music out of a dozen different tracks. As Roxy's career unfolded, there would be equally strong songs, equally emotional melodies, and undoubtedly better playing, technically. But no other Roxy Music album carries the same cultural kudos.

The album begins with "Re-Make/Re-Model", a startling statement of intent. To the sound of muffled conversation and clinking cocktail glasses, Roxy make their debut: not to a pack of mud-splattered punters in jeans, but to a witty social elite. The music – untutored, riotous, in fact a bit of a muddle – is part avant-garde hoedown, part Bonzo Dog Doo-Dah Band freak-out. The ending, featuring these not terribly good musicians soloing, was part parody of prog-rock muso virtuosity, and part homage to the Bonzos' "Jazz – Delicious Hot, Disgusting Cold", on which a succession of terrible trad-jazz soloists destroy the genre in four minutes. Sinfield remembers: "Why don't we take every bit of the band, all the players, and do a précis history of rock 'n' roll? That's how those bits got into the middle, because there really wasn't a middle. Those bits in the middle, the Duane Eddy guitar and the 'Ride Of The Valkyries' and all that stuff, are there because there's nothing else, but it seemed a good way of showcasing the band...."

"I love 'Re-Make/Re-Model' just for its unpredictability and its humour," says Richard Williams. "The first thing I remember thinking about Roxy Music was, 'CPL5938?' How amazing to make a chorus out of a car number plate; what a fantastic thing to do.'" Derek Boshier's 1962 painting, "Re-Think/Re-Entry" may have been one source of inspiration for the song. David O'List recalls its origins more specifically:

At the time, Bryan Ferry and I were really good friends and we often drove around together in his girlfriend's Mini, planning the future of the group. On one drive Bryan told me about a gorgeous girl he had been following in his car. I said that sounded like a theme for a song, we should write it. At the next rehearsal Bryan had written words and I put down some chords. I was never credited or received any money for it, but I had more than a hand in writing "CPL" [a working title for "Re-Make/Re-Model"]. Phil copied me exactly on the album version. The ending is something I played for the Pink Floyd.

A huge fan of the first Roxy record was Paul Du Noyer, later to become editor of *Q*, and creator of *Mojo*:

I have distinct memories of sitting round in suburban Liverpool bedrooms listening to people's Roxy Music records and, I guess, although not knowing the term post-modernism, it was my first encounter with that way of working. On "Re-Make/Re-Model" there's very clearly a snatch of "Day Tripper", and this really struck me, because the Beatles had only just split up, and their music seemed very, very recent, and yet suddenly they just seemed to be turned into an archaeological fragment. Intuitively, I thought, that's a very interesting way of presenting rock. It's as if we're now recognising that a chapter has closed, and the future will be made of people assembling ready-made elements in new ways. All that stuff is now very conventional, but at the time it seemed blindingly new and strange.

A performance of the song was filmed as a project by art students, and became the band's first promotional film. For the trivia hound, CPL 9538 is a Surrey registration number.

The influence of Eno is everywhere on *Roxy Music*. If ever proof were needed that composition and arrangement are only part of the picture within rock music, then the early Roxy sound is it. Without the astonishing delays and sonic experiments, in part coordinated through Eno's anarchic approach to how rock music should sound, the first two albums would have been very much less thrilling. Saxophones and guitars were routinely reinvented with tape delay and weird phasing. Ferry remembers saying to him, "Oh, for 'Ladytron', can you make some sounds that, like, sound like the moon, like the lunar landscapes," and he'd say, "Yes, sure," and ... wisssh, y'know, it was very easy for him."

"Ladytron" is arguably the standout track on the album. Mackay's haunting refrain on the oboe is set against Eno's moon-landing "lunarcy" and cool castanets, while Ferry's vocal, initially exposed in the overall sound, picks out the song's most potent melody. According to academic and musicologist Allan F. Moore, Ferry's songs at the time were incredibly simple structurally yet incredibly busy instrumentally, and vocally bordering on the absurd:

The introduction, with its slow oboe melody over Eno's disorientating tape effects, giving way to Ferry's minimally accompanied despairing admission that, "You've got me, girl, on the runaround, and it's getting me down", sets up a complex frenetic surface. Its influence is felt throughout the song, with its rich, honking sax, fast tom-tom rhythms and pounding bass. The rich surface, however, hides the most minimal of structures, thus delivering a rich metaphor for glam rock itself. This is reinforced by Ferry's highly distinctive vocal style, in which he almost chokes the words out, with a tremble to the voice, which is apt to shoot out uncontrolled to an unexpected pitch at any moment ... The actual lyrics are ordinary, but within the strange environment, Ferry's agonised delivery of them suggests less the plaint of the lovestruck than the anguished cry of the possessed.

With a snook cocked at conventional rock structures, "Ladytron" has no real ending; the huge power chords from Manzanera dissolve into Eno synth mayhem, as the track is slowly sucked down the plughole in one of the weirdest fade-outs in modern pop.

"If There Is Something", many years later de-ironised by David Bowie's Tin Machine project, is three songs in one: the opening is jaunty country rock, the middle section a disquieting piano and oboe instrumental, and the finale, a rousing, melodramatic vocal *tour de force*. It also features the most bizarre singing Ferry ever committed to tape:

> "I would do anything for you I would climb mountains
> I would swim all the oceans blue
> I would walk a thousand miles reveal my secrets
> More than enough for me to share
> I would put roses round our door sit in the garden
> Growing potatoes by the score."

> (Words and music: Bryan Ferry, 1972)

This is the return of Ferry the lovelorn romantic, the bathetic final line brilliantly banal.

"2HB", a tribute to Humphrey Bogart (and, of course, a punning reference to a soft pencil), contains one of Roxy's most beautiful melodies and brilliant interpolative lyrics. For once, the words came to Ferry quite quickly as he composed one of his finest (though rarely performed) songs with a typewriter balanced on his lap. In many ways it's the signature song on the album, as Ferry's lyric encapsulates his cinematic fascination:

"Here's looking at you kid
Hard to forget
Here's looking at you kid
At least not yet
Your memory stays
It lingers ever
Fade away never."

(Words and music: Bryan Ferry, 1972)

Eno's tape delay on Mackay's sax gently caresses the sound in the middle instrumental section. Trivia alert: Madness wrote a tribute to Bryan Ferry based on this song, and called it "4BF".

The second side of the vinyl album showcased the band's experimental talents. "The Bob (Medley)", a song suite based loosely around World War II's Battle Of Britain, contains slabs of *musique concrète*, more oboe soloing, and a "Life On Mars?"-aping timpani denouement. Eno told the press that it was Roxy's attempt at systems music, particularly the end section when the band played the song live: "Each musician plays a simple part over and over again, so that the different parts overlap in a different phase relation at any given time. It gives the appearance of a complex piece of music progressing, when it is really very simple. The changes are not in the music, but in the perception of the listener, whose ear picks out more and more detail."

"Chance Meeting" is another extreme song, an art-rock ballad of the type Japan must have had in mind when they recorded "Ghosts" a decade later. Simpson's bass runs are played high on the fret board, while Eno's swathes of discordance give the whole a spectral air. "Sea Breezes" is cut from the same cloth, an exposed Ferry vocal accompanied by electric piano and Mackay's oboe. The middle section almost descends into musical breakdown, as Allan F. Moore observes: "In the central section of 'Sea Breezes' the voice is underpinned almost solely by a modally obscure bass pattern (in which 'wrong notes' predominate) and a kit appearing right in the foreground of the sound-box, playing a highly varied counterpoint with the bass beat, but eschewing its own normal time-keeping function." Quite simply, nothing else like this was being made in 1972.

There are only two slight misfires on Roxy Music. "Would You Believe?" is a more straightforward fifties pastiche, and Ferry's vocal, shouted mid-song at the top of his range, redefines "strained". The final track, "Bitters End", whilst jolly good fun, is again more pastiche than weird re-assemblage, a doo-wop homage and the sort of thing already carried off to greater humorous effect by Viv Stanshall and the Bonzos.

"Lennon describes his music as seventies rock," Mackay opined to *Disc* magazine in 1972. "Ours is fifties, seventies and eighties. It's inevitable that we're going to be influenced by lots of things, people and ideas. The combinations are endless." After Roxy's first album, it became clear that everything in rock *was* now possible. Liberated from the tyranny of trying to sound authentic, of trying to find space within the stifling idioms of American rock, Roxy Music were the future. Andy Mackay: "I think Bryan influenced a whole generation of British singers. Bryan, and Bowie to an extent, didn't sing in an American accent, and that liberated just about every British band since. I think our use of synthesisers was creative and exciting. And we certainly didn't invent eclecticism, but we did say and prove that rock 'n' roll could accommodate – well, anything, really.

The band knew that the album was so groundbreaking that it could, in fact, lead them anywhere. "I think what might happen is we'll get two nice directions together," said Eno at the time. "One is the 'Re-Make/Re-Model' direction, where you have a continuous wedge of sound with a lot of complexity inside it, and the other is the 'Ladytron' direction, which moves through a whole set of changes in four-and-a-half minutes. There's a fifties spaceship-type opening, then a cowboy song, then a kind of Phil Spector thing where an oboe solo like one of those organ solos they used to do, and a piece with synthesised guitars." He went on:

> The only style I'd like to have is one that deals with other styles, if you see what I mean. I'd like it to be said that our style is to be able to work with every style and integrate them into our way of playing. The Bonzos are great heroes of mine. I think it's partly because none of us could encompass playing the same kind of thing for a long time, and if we start off being expected to come up with surprises, and to come up with things we haven't done before, that seems like a very healthy business to begin on. If you begin on the basis that I imagine Deep Purple or Led Zeppelin began on, with a very definite style, the restriction on your movement is immense. Whereas our album is unspecific enough to allow us to go anywhere from there, as we wish.

Mention must also be made of the brief, and largely incomprehensible, sleeve notes written for the album by Simon Puxley. Puxley, a doctor of philosophy, would become, in Ferry's words, the "sixth Beatle", eventually taking over as the band's publicist from Island's BP Fallon. It requires a certain *nous* (and perhaps quite a lot of barefaced cheek) to write something as self-consciously meaningless as Puxley's effort. Rather than follow the normal pattern of introducing the band and its music, Puxley attempts to re-create, or mimic, the confusion of the music, with a jumble of words picked less for their literal meaning, than for their semiotic charge. Here's a sample:

> ... fantasising: phantomising: echoes of magic-golden moments become real presences ... dreamworld & realworld loaded with images (of a style & time & world of – celluloid artefacts? Heartrending hardfacts?). Monoaural & aureate fragments sea-changed & refined to pan, span the limits of sensation ... leaves of gold, crossing thresholds & hearts.

"Neologising" nonsense or inspired stream-of-consciousness, Puxley's (non-) introduction left nobody in any doubt that this was grown-up music for a thinking audience. It was to the band's surprise, then, that they would, within weeks, be corralled into the glam rock movement by the music press, acquiring some unwelcome bedfellows in the process.

Although the album now stands as one of the most thrilling debut albums of all time, Ferry himself has always had his reservations:

> My musical influences were so wide and so diverse. I'm the one who was into Fred Astaire on the one hand and Leadbelly on the other. And I think it worked at its best on the first album, when there were so many ideas that it was like, "Christ! Let's get them all down before they go away." Because you don't know if you were gonna ever make a second album! Later you start to compromise, for fear of your music going over people's heads. On *Roxy Music* it was like, let's do this thing right next to that, edit straight from this to that ... and so you never get bored with it. I mean, there are many flaws on the first album – the singing is terrible, and the recording isn't very good – it's also incredibly exciting.

Thirty-four years later, the debut Roxy Music album still holds up as one of the most beautiful in music history. Like Radiohead's *OK*

Computer, it manages to be both intriguing and melodic, the perfect blend of accessibility and outreach. "Certainly one of the interesting things was that by the time we got to do the first record, to me it all sounded completely normal," says Ferry. "And, in fact, I listened to that record recently and thought, 'God, I can suddenly see why people thought this was weird'. In fact, I was worried back then that it sounded too normal."

The Bryan Ferry story has only a certain amount to do with music. Roxy's first album might have been an astonishing piece of music, but it was also an astonishing piece of art. The cover was like nothing the rock world had seen before. Model Kari-Ann Moller, suggested to Ferry by Antony Price, was dressed like an extra from *Gone With The Wind*. Photographed by Karl Stoecker, her image adorned the cover where the band should have been. "When he showed me the proof of the very first album cover, with Kari-Ann Moller on it, I remember thinking how extraordinary and different and high-concept it was," remembers Richard Williams. "It was far beyond what anybody else was doing; what anybody else would dare to do." A mythology of sorts soon attached itself to the cover image. Was it a man in drag? Could it even be Ferry in drag? More trivia: Moller went on to marry Chris Jagger, brother of Mick.

The *Roxy Music* cover was the first in a long and increasingly controversial sequence of ever more brazen female images for Roxy albums. The band very soon came to be seen as being as important for their visuals as for their music. "Ferry came around and played me this tape, and these earphones were clonked on my head, and I heard the sound of the seventies for the first time," recalls Antony Price. "I remember being particularly struck by that track 'Ladytron', which is very me. The work thing then took off ... I suppose he was for me what Madonna was to Gaultier, but this was years ago and remember, it was difficult for music to handle fashion. They didn't like us; they saw us as snooty, and well, just out, not their scene. Fashion saw music as sweaty and disgusting and here was the first person to change all that.

Ferry imported high fashion into rock music, a mixed blessing if ever there was one. Without the 1972 Ferry/Price coup, the early eighties New Romantic movement would have been inconceivable, Duran Duran and Spandau Ballet impossible. Also inconceivable would have been the thousands of other boys in suits playing bad wine-bar music, the ultimate emetic end-product of what was originally conceived as a subtle and novel idea. Bowie, for all his astonishing changes in personae, was never much interested in fashion *per se*, as his damning 1980 song of the same name so clearly revealed. Yet Bryan Ferry's near-obsession with style, so liberating at the beginning, would, year on year, grate with the public, and become a prison of studied elegance for him. Like much else in the Ferry story, a good idea would be rendered banal through repetition.

With the record in the can by April 16, the next few months saw a virtually unknown band become one of the biggest acts in the UK. Enthoven and Gaydon had financed the recording sessions themselves whilst negotiations went on with interested labels. On Tuesday May 2, EG secured a recording contact with Chris Blackwell's Island Records, who had already turned down Roxy Music once before. Dave Betteridge in marketing and Tim Clarke in publicity loved what they heard, but the rest of the company were not convinced. "Just about everyone round the table was sceptical," says Clarke. "I said to Chris Blackwell, 'What do you think, Chris?' And he sat there and didn't say anything. We thought that was it; the rest of the people around the table had won the day." It was only when Enthoven brought in the stunning artwork for the album that Blackwell was finally swayed. "EG had a licensing deal with Island records," Manzanera explains. "Everyone had turned Roxy down, and because EG had a licensing deal for King Crimson with Island they managed to wrangle us on the label. It's difficult to believe, but nobody wanted Roxy. Poor Bryan spent a year trying to get a deal before that, but I wasn't involved in that bit, luckily."

With the album ready, Roxy revealed themselves to an eager, if somewhat bewildered public. The Great Western Express Festival, which took place in Bardney, Lincolnshire, over the Whitsuntide holiday on May 26 and 27, featured the boozy Faces, Irish virtuoso Rory Gallagher, guitar hero Carlos Santana, the folk-rocking Strawbs, authentic blues from Alexis Korner, honest wailing from Stone the Crows ... and Roxy Music, who looked like they were from a different planet, not just from a different musical era.

The band played the festival with a new member. Graham Simpson, a stalwart from Ferry's early days in the Gas Board, had by now been sacked by Ferry over "commitment issues". Simpson, co-founder of the band, has never been heard of in the music scene since, reportedly having left the UK to study Sufism in India. He was the first of Roxy's numerous bassists. The removal of Simpson might have made sense to

Ferry, given the bassist's less-than-enthusiastic approach to rehearsing and performing, but the band lost a little from the mix. Simpson's unusual bass parts, mini-solos high on the fret, and "walking" step-by-step runs that featured on the first album would be replaced by competent, though arguably less inventive, playing thereafter.

Producer Pete Sinfield's suggested replacement was Rik Kenton, a professional with five years' experience. Kenton had been playing jazz and blues on organ and guitar in Nottingham before filling the role of bass-player first in the London-based group Mouseproof in 1969, and then with Armada a little later. He befriended ex-King Crimson drummer Michael Giles, and eventually came to the attention of Sinfield. His Roxy debut would be something of a baptism of fire for Kenton, as the hastily drafted bassist had just days to learn the band's entire repertoire.

The English weather, that most capricious of phenomena, turned Bardney overnight into a mud-fest of almost Woodstock proportions. Rain and 50mph winds had destroyed the nine marquees erected to sleep the eight thousand music fans the night before, and, by the time Roxy took the stage at noon on Saturday, the audience were soaked through and freezing. Media reaction was muted. "Roxy made a fairly unremarkable impact on the muddy thousands at Lincoln," said *Disc*. "Despite their outward flamboyance, it was a quiet-ish and reasonably self-conscious set. Yet there was something lurking behind it all that suggests we might do well to keep tabs on this band."

A BBC radio session for "Sounds Of The Seventies" recorded on May 23 was aired a month later, featuring blink-or-you'll-miss-him Peter Paul, Rik Kenton's fleeting predecessor, on bass. By this point, Roxy were almost permanently on the road. On May 28 they were in Southsea supporting Rory Gallagher. This was followed in quick succession by a series of gigs including the Floral Hall, Hornsea and the Liverpool Stadium. At one of the Rory Gallagher support slots, the audience allegedly taunted the band, shouting out "pooftahs". They received their most enthusiastic receptions in the northern industrial cities, where the rather harsher realities of the everyday paradoxically meant that exotic acts such as Roxy found a more vocal support. "I remember the gig at the Liverpool Stadium," says Ferry. "That was a great place. We always had a very good audience in Liverpool because it's very similar to Newcastle; it's a town with a personality. I like that, and they liked us."

At the Greyhound in Croydon, Roxy opened for David Bowie. Ferry remembers the gig warmly: "Yeah, it was really exciting because he was on a roll at the time and just emerging in the Ziggy Stardust period, and I think he asked us to join him. It was a very good audience for both turns." From the outset, Bowie would be a vocal supporter of the band. Bowie's friend, the photographer Mick Rock, recalls: "David boosts Roxy whenever he can. He's always been a big Roxy Music fan. And to this day, I remember him telling me when he first saw them play, 'Ah, they're fantastic, Mick,' and he doesn't say that about just anybody."

Roxy Music hit the shops on June 16, 1972. It was a magical month for British pop. Bowie's *The Rise And Fall of Ziggy Stardust And The Spiders From Mars* had been released just ten days earlier, and was heading for the Top 10. "Roxy Music can bring pictures to your head like no one else and they've only just begun," raved Richard Williams in *Melody Maker*. Roxy Music "are a potentially enormous musical influence" was Tony Tyler's spot-on assessment in *NME*. "Altogether, this is the finest album I've ever heard this year and the best 'first' I can EVER remember."

All Roxy needed now was a single ...

MAKE THE BIG TIME: 1972-1973

It's not often that one song changes the pop world. "Rocket 88", "Tomorrow Never Knows", "Autobahn", "Anarchy In The UK", "Blue Monday", "Smells Like Teen Spirit"; all have strong claims to be genre-busting moments. Back in 1972, "Virginia Plain" was one such song. A single with no chorus and no obvious pop form, it established electronica and art-rock in the pop mainstream. Nothing sounded even remotely like it. The song tapped into all that was fresh and new and current in 1972 – insipient Krautrock experimentation, art-school intelligence, glam decadence, fifties nostalgia – to produce a brand new statement of intent. Appealing to both the head and the heart, it got you thinking and it got you dancing. Let's face it: pop doesn't come any better than that.

BBC DJ, broadcaster, writer and music nut Mark Radcliffe recalls the moment of the single's impact on him:

> I've got great affection for "Virginia Plain" because I'll never forget the initial rush of hearing it. I remember going into Boots in Bolton, and thinking, oh, I'll buy a record. "Virginia Plain" was on one of those *Top Of the Pops* albums, which were not the original artists. I really liked "Virginia Plain", but for your pocket money, you could get either a whole album's worth of tunes, or you could get one single; they were about the same price. You could still listen in those little booths in those days, and I said, "Can you put 'Virginia Plain' off this *Top of The Pops* album on?" So I went in the booth and listened to that, and came out and bought the Roxy single, because I thought, it doesn't matter if you've got a whole album's worth of other stuff, you just need one great tune.

A young Ferry wears a prototype Roxy outfit for his role
as Malvolio in a school production of *Twelfth Night*.

Gainsborough Avenue in Washington: the Ferrys moved here in the fifties.

Over the moon, Bryan Ferry wears the No. 1 shirt for his school team.

Pop Art guru Richard Hamilton: 'Bryan Ferry – my greatest creation.'

'Other bands wanted to wreck hotel rooms; Roxy Music wanted to redecorate them.' Roxy Music in 1972.

Ferry on Eno: 'He was undoubtedly very successful with women; I've never seen anything like it – unbelievable.'

'He looks just like a rock 'n' roll singer. I just wish he'd sound
more like one.' The *NME*'s verdict on Ferry in 1973.

Roxy ride again: the first reunion, for *Manifesto*, in late 1978.

Ferry on stage during the *Mamouna* tour, 1994.

The *Flesh + Blood* tour, 1980.

A great tune and a great lyric too, "Virginia Plain" works in a series of mini-slogans, with apparently unconnected fragments of imagery that capture the pioneering art-rock spirit absolutely perfectly. Its creator, Bryan Ferry, was the future of pop: how strange that this future would so soon be so different.

"What's real and make believe?" asks Ferry, and throughout "Virginia Plain" his lyrics play the autobiographical against the imaginary. His obsession with the American Dream is inextricably linked to his own quest for superstardom. Baby Jane Holzer, that Warholian fifteen-minute hero and a habitué of the Factory is mentioned – or rather, her huge hairdo is.

The first verse of the song was in fact a description of Ferry's own quest for the big time: "Make me a deal, and make it straight/all signed and sealed, I'll take it". Taken together with "We've been around a long time/to try, to try, to try to/make the big time", these words give the song a manifesto-like quality: an aspirational fire. "The first verse is about our solicitor," revealed Ferry to *NME*'s Ian MacDonald at the time. "It's a lot of throwaway lines that link up for me but maybe not for everyone else."

There are other images of America too: "the pale horizon" and the "desert strand" reference, almost ironically, the wide panoramas and endless vistas that make up so much of the stock of clichéd images of the pioneering spirit, now so much part of the mythic America. Then there's the glitz and the cool, filmic grandeur, a collage of images which could have been drawn directly from fifties' films: "Teenage rebel of the week", "Last picture show down the drive-in" and even a name-check for his old American car, last seen coughing and spluttering around the grimy streets of Newcastle five years previously: "Where my Studebaker takes me/that's where I'll make my stand". There's kitsch too, with the sound of the revving motorbike when Ferry sings, "Teenage rebel of the week", surely a homage to the Shangri-Las' "Leader Of The Pack". "We had a roadie riding up and down Piccadilly, with stereo mikes on long leads coming out of Command Studios to record him," Ferry told *NME*. Finally, there's just a hint of English absurdism in the line "just like flamingos look the same." However, the overall tenor of the song is pop *art* meets pop *music* – the blatant mining of cliché, for example, in "throw me a line, I'm sinking fast/clutching at straws can't make it" is so banal that it could only appear in a song that ironically pokes fun at the surface of everyday life.

The title of the song itself, which is the name of a person, a locale, and a brand of cigarette, has layers of meaning unusual for 1972. As journalist Caroline Boucher noted at the time, "Surprisingly, the idea for the single 'Virginia Plain' dates back to 1964, which was Bryan's first year at Newcastle University studying art. He did a painting, still in existence somewhere, of a girl with flowing, wavy hair on a vast cigarette packet with a dream plain background so that the title could have referred to all three subjects." Ferry told Boucher, "Lyrically the song is the best thing I've done but not the easiest to follow because there's lots of little ideas and bits of ideas. The overall theme is an American Dream type of thing that British people have, and I have. I don't know why I remembered the painting so clearly – I've just always had a strong thing about it. It was a part of the whole early Warhol movement of the time – of wanting to have a huge studio and live in New York. The face of the girl in my painting was based on one of Warhol's stars at the time, Baby Jane Holzer."

Richard Williams noted, "The painting consists of a large cigarette pack, with the motif of a girl, placed at the end of a plain; so the cigarettes are Virginia Plain, the girl is Virginia Plain, and the plain is Virginia Plain." "The painting was a sort of throwaway water colour," Ferry told Williams, "and the song has lots of little images and throwaway lines. The painting was done in '64 and, although the song was written this year, it reflects the feeling of that time – I was up in Newcastle, living with a guy who'd helped Warhol to make the Marilyn [Monroe] silk-screens. It's a whole American Dream thing, living up there yet constantly thinking about Warhol's Factory and Baby Jane Holzer. It's got some other things in it now: Vegas, Nevada, Route 66 ..."

The lyrics also revealed Ferry's moody, painterly approach to songwriting. "Flavours of the mountain streamline/Midnight blue casino floors" is the closest pop can get to recreating in words the imagery and intent of the artist. And let's not forget Ferry's brilliant vocal phrasings; when he sings, "Don't you throw my pride aside, beside", the words echo Eno's own synth-riff motif which opens the song and which pulses through it. Lyrically brilliant and musically, with Eno's unstoppable, linear groove, riffing and weird, it provided a blueprint for art-rock experimentation. Even Sailor's 1975 pop hit "Glass Of Champagne" had a touch of "Virginia Plain" about it. According to John O'Brien's excellent web site, vivaroxymusic.com, "Virginia Plain" has also been recorded by Spizzenergi, four dance versions have been made by

Slamm, and The Mission recorded it under the name of The Metal Gurus, making it one of the most-covered Roxy songs.

Had it not been for the changing promotional tactics of the early seventies record industry, "Virginia Plain" might never have even been a single at all. Back in 1972, it wasn't the norm for bands such as Roxy Music to even release singles. Pink Floyd and Led Zeppelin got along quite nicely with little or no singles play. Peter Sinfield explains:

> One didn't have to have a single. Traffic had "Hole In My Shoe", I suppose, us bands on Island didn't have to have singles; we made albums. It was just *turning* then, the business. The advice was that, to sell your album, a single was a requisite, and I was most definitely trying to make one. I think it was the first track, "Re-Make/Re-Model", but I couldn't get it into an obvious form. Fortunately, just after the album we were rehearsing, and Ferry was in the corner going "de de de de" in eighths. I said, "What's that? I haven't heard that before," and he said, "I've got this idea for this thing with the bass coming in ba-do-dah." He sang it to me, and I went "Wow!" It was a bit like hearing "Satisfaction" really, in so far as you could hear a fuzz bass at the front. And I said, "I can hear, it, I can hear it – what's next?" And he said, "Well, there isn't much more" (although there was). And I said, "Let's take it to the studio."

As a promotional tool, "Virginia Plain" was not a taster for the album but an adjunct. Although included on later CD versions of the album, "Virginia Plain" was originally a standalone single, an attempt to get the Roxy Music brand name into the singles charts, and a gift to the fans. Singles culled from albums were seen, at least initially, as short-changing the Roxy fan base: a "swizz", as Ferry would put it. Their second single, "Pyjamarama", released in early 1973, was also a non-album track.

Recording for the single began on July 10, after an intense period of gigging to support the just-released debut album. The single, and its B-side, "The Numberer", took three days to record and two days to mix in July. It took a little while to get right. "The first mix was nice and rough and had a lot of life in it, though the motorbike wasn't on it," Ferry told the *NME*. "Then we did another one which I thought was too refined, and finally, because it was a rush release, Peter (Sinfield) had to do a third mix somewhere in-between without us there. But I liked it." From the very beginning of their career, Roxy were happy to experiment: "Frequently the group go into the studio to do a new number without telling me how it goes so that I'll play with the spontaneity they like," Phil Manzanera revealed. "For 'Virginia Plain', I got into the studio and set up my amp and the time was getting closer to my solo and I still hadn't the faintest idea what I was going to do. And the break arrived and I just went, "Blaamm!" I could have put my fingers anywhere. I've since tried to reproduce that solo, and I can't work it out at all."

On June 30, Roxy Music found themselves last-minute replacements for the J Geils Band supporting Alice Cooper at the Empire Pool Wembley. The band then continued their UK tour in the provinces before taking part in what was seen as a potentially big breakthrough gig, at the Summer Garden Party at the Crystal Palace Bowl on Friday July 28. Reviews were mixed, but the debut album was already in the lower reaches of the Top 30 and, with continued serious support from Richard Williams at *Melody Maker*, who weighed in with a double-page Roxy spread, the ground was prepared for the success of the single.

In the week ending August 26, "Virginia Plain" broke into the British Top 40 at Number 26 (Alice Cooper was Number 1 with "School's Out"). Its progress ran as follows: Number 18, 8, 4 (at which point it looked as if it was destined for Number 1), 7, 10, 15, 24, 28, before its final week in the Top 40 chart at 36 on October 28 (by which time "Mouldy Old Dough" by Lieutenant Pigeon ruled/riled the roost). All in all, it spent an impressive ten weeks in the Top 40. Perhaps the real enduring image for those of us born too late to have seen the original Roxy Music was the band's *Top Of The Pops* performance: Ferry's manic smile, Eno's glittery gloves, and the studio audience dressed in wide-lapelled shirts and the sort of multi-coloured tank tops later to be immortalised by Keith Chegwin. If ever one needed proof of how a band had cut the emotional and sartorial umbilical chord between performer and audience, there was it. The band looked like it had been beamed down not only from another era, but also from another planet altogether. This was *Dr Who* pop for the *Dr Who* generation.

Such strangeness met with a certain amount of initial hostility. In 1972, opposition to Roxy Music in the media was stiff indeed. It's one of the more disappointing aspects of the Bryan Ferry story that, having gone out on such a limb and been so brave as to rail against such a large section of the *status quo*, he would later, bit by bit, seek accommodation with the mainstream. However, back in 1972, Roxy Music burned with the heretical fire.

Even at the best of times, Ferry has never had an easy ride in the press, managing to annoy journalists with his unwillingness to discuss either his music or his personal life to the point where, by the nineties, he had become one of the least co-operative interviewees in rock. Back in 1972, however, the problems weren't so much personal as *ideological*. Before punk concentrated everyone's mind on the ideological territories of us/them, heartfelt/contrived, true/false, the glam rock moment initiated a rather more nebulous but no less important debate about what constituted good music, and whether music which was so audaciously different, ironic and punning could be heartfelt and therefore admired. Hitherto, with honourable exceptions such as Frank Zappa and the Velvet Underground, music, usually rooted firmly in the blues tradition or a by-product of prog-rock virtuosity, was meant to encapsulate the honest outpourings of the soul for it to be considered serious and worthy. Blatant bubblegum/novelty chart hits from the likes of Benny Hill, David Cassidy and Middle Of The Road could easily be dismissed as mere entertainment; Marc Bolan and David Bowie were, however, already blurring the lines between pop and rock with intelligent forays into the singles charts. But nobody seemed quite prepared for the arrival of Roxy Music; a band so outrageously attired, and yet simultaneously demanding to be taken seriously. Pop had never before seen a band whose stage personae were so seemingly at odds with their serious, arty intent. Roxy Music, along with Marc Bolan, David Bowie, and those showmen from the progressive rock wing, Ian Anderson and Peter Gabriel, had changed the face of rock music completely. Look at footage of Woodstock, and the performers are dressed just like the audience, in the same counter-cultural garb. Just two and a half years later and the likes of Ferry and Eno had set new standards for the absurd in pop.

It's hard to overestimate just what a break with the past Roxy Music's first album was. In David Bowie and Marc Bolan, glam rock had its twin superstars. Bowie would outlast Bolan and go on to be undoubtedly the bigger star as well as a more versatile musician, an unstoppable pop virus changing and adapting so brilliantly to his environment, while Bolan was doomed to repeat himself. However, both had come from the mod and hippy eras; that is, they both had history. They may have helped redefine the seventies, but the Muddy Waters beat of "The Jean Genie" and the bluesy, folksy swagger of "Ride A White Swan" showed that their musical material was, in part, cut from an older cloth. Of course, the first Roxy Music album also had elements of past styles, but they were so unexpected, so rehearsed, so archly quoted, rather than simply borrowed, that they sounded articulate and new. Fan and writer Paul Du Noyer sums up the Roxy shock of the new like this:

> Ferry was always a great hero of mine, because I think I was initially attracted to, like so many people, the first two Roxy Music albums. That broke the mould of popular music, to my way of hearing. It was the first post-modern pop music ever made, as far as I was aware, in which they predated David Bowie and they made music that overnight made everything else sound at best traditional, at worst, obsolete. So, all of a sudden, it made all the other music around, some of which I liked, it made it all sound as if it was from a previous era now – Joe Cocker, Free, the Grateful Dead, everyone you wanted to name; as soon as you'd heard Roxy Music's first album, all that music sounded deeply traditional. Only Roxy Music's album seemed to belong to that year, and that year alone.
>
> Most people like me tended to take Bowie and Roxy Music as a double act almost. We tended to like Bowie, Roxy Music and T. Rex in a funny sort of way, we took them as a trilogy, and those three seemed to be the operating in their own field as supposed to everyone else. Even if you couldn't articulate it, you knew that *Ziggy Stardust* represented a change within the perception of pop music, but it was still a fundamentally traditional-sounding rock record. Mick Ronson was brilliant, and so forth, but it was still clearly within the tradition of garage rock, whereas the Roxy Music album was unlike anything one had previously heard. So, that was where the fascination began.

Roxy seemed to materialise in the summer of 1972, having apparently done away with the need to build up a live profile through constant gigging. This angered the rock Establishment to an astonishing degree. What outrage! The very thought of it – a hugely successful group which had not spent the last five years on the club circuit, paying their dues, building up a repertoire and some honest counter-cultural kudos! "People think that to be a success you've got to have served your apprenticeship on the road," complained Ferry to Steve Turner at *Beat*

Instrumental magazine that same year. "That's completely bogus." Eno shared his view: "We've always been conscious of making contacts, simply because we didn't want to do things the hard way; we didn't want to have to spend two years trucking around and living squalidly on the assumption that that was what made great music, because I don't think it is – I think there are other ways."

The result was that Roxy Music had articulate, loyal and very vocal supporters in the press from the outset. It wasn't every journalist, certainly, but as 1972 progressed, some of the doubters were converted, and, those that were converted wrote with a proselytising zeal. On the flip side of that, however, was an influential body of opinion that suspected hype. By the autumn of 1972, even Eno had realised the dangers: "Well, I was getting to the point where I was thinking we ought to pay someone to write bad articles about us, because I know how it affects me if I see all that written about other bands, you see, which is why I was scared about it. You remember when Curved Air came out? I mean, they're a good band, but because of all the stuff that was written about them I couldn't listen to them for four months or so because I automatically suspected hype – and I hate all that kind of thing."

In Roxy Music, rock writers saw a triumph of contrivance over content. *Melody Maker*'s Chris Welch damned "Virginia Plain", saying, "One's assailed by glitter and the ears by somewhat shallow, contrived music." "There was pretty much a blanket scepticism, and scepticism would be putting it mildly," remembers Richard Williams:

> I remember Barrie Wentzell, our photographer, going to the Speakeasy [a London venue] one night and coming into the office the next morning and saying, "I saw a really great band last night. Never mind your Roxy Music! Poxy Music! I saw this really, really great band last night – Fanny!" I mean, *Fanny*?! That was typical, absolutely typical. I'm not just singling out Barry here, his was simply a typical rock 'n' roll reaction; they haven't paid their dues, who the fuck are they, why don't their songs sound like the Eagles or Free?
>
> Artifice/authenticity? Yes, it was argued about hugely. I remember when *For Your Pleasure* came out, Roy Hollingsworth, who had been a sceptic, listened to it, and discovered that it was really very good. He reviewed it, and went on to interview Bryan. It was interesting to see the dominoes falling, as people recognised that they were worthwhile.

Some established and technically proficient musicians regarded Roxy Music with a certain disgust. Keith Emerson slated Eno in *Melody Maker* for his abject lack of technical ability, something remembered with not a little pride by Eno himself.

Perhaps the highpoint of the initial wave of media disgust/distrust came in the summer of 1972, when Roxy were booked on the BBC's flagship music show, *The Old Grey Whistle Test*. Artists appeared live in a studio with no audience, whilst presenter "Whispering" Bob Harris looked on in quiet groovyment. However, in a radically honest moment, Harris felt moved to announce his true feelings about Roxy Music on air: "I think he said something like, 'Oh, these aren't exactly my cup of tea (laughs), but here they are anyway,'" chuckles Bryan Ferry, looking back. "We thought that was really funny." Richard Williams, who had presented the first season of *Whistle Test*, admired Harris' honesty:

Roxy had no breeding! No, they hadn't paid their dues at all. People were very, very, very angry about that; it's extraordinary, but they were. It seems like terribly bad manners, but Bob made it very clear that he disapproved of them, and that they were on the show against his better judgement. I quite admire him for that because in the miserable year I spent doing the *Whistle Test*, what made me particularly miserable was having to introduce things of which I really disapproved. I just couldn't bring myself to introduce a David Crosby track with a glad heart. I felt awful about it. And you knew that the people who watched you would associate you with something that basically you despised. And, you know, fair play to Bob, he was wrong, but at least he was saying what he believed.

Mark Radcliffe was a very early Roxy fan, and remembers the Night of the Harris Long Knives very clearly:

They finished, and he was sat there looking woolly in his chair with his big teeth. He said something like, "Well, if this is the future of rock 'n' roll, you can keep it!" And I thought, "Well, you cheeky, hairy old bastard!" But in retrospect I admire his candour. He was quite clearly wrong, though. They were mistrusted because they were a rock band, but they were also considered glam. And for all those people like Bob Harris who liked the Little River Band and things like that it was greeted with some suspicion, because dressing up, together with also

86

being a real band with real songs, was also kind of unusual at that time. You were either a pop act, or you were an earthy rock band in the vein of Free, or Wishbone Ash, or something like that.

If the critical response was split, the impact the early Roxy Music had on those lucky enough to witness the band in their Eno-pomp was seismic. Many future musicians who saw and heard the first phase of Roxy Music would later go on to produce the most thrillingly bizarre music of the punk and post-punk generations. Roxy's influence was never as all-pervading as that of David Bowie, but many punks, futurists and New Romantics were Roxy fans. In all their randomness and inarticulacy, those early Roxy albums provided something vital. More obviously intellectual and less formulaic than Bowie's earlier work, less public school than Gabriel's Genesis, hipper than the Floyd, Roxy Music appeared to herald a radically new future.

The effect of the timing of Ferry's arrival on the music scene is crucial in explaining just why Roxy made the impact they did. Along with Bowie, Roxy Music were the first British pop act to rise to the challenge of attempting to replace the Beatles, the acknowledged masters of all they had surveyed for most of the previous decade. Although Bowie would go on to be the greater talent and bigger star, his early seventies music largely stayed within the format laid down by Lennon and McCartney, although with added avant-garde flourishes and cool Velvets references thrown in. It wouldn't be until the mid-seventies that Bowie made music which was not only equal to the weight of the sixties heritage, but radically different to it. But Roxy Music's very first album was equal to it, just two years after the Fab Four split.

What also gave Roxy and Bowie such distinctiveness was that they were a further pop generation removed from their source material. Ferry, born in the autumn of 1945, and Bowie, born not quite eighteen months later, were children in the fifties, and adolescents and young men in the sixties. They assimilated roughly the same set of influences: jazz, blues, early rock 'n' roll, Beatles, Stones and progressive rock. Both Roxy Music and, a little later, Bowie responded by making music that was as un-Beatles-like as possible, perhaps the *sine qua non* of musical development within rock. If anything, Roxy Music would pastiche, almost poke fun at the Beatles, for example on "Re-Make/Re-Model" with its brief "Day Tripper" interpolation. They were setting a totally new agenda for modern pop music.

Ultimately, what made both Bowie and Roxy Music so distinctive was their *in-betweenness*, their discomfort in their new roles. Succeeding such "authentic" singers as John Lennon and Mick Jagger, the new breed sounded artificial and contrived. Ferry's extraordinary voice can in no way be considered authentic, unlike Jagger's impeccably Americanised delivery, a signifier of earthiness and emotional depth at the time. Paul Du Noyer sums it up like this: "Bowie and Ferry weren't that much younger, but their careers got going that bit later than those of the first wave, so they're two steps removed from the original source. You've got Muddy Waters, then you've got Jagger and Richards, and Bowie and Ferry are third in that line. Bowie and Ferry are responding to copies of copies in a way, which I don't mean disparagingly; I'm just saying that, objectively, they were responding to music that had completed another cycle of its evolution. That's a process that continues to this day."

In 1972, many of Bryan Ferry's borrowings from previous musical eras looked fresh and new. However, from the very outset, there was a sense that whilst Eno, the gadget man, was progressive in the literal sense, Ferry was something of a throwback. He saw in old music a simplicity he thought was missing in Roxy Music. On the subject of old Gary US Bonds records, Ferry spoke misty-eyed and reverentially of the joy of songs which "sound as if they were recorded in a fish and chip shop. The idea is to sound raw and exciting and still subtle, not to become too clinical, not to fade up the nice bits but let them stay hidden." Ferry would tell the press that his favourite songwriter was Smokey Robinson, yet his own lyrical style seemed so much more self-conscious and arty by comparison. Eno seemed to be setting himself a futuristic agenda whereas Ferry appeared to be struggling to move in the opposite direction, to an imaginary world of sweet innocence, wistful melancholy, filmic romance and simple songs.

Ferry himself certainly considered Roxy Music to be a very different sort of musical entity at the time, and quickly grew frustrated at being considered a mere *pop* band. Did Ferry regard himself as being part of a glam (or "glitter" as it was more often called in the press at the time) rock movement? Apparently not:

Not at all, no. It's strange, and it's always irritating to see people lumped together when they don't really feel … I guess people just see other things and feel, oh, that's working for them, and there's a lot of imitation that goes on, and cross-fertilisation. When we started to play, I'm not really sure how aware we were of what other people were doing. I suppose we were conscious of Marc Bolan and Bowie, but I think that we felt that we were very much doing our own thing. If you wanted to make some sort of pattern out of it, you'd say that King Crimson were one polar extreme, and Bowie was the other, and we were in the middle, because we were more commercial and populist than King Crimson, but not as much as David. That's why I'm not as rich as he is!

"I think Roxy Music were art rock," is how Richard Williams puts it:

They were the absolute epitome of the sort of music that came out of art schools in England in the mid and late sixties, the two Brian/Bryans being the perfect example, and Andy Mackay and Phil too, although I don't think either of those went to art school. The whole thing was about making art, and that was what was different about them. I don't think anybody else, with the possible exception of the early Velvet Underground, was quite so focused on that, quite so aware of what they were doing.

"I think we felt we were providing a different musical thing from any of the other people," is how Bryan Ferry sums it up. "We didn't think we were as commercial as what other people were doing. I mean, I was astounded when we had a hit record [with 'Virginia Plain'] and a hit with the first album ever, which was slightly before 'Virginia Plain'. When we started, I think we thought we'd be a kind of art student band, and that's as far as it would go. I didn't have a clue really; just the fact that we could make some records and have any kind of audience seemed really exciting."

Brian Eno also agrees that the "glam" part of "glam rock" was the wrong aspect on which to focus: "For me, it wasn't about glamour so much as about the idea of changing identity, or thinking up your own identity," he said in 2001. "Whether it was glamorous or not was actually accidental. In fact, I think it's called glamorous in retrospect. So 'glam' doesn't really mean much to me." Eno was only too aware that Roxy Music were attacking the codes of authentic rock performance, establishing a new way. In 1972, Eno told *Sounds* that there was:

... this kind of assumption that, if you played the music in the clothes you spent the day in, there was obviously something more sincere about it, which I can understand. It obviously sprung from the Crosby, Stills & Nash country-type influences, where a lot of the people were simple – I don't mean naïve, but simple – people, who naturally played music, and it was a natural form of expression for them. For us to do that would be so dishonest and unsatisfying, because there are so many other things going on in our minds at the same time, and we're surrounded by so much. If you're intensely conscious, as one must be living in London in 1972, of the history of music and the history of style and theatre and so on, to neglect all that is just unsatisfying after a while – you want to do something about it and you want to make a statement in that area.

Both Ferry and Eno regarded the likes of Marc Bolan as *pop*. "We're not a singles band, really," said Ferry in 1972. "I certainly don't want to find myself sliding down the Slade/T. Rex corridor of horror." Even David Bowie, who many saw as being in the same camp as Roxy, was regarded as being a more commercial act. "I think it was too poppy for me, but I think I've changed my mind on that," Ferry has told me. "His music from that period was really good, some of those songs, such as 'Life On Mars?' I think that's really nice, and he pulled it off really well … I think I was suspicious of people changing their names, like David Jones to David Bowie, but, fair enough, perhaps I should have changed mine!" With hindsight, Eno admits that, although Roxy Music were certainly different from the glitter acts such as the Sweet, there was always a connection between them: "I think all those things were a sort of reaction against what had happened immediately before, which was an idea of musicianship where you turned your back on the audience and got into your guitar solos. So I think all those bands – us, and Bowie, and so on – were suddenly turning round towards the audience and saying, 'We are doing a show'. And in that sense there was a unity. But it wasn't very obvious at the time."

Perhaps the best summation of what Roxy Music were about is also the simplest. In his book, *Black Vinyl, White Powder*, pop manager Simon Napier-Bell dubbed Roxy Music "glam rock for adults." Roxy were intentionally elitist and Ferry actively sought out a more learned, bookish and intelligent audience, one for whom personal style mattered. "Roxy Music came along and seemed to pull together a lot of threads and show a way forward," is how Martyn Ware, a Sheffield lad soon to become one of the founders of the Human League, put it.

"Their music was very futuristic; it incorporated everything that we loved about synthesisers. You've got to realise that at this stage, you may as well have said that you wanted to be an astronaut as be a pop star. We were not interested in fame or in a group because it seemed so unobtainable. It wasn't like it is now, where every child wants to be in a pop group and is led to believe they can do it, on television, without any talent."

What really persuaded observers of the scene that Ferry was something different was that he seemed to possess none of the animalism of Jagger, the degeneracy of Lou Reed, the drive and ego of Bolan or the charisma and outrage of Bowie. Mick Rock, court photographer to Bowie and a perspicacious reader of the scene he lived in, has this to say about the young Bryan Ferry:

> His art was a lot more interesting than he was, whereas people like David and Lou were as interesting as their art. I don't know how interesting the story of Bryan Ferry actually is, but it's probably not going to be quite as absolutely whacked-out torrid as Lou Reed's, David Bowie's or Iggy's because he's not that kind of person. He's a coal miner's son from Newcastle – not that you'd ever have known it. He had, I wouldn't call them pretensions; they were more aspirations, *interests* that he glued together. I think he was extremely talented, Bryan Ferry, if you listen to the first Roxy Music album, and it's a fantastic album to this day. Bryan is, by nature, quite a shy person, unlike David, who's a character. Bryan Ferry was always a more reserved personality.

On stage, Roxy Music were arguably the most excessive mainstream pop group the British scene has ever witnessed. As a stage act, though, they were also a simmering pot of discontent waiting to boil over. Seldom has a rock group possessed two such dissimilar front men. As lead singer and sole songwriter, Ferry obviously should have been the central figure. Mott The Hoople's Ian Hunter, that summer in the Top 3 with the Bowie-penned "All The Young Dudes", called him a "Dracula-type Presley" and it was true: his stage presence was both elegant and leery. However, as lead singer he didn't appear to actually do very much leading, being somewhat uncomfortable and slightly marginalised, the John Major of glam rock. Increasingly, it was Eno who stole Ferry's thunder, both onstage and in interview.

By early 1972, Eno had transformed himself into the most outrageously attired man in rock. Neither Alice Cooper nor even David Bowie were ever as excessive as Eno in his preening pomp. At the start of Roxy's live career, he had sat where the sound-mixer was usually positioned, treating the music using a VCS3, a state-of-the-art synth operated by knobs and switches. "I would be fiddling with the whole sound of the group, and sometimes putting in backing vocals," said Eno. "It was very bizarre. People in the audience would wheel around when I started singing." It was all most odd, as Phil Manzanera, newly installed on guitar, records: "At the very early gigs, Eno was seated in the audience, mixing the sound, playing his synth and singing. No wonder people thought the band was weird! And at that time, we had no amps – everything went into the mixing desk to be treated. It must have looked very strange with no amps on stage."

Roxy's rudimentary version of "surround sound" had its precedents, though. Earlier, Pete Sinfield of King Crimson had positioned himself in the same space to bend sound. Following in the same tradition, Eno wasn't a player *per se*, but a sound-tweaker, a sonic technician. Later in the seventies, the Human League would have Adrian Wright as the non-musician, visual-effects guy, this time playing the slide-projector rather than the synth, but the effect was quite similar, as art bands now expanded the idea of what being in a band actually meant. Punk made a big thing about the importance of ideas above technique, but Roxy Music had been singing from that hymn book half a dozen years earlier.

However, the impulse to perform on stage being what it is, by early 1972 Eno had assumed an on-stage role, with devastating effect. At the time, Bowie had powerhouse guitarist Mick Ronson to play off and pose with; Bryan Ferry, who has subsequently admitted that he himself would have loved a wild lead guitarist to beef up the sound, had a gaunt non-musician instead, who was a rival not a foil, and who, so it might have appeared, was sniping away at him from the opposite side of the stage. Eno's tweakings were legendary. According to Robin Denselow:

> He plays synthesizer not as a melody instrument, to reproduce the sound of, say, fake French horns, or as a freak box to make strange noises, but to modify the sound from other instruments. Such experiments are difficult in a travelling rock band. The sound signal has to travel from the instrument that is to be modified (piano, guitar or saxophone) to a mixer at the back of the hall, then back to Eno on

stage, back to the mixer, and back to the amplifiers – a journey of nearly a mile. Special equipment is being built to cope.

Later, bedecked in peacock feathers and make-up, his hair thinning on top but long and languorous, Eno looked more *other* than any of his contemporaries in the pop world. "In terms of his appearance, he really blossomed when he was in Roxy," says Ferry. "And Carol McNichol, his girlfriend at the time, was a very clever artist who had a lot to do with the costumes." Eno agrees: "I was living with a woman at the time who was a sculptor and also a clothes-maker, and she was very important in that respect. I could sort of think up ideas for clothes, and she would improve on the ideas and then actually make them. I think we were really thinking in terms of sculpture rather than clothing. They were clothes that you could only really wear on stage. It was impossible to do anything normal, like making a cup of coffee, in them. Probably because of what I did, which was a very unphysical job, I was the only member of Roxy who could have worn those kinds of clothes." Eno continues: "The only decision I can consciously remember making was this: what I do involves standing still a lot of the time, because I'm adjusting these tiny little knobs, so I thought it would make sense to wear garments that magnified my movements. Hence the feathers, and so on. So I wasn't doing very much, but it looked quite good." "He was very sober, even more so than he is now," says Ferry. "The audiences assumed that he was on acid, but if there was a joint in the room he'd start getting giddy!" "The constituent part that was Eno was all about sexual ambivalence, and he seemed more alien than gay," is Martin Ware's assessment. "At that time, the dressing-up and the glam thing had no gay connotations, or very few. It was all about an escape from the humdrum as far as we were concerned. And also, he was bald and looked like Max Wall; the hair, at least."

"Eno looked fabulous," enthuses Mick Rock:

I don't think I thought that much about Brian originally, other than that he probably hit on my first wife Sheila a couple of times. But that's all right. In those days everybody was hitting on everybody else. And she [his ex-wife] was very close to the lady that he lived with for a long time, who made this amazing pottery, very Alice In Wonderland sort of stuff. Eno did look pretty extraordinary in those days because he still had his hair. It was kind of fluffy, and the fact that it was a bit thin on top worked with the way he looked, which was slightly extra-terrestrial. I've never heard anything but nice things about Brian, other than the fact that he might tap up your girl if you weren't looking.

With Roxy Music, though, there was none of the grand theatrical design or personae-switching, identity-blurring ideology of the Ziggy shows. In this new era of the pretend, Ferry downplays any suggestion that he was a character on stage. "It was just a bit of a lark," he says:

> I just thought it was kind of boring how music was presented. You see, going back to my jazz days, as a young jazz fan I'd go to see the Modern Jazz Quartet and they'd be in black tie, immaculately dressed. In fact, all the jazz players always looked really cool, in suits and dressed up to go on stage. I liked that tradition. When I went to see Otis Redding and the Stax Road Show, they looked fantastic as well as sounding great. They jumped around and the presentation was very strong. And I thought, well, Roxy is going to be like that as well. You wear *this* and you do *that* so there was quite a lot of direction involved. Not with Brian and Andy, I would say, but the others, you had to try and help them out a bit. But Andy and Brian were always pretty cool dressers themselves.

"People tend to overlook the humour that was there," said Phil Manzanera in 2001:

> At first it was just us and Bowie doing it, in a context of everybody else *not* doing it. The more extreme we got, the bigger the reaction. It was a bit of theatre. And it sounds crazy, but hardly anyone was using proper lighting before then. It was a big deal, as were synths. It also gave us something to do to conquer the nerves and the feelings of amateurishness before we went on. It'd be: yes, more make-up, more outrageous costumes! We had lots of friends in fashion. It was never pre-arranged, we never saw each other's stuff until five minutes before the set, so we'd turn up and freak each other out. But by the eighties, it was all designed.

"Brian started to get into his look, lots of make-up because he had this long hair and looked like some sort of *Star Trek* professor or something," remembers Ferry. "Andy had his high cheekbones, this sort of matinee idol, glossy Valentino look ... and Phil, we, er ... Antony [Price] had made these glasses which looked like flies' eyes which were really good. Paul, we did him as a sort of circus strong man complete with black eye. It was all done on the cheap of course, but it really helped because we were all fairly sort of retiring – we weren't pushy, outgoing people."

Very little early television footage of the band remains, and there is hardly any film of them in action on stage back then. In a way this has aided, rather than diminished, their importance. Perhaps this is why Roxy Music, like David Bowie and some of the experimental progressive rock acts such as Genesis and Pink Floyd, made such a visual impact. In the era before pop video, their live performances attained a mythic status, their photos in the music weeklies and the very occasional sighting on television being likewise big events. And their songs came to us straight: without MTV and blanket music promotion, they took on a vibrancy of their own, the meaning of a song a private negotiation between performer and fan, with just the album sleeve or that rare television performance to give any additional information to complete the picture. Early Roxy Music, like the classic Ken Scott-era David Bowie, made its impact because of its sense of incompleteness, a mystery which we can only dream about in the supersaturated pop culture of today, in which the stream of images renders the message bland.

In a brilliantly apt description of the disordered musical world of 1972, Michael Stipe once referred, affectionately it has to be said, to "the car wreck that was Roxy Music". This was before Ferry was transformed into the cool sophisticate in search of musical perfection. This was an era of musical imperfection, and all the better for it. Roxy were by no means the finished article, playing-wise. Listen to any early live gig and you can't deny the bum notes, missed cues, and strained and occasionally off-key vocals. Webmaster and Roxy historian John O'Brien sums it up like this: "Technically the guys weren't that good, and you hear it on a lot of the early bootlegs – Bryan is terrible in places, Andy Mackay hits duffers all over, Manzanera hits duffers all over, and it's that fragility that I like about them, actually." No wonder Roxy were something of an inspiration for both punk and the electronic bands that followed.

Eno's first experiences on the road with Roxy had a formative effect on his musical philosophy: "honour thy error as a hidden intention", as he said in his Oblique Strategies, his famous box of cards offering a series of suggestions, commands and aphorisms for the would-be artist.

This lateral thinking was the polar opposite of the painstaking, fastidious Ferry, obsessed by good playing, impeccable presentation and pre-planning. "The main thing about being on the road," Eno told *Sounds* in 1972, "is being confident enough to make mistakes and live with them, because in a sense you reach the stage where there's no such thing as making a mistake; all you do is take a new departure and decide to move in another direction."

Despite the fluffed lines, what an astonishing event a Roxy Music gig in 1972 must have been: a mixture of visual super-excess and musical derring-do, topped off by the barely disguised tension between Ferry and Eno at opposite sides of the stage. Producer Peter Sinfield:

> Of course there was a clash. Bryan was singing, but Eno is very clever. And Ferry on stage – especially in those days, not so much now – looked well awkward. I remember the first time I saw them, and I thought, "My God, it's like Joe Cocker on a bad night." I mean, his performance was so uneven; the positions he took. His stances were so odd, a bit like somebody had gone mad with one of those little artist's models, do you know what I mean? He just had very, very odd stage movements. He's cooled it all down now; he's famously Mr Smooth.

Ferry's Frankenstein-monster movements, coupled with sudden changes in register, a rather idiosyncratic relationship to pitch, and such wildly contrasting moods, often within songs, made him unique, and sometimes self-conscious to boot. "When we do 'If There Is Something' live, people always seem startled by the juxtapositions," he said in 1972. "It's tilting along pleasantly and suddenly this agonised voice bursts out. I find doing it quite embarrassing sometimes, because it's just raw emotion and you can't be in twenty different moods in one night. You have to be an actor, project yourself into it."

The lucky few who witnessed Roxy Music back in 1972 and early 1973 were treated to rock spectacle at its most extreme. "Early photographs of the band recall 'The Clangers' on dangerous drugs," is how writer Barbara Ellen wittily put it. However, the Eno/Ferry face-off was becoming more gladiatorial as the gigs went by. As the Roxy Music shows became wilder they also became more partisan. The pro-Eno faction would tend to gravitate towards his side of the stage, and they weren't bashful about voicing their support. It would become an issue.

Here's Martyn Ware on the colossal impact the band had on his teenage consciousness, and on the unease between the two:

> There was an enormous amount of tension between Eno and Ferry right from the start, as far as I could tell. They were always at opposite sides of the stage and they were always trying to upstage each other. They never talked to each other on stage, and I saw eight gigs before he [Eno] left. The first time I ever saw Roxy Music was at Sheffield University Students Union. They used to have a free concert for new bands every year. Of course, it was meant to be for students, but we always managed to blag our way in. And at this particular concert – a free concert in a hall that held 300 people – Roxy Music were top of the bill because they had literally just brought their album out two weeks earlier. Working backwards, it was Kilburn And The High Roads, Dire Straits (they were fucking terrible, really dull), Leo Sayer (we thought, who is this bizarre muppet with the hair?), and there were about three or four other very well-known acts. I think Gary Glitter was on that bill too. It was a formative evening of my life, actually.
>
> Then a month later, Roxy were booked into a hall of residence called Ranmore Hall, which had a kind of refectory that held 250 people. It had quite a big, wide stage and you were literally about five yards from these people. They simply didn't need a light show: back in those days it was all about flashing lights because the performers were so dull, in their waistcoats and faded denims. They came on stage and I'd never seen anything like it. As far as I remember, Ferry's outfit made Gary Glitter's look sedate. It was like silver lamé, with enormous pointed, padded shoulders. Eno was wearing the legendary feather boa-shouldered bolero jacket, and high-waisted loon pants.
>
> In the wildest excesses of rock iconography, I've never read about, let alone seen, anything as excessive. I saw T. Rex at their peak and it was nothing like that, and neither were Genesis with Peter Gabriel. If you had taken a photograph of them and showed it to someone in America at that time, they'd had probably have gone "faggots"! But that's not the message it was saying to us: it was saying "the future". It's an exciting thing when you're 16 years of age.

Mark Radcliffe was also in the queue to see Roxy take off:

I saw Roxy at Manchester University. It must have been well early on because I was under-age for getting in, but my dad worked at the university so he got someone to sneak me in at the back, you know, to watch Roxy Music and Eno at the Main Debating Hall at Manchester University. It was the best thing I'd ever seen.

I think Eno was a real sonic architect, at the risk of sounding precious. Ferry could also obviously write good pop songs and good rock songs, but Eno just had that fairy dust. The only other band who had that, but hadn't been able to channel it in any way commercially, was Hawkwind, who had a guy called Dick Mick who used to play what they called the audio generator. The rest of them did a song, and then he'd go on and put a load of burbles, squeaks and farts over it. And in some sense, Eno was that: it just broadened the sonic spectrum of what a pop song could be. Perhaps you could trace it back to the first kind of sonic experiment and Joe Meek. There was an element of being at the forefront of what a pop song could be, I think, and yet still there was a great Ferry pop song under there.

Another eye-witness at the early Roxy gigs was future rock journalist and Bolan and Siouxsie and the Banshees biographer Mark Paytress. Enamoured of the first brace of Roxy singles and albums, this teenager saw the gig very much as the Bryan Ferry show:

My first live experience was Family at the Bournemouth Winter Gardens in December 1972. Four months later, on April 13, 1973, Roxy Music came to town, supported by Sharks, another Island act, featuring Andy Fraser (ex Free), Chris Spedding and singer Snips. They weren't too exciting, but the audience was. I was just 14 and, together with three of my fellow third-formers, I marvelled at the array of sparkly-costumed seniors in attendance. I also recall a girl in the row in front was bra-less with a see-through blouse, which prompted much spluttering on those surreptitiously-purchased Consulate cigarettes. I remember Eno being fairly static, surrounded by hardware, but Ferry occasionally veered off to the side of the stage, arms outstretched like Frankenstein's monster in desperate need of an energy re-charge. In fact, he was only going to play his electric piano, but he cut an incredibly dashing figure and dominated the stage. His face, his voice and above all his movements gave him a strangeness that seemed far more elusive than

Eno's obviously "weird" visual appeal. Ferry was incredible back then; Eno was merely his sidekick.

Expectations had been high. I think I saw photos of Roxy in the music press before I heard them. They were definitely "next big thing" material. I was in bed with Radio Luxembourg and on came "Virginia Plain". It sounded like nothing else I'd ever heard before, and you couldn't always say that about the early seventies: it was strange, stylish, and a perfect match for the band's alien image. I recall a photo in *Music Scene* – I think it was in colour – of the group backstage at a festival. Groups just didn't look like that in those days! There was some suggestion that Eno had come from outer space and, eager for any morsel of oddity, a few mates and me half-believed it.

I was disappointed that Rik Kenton was no longer with the band by the time of the concert. We all had too much hair and not enough sartorial imagination to imitate Eno, but we could all have a go at a "Ferry" – arms outstretched like Jimmy Cagney and loads of teeth-baring. And that mannered vocal style was a cinch too. This was someone operating at the other end of the scale to Mick Jagger. There was, I suppose, elements of Hollywood there, but the over-riding feeling I got from this man was strangeness. And, so *Popswop* magazine told us, he'd been an art teacher and was a bit old for a pop star.

Of all the gigs from 1972 and 1973, however, it was another high-profile support slot that would do more to cement the band's future than any television appearance or radio session. Roxy had already toured with David Bowie, the face of 1972, when he asked them to support him on a few British dates. The first was at Croydon Greyhound in June 1972, but the really big show would come at the Rainbow Theatre, where Roxy opened on August 19 and 20. Amanda Lear, a striking and disturbing glam-era figure, announced them in high-camp style. Whereas so many of the boys were playing at being girls, Lear appeared the real deal – a genuinely indeterminate figure sexually. Mick Rock:

She's definitely a lady now, and has been for a long while. Let's put it like this; I've heard a number of different stories, from a number of different people, including friends of hers like Anita Pallenberg. Anita tells me that she remembers her in Rome in the early Sixties, and she was called ... I think she said she was called Richard. But then someone else told me that she was born essentially hermaphroditic, somewhere straight down the middle, a little bit of this and a little bit of that, and she took hormone treatment. She's quite a curvy lady hip-wise for someone who was a full-blown man. She had the hoarse voice, but her hips seemed to tell you that she was never a full-blown man, that there was always something essentially female in her genetic makeup. I can't say that for sure, because you'd have to be there to know it! But I'm giving you hearsay and that's what somebody told me; you had to glug down hormone treatment every day just to make sure that you stayed in the neck of the woods where you wanted to be!

Ferry remembers the two Rainbow shows with some affection. For him, it was visually exciting, the mixture of high art and pop trash that Roxy so stridently advocated:

The Rainbow gig? That was really successful for everyone, I think. I had Amanda Lear on stage, kind of gyrating in the background, with a couple of other girls, rather slaggy girls as I remember. I can't remember where on Earth they came from. Vulgarity, I think, is quite amusing. There was always an element of that in Roxy – vulgarity mixed with sophistication. It's nice to have opposite elements and create some sort of dynamic when you have that.

"David Bowie's songs I like a lot," was Phil Manzanera's assessment. "His management were rather disagreeable at The Rainbow, but Bowie and the Spiders were very nice people and I enjoyed what they were doing." For his part, Bowie genuinely thought Roxy Music were something special. He saw them as one of the few credible artists of the period. Much has been made of the Bolan/Bowie rivalry of the glam-rock period, and there's no doubting that their careers mirrored each other in many important respects. But, really, only Roxy Music carried the weight to rival Bowie.

With a single in the charts and the album climbing to Number 10, Roxy Music became a huge live draw. They could always count on the most enthusiastic responses in the north of the country, in Liverpool, Sheffield, Glasgow and, of course, Newcastle. "We've had some really nice audiences recently, especially up north, and they come with just the right amount of expectation about it," Eno told *Sounds*. "They know the numbers aren't going to be the same all the way through, most of them chop and change quite often. So the thing that used to happen doesn't any more, where people used to start dancing and then an oboe and piano bit would come, and they'd be left hanging over the edge."

Richard Mills, an early fan of the band, captures the thrill of it all for pop fans desperate for something new, something to follow in the wake of the Bowie breakthrough:

In 1972, I was 14 and just the right age for the onslaught of glam rock that was to follow. For me, despite the increased use of tinsel and glitter worn by the New Seekers and other "pop" acts, it was always Bowie that mattered. But as soon as the shock value of Ziggy had sunk in, there was an appetite for more of the same. And that's why anybody trying to ply their trade soon found themselves applying mascara and squeezing into tinfoil catsuits. But I know that my friends and I applied our own league table system to the bands and artists that came out, with First Division places going to Bowie, Roxy, Sparks and Queen, with Jobriath and others in mid-table and Gary Glitter, Sweet and Suzi Quatro well down the pecking order. Roxy were a breath of fresh air – completely innovative. Each of the members had their own strong personality and it seemed to me that not since the Beatles, or maybe the Monkees, had any band boasted such disparate characters.

Success changed the individual band members; well, almost all of them, one suspects. At first, though, the money did not exactly pour in. By September 1972, Roxy were still on just £20 per week. "The album was done cheaply," confirmed Ferry in 1972. "That only took five grand. But we're twenty grand in debt still. We've got three roadies now, six of us in the band, our PR man, and a lot of our equipment is still in its infancy; it could be much tighter than it is." For Eno, Ferry, Manzanera and Mackay, success would ultimately bring financial security and an enhanced prestige, providing the chance to further their musical careers as solo artists or in collaborations. Eno was to emerge as the dominant figure as band publicist, as Ferry proved a reluctant interviewee. "Arranging interviews with the others will be no problem," Adrianne Hunter, Roxy's publicist would say. "But I can't guarantee Bryan. You know how he is." Yet for 22-year-old Paul Thompson, success appears to have changed very little at all: "I knew I had arrived when I came back to Tyneside. I went to see a mate of mine playing at a social club in Gateshead. I didn't have my club card and I expected a grilling from the doorman, but he looked at me and said, 'It's all right, son, you can go in. I saw you on *Top Of The Pops*!'"

This was a far cry from the years of struggle that the likes of Bolan and Bowie had endured. Success made Roxy giddy for more, yet there was still an air of disbelief and a certain innocence: "We'd be travelling in the van at five in the morning, coming back from somewhere, and hear a Roxy track on Kid Jensen's Radio Luxembourg Show," recalls Phil Manzanera. "We'd all go, 'Wow, we're on the radio, wake up!' Bryan and Andy would be swerving along the white lines, while Eno was slotted in amongst the Marshall stacks at the back because he was the smallest."

Roxy may have been heavily in debt but their personal circumstances hardly hinted at penury. Ferry had spent the summer moving house and writing songs for the second Roxy Music album. He left the terraced house in Battersea he shared with Andy Mackay and moved into a sizeable elegant flat in Chelsea's Redcliffe Square. A Steinway grand piano would now be the instrument on which future Roxy classics were composed. Andy Mackay lived in a Victorian cottage in Battersea, Eno had two mansion flats in Maida Vale and Kilburn, Thompson was based in Putney in a flat and Manzanera had a penthouse near Clapham Common. The Roxy life was one of bachelor airs and graces, set against the backdrop of a vibrant London artistic scene. Eno's playboy bachelor flat in Maida Vale was, unsurprisingly, a place of rare charm and no little eccentricity. The music room was "festooned with all manner of bizarre technological innovations," recorded *NME*'s Nick Kent in 1973, "keyboard instruments, sprawling tape equipment and suchlike." He went on:

> The walls are decorated with *objets d'art* as diverse as the cover of a "True Hollywood Confessions" mag, a grim article on a child-killer and a series of out take shots of Kari-Ann posing for the legendary first Roxy album cover. Directly adjacent to all this hangs the maestro's current fave stage costume – a rather remarkable black jacket embellished with garishly coloured peacock feathers pointing out in all directions. I hesitate to further describe the oddities to be found in other rooms. What was the sponge frozen for posterity in a jar doing in the fridge? And those ducks on the wall?

However, an autumn that promised to be gig-filled and full of further conquest hit the skids pretty early on when Ferry was taken ill. "Roxy

Music deeply regret that they are unable to appear at the following venues due to Bryan Ferry's tonsil operation," began a flyer. Sure enough, after months of pain and suffering, Ferry had been taken into hospital to have his tonsils removed. An estimated £10,000-worth of gigs were cancelled. Journalist Ian MacDonald was despatched to inspect the fragile singer, only to find him propped up in bed wearing 'RM'-monogrammed gold-trimmed black pyjamas and sipping champagne. Now even a hospital stay for a routine operation could make the front pages of *Melody Maker*. "I feel fine," Ferry told the press. "I may never sing again, but I can't promise anything. I've got some numbers in the pipeline, and one of them might make a good single eventually; it's a ballad called 'Beauty Queen', and will be grandiose and heavy in the Walker Brothers' tradition."

An eighteen-date late-autumn UK tour was arranged as soon as Ferry was fit again. Starting on October 28 at the Winter Gardens, Weston-super-Mare, the tour climaxed at Lancaster University. Roxy's fame meant that they had outgrown the venues they had been booked into, as ex-university friend Michael Brick remembers:

> Nothing surprised me less than when Bryan became a pop star. I saw Roxy for the first time when "Virginia Plain" had just come out. I was artist-in-residence at York University and they came to do a gig there, no doubt booked months before. They were, by then, too famous for the venue, and I remember being besieged in the Senior Common room with them while most of the youth [female] of Yorkshire banged on the windows. It was a great concert and we got very drunk afterwards.

The set consisted of songs culled from the band's debut album, with "Virginia Plain", of course, left for the encore. The audience would go ape-shit as the song revved up, shouting out in unison to Ferry's very white call-and-response: "What's her name?" (slight pause), "Virginia Plain!" (shouted by the assembled Roxy brethren). Nick Kent liked the music, but found fault with the presentation: "There are no new numbers and the band could loosen up. Bryan Ferry always looks to be on the verge of the peppermint twist, but never does." However, Richard Williams penned yet another sturdy defence of the band in *Melody Maker* in November. Responding to the repeated claims that Roxy were hype, he wrote:

It's a claim I've heard many times, and always from people involved with the kind of unimaginative loser bands who nearly strangled rock a year or so ago. You know the kind I mean: those bands and managers whose "honesty" and "integrity" last just as long as their obscurity, and are banished by one hit record. Roxy Music never claimed any honesty. The concept would be meaningless to them, because they have a clear vision of what rock entertainment is about, and it's not about integrity or any other sort of facile morality.

As an aside, Williams also praised the venue in question, Manchester's Hard Rock Emporium: "Built in a semi-circle, the theatre is half-seating and half-standing, but the latter half sat on the floor anyway." Ah, the old hippy values were obviously taking some time to die. It was obvious that the times were changing rather more slowly than had been hoped.

In America, the times hadn't changed at all. Rock culture in early seventies America was the direst in music history. Much has been made of how Britain needed punk to oust the old guard in the UK, but America had it ten times worse. Soft rock, country rock, hard rock, singer/songwriterly pretension – music in America in 1972 was the sound of remorseless, unforgiving tedium. Americans liked music played by people who looked like them and who played honestly, with technique and skill. When the new wave finally crossed the pond, its job was a lot harder than it had been at home. Apart from Alice Cooper's brand of vaudeville, anything that looked like a show was also beyond the pale. And one other thing was for sure: in 1972, America preferred its music irony-free.

Roxy's attempt to make inroads into the American market in late 1972 was little short of disastrous as they opened for Jethro Tull, beginning on December 7 in Athens, Ohio. True, Bolan and Bowie had also found the US going tough, but Roxy Music appeared to give up almost at the outset. The decadence, the gender-bending and the artiness of their music did not endear them to their would-be audience. Their repeated failure to break the America would be the open sore, the canker in Ferry's career.

Whether as a member of Roxy Music or as a solo artist, the American public simply did not warm to Ferry's arch command of the ironies of life in the same way as the Europeans did. He had some successes and, late in his career, he could tour in the States and sell out medium-sized venues, but he never had a big album or single. Given his talent and the sheer longevity of his career, that can only equal failure. Perhaps it was the lack of touring commitment, the absence of the power-chord and the grand rock pose, or perhaps it was simply the fact that Ferry was too much the patrician English gent for the uninterested gaze of the average all-American boy in jeans and t-shirt. Despite several quite conscious attempts to curry favour with the US mainstream through the recording of American FM classics such as "Eight Miles High" and "In The Midnight Hour", not to mention the raft of Dylan covers which would make up such a large part of the Ferry repertoire, only once would Roxy Music dent the US Top 30.

Since then, it has often been said that Roxy Music failed to find the key to American success because their music tended to fall between several stools. Unlike the music of David Bowie, Elton John and the Bee Gees, it was obviously not black, funky or dance-y enough to be played by non-white-orientated stations. It wasn't loud, angsty or basic enough to be played by the incipient college radio in the late seventies, who supported the new wave, and it wasn't conventional enough to fit easily into FM rock programming, where Steely Dan, Led Zeppelin and the Rolling Stones were kings. It was too nebulous a body of work in all respects.

When Lisa Robinson of *Disc* magazine caught up with the two Brians/Bryans just before the tour opened, spirits were high. Ferry, one of the biggest Yankophiles in the business, told her:

> The American thing is so important to me because at least fifty percent of the things that influenced me were American things. The best films were American films, the best stars were American stars, because there were no English equivalents really – and the best music was American, until the Beatles came along. That's why I sing in American voices on some of the numbers ... at least I try to have an American inflection.

If anything, Eno would be even more openly enthusiastic, going so far as to claim a sort of spiritual kinship with the land of opportunity. Given his subsequent highly critical stance on all things American, his initial enthusiasm is revealing:

> I feel terribly excited about going there because I feel that that's my emotional homeland. I feel that there are two places I'm emotionally based in, and one is the English countryside, where I was born and

bred, and the other is the heart of New York City. Partially because in the English countryside where I grew up there were two American air bases which left their mark on me, in terms of music particularly, and I kind of lived with that mood. So all my nostalgia is for American records rather than English ones.

However, the reality did not live up to the dream. By the end of the tour, Ferry was openly dismissive of the American public. While a contemporary like Bowie gaped in awe at Detroit, paid homage to Warhol at the Factory and got backstage to meet the Velvet Underground, Ferry thought the American public unsophisticated and backward. A trip to the observation decks at the top of the Empire State Building aside, it seems the band found the Big Apple a bit of a disappointment. "I don't find New York at all freaky," said Ferry to *Sounds*. "We made a ritual pilgrimage to Max's and Nobody's and it was all very squalid, rather like the Chasse [a small, downmarket drinking club in Wardour Street, London] on a bad night." Not even a good-luck bouquet of poinsettias courtesy of David Bowie could lift the heart.

Ferry was understandably peevish, seeing Roxy bottom of the bill below the likes of Jethro Tull, Edgar Winter, the Allman Brothers, Ten Years After, Steve Miller, Humble Pie and Jo Jo Gunne. But could this really excuse the following overly candid remarks? "They [the Americans] appear to be three to five years out of date, behind England ... and I think it's basically to do with communications; they're just not informed." Or this: "It's very interesting seeing all these different towns, but most of them you can do without – they're so characterless, so featureless, and so similar." Always with an eye for the pretty, some might say cartoon-like stereotypical girl, Ferry did, however, approve of the Texan cheerleaders at a local football game: "... all these Texan girls in short, bright red costumes and high boots and Stetsons doing these sexy dances, while all these huge men lumber around on the sidelines waiting to come on again. It was the most amazing spectacle I'd ever seen."

The tour had kicked off with a grand reception at Warner Brothers in New York, to whom the band were now signed for the US, before Roxy were sent off round the States to play to indifferent and bemused audiences. A few rave reviews of the debut album aside, the press were nonplussed, particularly with Roxy as a live act. Dick Saunders of the *Chicago Sun Times* was typical:

The big disappointment of the evening was Roxy Music – another of those groups who try to hide their mediocrity under outrageous costumes. There were sequins, ruffles and rhinestones; a Flash Gordon type with two-toned hair who made a few good sounds on the saxophone, and one little thing in black feathers and thinning blond pageboy who occasionally removed his hand from his hip to flip some electrical switches and add to the noise.

Playing to 26,000 people at Madison Square Gardens, all of who had come to see Jethro Tull, was too much too soon. In reality, America wasn't ready for Roxy and Roxy weren't ready for them – equipment failure and dispiriting bottom-of-the-bill slots meant that even some of Roxy's fans barely registered that they were in the country at all. For Eno, the experience was more mixed. He managed to pick up a new girlfriend, an actress called Cassandra, when the band played the Bay Area, and he really enjoyed getting out and about, but the food was terrible and the gigs highly variable. At a festival in Miami, he kicked down the speaker system in disgust, and had a can of beer thrown at him when he was at the front of the stage doing the harmonies for "If There Is Something". "It's a particularly dispiriting feeling having stale beer running down your stage costume," he told the *NME*:

> Another thing about the States was the lack of promotion meted out by Warner Bros. We had a reception in New York but otherwise we kept to doing a few radio spots, which were quite farcical. On one of them it was obvious that the interviewer knew absolutely nothing about us and had just been given a promo sheet beforehand. He asked me about an album I was supposed to be recording with Rupurt Frupp (*sic*). I informed him that the name was in fact Rodney Frock.

Roxy played their final gig of the tour in Washington on January 4, 1973, arriving back at Heathrow the following day. Their return was followed by yet another change in personnel, as bassist Rik Kenton was dropped. The decision was also made not to use Pete Sinfield to produce the next album. "I still like a lot of the production on the first record but this time I want a more ... punchy attack," was how Ferry explained it. The task now was to make a follow-up album. The "difficult second album syndrome" is well known in pop: the first album the result of months, if not years, of careful planning, the follow-up a pressured disappointment. However, for Roxy Music, their second album was arguably their greatest. 1973 would be the year that Roxy Music secured their future – but at what price?

PART TWO

1973-1978

TA-RA: 1973

It was 1973 that was glam rock's *annus mirabilis*: twelve months of exhilarating foolery that presented British pop at its most theatrical *and* its most showbiz. At the extreme end of glam there was some serious experimentation but, in the main, it was the year that pop stars became as much a part of the fabric of light entertainment as Mike Yarwood, the Two Ronnies and Bruce Forsyth's "Generation Game". If you were looking for sensuality, originality and truthfulness, you needn't have bothered: 1973 was the year that British pop became a clown.

The year was unrecognisable when compared with the late-sixties musical scene: there were no Beatles, no Kinks, no ska and hardly any Motown. The year that began with Sweet's "Blockbuster" and ended with Slade's "Merry Xmas Everybody" also featured Number 1's by Suzi Quatro, Gary Glitter and Wizzard, plus two more from Slade, as well as all manner of trashy fun in between, from Alvin Stardust through to David Essex, Mud and Elton John. It was an age in which heterosexual men with brickies' bums and a fashion sense which, even by the standards of the day, looked horridly naff took to the *Top Of The Pops* stage with a sprinkling of glitter, a dab of blusher, stupid flares and a camp grin. As the nation slid towards the end of the year into dispute and recession, and talk of miners' strikes and three-day weeks, the pop world danced to a beat of extroverted, gender-bending pop silliness.

Of course, there were those who demanded to be taken seriously, and who found in 1973 all the nihilism, discontent and end-of-the-party decadence they needed to create remorselessly powerful and complicated art. David Bowie's six Top 10 singles and two Number 1 albums made him the biggest selling act of the year, and his brand of proto-punk androgyny bespoke a far more serious agenda. By the end of the year, he had, so it seemed, sped through three or four cycles of the pop evolutionary cycle and was planning *Diamond Dogs*, an apocalyptical theatrical *tour de force* that single-handedly brought the glam rock juggernaut to a shuddering halt. In 1973, former Godhead Marc Bolan saw his star in the descendant, although he still managed to crank out "Twentieth Century Boy", no mean achievement in itself. Then there were the likes of Cockney Rebel, who were preparing to make their assault with songs such as "Sebastian", a key song in late-period glam. With "serious" (although no less theatrical) music from the Floyd, Mike Oldfield and Genesis, 1973 appeared to have something for everyone who liked their music dressed up and ready for the theatre. Roxy Music, the most extreme and the most cerebral of all the rock acts, would also up the ante in 1973. It was a year that would see prodigious creativity, with two band albums, Ferry's first solo recordings, more tours, and more hits. It was also a year of significant interpersonal ructions that would ultimately send the band off in a completely new direction.

Roxy started the year busy recording a new single, to be released a month before the new album. The song, "Pyjamarama", was a surprise. "We took a radio to school so we could hear the Tuesday lunchtime chart rundown, and we were amazed to discover that the follow-up to 'Virginia Plain' was so subdued," remembers fan and writer Mark Paytress. "It was a fantastically radical single: that weird sax break, and such a mannered vocal again, with lyrics that were instantly memorable. You could just visualise Ferry, with his fantastically forced Gloria Swanson smile, rolling the words out."

"Pyjamarama" is the great "lost" Roxy Music song. Hardly ever played live and hardly ever discussed, it's one of Roxy's finest singles. Totally unique, it is very different from the art rock excursions of the first album, yet so sedate and mild compared with the brash chill of the second album. It's a perfect pop song, with superb, Keith Moon-influenced drumming at the rousing, chord-crashing opening, Eno's nifty Morse Code-synth throughout, arguably Mackay's best-ever sax fill and a fine guitar section at the end. Sadly, it seems that it was destined from the very outset to be the unloved runt of the Roxy litter: "We should never have put that out as a single," said Eno, just under two months after its release. "We did it in a rush after our American tour. We were still musically disorientated at that time. 'Do The Strand' would have been far better, but we hadn't recorded it at the time. We will never rush a single like that again."

The single was another tidy-sized hit for the band. Not quite matching the success of "Virginia Plain", it entered the UK Top 40 on March 17 at Number 31. Its chart progress was then as follows: Number 23, 17, 13, 10, 10, 10, 14, 25 and 30, before it ended its impressive eleven-week Top 40 residency in the Number 39 slot during the week ending May 26, by which time it was just another star in the glam rock heaven that was the British charts: Wizzard's "See My Baby Jive" was Number 1, Sweet's "Hell Raiser" was Number 2, "Can The Can" by Suzi Quatro was at Number 5 and Gary Glitter's "Hello! Hello! I'm Back Again" was at Number 8. For the glam intellectuals, Bowie's "Drive-In Saturday" was still clinging on at Number 16, whilst his sometime buddy Lou Reed was at number 17 with "Walk On The Wild Side". The late spring and summer were, it has to be said, the very pinnacle of pop poncery.

Roxy Music, buoyed by the vibrancy of a glam scene to which they felt only very loosely attached, were having the most successful year of their career, and it was their second album, *For Your Pleasure,* that made it for them. Looking back now, most critics regard *For Your Pleasure* as Roxy Music's finest hour: still pushing the musical envelope, yet more strident and more confident than on their quirky debut. "*For Your Pleasure* is my favourite," says Mark Radcliffe. "It seems to hang together perfectly; they seem to know exactly what they are doing. I think with the first one, they're still getting there. Isn't "Do The Strand" the best opening track of an album ever? I mean, you couldn't better that." "For me, *For Your Pleasure* is the peak, I guess," is Richard Williams' assessment. "'In Every Dream Home A Heartache' is a perfect piece of pop art, as perfect as a Lichtenstein." Julie Burchill and Tony Parsons, in their book *The Boy Looked At Johnny,* announced that the first two Roxy albums contained "the only truly timeless rock music ever recorded." For Bryan Ferry, the album is his personal favourite: "*For Your Pleasure* sounds a lot better, and the songs are more developed. It's awful to think that that's your high spot, only your second year of doing anything. If I were to have just one album though, I'd probably say that one."

Recording took place in February 1973, at London's Air Studios in Oxford Circus. The new bassist was John Porter, who had previously played with Ferry and the Gas Board. Although a lead guitarist by temperament, he filled the revolving-door role of temporary bassist for the new album and tour. This time Roxy would produce the album themselves, with the aid of Chris Thomas, whilst John Middleton and

John Punter engineered. The band had, in fact, been keen on producing the album entirely on their own, but had been talked round by their management, and rightly so.

The arrangement with Chris Thomas was the start of a four-album liaison with one of the top producers in the music business. Having been involved with the Beatles' *White Album* in the sixties, Thomas would go on to work on *Never Mind The Bollocks* in the seventies, *The Pretenders* in the eighties and Pulp's *A Different Class* in the nineties. Production work for Procol Harum, John Cale, Badfinger, Paul McCartney, Tom Robinson, Pete Townshend, INXS and Elton John are also on the Thomas CV, one of the classiest in rock production. "Roxy Music, after their first album, contacted John Cale to produce them, and they said, 'Which studio would you like to produce us in?'" Thomas remembers. "And John said, 'Air Studios'. Well, I was doing some stuff at Air with Procol when Bryan Ferry came by to look at the studio. I met him, then the thing with John blew out, so Bryan asked me to produce them."

Whereas Peter Sinfield had captured Roxy Music in all their eccentricities and with all their flaws still evident, the band Thomas was to work with was well-drilled. A year of almost constant touring had sharpened Roxy Music. They had lost some of their freewheeling wildness (Graham Simpson's bass playing had certainly been more extreme than that of John Porter, described as a "guest artiste" and not a full band member) but they had gained something Ferry in particular was very much keen to have, and that was a tighter, warmer and less experimental sound. The first Roxy Music is arguably the better record, but its eclecticism put some people off. *For Your Pleasure*, as Eno said at the time, was not so on the hoof; it stopped once in a while to take on water rather than bolting rider-less into a new musical field:

> I think the first album stressed all the things about us that are esoteric, ethereal and spacey, but as far as I'm concerned those things don't come off unless they're anchored to a strong base. I think that one of the things that attracted people to the band before was that feeling of dilettantism – a lot of the ideas being just touched on – but I felt that nothing was really taken far enough, and this album's got over that to an extent ... The album might be criticised for not showing enough ideas, but the ideas in there have been investigated much more thoroughly.

Most of the material that made up side two of *For Your Pleasure* had been left over from the first record, and was updated for the new album. However, a good portion of the rest had been conceived and written in short order by Bryan Ferry that winter:

> I had to sit down and try and write a kind of follow-up to the first one which got such great plaudits and I managed to do what I think was probably the best album overall. I think I was just so completely centred and focused on it, perhaps more so than I ever was afterwards. I had nothing else to do. I had no other life except this. I borrowed a cottage in Derbyshire from Nick De Ville and filled my ... what was I driving? I was driving this kind of very bourgeois Renault 4, a white Renault 4 ... and sort of drove up with these keyboards and things in the back. I was just on my own in this cottage for a few days and I bashed the songs out.

Given the tortuous compositional process that was to become so much a feature of Ferry's work from the eighties onwards, it's good to recall a time when the basics of one of the seventies' greatest albums could be written so quickly. Indeed, the whole album was tracked in just two weeks.

"Do The Strand" is, of course, the single that never was – in the UK at least. Released as a single in most world territories, it remained an album track in the homeland, eventually to be issued during a lull in Roxy Music recordings in 1978, when it failed to chart. Ferry told *Melody Maker* in 1973 that "it would be cheating kids, putting a single out from an album." It's probably Roxy Music's most performed song live, and it continues to find its way into Ferry solo sets to this day. The opening salvo: "There's a new sensation, a fabulous creation/A danceable solution, to teenage revolution" is not simply brilliant poetry; it's a Roxy manifesto, an art-pop slogan. In fact, the entire lyric – allusive, literary, punning, silly – is classic Ferry. Publicist Simon Puxley penned a 900-word dissection of the song, revealing the astonishing range of cultural references. Here's his analysis of the song's title:

> "The Strand": first and foremost a dance, depicted as a new craze ("new sensation", "the new way"). However, in the dictionary "strand" can mean "walk" (verb), a place to walk, a stretch of beach, or "to leave high and dry". "Strand" was also once a brand of cigarette. And the Strand is of course a famous London street, once highly fashionable:

this is the meaning that the title immediately calls to mind, if any. BUT the Strand is none of these things. It's without precedent and unique. It's not even a dance-step. It is, as the lyrics demonstrate, everything; or more particularly it is – to use inadequate platitudes – where it's at, whatever turns you on. The buzz, the action, the centre, the quintessence, the energy. The all-embracing focus, past, present and future, the ineffable. The indefinable. And in the context of performance the Strand is also something else, the here-and-now, i.e. the song, the music and the atmosphere themselves. The song metaphorically conceives of the Strand as a dance. No ordinary dance, but an eternal, universal or a tangible image of an indefinable aesthetic and emotional perfection.

The centrepiece of the album is, however, "In Every Dream Home A Heartache." Producer Chris Thomas recalls the birth of what must be one of the greatest art rock songs ever recorded: "That was one of the songs where we didn't know what was going on in the sense that we didn't know what the lyric was going to be. So we did the backing track as the sort of soundtrack, and then the idea was for this sort of psychedelic bit to happen at the end, but Bryan didn't tell us why. I mean he just said this is what he wanted. So we were just, y'know, flying blind."

"I don't think 'Dream Home' would have been written had I not been working with or in the same place as Richard Hamilton," says Ferry. "I think he influenced me. And also, I suppose, the title of 'Dream Home' was influenced by Richard as well, although I never discussed music with him." The Hamilton piece mentioned earlier, *What Is It About Today's Homes That Makes Them So Different, So Appealing?*, is one of the song's prime inspirations. The new consumerism, collaged by Hamilton, became the subject of Ferry's lyric. What Ferry does, however, is to discuss images of luxury consumerism within the framework of the early seventies, which is portrayed as a godless, soulless, depersonalised reality:

> "In every dream home a heartache
> And every step I take
> Takes me further from heaven
> Is there a heaven?
> I'd like to think so"

Before later concluding:

"Penthouse perfection
But what goes on there?
What to do there?
Better pray there."

(Words and music: Bryan Ferry, 1972)

This was Ferry at his most superb as a wordsmith. Gone are the sometimes rather trite juxtapositions of "Do The Strand" to be replaced by words that are so poetic, yet so economical. It's almost prayer-like in its construction. "It was twice as long when I first wrote it," Ferry revealed to *Melody Maker* immediately prior to its release. "But with it being a recitation rather than a song, I had to cut it quite a bit." The music is likewise minimalist and chill; a slow organ figure repeats through the first section, placing this song of godlessness on a more holy, spiritual plane of ideas and contemplation which mirror the sense of spiritual questioning in the words. Ferry's singing is, again, perfect for the subject matter – expressive, idiosyncratic, contrived, distanced yet heartfelt, it's the perfect summation of the best (and some would say worst) of the seventies.

The new consumerism, the "standards of living" that are "rising daily" are just show, just froth. The soul and spirit are corrupted, and whilst Ferry intones the legacy of uselessness that is modern life, he almost causally introduces the result of this soullessness – love not for a real human being, but for a blow-up doll:

"Open plan living
Bungalow ranch style
All of its comforts
Seem so essential
I bought you mail order
My plain wrapper baby
Your skin is like vinyl
The perfect companion"

In this hell of loneliness and contrived elegance, with no God or even a human being with whom to make any meaningful spiritual or physical contact, a man-made approximation of the human form, designed for instant sexual gratification by proxy, becomes the only Truth:

> "Inflatable doll
> My role is to serve you
> Disposable darling
> Can't throw you away now
> Immortal and life-size
> My breath is inside you."

The artificial has now become the real; the disposable and dispensable is the new reality (both very glam ideas). In a *Pygmalion* or *Frankenstein* scenario, the creator has lost control over the created:

> "Inflatable doll
> Lover ungrateful
> I blew up your body
> But you blew my mind!"

> (Words and music: Bryan Ferry, 1972)

Cue guitar freak-out, and the inevitable moment when all the incredible pent-up tension is released. An astonishing piece of pop art, "In Every Dream Home A Heartache" is the sort of grand dramatic gesture that pop music has now largely forgotten how to make.

With Eno's *outré* synth solo (so *outré* that "solo" is really a misnomer), and Mackay's sax blast (accompanied live by his update of Chuck Berry's duck-walk) with its frantic energy, "Editions Of You" points to punk and forges a link between glam pretence and new wave messing around. Glam rockers preened and posed and pretended to be other: punks assumed false identities to rail against the bourgeoisie. Bowie was Ziggy Stardust; John Lydon was Johnny Rotten. Yet ultimately, even if one strategy was arty, and the other cartoon-like, it was all part of the unpacking of different "editions" of oneself for the public:

> "I hope something special will step into my life
> Another fine edition of you."

The country and the city, that age-old divide, is the theme of the silliest and campest verse in Roxy history:

"Sometimes you find me yearning for the quiet life
The country air and all of its joys
But badgers couldn't compensate at twice the price
For just another night with the boys, oh yeah
And boys will be boys will be boys."

(Words and music: Bryan Ferry, 1972)

Ah, the silliness, the hedonism, the partying, the fun, all served in a cocktail with liberal dashes of the commodity of which there was a superabundance in the seventies: irony. It was not without its risks, however. "I always knew irony in pop was dangerous," says Phil Oakey of the Human League and an early Roxy Music fan:

> The line was exactly drawn by Bryan Ferry with, "But badgers couldn't compensate at twice the price." He was as funny as you could get and, when I came to make my own records, I knew people didn't want to buy comedy records. If they were going to lay out a proportion of the money they had sweated to earn, they didn't want to think you were in the studio laughing at them for buying it. So, I've always erred on the side of being serious.

"The Bogus Man", which was already being performed live before the recording of the album began, is Roxy Music at their most extreme and, arguably, their most indulgent. "We've done one very weird thing with a reggae drum beat and completely atonal sax," said Andy Mackay. "I stopped myself playing in key." A particular favourite of Paul Thompson's, the song repeats and repeats in a circuit of self-regard. It's the track that borrows the most from the Krautrock scene and the avant-gardists working in art music and, as such, its daring is matched by its aloofness. Eno loved it: "We had an underdeveloped idea of making something that had a sinister feeling to it, but with an under-tone of a fairly happy sounding riff; it was just meant to sound uneasy ... All the elements are very strange but they do work together to give this feeling of something very uneasy proceeding in a direction it's not quite sure of. For me, it's probably the most successful track."

More eloquent, and less lauded, was "Beauty Queen", another potential single and fan favourite (the "Valerie" mentioned in the first line was a model who lived in the Newcastle area in the late sixties).

Bryan Ferry songs are just made to be sung in the Vic Reeves pub singer style in karaoke bars, among pissed friends. Of "Beauty Queen", Ferry said at the time: "This one has a distinct northern working men's club feel to it." Eno loved it, too.

If the call to arms of "Do The Strand" was the perfect album opener, then the languid, crooning space-rock of the title track is surely the perfect closer. "For Your Pleasure" was in fact one of the numbers Ferry had penned at the time that he was stockpiling songs for the first album. So sings Ferry:

> "For your pleasure in our present state
> Part false part true like anything
> We present ourselves."

He is re-affirming those holy tenets of glam rock: "What's real or make-believe?"

The wonderful ending "Ta-ra, ta-ra", as the song dissolves into trippy white noise and Paul Thompson's rebounding drum figure, is exquisite. "The final psych-out is excellent on LSD," is critic Jon Savage's opinion. "I can't think of anything in rock like it, before or after, except perhaps Nico's 'The Marble Index' and Joy Division's 'Atmosphere'," wrote Simon Reynolds in *Uncut* magazine:

Ferry's hieroglyph words and stilted, stately phrasing (a frieze of emotion), the reverb-hazed piano, the stop-start rhythm, all conjure a gothic tableau of macabre elegance ... Halting for the impossible gravitas of Ferry's adieu ("Old man/Through e-ver-y step I change/You watch me walk away/Ta-ra"), the song then mutates into a mind-blowing extended coda, with multi-layered piano (Terry Riley/Steve Reich-style one-note riffs and upper octave trills) pointil-listic-painting a Milky Way skyscape mad with stars. Finally, the song expires like a galaxy swirling down a black hole's funnel.

For Your Pleasure entered the UK album charts in April 1973 and reached a thumping Number 4. It remained in the charts for 27 weeks, thus improving on the more-than-respectable performance of the debut, and garnered enthusiastic reviews. Surprisingly, it was Roy Hollingsworth, not band supporter Richard Williams, who was given the task of reviewing it for *Melody Maker*. Hollingsworth, initially sceptical of the band, was completely charmed. Long-standing supporter Caroline Boucher called it a "huge and lovely improvement on their first album" in *Disc*, whilst Charles Shaar Murray wrote this in *NME*:

> There are a large number of people in the music business who would be delighted to hear that Roxy Music had blown it. Their sudden rise to prominence offended many people who believe in dues-paying as the only acceptable prelude to success. That the Roxy personnel had all paid their dues in other fields is a fact often ignored by the band's detractors. And, indeed, if their second album had been a bummer, then all the hopes of the Anti-Roxy Brigade would have been fulfilled. Happy to state, they gonna have to close down operations for some little while, because the new Roxy album is here, and it's a staggeringly fine piece of work, easily outstripping the first album.

There were still pockets of resistance within journalism – those who continued to regard Roxy Music as a contrivance to cash in on glam rock, or simply as poor musicians whose ideas outmatched their limited technique – but as 1973 progressed, these voices of dissent became ever fainter.

However, in the period leading up to the album's release, the first signs of unrest within the Roxy Music camp began to be felt. One source of irritation was the album cover. Here was the first real flashpoint in the Roxy world, and it centred on what the band perceived, possibly, as Ferry's quest for stardom. The cover depicted Amanda Lear in a leather dress, pillbox hat, and stilettos, set against a city skyline; a black cheetah on a leash snarls out of the sleeve. Open the artwork out, and there's Bryan Ferry, smiling, standing behind the open door of a showy limousine. True, the gatefold inner cover shows the rest of the band posing with electric guitars, for "balance" as political editors might say, but the overall effect was pretty unambiguous – Bryan Ferry was the figurehead of the band. Eno was sniffy:

> Oh God. I'm really fed up with all this thing about glamour. We had to get a girl in to pose for the cover of the new album, which I thought was a drag because it's all becoming too stereotyped. Personally I'd prefer a nice unpretentious unglamorous picture of the band, wearing false beards and denims and standing around a tree, with "Support Ecology" on the back of the sleeve.

For Eno, there may have just been more than the slightest hint that style was in danger of becoming a prison for Roxy Music. He obviously didn't share Ferry's vision of cool and, in its place, he projected a much more radical and low-key future; a future away from the limelight, in the margins, where all the interesting things happen. So began the disintegration of the original Roxy Music. By spring of 1973, relations between Eno and Ferry were frosty. By the summer, the partnership would break apart and, a couple of low-key collaborations aside, it has never been re-established. And, despite Ferry's championing of the album as Roxy's finest, and the critical plaudits then and since, Eno, perhaps correctly, regarded the second album with rather mixed feelings:

> The second album ... was just slung together, not worked on like the first one. "The Bogus Man" could have been really good, but it was just left as it stood, and I thought "Grey Lagoons" was a very trivial track, our fifties gesture type thing. I thought "Beauty Queen" – which Bryan did practically by himself, incidentally – was spectacularly beautiful: my favourite Roxy track. But the rest ... well, I would like to have seen the experimental stance maintained a bit. Because "Bogus Man" was almost like some of the things Can were doing at the time – you know, open-ended, improvisatory, and not just thoroughly rehearsed performances with bits for the band to fiddle around with. But we didn't go that way and, instead, went for the zippiest, slickest option of just hitting the audience with the most exciting succession of ideas and images. Because you can't handle those huge tours without working to a safe formula, you know. You just get too tired to be creative every night, so you settle for a crowd-pleasing act that you can sort of sleepwalk your way through. So, for me, Roxy lost it somewhere around the middle of 1973.

Meanwhile, on the eve of the album's release, the band played British and European dates in spring 1973. For the tour, yet another bassist was brought in, in the shape of 6' 4" of Salvatore (Sal) Maida. Nottingham University Sports Centre launched the tour with one of the worst sound systems of Roxy's career, but from a wobbly start, the band powered through the provinces, terrifying the country once again with an unfettered hit of art rock. The costuming (Eno aside) had been toned down slightly from the extremes of 1972, but the new material was perfect for showcasing Ferry's melodramatic style, with high camp for "Do The Strand" (now with a ¾ section for the line "weary of the waltz?") and "Editions Of You". Of the earlier material, only "Ladytron", "If There Is Something", "Re-Make/Re-Model" and "Virginia Plain" were regularly included. What was also certain still was that the band was continuing to convert the press to the Roxy cause.

"I always remember seeing Roxy at the Rainbow, just when the second album came out," recalls former *Melody Maker* journalist Chris Charlesworth. "I thought they were terrific. 'Do The Strand' was the highlight. Bryan was in a red toreador outfit, as I recall." The *Observer's* Tony Palmer, who hadn't cared much for the albums, thought the presentation was astonishing: "demonic, sinister, apocalyptic, monstrous, dazzling, flashy – what opera might have been in the seventies before it lost its nerve."

The support for the tour was provided by the Sharks, whose line-up included Chris Spedding, perhaps the hottest session guitarist in the UK in the seventies, who went on to play with Ferry and Roxy Music, and remains a regular member of the touring band to this day. "Eno was one of the more sociable members of the band, he got on well with us," recalls Spedding:

> Not many headline bands even talk to the support act. I remember getting on well with Phil, Andy and Brian Eno. Bryan was always very pleasant, but, of course, Bryan being Bryan, he was always a bit less easy to hang out with.
>
> I was interested in the audience's reaction to them. At the time it wasn't really my kind of music. I became more sympathetic to that type of music after I left the Sharks. We were more a rhythm 'n' blues sort of band. I never thought that I'd end up working with Bryan, but it happened ...

Bravely, the concerts began with a big chunk of new material before climaxing with "Editions Of You" and "Re-Make/Re-Model". The two singles, "Pyjamarama" and "Virginia Plain", provided the rapturously received encores. Critics agreed that the playing was altogether more competent: Mackay was emerging as a much more powerful performer, whilst Ferry too now played with the audience, inviting them to get up, stand up, and dance their way to the front of the hall to share the music's exuberant pull. Martin Kirkup, reporting from Nottingham

University for *Sounds*, mentioned that, "Eno's had a haircut, Bryan sports a guitar, and the audience is full of Andrew Mackay look-alikes." But even though some critics could see the merits of a group that killed off the slack ideas and dull presentation of the period for good, there were still musical issues for many. "Musically, drummer Paul Thompson and guitarist Phil Manzanera came over best," said the *NME*'s Steve Clarke:

> But there were too many instances when the sounds became confused and just a mess, though things did improve towards the end when the band played several short, tighter numbers which just about worked. I've never liked Ferry's voice but he looks just like a rock 'n' roll singer. I just wish he'd sound more like one.

The tour of the provinces hit a moment of sublime absurdity up in Scotland, always a Roxy stronghold, when the band played Green's Playhouse in Glasgow. The band's performance was prefigured by a bagpipe medley of Roxy favourites played by three pipers. Unexpectedly, the trio dramatically took to the stage during the main set to play what must be the world's only version of "Virginia Plain" in the style of the Royal Scots Dragoon Guards as the band thrashed out the encore. Puxley, not one to miss a photo opportunity when it came piping to the front door, had the band snapped with the bagpipers for the *Sunday Mail*. The bagpipers also blew their way through a second gig at Edinburgh's Odeon. This was pure rock 'n' roll Dadaism.

Next up was the spring European promotional tour, which included the Golden Rose Festival in Montreux and Germany's *Musikladen* television show, where the band played live. They didn't make any money on the European tour, nor had they done on any of the UK tours to date, despite their undeniably strong box-office appeal. On tour in Paris, they demanded to stay at the George V Hotel. This was a band on the make living like the upper class.

However, what should have been the real coup, and proof positive that they were serious players on the high cultural scene, was their meeting with the grand old man of surrealist art, Salvador Dali. Amanda Lear had arranged for the band to meet Dali at his permanent residence at the Hotel Meurice. A TV producer and camera crew failed to show up, but plenty of media coverage was guaranteed as they took tea. Roxy, however, seemed unimpressed to be in the company of greatness. "Dali seems to have deteriorated into someone who hangs around with bands just to get publicity," said Ferry, rather snootily, just after the meeting. "His current output is quite meagre – certainly nothing to talk about over dinner." Such was the disappointment that Roxy's manager Mark Fenwick reportedly scribbled the word "asshole" over a photo of Dali in Andy Warhol's *Interview* magazine.

As on the British leg, slide-guitarist and singer-songwriter Lloyd Watson opened for the band, who played confidently through a set-list almost identical to the one used in the UK. Ferry, meanwhile, found himself several suits lighter after some of his specialities had been stolen during the UK tour: for the gig at Olympia in Paris he took to the stage wearing a "flared gold brocade D'Artagnan coat hired from a theatrical costumier," reported Richard Williams.

The slide towards the disintegration of Roxy Music Model I was, of course, accelerated by that age-old music biz cover-all: musical differences. This time, though, there really were important differences in how the two main protagonists saw the future of the band. Ferry wanted to foreground the songwriting, to improve both musically and technically, and to lose some of the art-school pretension of the early Roxy. He wanted rounded, romantic songs. Captain Eno, on the other hand, wanted to keep foraging for rare musical truffles, to seek out new life and new musical civilisations, and, indeed, probably to boldly go where no rock star had gone before. From early 1973, Ferry and Eno's careers took wildly divergent routes. Ferry established himself as a mainstream star, a crooner, an interpreter of the work of others yet a witty and talented songwriter in his own right, and, most importantly, a style icon for the soul boys and punks to be found roaming suburbia from late 1974 onwards. Eno, by contrast, became increasingly abstract, increasingly random, and increasingly *outré*. Yet even though he was working at the margins of popular culture, it would, ironically, be Eno and not Ferry who would have the greatest impact on the mainstream and who, through a series of high profile and hugely successful musical productions over the next thirty years, would become presumably the much wealthier man. Eno fulfilled all his potential and more; Ferry never quite became the huge star his talent deserved.

To many back in 1973, and many still in 2004, Eno was an essential part of the overall Roxy master plan. His removal, in the summer of 1973, was a blow from which some claim the band never recovered. Although at that stage not a credited songwriter, Eno's presence in the studio as a creative genius working on the sound of the band, plus his astonishingly flamboyant and alien stage presentation, made him into a figure at least as important and as resonant as Ferry. Just what was it that Eno did? Peter Sinfield:

> Eno, in some ways, is one of the world's most brilliant frauds in so far as he's made an art of not being a musician. That's to say, he puts coloured dots on piano keys and he used tape loops. It's quite brilliant to invent something like *Music For Airports* where you don't play anything – you just play one note and let it hang around. It's like a conjuring trick really ... yet it's very, very intelligent, as is Brian, very intelligent and Machiavellian. I think it was clear that Brian Eno in his feathers was becoming the centre of attraction, yet he wasn't really doing very much to the music except making the guitars wobble and doing the backing singing – the most glamorous backing singer with a small synthesiser that there had ever been!

For many fans, too, it was Eno, not Ferry, who was the star attraction. "You can't hide the fact that Eno appeared to just materialise out of nowhere, and that David Bowie materialised out of 'The Laughing Gnome'," is how Martyn Ware puts it:

> Bowie and Eno were entirely different as far as I'm concerned. It was a conscious decision of Bowie's, that transitional phase into alien rock icon. It was fantastic, but it was a gradual process, whereas with Eno it was like, what is that mane? How long is it? Where did he come from? And does he have a passport? Why does he have feathers coming out of his shoulders? And why is he wearing white glittery gloves? And what's he twiddling that knob for? And why is he right on the outside of the stage? How does he make those sounds? What is that synthesiser?
>
> I'd always been a fan of synthesisers in pop music. And of course, Eno came along and fulfilled all the dreams of what we thought possible. He rarely actually played a tune, in fact he didn't play a tune, that's what we loved about it, it was a series of bleeps and blobs and science-fiction stuff which married perfectly with our bizarre futuristic vision.

It wasn't just the fact that Eno was such a strong and forceful ideas man within the band, or even that he was becoming the bigger star. Eno got at Ferry in other ways, too. Despite Ferry's raven-haired good looks, he couldn't even begin to compete with Eno's enormous sexual appetite and incredible success in the bedroom. A balding man in make-up, Eno could literally charm the pants off the "laydeez". Was Ferry jealous? "Oh, probably," is the candid answer. And how true are those tales (and they are now part and parcel of rock mythology) of Eno suffering a collapsed lung in 1974 after a particularly strenuous shagging session? "Well, I wouldn't put it past him," continues Ferry. "I think Brian had a very strong personality, but he wasn't really threatening to women, you know? And I think that was possibly part of the secret of his success. He was undoubtedly very successful with women. I've never seen anything like it – he was unbelievable." On the road in Europe, Eno told Nick Kent that it was "marvellous" to be thought of as a sex symbol, "particularly as I'm totally useless at playing music." One fan letter read: "Hi, I'm 18 years old, and a good screw." Eno's only regret was, "I wish these girls would send photographs."

Back in 1973, the best thing you could do to attract the girls was to apply a bit of slap. Maybe 1973 was rock's 1773, with wigs, corsets, ludicrous powder-puffery and rakish libertine excess the order of the day. Eno was pop's most preening of rock stars: "My make-up is the same both on and off stage," Eno would claim at a time when even David Bowie could be seen in mufti at recording sessions. "It consists of a large selection of things including Quant, Revlon, Schwarzkopf and Yardley. I just choose whatever colours appeal to me at the time. On my eyes I use six different colours by three or four different makers." Eno's striking looks, his femininity, his oversized libido, his rock star appeal and, of course, his money turned him into one of rock's most voracious sexual magnets. In fact, it's hard not to feel a certain admiration (and perhaps more than a trace of envy) for a man who has led such a dissolute and yet intellectual life. No wonder, given the private lives of so many of our politicians, that he would eventually make such a perfect panellist on BBC TV's flagship question-and-answer political programme *Question Time*.

Naturally, Eno intellectualised his role-playing. That was the fun of it. He might have lived the lifestyle, but he never lost sight of the real objective: to take life as everyday lived experience and seek out new ways of living – to *pretend*. At the core of Eno's art, and at the core of his music, his singing, and some of the almost excruciating naïvety of his music, is his essential childish theatricality: "I've got plans for some fabulous new costumes," he told *Sounds* in early 1973:

They're going to be rather difficult to construct because they're made from totally outlandish materials that have to be gathered from all parts of the globe. One actually requires feathers from the tail of a lye bird, which might be a bit difficult – I've never actually seen one, just in children's encyclopaedias and things, so they might be extinct for all I know. But I need three and then I'll be away. I do love the whole costume bit – its very important to me musically, not a superfluous thing in any way.

Eno was also, from the start of his media career, astonishingly open about sex, nudity, pornography, and all fleshly matters. Intensely cerebral, he was also insanely sexual. In 1973, publicist Simon Puxley cajoled a photographer, hired to take photos for the rock mag *Creem*, into taking some nude photographs of the waif-like Eno stretched out on his bed, posing coquettishly for a series of test shots for *Viva*. "I could never do this for a male photographer, I'd be too embarrassed," Eno said to the female snapper: "Don't be coy, thousands have seen me naked." Eno's offer to be photographed "with all my rudeness showing" was, however, flatly turned down. Eno concluded the session thus: "Forgive me if I have a hard-on; it is certainly the way of nature. I can't sit up." Then he found a solution: "I'll cover it with a book."

However, what ultimately annoyed Ferry the most was the fact that, while he wrote the songs, it was Eno who won the critical plaudits. Ferry bitterly resented the fact that print journalists found Eno utterly charismatic, the perfect combination of intellectualism and alien outrage. Almost thirty years after the split he told *Guardian* writer Dave Simpson: "We were young and foolish. But at the same time, we worked well together. I just didn't like being portrayed as the glamour-boy singer when I was writing this stuff. Back then I felt threatened, but that's changed."

Eno also appealed to the hipsters at the *NME* because he possessed a sense of outrage that was obviously so different to Ferry's increasingly sedate charms. Seldom has a rock band had two leaders, and the bipolarity within Roxy Music was, with hindsight, never going to work forever. This is a shame, since this challenge to the front-guy rock format was so refreshing. The Brian Jones-era Stones and the Beatles obviously helped change the way rock groups presented themselves, but, as a rule, most groups had dominant front men who garnered ninety percent of the attention. Eno recognised the problem, and was not unsympathetic:

> Some of the papers seemed to think that I was the leader of the group, which was very embarrassing and quite unjust to Bryan. But then he went off and started doing interviews where he'd try to re-establish the real position and started saying completely over-the-top things like "This band is my baby and I could have done the same thing with any other group of musicians", which was blatantly untrue.

Ferry originated the material, yet he saw himself upstaged night after night by the peacock-feathered Eno. By day, the press would clamour for an Eno interview. Journalists loved Eno; he was a futuristic dandy and he gave great copy. With a knack for media sound bites Ferry has never possessed, he would famously tell *Disc* magazine that he was an alien. Some of his fans almost believed him.

The situation between the two deteriorated very quickly in the course of the first six months of 1973. One important factor was the perceived inequitable share of the Roxy revenues, as Eno would later reveal:

> Even taking into account that Bryan deserved more than the rest of us, having written all the material, to me the revenue was unfairly divided. He took all the music and lyric royalties and a sixth share in arrangements – which meant he ended up with over seventy percent of what we were collectively earning. I'm not saying we should have split it equally, just that he could have given away a little more than he did.

There was increasing pressure by management on Ferry to move centre stage: quite literally, in fact. Phil Manzanera:

> He was pushed to do it, by the management and everybody saying, "You've got to have someone focused in the middle or the band won't be successful". I remember the first time we did *Top Of The Pops*, and Eno being terribly upset because the only thing you saw of Eno if you watch it back now, is his glove, which was a terrible waste, actually. There was much more pressure on Bryan than on anyone, I think at that time, because he was sort of lauded as the Great White Hope, and, obviously, Bowie was happening, and there were always

comparisons with Bowie. He must have felt very special, but under a lot of pressure.

Eno himself agrees that, "silly things, like whose photographs were the biggest, seemed just gigantically important at the time."

Fan power played a part in all this. At certain concerts, Eno fans would assemble at his side of the stage, cheering and chanting his name, and attempting to drown out the lead singer during the quieter sections. There are also unsubstantiated tales of Eno deliberately extending his synth solos and turning up the volume to drown out the singer. It's hardly surprising that Eno and Ferry fell out. They had been living and working together almost continually for over two years. Hardly a day would go by without them being in the same space. A few months before Eno's departure, Ferry hinted at the dangers of being in a band: "It's the same as a love affair really – up and down when you're in each other's company for ninety percent of the time."

But what really seemed to do for Eno was Ferry's jealousy, mixed with a profound sense of insecurity. Eno didn't help, flaunting his ideas to the press as he did at every available opportunity. But the basis of the Roxy split appears to be Ferry's inability to cope with Eno as such a powerful backseat driver. "Brian and I seemed to fall out," says Ferry:

I think it was over some interviews when we were playing. You see, I didn't really like the interview process and I'm not that great at it now, but I'm less shy than I used to be. I used to be really tongue-tied. I guess that's what made me a singer; it's a way of overcoming this verbal insecurity, verbal shyness. Brian, of course, had confidence in spades. He could give a lecture; stand up in front of any number of people about anything. He's so full of himself and full of words and he's really good at that.

So, at the end of the shows we did over Europe in particular, I'd be kind of flat out in the dressing room gasping for air, really exhausted, and Brian would be fresh as a daisy in a room next door with, like, twenty Italian journalists around him or something saying, "Oh well, we did this because ..." and it just kind of got to me, I guess. I suppose I was young and foolish and full of ego like a lot of young musicians are. I just felt it was my baby and I think he was maybe wanting to do more, more than I wanted him to do perhaps at that point.

"Oh yeah, we had a very big rift," confirms Eno:

> It was a typical clash of young male egos I think, really. What had happened was that because I was visually so bizarre-looking I got a lot of press attention. The press are always interested in people who make good photographs and I made good photographs. That did rather distort the impression of where the creative leadership of the band was. It was definitely Bryan's band, y'know, and I probably got more attention than I deserved, or perhaps I should say that he got less attention than he deserved. So this created a real problem in the band.

By the early summer of 1973, Ferry had decided to take action. Roxy's gig at the York Festival in June was the catalyst. Ferry arrived at the site to find the journalists more interested in Eno's collaboration with Fripp than in Roxy Music. His hackles already rising, he was further provoked by the fact that Eno was also scheduled to play with the Portsmouth Sinfonia before Roxy took the stage, which would have the effect of mobilising the pro-Eno faction in the audience. Then, during Roxy Music's set, Eno fans drowned out Ferry's vocal on "Beauty Queen". Eno left the stage in an attempt to diffuse the situation, signalling his annoyance at the fans' behaviour, but his absence only made matters worse. At the end of the gig Ferry told his manager that he would never work with Eno again, although there would be no face-to-face discussion of the situation. Ferry's style was to avoid confrontation, to avoid full discussion, and to let management handle interpersonal disputes. On returning from holiday in Corfu, he found that Eno, fed up with his underhand tactics, had called a meeting with his management and told them that he had no alternative but to leave. "I was pissed off at the subterfuge and wanted Bryan to actually say it to my face. But he didn't. So eventually I just stood up, said, 'OK, fuck it, I'm leaving,' and walked out." So, perhaps like football managers who "agree to terminate their contracts by mutual consent", Eno's was neither strictly a sacking nor a totally voluntary departure, but something in-between. The final decision to leave was Eno's, but he had no choice, given Ferry's intransigence. Eno himself greeted the news with a huge sigh of relief. After a meeting with the band management that sealed his fate as an ex-band member, he ran down the street, bounding giddily like a schoolchild with a good report at the end of term, and wrote "Baby's On Fire" the very same day: June 21, 1973.

Eno, for his part, later claimed that he quit Roxy Music when he found himself on stage thinking about his laundry. As Eno has been a most reluctant performer ever since, we must give some credence to the notion that he was simply bored with the whole touring process. In fact, almost all his work, from the late seventies onwards, has been made with the express purpose of being unplayable in a live context, in real time, by real musicians. Eno had simply outgrown not just Ferry and Roxy Music, but the whole idea of what it was that a rock musician was supposed to be. "I think I'll probably just give up music altogether and become a full-time poseur," he joked to Nick Kent in *NME* just after the split.

What is certain is that Eno left with dignity intact. "People who do hatchet-jobs on the members of their old bands usually come out looking like losers when it all appears in print," he said. "I started off wanting to call a press conference so that I could state my case, but that's all so pointless. Another reason for my reticence is because I don't want to damage Roxy, for the sake of the other people in it. I mean, I really like the other members, and I (pause) really like Bryan, in a funny way."

Eno's solo career was already a viable prospect before his forced exit from the band. At the beginning of 1973 he had recorded the experimental electronic album *No Pussyfooting* with King Crimson's Robert Fripp. "Fripp and I tend to complement each other greatly in the sense that I am by no means a musician, whereas Fripp most certainly is and can therefore form my fantasy ideas and turn them into some of substance," Eno told the *NME*. He was also developing a more than passing interest in what was then the unhippest music around: muzak. In fact, to many, this was "non-music". Eno would tweak and reshape, develop a newer form, and re-brand it as "ambient", perhaps the most important development within popular music of the last twenty years. "I used to suffer from long stretches of insomnia and was forced to construct a piece using tape loops that took the form of muzak which, in turn, was conducive to sleep. Really, the potential to be found in the use of electronic music has only just begun to be mined." However, for now, Eno was still attempting to make pop music.

Eno's first solo album proper was 1974's *Here Come The Warm Jets*. He felt liberated. Before recording began, he told *NME*, "My main plan is to record as much as possible with as many different people as possible. Muff Winwood has offered me free time at Island, so it should be a cinch." He continued to be managed by EG, who told him that he was personally in debt to the tune of £15,000 despite two years of gigging and chart success. "That's what you get for trying to be a rock star," was his wry rejoinder to journalists.

No longer having to throw his ideas into a band environment, to compromise, dilute, and reshape, Eno began establishing his own eccentric agenda. At times, his music sounded unmoving, unlistenable, and obtuse; however, at its best, the wild flights of fancy, unexpected melodies and silly, punning lyrics made the unfettered Eno a precious delight for the aficionado. Eno was already thinking about how to make music out of unpromising or seemingly oppositional musical forces. At the beginning of the year, he had already promised some changes: "On my next album I will follow my idea of using musicians who are not compatible with each other." Two years later, together with Peter Schmidt, a British artist, Eno would work on his *Oblique Strategies* cards.

Subtitled "One Hundred Worthwhile Dilemmas", these cards provided a fascinating insight into the workings of the immediate post-Roxy Eno. The idea was simple, almost childlike, but at the same time devastatingly effective: Eno and Schmidt provided a list of mini-rules and directives to aid the creative process. *Oblique Strategies* codified Eno's working practices for us all to see: "Ask people to work against their better judgement", "Abandon normal instruments" and "Use 'unqualified' people" are just three Eno aphorisms which appear central to his idea of using incompatible musicians. John Wetton, one of rock's most enduring musicians and doyen of Uriah Heap, King Crimson, Asia and many solo albums, played with Eno, Ferry and Roxy in the mid-seventies, and recalls Eno's idiosyncrasies only too well:

I find Brian Eno an enticing subject at the best of times. He's really great to work with, totally off the wall. Bryan Ferry is naïve, and so is Brian Eno for that matter, but in a different way. There's an old story of me going to play on "Baby's On Fire" from *Here Comes The Warm Jets*. Such was my naïvety; I didn't even get the significance of that album title, so that showed you where I was at the time. I got a call from Captain Eno and he said two o'clock at some bloody place in south London. I had to borrow a mate's bass because mine was in America. So I turned up there with a bass I'd never even played before. And did what I normally did, which was to tune up to the track. And I was playing this outrageous EB3 bass with a fuzz box, just playing all the way up from the bottom fret to the top fret very loudly. I got to the end, and I said, "Yeah, I'm in tune now, are we going to do a take?" And he said, "No, that's alright, we've already got it." It made me chuckle that he could be so straightforward and sure about what he was doing.

Brian Eno is willing to tackle anything, and he'll go in at it at an oblique angle, and sometimes you get some really good results with that: as in art, music is no different. Sometimes when people have the rudiments, and they attack it from a different angle, they can come up trumps. Björk is one such case – no formal musicality, but she comes up with some outrageously good stuff. Like Eno, like Pete Gabriel – it's the same thing. Sometimes those oblique ideas really work.

Released in January 1974, *Here Come The Warm Jets* is a minor classic. Neither glam nor progressive rock but containing curious references to both, it actually points the way to the new wave. "Baby's On Fire" and, in particular, "Needle In The Camel's Eye" are so startlingly different that they sound as if they belong to 1977 rather than 1974. In fact, the whole album has a timeless quality. Moorings to the Roxy mothership successfully snapped, Eno had seemed to have found his own voice very quickly.

And what a peculiar voice! Although five years later he would largely forsake vocals altogether, the first and arguably the most enjoyable phase of the solo Eno saw words tumbling out of the speakers. Eno's thin voice, always more suitable to backing rather than lead vocals, is still enjoyable, whilst the lyrics themselves are very often jumbles of words and short phrases, chosen for their sound and rhythm rather than for their meaning. Unlike Ferry, Eno was no craftsman, but the result was just as enjoyable in its playfulness.

Eno-less, Roxy would ultimately reposition towards the mainstream and, as a result, many of the group's original fans began to lose interest. Martyn Ware puts it bluntly:

When Eno left the band, I thought it was all downhill from there. They lost a huge amount. The songwriting was still very good, but they just became more normal. It's a bit like when Peter Gabriel left Genesis – nobody could argue about the proficiency of what's left, it just wasn't as exciting or as dangerous or as daring. With everybody I knew, if it had been down to a loyalty between Roxy Music and Eno's output, we all knew which way we would have jumped. We were great fans of his albums and of his ambient stuff as well. Just the general kind of thought that it was a bit more than a strive for fame and wealth. It was actually *art*. And art has become a dirty word. Even thinking that is taboo now: I would be deemed old-fashioned, or naïve.

For Jon Savage, however, the change in the post-Eno Roxy led to equally intriguing music: "Ferry was now in control, and the wilder outreaches of *For Your Pleasure* were abandoned, all with ultimately very little loss to the Roxy blueprint." Whilst Richard Williams describes the "new" Roxy like this: "The music became more predictable, which immediately removed one of the things I liked about it. It became much more consistent. I don't think the quality declined, in fact. I think the creativity did, to some extent."

But Eno's career as a pop star was to be comparatively short-lived. Touring to support his first solo album in 1974, he was literally shagged out. Enough groupies to keep even the most voracious sexual appetites satisfied and constant gigging resulted in a collapsed lung and hospitalisation. "The momentum of my career had been towards becoming a sub-David Bowie," is how Eno put it. "But what I like is sitting in little rooms and fiddling with things until they suddenly hit a chord." Whether it was stage fright or boredom, or simply the fact that Eno saw his future not as a pop star but as a studio artist, Eno was mightily relieved to be out of Roxy Music and, very soon after, to become almost invisible as a live act: "I was happy when my lung collapsed."

Swapping the studio for the stage, Eno established himself as one of rock's most important artists. But that's for the future. For now, Eno was out of Roxy Music, but Roxy Music would endure. As Eno's career followed a wholly unpredictable, but ultimately hugely successful path of astonishing changes and freewheeling invention, Ferry and Roxy were headed for calmer waters and, perhaps, greater acceptance and broader appeal. Yet even Ferry admits he has regrets: "At the time, I didn't think Eno was as important as Mackay and Manzanera, but I think, looking back now, he definitely was. I do have a soft spot for those albums." In 1994, he told the BBC:

Looking back, I think I sort of underestimated what he did do, which is strange for me, because I'm usually the hyper-fairest of people but, er, I think circumstances just got too much, and anyway we went our separate ways, sadly I think for too long. What we probably needed was just somebody to ... and I don't think the management were focused enough at the time to do that, to just get us together and say, 'Hey you guys are great together and you should resolve this, and ...

When I fall out with people I tend to freeze them out, and I froze him out. I don't like a scene so much, but I do a very good sort of Garbo freeze-out technique. And Brian left. I think looking back it was probably the best for all concerned, even though I'd like to go back and remake all those [subsequent] albums with him to see what it would sound like ...

ROXY MUSIC
PHASE 2: 1973

For a few weeks after the removal of Brian Eno, it seemed as though Roxy Music were on the verge of splitting up altogether. In the summer of 1973, the music press reported that Andy Mackay was close to quitting and that Manzanera would surely follow suit. To the press, Ferry once again cited musical differences in defence of his decision to remove Eno. Roxy was simply not a broad enough church to accommodate the musical heresies of Eno. "Groups kind of break up – it's a very sort of natural process, in the same way as you grow apart from friends, girlfriends or whatever," Ferry told the BBC's Paul Gambaccini in 1975:

> People just change all the time, and their relationship to each other changes all the time. And if you feel that a break is the right thing to do at any time then you have to do it rather than keep it together under any kind of pressure. After *For Your Pleasure*, we'd done as much as we could with that line-up.

Andy, Phil and Paul were, indeed, shocked by Eno's removal. They hadn't wanted it to happen, and were alarmed when it did. However, after considering their positions, a "heads down" mentality prevailed, and the band were very quickly back to work. However, it was plain that the first version of Roxy Music was over. A new era had dawned.

The year 1973 would be a turning point in the history of Bryan Ferry and Roxy Music, and not only because of the exit of Eno. It was the year in which the "Bryan Ferry" brand name was launched. For all but the hardcore fan, the result was a muddle; by the end of the decade, many were unsure about which song fitted where, and this confusion persists to the present day, where Ferry fans attending a Roxy concert fully expect to hear "Let's Stick Together". Two repertoires, one singer: it served only to dilute the power of the "Roxy" brand, whilst the impact of the band lessened as Ferry's own solo work became increasingly less radical.

However, with Eno gone, the most pressing need for Ferry and Roxy was to find a replacement, and to find one quickly. Work was about to begin on Bryan Ferry's first solo album, a collection of covers called *These Foolish Things*, and, soon after that, on Roxy's third album, planned for autumn release.

This meant that 1973, the year of the three albums, was the most productive in Ferry's career. He had been planning a solo album for several months. Back in January he had told the *NME*, "I'm very interested in doing a solo album of things not written by me, but which I like very much." According to Ferry, most of the great songwriters were American and, moreover, most of the true wordsmiths were professional songwriters rather than performers. For Ferry, the impulse for singers to originate their own material had produced a lot of substandard music. By recording standards, he felt he would be more faithful to the original spirit of popular song. "Pre-Beatles, singers would pick twelve songs by songwriters they liked and go ahead like that, which is what I did," he explained shortly afterwards. Even as early as 1973, Ferry was a bit of a musical nostalgist.

It's actually unclear whether Ferry had decided upon a replacement for Eno while Eno himself was still in the band. As the replacement, Ferry opted for youth in the shape of Edwin "Eddie" Jobson, already an experienced musician but, on the surface, much less of a "threat" than the deposed Eno. "I felt that the group needed another virtuoso instrumentalist/soloist, which we didn't have. I thought it was better for all concerned if he were to kind of join the group, which would enable Eno to go and do his own things, because there wasn't room for them in Roxy Music. It's as simple as that," he explained. Not long afterwards, however, Eno revealed that Ferry's alleged Machiavellian dealings to bring Jobson in had caused great disharmony: "I know both Andy and Phil are very annoyed about that. I don't know what Paul thinks – Bryan is obviously pleased about it. One thing I'm personally very annoyed at is that when Eddie Jobson was brought up to York [the last Eno-intact Roxy gig] to study my style and form, Bryan didn't tell anyone up until the last minute." It is undeniable that Jobson's unexpected appearance when the band played the York Festival made it seem to Eno that Ferry was contemplating a change of personnel, and was in fact already grooming his successor in a quite calculated manner.

Eddie Jobson was born on April 28, 1955 in Billingham, County Durham (the same county as Ferry), and was something of a teenage rock prodigy. He had joined Curved Air, the progressive rock outfit fronted by Sonja Kristina, in 1972 and had worked on their album *Air Cut*, released in April 1973. In stark contrast to Brian Eno's non-musicianship, Jobson was a talented multi-instrumentalist, arranger and composer. "Actually, I think Bryan first heard of me from his sister, Enid, who shared a room with my sister, Ann, in college [at Durham]", says Jobson:

Bryan presumably became more aware of me once I was a member of Curved Air, and he did show up at a concert in London to check me out. As one of the few VCS3 synthesizer players around, I could obviously cover Eno's parts, as well as take over Bryan's piano parts, allowing him to move to centre stage for the first time. I also brought the electric violin and my keyboard skills and flair for orchestral arrangements. Best of all, I was from the Newcastle area, a northern lad.

The prevailing line was that nobody could "replace" Eno and that was obviously true. However, I brought my own form of teen-appeal and could add another "classical" element [along with the oboe] with the plexiglass violin. The main reason for Eno's departure and my joining was that Bryan wanted to remove the distraction of Eno's ever-increasing recognition. Eno was becoming a bigger media star than Bryan, and Bryan was the one writing and singing all the songs. By bringing me in, much to the protest of Andy and Phil, Bryan got to have all of the above, without competing with Brian Eno for the attention. As a rather green 18-year-old, I was no competition in terms of becoming a media darling.

At first, I was extremely hesitant to accept Bryan's invitation, partly because I didn't want to split up Curved Air. But then I found out just a few days later that both the guitarist and the drummer were planning to leave the band. I was offered the option of taking Curved Air in the direction of my choosing but, very hesitantly, I just had to take the opportunity with Roxy. Unfortunately, having made the bold move, I was then greeted by Andy and Phil with complete hostility. In fact, they told the *New Musical Express* that if I joined, they would leave! This made me feel pretty bad. Obviously, if Bryan could pull this kind of power move without their consultation, then the days of the Roxy Music democracy were over.

For his solo record, Ferry picked thirteen classics; pop songs he remembered fondly from his youth and teenage years, and also pre-rock-era songs. He had always admired songs from the past, from his youth, his childhood, and even further back. However, in this reclamation of a pre-rock heritage, he was, by the standards of the time, unique. Writer and fan Paul Du Noyer recalls the impact of the solo albums:

I remember his first few records were cover versions, in parallel with Roxy Music. What was seductive about those was that it was the first recognition by the rock 'n' roll generation of popular culture before rock 'n' roll. His reference points were Sinatra and Bogart and torch singers of that era. Again, in retrospect, this is also probably the first stirrings of postmodernism within pop music because, before Ferry, the general conceit was that Elvis Presley's first record was year zero; nothing of any consequence had existed before that, unless it were an obscure blues record or something. Mainstream popular culture had nothing to offer before Elvis Presley. Now Ferry tuned into the burgeoning fashionability of thirties and forties style in London at that time. This was the era of Biba in Kensington, who specialised in basically art deco style but reworked for the seventies. This was the time when Oxford Bags made a return, and fashion was beginning to show certain stylistic traits from the thirties and forties, which Ferry was probably the prime mover in. But he paralleled that in his music: he acknowledged that there was worthwhile music before and outside of the rock 'n' roll canon.

The project afforded Ferry the chance to collaborate with an array of different talents, including David Skinner on bass, a horn section, and backing vocalists the Angelettes. Eddie Jobson played a major role. "Did you know I was the entire orchestra on Bryan's first album?" says Jobson today. "Or that Paul [Thompson] and I created the complete reggae arrangement of 'These Foolish Things' and the rock arrangement of 'Hard Rain's?'" Jobson continues:

I think I was transitioning from Curved Air at the time; it was Bryan's way of bringing me into the fold. I guess that Bryan couldn't afford an orchestra at the time, because I ended being the orchestra. My credit casually says "strings", but I don't think people realise that I not only wrote all the string parts, but I individually overdubbed the violins, violas and cellos until my fingers were blistered. I also added the double bass parts by playing them on viola at double speed and then slowing down the tape.

If I remember correctly, "These Foolish Things" started with Paul and me laying down a piano and drum track in a reggae/lounge style. Everything else, like the bass, was laid on top of that, including the multi-tracked synthesizer "flute-tones" which provided the harmonic texture. Actually, playing something that musical on a VCS3 synthesizer was trickier than it sounds; it was a machine that was very easy to make electronic beeps and bleeps on but was much more difficult to make tonal music with. It was a huge pain to tune. "A Hard Rain's ..." started with Bryan on the electric piano and Paul on drums. I came up with the choppy strings, which I then overdubbed to death.

"When I started doing cover versions, I remember saying at one time that they're a bit like 'ready-mades', which is obviously what Duchamp did," explains Ferry:

He would take an object, which he thought was beautiful or interesting, and say, well, this is art, and basically just put a signature on it. And I sometimes think that's a kind of cute description of how I take a song from another period and do my interpretation of it. Sometimes they're more successful than others, of course.

It's certainly the case in Ferry's own solo recordings that the overall quality is very uneven, and nowhere is this more apparent than on *These Foolish Things*. At one extreme, "A Hard Rain's A-Gonna Fall" was tremendously hard-hitting and justifiably a hit single, reaching Number 10 in the UK in October 1973. Ferry had transformed a caustic, acoustic protest song from *The Freewheelin' Bob Dylan* into a great *pop* record. The orchestration, the ballsy vocal accompaniment, those jagged, repeating violin phrases like lashing rain, and the absurdly mannered, yet highly effective (affected) vocal delivery reveal a depth of emotion absent from Dylan's original. Ferry had joined the growing ranks of singers who had improved on the Dylan blueprint, extracting a great tune from relatively unpromising ore. The sound effects – thunder, waves crashing, whispering, laughing, aahs, howling dogs, etc – added to many of the lines give the record a clownish, camp feel, as did the famous promo film for the single. A coolly T-shirted Ferry sang the song glaring at the camera as he bashed out its chords on a piano, accompanied by three female backing singers dressed, in best camp tarty fashion, in plastic macs, shades and forties' head-scarves. One of their number was, apparently, an unidentified man in drag: Roxy webmaster John O'Brien believes it to be band photographer Eric Boman.

So began Ferry's on-going love affair with Dylan's music. "Along with the Beatles, he raised the standard of lyric writing probably quite a lot," Ferry said in 1974. "I think he's a great emotional writer, you know. He's one of the best image-conjurers as well. Some of his love songs as well, which are very simple and don't have these sort of surrealist images, are also very good. I think he's a terrific writer, and a great singer. Although he doesn't have a great vocal range, he sings with a lot of conviction, which is the main thing."

But Ferry was little interested in Dylan as a political commentator: in fact, judging by the tenor of comments made later to the press, Dylan's progressive agenda was anathema to Ferry's increasingly patrician stance. At the time he said of "Hard Rain": "I think it's a beautiful song, although I can't be bothered with all that Cuba crisis stuff. I like the images."

If we're honest, the rest of the album is at best mildly diverting, a period piece produced at a time when irony and camp were kings: nowhere else on the album does Ferry actually improve on the original recordings. He starts "River Of Salt" in what sounds like almost completely the wrong key. The original, a 1962 Ketty Lester B-side to the single "You Can't Lie To A Liar", had been the second follow-up single to her big hit, "Love Letters", and had limped to Number 90 on the *Billboard* chart. Ferry took the chance to re-popularise a minor song, but his effort remains slight. "Don't Ever Change" was presumably remembered from his teenage years. The original was a Number 5 UK hit in 1962: Ferry's is a faithful cover, save for the fact that he doesn't have the vocal range to hit the high notes of the Crickets' original.

Sadly, the same charge can be laid before many of the tracks on the album. Ferry's voice was perfect for his own songs, where he could shape the contours of the music to suit his ululating and highly distinctive delivery, but when pitted against some of the technically finest singers in pop history, his interpretations were destined to come off second-best if he tried to match them note-for-note. The chorus of "Piece Of My Heart" is transposed down to accommodate Ferry's vocal, and he cannot compete vocally with either the original, by Erma Franklin from 1962, or the more famous cover by Big Brother And The Holding Company. Presley and Buddy Holly oozed confidence in their versions of "Baby I Don't Care", but Ferry's version sounds flat by comparison. On the Beatles' "You Won't See Me", Ferry ends the line "When I call you up" on a note alien to most peoples' interpretation of what constitutes perfect pitch.

It is curious, then, that a man with a voice which, in conventional terms, is so technically flawed should try to compete with so many of the great singers of the past. Some might regard Ferry's attempts at reinterpretation as bespeaking an ego happy to take liberties with both the material and his own voice: others simply enjoyed Ferry's very singular approach to redefining classic songs. Ferry knew the potential pitfalls of the exercise even before recording began. As he said to Richard Williams: "The trouble with doing something like 'The Tracks Of My Tears' is that the original was so brilliant and it's hard to touch it." And he's correct; his own version is a pallid imitation. But the nadir of the album is his misjudged cover of a record that could never be improved upon: "Sympathy For The Devil". The original was full of demonic power and orgiastic grooves which would influence many indie records in the eighties and early nineties. Ferry's version just can't compete, and sounds flimsy and half-baked.

A little more successful was Ferry's take on Leslie Gore's 1963 teen-weepy, "It's My Party", which does, at least, exude a sense of fun. In fact, throughout the album we can hear the sound of Bryan Ferry lightening up and, indeed, camping it up a bit (notice that Ferry doesn't change the gender of the song from the Gore original):

Roxy Music did have a gay following, I guess, because of all the camp clothes and the dressing-up. It was the camp sensibility that I had, and Andy had, and Brian had when he was there. We were sort of *artists*, so we had sort of artists' friends who were kind of gay, and we knew the sensibility inside out. That's the only reason I did "It's My Party" on the first solo album – it was for my gay friends. It wasn't intellectualising or anything, it was just fun. Part of the reason for doing that song, and some of the songs on my first solo album, was that they were really fun songs with a hint of Broadway in them. Whereas my work up until that point was really very dark – well, most of it anyway. And I thought, well, this is a nice sort of holiday from my dark, gloomy songs, doing something a bit lighter and frivolous. But it turned off a few people as well; a few of the critics didn't get it.

Thankfully, the album finishes, as it began, on a creative high. Ferry's reading of "These Foolish Things" is inspired. He was, as ever, on dangerous ground. The song had been covered several times; the most famous versions, by Billie Holiday and Benny Goodman respectively, had lodged it in the public's consciousnesses. With the advent of World War II, the images of loneliness and separation further enhanced its stature. Ripped up and remade as a reggae-tinged torch song, it becomes a vehicle for Ferry's absurd yet effective vocal mannerisms. He reinvents the song and stamps his own personality on it; his stop-start delivery utilises the space in the on-beat reggae beat. Music critic Robert Cushman writes about how Ferry's stylised vocal phrasings surprise us: 'There is a point in each of the song's lines where the tune turns a corner; Ferry pounces on and isolates each of these moments, almost regardless of what the lyric might be doing at the time. We get 'the winds of March that make my – heart a dancer' and even 'first daffodils and long ex-cited cables' … All the elements of the song are laid out – the elegance, the nonchalance, the driven misery – but dislocated and jumbled, so that Ferry seems simultaneously to be commenting on traditional pop style and re-enacting it. In this he was a harbinger. [Jazz critic] Francis Davis calls him "the British post-modern crooner …"

These Foolish Things was predominantly Ferry's take on American pop classics. "There are very few English groups I like," he was to tell BBC Radio One's Brian Matthews. In July 1973, a month after Ferry had recorded *These Foolish Things*, David Bowie set to work on a cover versions album of his own, entitled *Pin-Ups*. Bowie, however, chose to pay homage to his sixties English roots. Ferry was concerned about Bowie's project. In the summer of 1973, it seemed that both Bowie and Ferry were heading along worryingly similar musical paths. Ferry was perhaps right to be worried; such is the jealous and competitive nature of the music business where innovations, plans and tactics have to be kept tightly under wraps. (In early 1974, Bowie would clock the cover art to the next Rolling Stones' album, *It's Only Rock 'n' Roll*, and note the name of the creator of the impressive artwork, Belgian Guy Peellaert. Bingo! Bowie not only managed to tease an even better cover out of Peellaert for his own new album, *Diamond Dogs*, but also succeeded in getting it into the shops before the Stones' effort).

There were phone calls between the two camps, and a certain anxiety on Ferry's part. Bowie's initial call was simply to ask Ferry's permission to sing one of Roxy's songs on his next album. The song, rumoured to be "Ladytron", never appeared, but, during the course of the conversation, Bowie informed Ferry of his own covers project. Did Ferry feel that Bowie had aped what he had originally set out to do? "Well, I think I did", he says:

> I've got a feeling he rang me, unless I'm imagining it, but I'm sure he telephoned me to say he was doing it, that he'd heard I was doing this thing and that he was going to do something similar. I wasn't sure, but he just did songs from the sixties, so it ended up being a completely different type of record. But at first, I was a bit apprehensive before I heard it, wondering what it was going to be. I was always kind of anxious to try and, I suppose, be different from other people, to forge my own furrow.
>
> He's a great opportunist is David. He's very bright, very clever, I think, at getting the best out of himself. I don't really know him well, but there doesn't seem to be any great self-doubt there, which I think is to be commended. Whereas I'm always riddled with doubts and self-criticism and God-knows-what.

Ferry wasn't alone in noting the magpie tendencies of David Bowie. "There were a lot of pictures of him looking very similar to Andy Mackay, I must say; same suits," claims Ferry. "Andy used to raise his eyebrows at some of them."

Mick Rock points out the fundamental differences between the two main British rock songwriters of the day:

> Ferry was kind of shy. We all thought he was bit straight, I mean chemically straight. He wasn't a hustler, you see. David always had that marvellous street instinct. If he saw something he liked, he went

145

for it; that was his nature. David being this marvellous magpie and very instant about his influences, if he sees something, he absorbs it; it becomes his. And I would hear tales of Ferry saying, "I'm not here, I'm not here", when David would phone wanting to check out what he was up to. Partly because I think Bryan might have been overly paranoid in a way, but also because he might have had good reason. When David did *Pin-Ups* that was after Bryan did *These Foolish Things*. Remember, Roxy had only just got rolling. So the idea of this retro thing, despite David being a completely different animal, probably was inspired by Ferry. Of course, David got his own tilt at things.

In the end, both *These Foolish Things* and *Pin-Ups* would chart in the UK on the same day: November 3, 1973. Ferry's record would reach a highly creditable Number 5 and stay in the charts for 42 weeks, making it as big a seller as Roxy Music's concurrent product. Bowie's album would be Number 1 for five weeks, which was unsurprising given his huge media profile in 1973. In truth, neither record could be thought of as consistently listenable throughout, yet both marked a profound shift within pop culture. For the first time in the rock era, cool pop icons were making albums that reclaimed pop's past: a trend that would accelerate thereafter. This development also showed the two most important artists of their time to be open about their influences. Both Ferry and Bowie were huge music fans and voracious devourers of pop styles. The big difference between the two was that Ferry never cared overly for the present, whilst Bowie remains to this day a committed and enthusiastic listener of new music. As a result, Ferry would emerge as being quite content to plunder nostalgia for creative ends, whilst Bowie would continue to attempt to capture the "now". Ferry the archivist, Bowie the innovator.

A comparison of the album covers for *These Foolish Things* and *Pin-Ups* provides evidence of the two different approaches. Bowie chose a stunning photo of himself and Twiggy that had been rejected by *Vogue* magazine. Featuring his brown-crimson spiky cut and frozen, mask-like expression, the cover captures everything that was cutting-edge, dangerous and contemporary within popular culture. Ferry's cover, however, is a portrait in nostalgia. Wearing a black t-shirt (what Ferry would call a "motorbike look"), his head slightly turned away from the camera, Ferry fixes the viewer with a coy sideways glance: a study in filmic, faded fifties Hollywood glamour.

"I always felt like an inspired amateur, you know, rather than someone who had been playing music all his life, which I hadn't been doing," said Ferry in 1977, "and I feel very much a fan of music." Both *These Foolish Things* and *Pin-Ups* were basically the equivalent of compilation tapes put together by stars as fans. They were the equivalent of the *Under The Influence* compilations of today; pop stars picking moments from their heritage and laying bare their influences. Back in 1973, such tribute compilations were a novelty, but they were one of the first signs of popular culture folding in on itself.

These Foolish Things was also the sound of a man nearing thirty looking back, perhaps with a certain regret, to more innocent times. Though he was still young, Ferry's natural emotional bent was to look back rather than forward. Of "River Of Salt", he said, "I'm probably the only person in England with a copy of that. It reminds me of when I used to be in the Gas Board in Newcastle; in fact, the whole LP does. Did you know I once sang 'Strangers In the Night' in a talent contest in a working men's club? Didn't win any prizes, though."

These Foolish Things would have a profound effect on the future of Roxy Music and its singer. Ferry now had a successful solo career, and this meant that there would always be a refuge for him should Roxy become unworkable. It was a busman's holiday from the band that would, eventually, prove to be the more alluring option. Perhaps more importantly, working with a repertoire of covers affected Ferry's own songwriting style, not always with positive results, as he himself acknowledges with refreshing honesty:

> After I started with my solo career, doing classic songs written by other people, I think that had a bit of influence on my work. I became more interested in songwriting as opposed to making records. After a while, I seemed to get into a world of trying to write more conventional songs, which is why when I look back at the work of Roxy, the earlier period I'm slightly fonder of myself. Even though albums like *Avalon* had a certain atmospheric mood that was rather interesting, they weren't as groundbreaking.

By the late summer of 1973, recording sessions for the third album were already well under way, Roxy Music having in the meantime mutated into a very different band. The wilder musical acrobatics of the first two albums would now be tempered by a driving new musicality. The period between this third album, *Stranded*, and their sixth release, *Viva!*, provided arguably the most balanced material in the Roxy Music canon. Ferry's songs became more structured, and the weird sonic trickery, which formed such an integral part of the early Roxy, would now be a garnish rather than an essential ingredient. Speaking just before *Stranded* was released, Phil Manzanera told *Sounds*: "I suppose people will think we've changed because Eno left ... but we were preparing for quite a dramatic change anyway."

For the band to win a mainstream following outside of Europe, however, a certain musical conventionality and confidence were missing, as was a more clearly defined musical structure. Was Ferry aware of this? Eddie Jobson is in no doubt:

> Clearly, from the fact that Bryan has continued to surround himself with top-level session musicians, at least he obviously recognised that, even back then. However, there's also the argument that the idiosyncratic charm of what Michael Stipe described affectionately as "the train-wreck that was Roxy Music" came from a daring experimentalism born of a lack of ability. After the departure of Eno, and the introduction of myself and John Porter [and, later on, John Wetton] a certain amount of that "bleeding edge" was lost in favour of a more "professional" balance. I think this actually helped the band a lot commercially, especially in the United States. This, unfortunately though, probably explains why Bryan continued to get less and less experimental and edgy. Although I personally loved the first two albums, I can see why many people consider the '73-'76 period the band's best period, because of that balance.

While Eno is widely accepted as a visionary, and the two Roxy albums he worked on have equal claim to be the two most important Roxy albums, Jobson's input into Roxy Music has been consistently downplayed. His contribution was essential, not conceptually or in terms of performance, but certainly in terms of musicality. He was with the band for longer than Eno and helped make many of the classic cuts from the middle-period Roxy Music possible. Fan and webmaster John O'Brien assesses the role of Jobson as follows:

> The addition of Jobson gave them some level of virtuosity that they needed to blend with Phil and Andy's particular style. Paul Thompson is the one solid rock throughout the whole of the seven-

ties period. I have lots of live recordings from the seventies, and Bryan Ferry, Phil Manzanera and Andy Mackay all hit duff notes and had a sense of vulnerability about their performances (which I liked), but Paul Thompson was always there holding it all together, never putting a foot wrong.

For *Stranded*, Johnny Gustafson was brought in as bassist. If you were looking for professionalism, then this 29-year-old Liverpool-born rock guitarist was about as authentic as you could get, having played with the Big Three and the Merseybeats. "I was in my flat in Wilson Green in London when the phone rang and it was John Punter, the engineer in the studios where they were recording," recalls Gustafson:

They didn't have a bass player on that day so he said, get down here, we need a bass player. I went down there and immediately began work that day. I was doing a lot of sessions in those days, two or three a day. I'd seen them on the television dressed up in all this glittery stuff with weird Elvis haircuts and spiky things. I wasn't impressed with their playing, to be quite honest: it sounded like a bloody awful mess to me.

The drummer, Paul, was just a rock basher, in the sense of John Bonham, which is fine by me. He could play, and he had his licks down tight. The other guys, I wasn't impressed with at all. Ferry was just banging away on a piano, just thumping chords. I wasn't very impressed with Phil Manzanera's playing. He depended on a whole lot of Revox backup and two or three echo things all joined together for various effects. But I wasn't bothered any way. I was there to play for them, and it was a paying job, and that was it. Andy wanted to be a rock 'n' roll sax player, really: "Yakkety Sax", that kind of thing. He was probably on the greener side of things. Everyone was still learning all the time, that's the impression I got. Eddie Jobson was a good keyboard player; he was very musical. He could read music and play the violin. Ferry's style of singing was stylised. I've never been a particular fan of the French, Edith-Piaf style of singing where the vibrato is very fast. If I were being rude, I'd call it sheep singing, or goat singing, but it's immaterial to me: he was very popular, so why knock it?

Andy was quite an intellectual; he was quite a deep sort of chap, although he had a bubbly, bouncy front. As for Phil Manzanera, I never got near to him at all. I just didn't understand the man, I guess. That didn't mean there was anything wrong with him or he was unfriendly – certainly not, he was a very friendly guy – but I couldn't get under his skin at all, partly perhaps because we were never together very much at all anyway, only on tour. We didn't socialise other than at the gigs. Ferry was a real gentleman, a really friendly guy. A bit quiet; some would say shy, but I didn't think so. He was just a nice man.

Also in mid-1973, a further important shift took place within the band. Realising, perhaps, that Eno's departure had partly been occasioned by creative frustration, Ferry for the first time deigned to include musical ideas from other members. Quality control and the final decision would be his, but from now on, Phil and Andy (and, on the odd occasion, Eddie and Paul) were offered the chance to compose. As a result the ship steadied, and Roxy Music became more traditionally musical. Andy Mackay would help write the classic "A Song For Europe" whilst Manzanera wrote the funky music for the slinky "Amazona", with Ferry providing the lyric and the title. With its rolling piano figures, romantic sweep and beautiful melodies, *Stranded* may lack the youthful drive and ambition of the first two albums, appearing detached from the glam rock scene and setting out a different agenda as Roxy Music moved towards a more mature sound. But Eno, graciously, said it was their best album.

Gustafson unfortunately never quite felt part of the team. He realised that he wasn't a full-time member of the band, nor did he seek a more permanent residency. He became just one of the dozen or more musicians to fill the gap over the decades. Yet his bass parts on the three albums he played on provide some of the most memorable moments in the Roxy canon. Gustafson was unhappy, in any case, with the financial deal offered to secure his participation for his first album with the band. "I was having problems," reveals Gustafson: "my agent was asking, so they said, too much money. The band were never involved in this at all – it was their management. We agreed that I would just do it on straight session fees. I thought they were being tightfisted: the office that is. Session musicians are abused, and have been for generations."

Gustafson got on well with the engineer John Punter, working on overdubs and minor embellishments, and also enjoyed working with producer, Chris Thomas. "Chris Thomas is a great, funny guy, down to earth, up for a laugh, just one of the boys. I went to the studio and I had this array of songs which I learnt on the spot by rotor, and we just recorded them one at a time. 'Mother of Pearl' was quite fun to play – kind of semi funky."

Several of the songs on *Stranded* have since gone down as Roxy Music classics, and justifiably so. "Street Life" would break Roxy tradition in being the first single to be drawn direct from an album – but *what* a single! Their *Top Of The Pops* performance of the song "reduced the teenies to matchwood", as writer and fan Jon Savage put it. The cool finger-clicks, the presence – this was Roxy at their finest. And it was, in truth, the final rush of Britain's glam era. "Street Life" was the only song on *Stranded* to carry any of glam rock's perverse fun, and 1974 would get safer: Mud at Number 1, the Wombles the biggest-selling singles act of the year, and Kenny showing us "The Bump". Eventually the showbiz side of pop would take over completely, but, in December 1973, it was still pure, unsullied, glam rock at its most *mentale*. There was "Sorrow" by Bowie and "Roll Away The Stone" by Mott The Hoople: there were Slade and Wizzard with two of the best Christmas records ever. We entered 1974 safe in the knowledge that John Pertwee was still Dr Who and that comet Kahoutek was a mere milky millimeter smudge on even the sharpest of telescopes. British pop has never been quite so silly since – and, it has to be said, Roxy Music were never again quite as important as they were in 1973.

Eddie Jobson played a crucial role in the recording of *Stranded*:

The intro (and outro) to "Street Life" was my way of keeping the Eno-style electronic beeps and bleeps alive. It was the first sound on the first track of my first Roxy album. The other strange noises were made by playing minor-second dissonances with Mellotron brass samples (the same sound as for the brass "hits" throughout the song). In keeping with the "train-wreck" approach, the distorted solo in the middle is me playing my electric violin through the ring modulator of the VCS3. This was definitely not a sound anybody had heard before.

"Street Life" was Roxy at their most musically heavyweight which, admittedly, is not very heavyweight at all compared to *bona fide* hard rock, but it was still a punky sort of effort. Ferry sings, sounding panicked, in staccato phrases:

"Wish everybody would leave me alone
They're always calling on my telephone
When I pick it up there's no one there
So I walk outside just to take the air."

What was he on about? Well, now, at long last perhaps an explanation can be offered. In 2004, on New Zealand's *The Holmes Show*, long-time Ferry fanatic Denise L'Estrange Cobert was given the chance to interview her idol. L'Estrange, now a top fashion designer, revealed to a bemused but courteous Ferry that back in 1973, as a teenager from Tooting, she and her school friend Jackie would get the bus every week to 10 Redcliffe Square, Chelsea, where Ferry lived. Across from the flat on an area of grass was a red telephone box, from which Denise and her friend would call their idol. They would watch intently as Ferry moved past the window to answer the phone, and then they would hang up. Were the opening lines of "Street Life" inspired by this fanatical behaviour? "More than likely," smiled a mildly nervous Ferry in 2004. "Don't you want to sing a bit of 'Street Life' for me?" asked L'Estrange at the end of the short interview. "No, I certainly don't," came the reply.

Back in the seventies, rock stars' private lives were just that little bit more visible than they are now. Boy George, for example, recalls, not without a little pride, waiting outside Bowie's home, Haddon Hall in Beckenham, and being told by Angie to fuck off. Ferry lived the life of a private, although not too private, bachelor, as *Disc* journalist Ray Fox-Cummings found out:

> Bryan Ferry has obviously not yet found it necessary to adopt strict security measures to avoid his Earls Court flat being invaded by hoards of admirers. His doorbell is clearly marked FERRY in black felt-tip capitals. There is an intercom device that could, of course, be out of order, but at any rate he does not use it, and answers the door himself. Inside, the flat is unpretentious, similar to that of any other reasonably well-heeled SW 10 dweller – high ceilinged and sparsely furnished, with only a sturdy white grand piano in the living room to give any hint that the occupier might be a musician.

"Street Life" did well, becoming the third consecutive Roxy single to reach the UK Top 10. Entering the Top 40 at Number 21, for the chart week ending November 24, 1973, its progress was steady, from Number

16 to 11, peaking at 9 then holding firm over the Christmas period before dropping out of the charts in the week ending February 2, 1974. These, of course, were the days when singles stayed in the charts for weeks on end, rising steadily, falling gracefully and selling heavily.

The second classic Roxy song from *Stranded* was "A Song For Europe', arguably the most successful slow-tempo number the band ever recorded. Luxuriant piano figures, Ferry's most tortured of vocal deliveries and, overall, a sweeping orchestral sound make it one of the most beautiful melodies in pop. Eddie Jobson:

> I played the piano alone. Everything else was overdubbed to the piano, including the drums, timpani and the electric piano, which I also played. Andy came up with the basic chords. Phil added some nice George Harrison guitar. The piano approach was European classical mixed with a little Charles Aznavour lounge. Remember, this is only two years after I was a strictly classical player: I hadn't quite figured out how to play rock yet.

The lyric is one of Ferry's best. The title is a pun on the Eurovision Song Contest: Mackay's music, which struck Ferry as being quintessentially European, had inspired him to write this most romantic of lyrics. In keeping with the continental theme, the song concludes first in Latin then in French, the denouement (*"Jamais, jamais, jamais, jamais, jamais, jamais"*) quite simply one of the most wonderful moments in seventies pop. Earlier in the song, we find Ferry sitting by the Seine ("Though the world is my oyster/It's only a shell full of memories"), then lovelorn and in punning mode in Venice:

> 'These cities may change
> But there always remains
> My obsession
> Through silken waters
> My gondola glides
> And the bridge, it sighs."
>
> (Words and music: Bryan Ferry and
> Andy Mackay, 1973)

"Mother Of Pearl", another classic, starts with an adrenaline rush of partying:

'Turn the lights down, way low
Turn up the music, hi as fi can go
All the gang's here, everyone you know."

Then part two of the song details the restless, wearied comedown as the frantic music stalls, a mournful piano figure introducing the exhausted partygoer's sense of emptiness:

"Well I've been up all night again, party-time wasting is too much
    fun
Then I step back thinking of life's inner meaning and my latest fling
It's the same old story all love and glory it's a pantomime
If you're looking for love in a looking glass world it's pretty hard to
    find."

(Words and music: Bryan Ferry, 1973)

It would be difficult to find another pop song as perfectly written, cleverly expressed and elegant as "Mother Of Pearl". The themes of emotional retardation are similar to those in "In Every Dream Home A Heartache", yet here there's something more sleazy, more decadent to the overall picture. Throughout the entire album, the quality of songwriting is almost equally high: "Just Like You" is a simple, winsome pop tune, "Psalm" a slow-moving tableau of melancholy, "Serenade" a gorgeous melody and "Sunset" another stately, piano-led piece of near-melodic perfection with delicate cello phrasings.

Ferry took songwriting very seriously. He would usually originate the idea for a song, work out the melody line, than take it to be developed by the rest of the band. The lyrics would be fretted over and worked and reworked until they were right: "I feel the lyrics should always stand up to reading; I take a tremendous amount of care with them. It's very rare that I leave a verse unaltered from inception." Ferry didn't have a stockpile of lyrics awaiting a musical accompaniment. Rather, he tended to work on the words once the melody was in place. "When I'm writing songs, the idea comes first and then the melody," he said. "I'm not one of those writers who has a whole lot of poems waiting to have music set to them. When I go into the studio to record, I usually have the whole song pretty well worked-out, though sometimes I've sat up the whole night before typing out final lyric sheets."

If Ferry's lyric writing was painstaking, his actual method of composing was peculiar. Musician Ian Burden, who found fame as part of the Human League, worked with producer Chris Thomas and offers this fascinating insight into how Ferry's songs were constructed:

Roxy blew me away when I first heard them, but I couldn't quite figure out why. They just sounded so different. But then later on, around 1983, I had the privilege of working with Chris Thomas. He said he wasn't sure at first [about working with them]. And neither were Island Records, who'd sent him some demos. The fact that he subsequently agreed to produce Roxy was down to the compelling quality, which was difficult – if not impossible – to grasp. But a vague amount of musical insight can be had.

We sat at the piano one day and Chris showed me the bizarre secret of Mr Ferry's writing. Basic chords, as you may know, are formed using three-note inversions – of which the first is usually a straight-forward root note, played with the thumb, together with added third and fifth. Our Bryan played with two fingers, leaving out the middle finger. Since the middle finger should've been sounding the third, then, obviously, the third was missing. Since it's the third which determines whether the key is major or minor, the other band members were open to interpret either way, the result being that most early Roxy songs are essentially major but with minor intrusions.

"Bryan's missing thirds? Yes, Bryan *did* miss out the third note of the chords he played," affirms Guy Fletcher, a talented multi-instrumentalist who played with Roxy Music in the *Avalon* period and with Ferry in the nineties. "In this, he was similar to Mark Knopfler, who often demands of the band that there should be 'no thirds' in his songs. Because of this, Bryan often found himself writing in the black keys (F sharp, A flat, B flat, C sharp and E flat) simply because the hand shapes suit these keys well."

At the end of 1973, Roxy were under pressure. Recording for the third album had finished, but Island told the band that mixing had to be completed within a fortnight or else the release would be delayed until February 1974. At the same time there was also the little matter of rehearsals for a major UK tour, so the band entered a frantic period of work to prepare to launch what Phil Manzanera called "Phase Two" of Roxy Music. Although used in the sessions for the album,

Gustafson was passed over for live work in favour of the return of Sal Maida on bass.

And it was in that autumn of 1973 that the phenomenon that was Roxymania broke out. The band played to ecstatic audiences the length and breadth of the UK. Eddie Jobson recalls the mob scenes:

I think it was the second gig I ever played with Roxy, in Birmingham; I was eighteen. When we got back to the hotel from the concert there was a pretty hysterical crowd waiting there. Against advice, I stopped and signed a few autographs until it got a bit too "pushy". Half an hour later, I went out onto the balcony of my room to see if the fans had left so I could go downstairs to the bar, and I was greeted by this almighty scream of "EDDDIIIEEEE!!" from the mainly female crowd below, which had grown considerably. Quite shocked at this, I didn't quite know what to do, so I called my mother and went back out on to the balcony so she could hear the girls scream on the other end of the phone. I felt like Paul McCartney. This was only a little more than two years after I had been the corny violin kid at school, the leader of the school orchestra, so I enjoyed it immensely! I then called the other guys in the band, who had heard the screaming, and who started to appear on their respective balconies. The hotel called the police.

The next morning, I remember a disgruntled head housekeeper presenting us with a bill at breakfast for all the towels, washcloths, and other hotel items that we had thrown down to the fans. Ten years later, I met John Taylor and Nick Rhodes of Duran Duran, who told me that they were two of the fans for whom I had signed autographs that night, and that they remembered that I was the only one who had stopped to greet the fans.

But it always seemed to be the case that Roxy's warmest reception would be found in the industrial north. Recession-hit cities full of disaffected teenagers seemed to find the ultimate release in Roxy. "We also had some pretty wild scenes in Glasgow," confirms Jobson:

We used to leave the concert right from the stage, still in costume, while the house lights were still down; otherwise we would get trapped in the hall. Fenwick had some deal with the police chief – if he delivered a case of whiskey to the station, they would provide a police escort from the show to the hotel, and, impressively, have officers at the traffic lights stopping traffic. One time, we had left the audience chanting for a third encore and had been hustled through the crowd outside (the ones who couldn't get into the show) onto our bus, which belonged to the English soccer team. We went screaming down the hill with the police escort, but when we arrived at the hotel, there were already too many people outside. So the police took us down one-way streets the wrong way, to get us to the back of the hotel. By the time we got around to the kitchen/loading area of the hotel, the crowd from the front (and the people following the bus on scooters) had surrounded the freight-elevator entrance. One at a time, we were almost carried from the bus to the freight elevator by two bodyguards. Unfortunately, the crowd got the routine and by the time the last man came off, Phil, they heard the "1 ... 2 ... 3 ..." and leapt forward, pulling Phil off the bus. Phil was carried into the lift with a broken leg. He spent the rest of the tour on crutches, sitting on a stool on stage.

Leo Sayer, soon to have a huge hit with "I Won't Let The Show Go On", was the support act as the band played a set that drew heavily from the new album. "Street Life" was the opener, "Re-Make/Re-Model" the encore. Tony Tyler of the *NME* recorded for posterity the change in the new, mature, debonair Roxy at the Manchester Free Trade Hall:

I've never really seen the band go down as well as they did with any audience, and it can only be a measure of the new stature they've attained since Bryan Ferry re-grouped his shell-shocked battalions around him after the Eno departure. The trash element – an important part of Roxy's earlier breakthrough – is now Out of Favour with Mr. F. [Band attire] ranged from Ferry's own lower deck Lothario look (a cruise ship white tux ensemble) to Jobson's March Hare tail-coat. Both Phil Manzanera and the current stand-in bassist sported soft leathers, garnished with slightly effeminate studs, while The Great Paul Thompson (as Ferry introduced him) favoured his suede 'n' cloth look as of yore. Andy Mackay appeared in a distinguished suit of broadcloth with a string tie that gave him an undeniable air of fried chicken emporiums."

Tony Tyler noted that Roxy Phase Two were musically quite different, too: "Jobson was, for me, the surprise of the night. His approach to elec-

157

tronics is more technical and less individualistic than Eno's. Jobson's piano work, too, enabled El Ferry to cavort more than before."

The lack of glam and the injection of suavity confused some of the audience on the tour, as fan Carol Johnstone recalls: "[Ferry] appeared on stage in a tuxedo: there were other men dressed exactly the same at the side of the stage. When the show started, I thought, is that *him*? He looked like one of the bouncers." *NME* critic Bob Edmands was similarly unimpressed by the Leeds show on the tour:

> Lacklustre would be unkind – although maybe an accurate description. Some of the kids in the audience had a more stylish dress sense. Bryan Ferry is still the trendiest advert for Brylcreem in the business, and he looks more like a villain from a Hong Kong kung fu movie than ever. But where had all the finery gone? Ferry used to sport epaulettes, at the very least, as was only befitting a man of his status. Now he's chosen a white dinner jacket ensemble complete with black bow tie, making him somewhat less chic in appearance than the crumpled Mr Robin Day [a famously cantankerous TV politics show host of the time].

Roxy were regarded as shape-changers, stylists and ambitious re-inventors, but there was now just a hint of a backlash, set against the far-off sounds of disgruntlement. That other great stylist of his day, David Bowie, had ended the year as Britain's best-selling and most important artist and Roxy Music, in terms of culture shock if not actual sales, were not far behind. Back in late 1973, Roxy fans were quite often also Bowie fans, and vice versa. Although Ferry claims that the Roxy Music project wasn't pop, that it was separate from glam rock and very much a singular inquiry into fashion, art and pop history, in reality the music of Roxy and the music of Bowie shared many common themes and values, including the obsession with self, the nihilism and decadence, and the sense of irony. These shared cultural cells produced a shared taste community. Writer and Roxy fan Mat Snow puts it like this:

> The very fact that they had overlapping fanbases suggests that they pressed very similar buttons. However, I think the thing about Roxy Music was that they always spoke to the intellectual in the teenager. They didn't have very many *lumpen* fans. Bowie actually had a fair few who just got into the rock 'n' roll aspect of it, but you'd have to go

some distance to find a thick Roxy fan. Because what was so exciting about Roxy Music was the range of references, which was, of course, far beyond rock music, and far beyond even pop culture. It was the classic *gestalt* of high culture and low culture. In some ways, and this is with the voice of retrospect, there isn't that much difference between the intellectual sensation of listening to "Do The Strand" and that of listening to a mid-sixties Dylan track, because you were being hip to history and poetry and modern art. It was treating you as a grown-up, in an extremely flashy way of course, but also in a way that was tremendously elegant and inventive.

Richard Williams commented that, from very early in his career, Ferry surrounded himself with a set of creatively minded people; it was impressive to see Ferry, the director, so astutely moving Roxy through so many startling musical, visual and conceptual stages. As the Roxy machine grew, so did this entourage. By the beginning of 1974, Ferry and Roxy Music had assembled an extended family of publicists, stylists and management who played a crucial role in maintaining the Roxy brand in the public consciousness.

A key figure on the road was Christian Wainwright, the dresser who minded Ferry on tour and kept him spick and span, elegantly attired and ready for action. Wainwright is remembered fondly: "He was a white Trinidadian queen who functioned as group mum," says Eddie Jobson. "He brought a lot of camp and a lot of laughs to the group." "Christian, the gay dresser, was very, very funny," recalls Gustafson. "He was this little curly-haired major-domo and he arranged all the shirts and the suits, ironed things and arranged things, and cracked ridiculous gay jokes." "He is actually French Trinidadian. Exceedingly gay, very camp, very funny," recalls Guy Fletcher. "He would always wash Bryan's smalls in his bathtub by hand, wearing washer-woman headwear. I remember he had a big book that listed every gay bar in the world. This was at a time when AIDS had just been discovered. Christian was seriously worried by this, and announced his retirement from promiscuity." John Wetton adds, "It was such a reassuring thing to walk into the dressing room and to know that Christian was there. He had these wonderful ways of getting rid of women in the dressing room as well, as only a gay man could. And, for some reason, they would take it."

When it came to packaging and design, Antony Price was Ferry's ideas man. Each new look would be conceived in tandem with the *simpatico* Price. "Antony Price, of course, is gay, but like many gay people he's tremendously astute about appearances and about people's motivations and that sort of thing," says Mat Snow. "He spoke about how Bryan was absolutely homosexual in every way but his sexuality. In every other aspect of his thinking and feeling and his attention to detail in matters of clothes and in matters of any kind of presentation, he was a gay man. Basically, his sheer fastidiousness is unusual in a straight man." For his part, Ferry attests that "I've always liked interesting presentation. I've always been interested in how things look, whether it's the décor of a room or how people dress and so on." Of Antony Price, he adds, "this [Roxy] was an area in which he could act out his more bizarre fantasies in clothes; things that he wouldn't sell commercially, he could design for us to wear."

Then there was Simon Puxley, Ferry's confidant and the intellectual ideas man who helped give form to Ferry's pretensions. Indeed, Ferry has admitted that the good doctor even helped out with some of the lyrics for the classic "Mother Of Pearl" "Puxley was a friendly intellectual who manipulated the press to Bryan's benefit rather cleverly," is Jobson's succinct summation of the role of the Roxy PR man. Under the pseudonym of Rex Balfour, in 1976 Puxley penned *The Bryan Ferry Story*, a slight and brazen biography of Ferry for Michael Dempsey Press. For rock stars, who almost to a man (and women) are keen to portray their version of the truth at the cost of anybody else's, what better than to get your press guy to write it for you under an assumed name? "Yes, the good Dr Puxley – the only man I know who paces back and forth in elevators puffing on his cigarette," is how Guy Fletcher remembers him. Peter Sinfield saw Puxley's role as perhaps the most important within the Roxy camp:

He was about 5'10" with a cherubic face and long hair, and he was always smiling and always very gentle. I didn't have that much to do with him because he didn't really come in to my part of it. Simon, in many ways, knew all the right things to say to Bryan. Bryan, like many artists, had to keep proving himself. He was insecure, and Puxley was his prop. He was a better person to have around than Fenwick, who was too ready to please. Simon had the ability to question. It's very, very important for stars like Bryan that they have at least one person around who would say no.

"For some reason, they were secretive to the point of paranoia about anyone knowing anything that wasn't processed by the good doctor," is John Wetton's take on the veil of secrecy that covered the entire mid-seventies Roxy operation. "That gave Simon a great deal of power within the fold. He always used pseudonyms: 'Rex Balfour' was one of them, which wasn't quite up to 'Mr Bagley' (Ferry) or 'Baron Landscape' (me). We only used them for hotel aliases, but Simon was hardly ever quoted under his own name."

Later the PR man for David Bowie, and currently senior commissioning editor at Omnibus Press, one journalist who remembers Simon Puxley and the Roxy Music of the glam rock period is ex-*Melody Maker* man Chris Charlesworth:

It was as if Ferry needed Simon to guide him through the cultural and intellectual jungle he would face as frontman in a group as elitist as Roxy. They set out with an intellectual agenda far higher than most, the opposite end of the spectrum to Status Quo, and Puxley was crucial in making sure Bryan got his cultural references correct. His role as PR was secondary to this; PR was just something useful he could do at the same time.

Puxley was an odd character, big on hedonism. Known as Dr Puxley, the word was that he was an Oxbridge philosophy graduate, a Ph.D. no less. Obviously very well read, he was a bit of a theoretician and someone whom Bryan looked to for ideas, and probably for help with lyrics. He was always very quietly spoken, vague, the typical absent-minded professor sort, not the usual snappy, fast-talking PR type. He'd ring you up with some Roxy story he wanted printed in *Melody Maker* and you'd take it down, and then he'd ring you up half-an-hour later and tell you he'd got the wrong dates, or given you the wrong information, and you had to start again. Then he'd call the next day and it would be completely different. He took over doing Roxy's press after BP Fallon became Marc Bolan's constant companion and full-time press agent. I remember spending time with him in both LA and New York. He was much liked by the gay crowd that hung around Max's, probably because he was quite pretty, with long, shaggy hair, but to the best of my knowledge he was one hundred percent hetero.

When Roxy first arrived in New York, Atlantic Records threw a party for them in an artist's loft downtown, which was unusual in that such parties were normally held in restaurants or bars. This was obviously done to maintain their arty image. Puxley was there and was probably behind it.

At EG on the King's Road, Mark Fenwick was Roxy's first point of contact and would remain Bryan Ferry's manager until the mid-eighties. A dedicated, talented and efficient operator who fought tenaciously on Ferry's behalf, Fenwick – whose family owned the famous department store of the same name – was eager to please. There are some who are less-than-complimentary about him, Eddie Jobson for one: "Fenwick was wily and critical. His only interest was in promoting and protecting Bryan. After my very first gig, he told me to stop playing it up for the girls who were shouting my name, or I would go the way of Eno." Chris Charlesworth adds:

Yes, I remember Fenwick. He was awfully posh, a real public-schoolboy type: accent, hair, clothes, the lot. Very smooth: reminded me of an upmarket estate agent, probably went hunting at the week-ends, or at least weekended on someone's country estate. Very different from BP Fallon, who used to do their PR. Beep would always ring up and say, "Hey, man, I wanna lay a verbal on you." Everybody involved with EG was posh apart from BP Fallon.

For Johnny Gustafson, Fenwick was quite definitely not his sort: "He was this medium-build, very dapper man, very coiffured, and he had ostentatious jewellery. He had a ring with his initials in diamonds. Fenwick used to dog Bryan, be at his heels all the time and hovering, being sycophantic and so on, fawning slightly." However, session man Paul Carrack, who was to play with Roxy in the eighties, remembers Fenwick fondly as "completely mad, but an absolute hoot. He was a great laugh … I always felt that I was taken care of." It's also certainly the case that Ferry's most successful years came with Fenwick as his manager.

In an *NME* interview in the summer of 1973, Nick Kent enquired of Ferry: "Are you currently the lounge lizard of the ensemble?' "I certainly have pretensions in that direction," was the reply. "Mr Fenwick and I are rather fascinated by the lifestyle." For Pete Sinfield, Fenwick was not the sort of person to bring out the best in Bryan Ferry: "They were very good pals. The Fenwicks were quite high up in the social structure; they've got a lot of money. Bryan liked to mix with the *cognoscenti*, as he would put it. I think they just got on really well. Bryan is not the easiest person to manage because he is very much an artist.

He's a painter in some ways. Originally, he was a painter who happened to sing: I think he paints songs rather than sings them."

Ferry's surrogate family was now firmly in place: meanwhile, his real family had not been forgotten. Audrey Fletcher recalls the moment when the first fruits of his financial success were seen in his hometown:

> Bryan was always close to his Aunt Clara, and Bryan's uncle in Raeburn Avenue told the story of how, when Bryan first became famous, he rolled up in front of his Aunt Clara's house in a silver Rolls Royce. The whole street turned out to have a look. When Bryan bought his mum and dad a big house at the foot of Heugh Hill [pronounced Yuff Hill] at Springwell, Emily Daglish [a long-standing friend of the family] asked his dad if he enjoyed living there. "Whey aye," Fred replied. "Aah would hardly hev moved up there if aah didn't like it, noo would aah."

When *Stranded* finally appeared, in November 1973, reviews were mostly positive. *Melody Maker* contrasted Ferry's "lack of interpretative talent" on his solo record with the "highly idiosyncratic and original intelligence" of his own material, declaring that "*Stranded* is Roxy's third album and immeasurably the best so far." Ian MacDonald at the *NME* was again spot on with his verdict: "*Stranded* is a classic, the album Roxy have been aiming at for two years, and the long-awaited firm ground for the group's fans to stand on, even if some of the subtleties of the earlier approach have had to go in order to get there."

Stranded became Roxy's first UK Number 1 album, knocking David Bowie's *Pin-Ups* off its perch. Attention once again focused almost as much on the packaging of the album as on the actual contents. This time it was 24-year-old Marilyn Cole, the first British "Playmate Of The Year" and Ferry's new love interest, who was the cover girl, an Amazon in a red dress, supine in the jungle, dress torn, body beaded in sweat. Cole had moved onwards and upwards from her £12-per-week job in a Co-Op coal yard in Portsmouth to become the wife of *Playboy* executive Victor Lownes. *Playboy* published full-frontal photos of her, and she was perfect for the series of upmarket Bond girl-meets-rock chick covers that Ferry had embarked on. By the standards of today, the cover of *Stranded* is simply mildly sexist, the decadent glamour of the first Roxy Music cover and the sense of fun of the second having been stripped away to be replaced by a more brazen attempt to woo the punters with soft porn. Said Ferry, "The idea comes first and the cover then has to express the idea. You have to find the right chick for it."

In one music magazine at the end of 1973, under the headline "A Ferry Merry Christmas', the singer was photographed, cocktail in hand, wearing a Dannimac jacket and surrounded by three Hugh Heffner-style bunny girls, one of whom was holding a huge bush of mistletoe over the scowling, rakish Ferry. Perhaps this was the real legacy of Roxy Music Phase Two. Phase One had been full of playfulness and irony, whereas with Phase Two, the worry was that Bryan Ferry was beginning to live the luxury lifestyle for real. Was he about to become part of the rock aristocracy?

THE THRILL OF IT ALL:
1974-1975

The moment the public saw the cover of Bryan Ferry's second solo album, 1974's *Another Time, Another Place*, was the moment he became a prisoner to style. Luxuriant, decadent, smoothly sophisticated; in the eyes of the public, the look and the man became indistinguishable. More than any melody, lyric or performance, that image took over, and ultimately almost reduced Bryan Ferry to a caricature. It was franked, indelibly, on all of Bryan's subsequent endeavours: "Bryan Ferry: crooner".

The Eric Boman cover for *Another Time, Another Place* is one of the most striking in the history of rock, and is all the more striking for the very lack of any of the components traditionally associated with rock iconography. Ferry, with gold watch, black bow-tie and white sharkskin tuxedo (a look imported from the *Stranded* tour of 1973), stands impassively by the hotel pool, right hand in jacket pocket, left hand holding that obligatory signifier of filmic cool, the lit cigarette. He looks more like the next James Bond than a pop singer. For the mid-seventies, it was a startlingly fresh idea. It was "an image so powerful and seductive", wrote rock journalist David Sinclair, "that it virtually wiped out a decade of rock industry prejudice against 'straight' fashion at a stroke." However, the look would, in the eyes of the media at least, forever "fix" Ferry as "the sultan of suave", and would condition the lazier reviewer into dismissing each new offering as the product of a jet-set lifestyle of cool sophistication, all surface and no feeling.

The public would be "fooled" too. Ask anyone outside of the Roxy faithful about Bryan Ferry and they'll tell you he's a crooner, an elegantly good-looking man with an easy-listening repertoire. They'll remember "Jealous Guy" and "Let's Stick Together". They won't remember (or won't even have heard) "Ladytron". And it's that image (and Ferry's subsequent willingness to live up to it, particularly in concert) that set him on a course that would have been impossible to predict three years earlier, when Ferry was still the king of the new. If Ferry ever needed to find out why he has never been given the plaudits, media attention and cultural kudos of some of his peers, he should re-examine just what it was that made him so attractive in the first place: it was his avant-garde rock songs, not his forays into other people's catalogues and other people's lifestyles.

Yet the image also served Ferry well, and continues to do so. Writer, academic and poet Geoff Ward explains the significance of the famous poolside shot:

> I always thought the key moment in his career was not a song but an album cover, the white tuxedo on the second solo album. After that, he had an immediately memorable image, and – deliberately or not – a very clever one, in that he could age and keep it and not look ridiculous, unlike Jagger and Richards, or even Bowie. Ferry's look is also interesting in that, while there's a touch of Sinatra in the image, it's also very English, with a hint of European chic. Is he the only rock star to have exploited an upper-class style, however ironically (and it isn't entirely ironic)? You'd have to go back to Noël Coward to find a precedent.

However striking the image, there was always a sense that Ferry felt uncomfortable in his (shark) skin, as Mat Snow points out:

> Funnily enough, I don't think he ever entirely carried it off, and the *NME* at the time used to make hay at his expense. What they nailed was not just that he was ersatz, which he was, but that he really was gauche. It was odd that a former mod should be such a bad dancer. Ferry was actually quite a poor dancer, but that was sort of all right too, because he was getting the girls. He was sort of Jarvis Cocker before Jarvis Cocker!

As far as Ferry was concerned, the cover was to be seen in a fun, ironic way. Not for the first time, his intentions would be read literally, with generally negative results. "Antony [Price], like me, liked uniforms very much," said Ferry in 1994:

And he thought, oh well, this sort of cruise shark, lounge lizard sort of white tuxedo, that is kind of a uniform of sorts you know, and so we wore that, I think because at that point there was very much an edge to the music and it seemed ironic to wear something that was very MOR and Sinatra-ish. I'd always admired Sinatra, by the way. I always thought he was very cool for a grumpy old man. And, yes, we did that in Los Angeles. Eric Boman was the photographer and we had Manolo Blahnik in the background, who to this day has remained sort of the leading shoe designer in the world.

To original Roxy fans, the ones who watched in awe as Eno tweaked, Ferry grinned, and the whole of Roxy exploded into the most brilliant of art-rock calamities, the new look was incomprehensible, even mildly treasonable. Original fan Martyn Ware says this about the beast Ferry would become in the mid-seventies:

We all loved Bryan Ferry's voice, but frankly, he can't dance. He's curiously puppet-like in his movements. He did look amazing in those early concerts, with the slicked-back hair and the dazzling smile and the weirdness, and then it all turned into fucking Humphrey Bogart. I mean, what happened there? The *danger* of it just got ironed out of it very quickly for me. But the cover versions were at least true to his muse. The funny thing was that we didn't regard that as being as old-fashioned as Roxy Music's attempts to be up-to-date and new on subsequent albums.

Tellingly, when the album was released in the summer of 1974, a nation of viewers watching the *Cilla Black Show* on TV saw a pensioner pick Ferry's second solo album from a pile "our Cilla" offered, telling the world that "he looks like a nice boy". Ferry, so it seemed, had extended his fan demographic beyond youth and even beyond middle age.

Even before this infamous cover, and the increasingly safe solo music, some of the goodwill he had built up was beginning to evaporate. Not that Ferry needed to worry unduly, of course. At 28, he was now comfortably off and a household name. He was a major recording artist with a European fan base. He was, without doubt, one of the UK's best songwriters, if not the best. Had his career ended in 1973, he would still have contributed more to pop music than many artists now lauded as rock giants on the strength of far flimsier portfolios of recorded work. Yet, by 1974, Ferry appeared to be set on a course that would ultimately dismay his early fervent fans. Over the years, the sense of disappointment would be palpable as, step-by-step, he abandoned the edgy and eloquent music of the early Roxy period and replaced it with a safer repertoire. With Roxy, the quality seldom dipped (though the sense of outreach shown on those first albums was only occasionally matched) but, as a solo recording artist, Ferry would dip a toe in the lukewarm waters of the mainstream and paddle around aimlessly for much of the mid-seventies. The avant-rock god of 1972 would, by 1974, be appearing as a special guest on a light-entertainment show fronted by Twiggy. Ferry was testing the limits (and our patience) of just how ironic a "serious" musician could get without being dismissed as an opportunist of the worst kind.

By startling contrast, Brian Eno was heading in the opposite direction altogether. That most opinionated and peacock-like of men was actually doing something very daring: he was giving it all up. First to go would be touring, which he had always found exhausting and pointless. As the seventies progressed, Eno limited himself to the occasional public airing. He was also, equally bravely, abandoning rock music altogether. Aside from a modest chart position for *Here Come The Warm Jets*, Eno never managed to sell enough records to establish himself as a chart recording artist, but no matter. He sacrificed chart placings and public adulation for something far more important: cultural kudos. So began a trend that has lasted to this day: Ferry the celebrity, Eno the serious artist. A series of solo albums, little bought at the time but greatly admired by critics and musicians, established Eno in the eyes of the original Roxy fans as the guardian of the original Roxy spirit of adventure. The man dismissed by Ferry in 1973 would flourish as a radical solo artist.

Filled with dread and foreboding one dark cold day in January 1975, Eno walked in front of a taxi and was seriously injured. As the ambulance arrived, a passer-by was alleged to have commented, "He's a goner." It was whilst convalescing at home that Eno, drowsy on medication, was recuperating to the calming timbres of some classical music when one channel of the speakers went dead and the music became imbalanced and barely audible. Eno, however, liked what he heard: the sound of virtually nothing. He then became intrigued by the whole idea of making music for a specific environment that worked on a series of different levels, music that could be as listened-to as the listener wanted; music which could be background or foreground. Multi-purpose music for the seventies was Eno's great contribution to the cultural dialogue of the times. In the mid-seventies, he began building an astonishing repertoire of ambient instrumental pieces and incredibly catchy and wildly eccentric pop songs.

But what about Bryan Ferry the solo artist? What was his contribution to the same cultural conversation? With regard to his private life, Ferry would become that which he had always wanted to avoid – a tabloid favourite, written about in the gossip columns and targeted as rock's most eligible bachelor. To this day, Ferry tells the press that he wishes to keep his private life just that, yet he has consistently acted in ways that belie that assertion. He has dated models, society girls, backing singers: in fact, just the very people who attract the kind of media speculation he claims to disdain. He would record in high-profile studios, frequent the best eateries and increasingly be regarded as a member of the rock star jet set along with the likes of Elton and Rod. For an artist so fundamentally different from those two populist entertainers, this behaviour distorted what Bryan Ferry was about.

But what of the music to be found inside the most glamorous sleeve of 1974? The recording for *Another Time, Another Place* had taken place in the spring of that year, once again at Air Studios. Ferry's first solo album, *These Foolish Things*, and single, "A Hard Rain's A-Gonna Fall", had both sold in excess of 100,000 copies, so it was clear that a sizeable market existed for solo product. Produced by Ferry himself, along with John Punter, the album featured John Porter on lead guitar, Paul Thompson on drums and John Wetton on bass. "We just sat around at his house, and I virtually arranged the album," recalls Wetton. "If you notice, everything starts with a bass intro. I'm usually very mainstream musically. And it seemed like an opportunity for me to come back from King Crimson, which was very much avant-garde, and do something fairly straightforward."

The sound of *Another Time, Another Place*, named after the one Ferry original on the album, is much more confident and more complete than the slightly timid production on his first solo album. Yet the song-selection and performances are equally imperfect. On "The 'In' Crowd" it all gels perfectly, of course: Wetton's bass line is menacing, Davy O'List's powerchords are scorching and the finger clicks totally cool in the 45-second intro. Ferry is in total command: "But the originals are the greatest", he hisses, drawing out the sibilance of the final word in an act of bravura showboating. He takes over the song and, to all intents and purposes, reinvents it so completely that it sounds like an original. Dobie Gray's version, a minor hit back in the mod era of 1965, sounds flimsy by comparison. Cleverly, Ferry plays with the vocal hook ("How to have fun") and ends it a semitone down, rather than with the upward movement of the original phrasing.

Ferry's singing is likewise masterful on "Smoke Gets In Your Eyes" and, once again, the song's personality merges seamlessly with that of his own. The original, written by Jerome Kern and Otto Harbach, first featured in the 1933 Broadway musical *Roberta* and in the film version two years later. However, it was almost certainly the 1959 hit by the Platters that formed the blueprint for Ferry's cool rendering. Such was the success of Ferry's version that, later in the year, Australian Gary Shearston was able to score a UK hit with his version of "I Get A Kick Out Of You", in what can only be described as a pastiche of Ferry's own crooning triumph.

Both Ferry songs were UK hits: "The 'In' Crowd" reached the Top 20 in May 1974, the fag-end of the glam era. Peaking at No. 13, it rubbed along with other classic singles that spring such as Sparks' "This Town Ain't Big Enough For The Both Of Us" and Cockney Rebel's "Judy Teen". In the autumn of 1974, "Smoke Gets In Your Eyes", the second single culled from the album, also reached the Top 20. Ferry told *Melody Maker's* Allan Jones how he admired the songs of the pre-rock era. After applauding the poetry of "Smoke Gets In Your Eyes", the 28-year-old Ferry went on to say: "The people who did the best songs were, for me, pre-Beatles. After '64, and the Beatles and Dylan, it became more or less obligatory for performers to write their own songs, whether they could or not. And most often they can't, in my opinion."

The sharper, more forceful production and the more confident playing could not, however, rescue *Another Time, Another Place* from the mediocrity of the other tracks, comprising the half-baked (inconsequential covers of Kris Kristofferson's "Help Me Make It Through The Night", Sam Cooke's "Wonderful World" and Dylan's 1964 classic "It Ain't Me Babe") and the overdone (a bathetic and frankly quite terrible version of "You Are My Sunshine", first recorded in 1941 by Bing Crosby and covered by Ray Charles in 1962). The title track, a Ferry original, is a heavily stylised, schizophrenic song, part reflective ballad, part rocker, yet not quite successfully realised. Pleasant but ultimately pointless, Ferry's second solo album hasn't aged well, and to this day fails to reveal any hidden depths or unexpected twists. It was middle-brow music for a middlebrow audience.

That didn't, of course, stop people from buying it, or Ferry from liking it. "It's generally a lot heavier all round, I think," he said on release. "It's heavyweight where the first one was lightweight, or bantamweight, or whatever. The mood of the songs is quite heavy ... The first album, for me, was only half-successful because I tend to like more and more the songs I made changes to rather than those I left virtually the same as the original records. With this one I tried to do a totally new arrangement on every number, and put as much of me on it as possible."

Another Time, Another Place reached Number 4 in the UK and remained in the chart for six months. By way of promotion, in addition to the Cilla Black performance that summer, Ferry also appeared on BBC's *Twiggy* show in July, duetting with the show's host on "Wonderful World" while dressed in school uniform in a mock-up of a classroom. "Most people in the rock sphere tend to abhor those kind of programmes," said Ferry in 1975, "but I really like to kind of infiltrate into those areas and win converts. I have a lot of respect for television as a means to reach people. I'd much rather do a television programme than a tour."

Meanwhile, back in the early spring of 1974, Roxy Music had made a second attempt to win over the American market. A tour having been booked, two warm-up gigs were scheduled that April, in the arguably less-than-mythic locale of Southport on Merseyside. Just down the road, Red Rum was on his way to winning his second Grand National and Liverpool FC were heading for the FA Cup final (where they would beat Ferry's beloved Newcastle United 3-0), but it was Southport that had been chosen, presumably for its lack of cultural cachet, so that Roxy could get back into playing live without much media hoo-hah. However, such was their massive musical profile that the "secret" gigs were sold out allegedly even before PR man Simon Puxley knew they had been finalised. Eager for a scoop, the *NME*'s Nick Kent managed to track the band down for an interview. He discovered that Ferry's solo album was already in the can, Andy Mackay's own solo offering, *In Search Of Eddie Riff*, was also ready for release (promoted by a single, "The Ride Of The Valkyries"), and that a short US tour would be preceded by a media tour to be undertaken by Ferry and Puxley.

On the first night of the Southport warm-up, the town's Floral Hall witnessed scenes of near-carnage: "Well, there was supposed to be a particularly fearsome battle in the audience last night, and I was told someone's throat was almost cut," said Mackay. "The promoter had blood all over his face when he came backstage. I think it was someone else's, though." The second night passed off calmly, with the only real incident of note being Ferry changing out of his white tux into a grey Lonsdale sweatshirt.

Later in April, Ferry and Puxley departed for the pre-tour US publicity campaign. The twin charm offensive was utterly exhausting. Puxley claimed to average two hours sleep per night, Ferry little more, as the Roxy propaganda machine toured New York, Cleveland, Detroit, Chicago, Philadelphia and Boston in April. The band's tour followed on in May. Back in 1972, Roxy had played large auditoria but had been at the bottom of the bill: in 1974, the venues were small but at least it was *their* gig. Warner Brothers, who had released the first two Roxy albums, had not renewed their contract, but *Stranded* and *These Foolish Things* had been taken up by Atlantic. Chris Charlesworth caught up with them. "I travelled with them to Philadelphia to do a show review and story," says Charlesworth today. "I had known Jane [McKay's wife] from when she was married to Lee Jackson from the Nice before him, and I think she was at a loose end in New York while Andy was touring somewhere. I bumped into her at some lunchtime function thrown by Atlantic and we got pissed and ended up having a smoke back at my apartment." "My view of American audiences is that they are incredibly conservative," Ferry told Charlesworth:

I think that when they went through all the social changes in the sixties they seemed to create a new style which was equally as rigid as the one they left. Our things haven't been successful here in large numbers because we are something new again. We are too different for them. We were very fortunate to be successful from the first record on in England, maybe because of the mechanics of the English system. There isn't a huge rock press over here, and in England we were always written about from the very beginning, so people were aware of us before even the first album came out. Here people are more influenced by FM radio and they're more unadventurous in their outlook. There seems to be a dreadful snobbery between AM and FM radio, and Roxy doesn't seem to fall into either of these accepted categories. We're too weird for AM and considered too flash and image-conscious for some of the FM stations.

Whilst Ferry and Puxley were in the States, Paul Thompson took advantage of the lull in the schedule to get married. Susan Smith, just 17, from Lanarkshire was snapped by Scotland's *Daily Record*, resplendent in white, carried by Manzanera and a dapper Paul Thompson, sporting a white carnation.

The US tour was in fact hardly a tour at all, just half a dozen nights at 2,000-seater halls along the East Coast, ending at the New York Academy of Music. Roxy essentially played the same set as on the autumn 1973 *Stranded* tour. The audience response was enthusiastic, but it was hardly the sort of strategy to win over the biggest market in the world. *Stranded* was Number 99 on the *Cashbox* charts. "One can't help feeling that there's a certain unwillingness to work within the Roxy camp," wrote Chris Charlesworth. "Their stablemates King Crimson, on the other hand, seem to be permanently on the road in America at present. Mott The Hoople have made it into the Top 30 with *The Hoople*, a fact that surely reflects the hard work they've put in on numerous trips across the Atlantic."

Roxy Music were in part relying on curious David Bowie fans to swell the numbers in the halls. Unlike Roxy, Bowie's attempt to crack the American market was far from half-hearted. He left the UK in April 1974 and didn't return to work in Europe for two years. He toured for six straight months exclusively in the US, made *Young Americans* with an eye to the US market, starred in *The Man Who Fell To Earth*, also in America, and guested on such staples of American television as *The Cher Show*, *Soul Train* and *The Dinah Shore Show*. Following another bout of intensive touring in early 1976, Bowie may have become an unhinged drug addict, but he had also made two groundbreaking albums, in the process becoming one of the biggest stars of the mid-seventies. "Fame" soared to Number 1 in the US in 1975 and *Station To Station* reached Number 3 in the spring of 1976. It was a lesson for all British rockers: success in America required bloody hard graft, not the mild dilettantism of the Roxy operation.

Ferry's attempt to woo the American public appeared lame in comparison, and was all the more surprising because he was so enamoured of American culture and song. Roxy Music simply couldn't make inroads in the US in the same way they had established themselves in the UK. Their initial British success had been achieved despite, or because of, their refusal to submit themselves to mindless low-key gigs and steadfast touring. But to be successful in the US they could not afford to forego months, if not years, of profile-building gigging, state after state, in order to get their records in the Top 40 and, most importantly, to get play-listed. This, Ferry and co. simply found beyond them.

In the States, Roxy Music never became popular enough to fill large stadia, which is where the real money was. They lost money on every successive tour, and they were viewed by their American record company, Atlantic, as an English art rock group, a minority taste, despite the European Number 1 albums. With a comparatively small promotional budget, Roxy stood little chance. As the years went by, Ferry and Roxy American tours became increasingly rare.

Yet although Ferry was a reluctant performer, his ambition to make it in America never quite left him, and his comparative lack of success irked him considerably. Perhaps there was something too arch, too contrived in the Ferry persona, something too alien to resonate with the general American public. It's no coincidence that, in the seventies, Britain's most successful exports to the USA – Led Zeppelin, Rod Stewart, the Rolling Stones and Elton John – all sang with an American accent. Bowie, on the other hand, either retained his Bromley tones or, at most, parodied blue-eyed soul, so in this respect, his success was the exception, not the rule. In an era of US shock-rock headed by Alice Cooper and Kiss, he was sartorially also just about acceptable. Ferry, however, with his designer suits, suave, European melodies and astonishingly mannered and mostly resolutely English singing style, found only minority support amongst the hipsters in America. His style of tortured romanticism played well in England and France, but translated poorly into a market dominated by the Allman Brothers and the Eagles.

Later, in 1982, when a 37-year-old Ferry probably realised that US success would probably forever elude him, he told the *NME*:

It's interesting that in America the simpler the image a star has – be it a movie star, television personality, whatever – the more successful they seem to be. That's not as true in England because the British are more prepared to accept weirdness and complexity, and I think that's because the hard sell principle doesn't happen quite as intensely in England. Things are just made available and the audience then makes a decision. In America there's the sense that things are much more important. There's more money at stake, so success is more important. If an American record company decides to break an artist, they put a lot of money into it and push it very hard. That never really happened with me.

'I do love the whole costume bit.'
Glam-era Eno says 'cheese'.

'I'm totally useless at playing music.'
Eno on stage with Roxy.

Roxy Music backstage at the Crystal Palace Bowl, summer 1972.

'Early photographs of the band recall the Clangers on bad drugs.' (Barbara Ellen)

Roxy Music perform 'In Every Dream Home A Heartache' on *The Old Grey Whistle Test*, 1973.

The inspired amateurs, five years before punk.

The GI look for *Siren*, 1975.

The controversial *Country Life* cover, 1974.

Ferry adrift in the solo years of the late seventies.

Back on form with Roxy on the *Flesh + Blood* tour.

Jerry and Ferry, the Posh and Becks of 1976.

The central issues behind Roxy Music's comparative American failure were not just promotional, but cultural too. "This is not an easy question, because to answer it fully you have to explain the difference between British and American culture," says Eddie Jobson:

I would agree that Roxy never really cracked the US and the simple reason is that the Americans like their rock music tougher. In the seventies, Robert Plant was the archetypal "rock star": raw, sensuous and earthy. The very broad American music spectrum embraced many artists who captured the myriad sides of the American culture, from Janis Joplin and Jimi Hendrix to Dolly Parton and the Beach Boys. The British bands who made it big there in the sixties and seventies either fit the commercial radio format, like, say, ELO, or captured something Americans related to in their rock music, like drugs (Pink Floyd), sex (Led Zeppelin) or maybe something less mainstream, like the decadence of downtown New York (Bowie). Roxy never quite hit that or any other pulse. We were viewed as effete, amateurish, tame, and Bryan as old and clunky with a funny, warbly voice. The black-leather Warhol crowd thought the whole gay/glam thing was decadent and cool, but the only places in Middle America that hit were the blue-collar cities of Detroit and Cleveland. Like Glasgow or Birmingham, these places needed some glamour in their lives, and Roxy, T. Rex, Bowie, Mott the Hoople, and even The New York Dolls, Devo or Television provided it. Other than that, Roxy spoke for a strictly Euro culture: Paris in the thirties, Berlin in the forties or Kings Road in the seventies. Americans could never put Humphrey Bogart and rock music in the same sentence, let alone the same theatre.

In his more reflective moments, Ferry himself admits that a different sort of sound, or perhaps a different sort of musical backing, just might have been the key to greater success. "I always wished I had a guitar player like Keith Richards, that would have been a lovely thing," he told me in 1999. "Or Mick Ronson, actually, I thought he was very good."

Was it a handicap that, at least initially, Roxy Music were not fantastic musicians? Ferry, again, is candid: "I think it was, certainly as far as America went. With all due respect to Phil – he was a different type of player, more a sound-effect man – I think if we'd had a real blood-curdling type of soloist, I think it might have made a bit of difference, but, then again, who knows? Or Jeff Beck, or someone like that, would have been quite useful to have in the group."

So 1974, like 1973, would be a year of constant work and promotion. It was also time for Roxy's fourth album to be recorded. *Country Life*, although not as big a success as *Stranded* and never as admired by the critics, saw no dip in quality. "*Country Life* is the great lost classic; I think it's a fantastic record," says Mat Snow. "It's really, really good throughout."

It's a heavier album than *Stranded*: the playing more urgent, the tone less reflective. Worryingly, there was one completely lame moment. A trite, plodding, boogie number, with harmonica to the fore and yakkety sax, "If It Takes All Night" sounded as if it belonged on a Ferry solo album. It was pastiche of the worst kind. The rest, though, was classic Roxy Music.

The adrenaline rush of the opening salvo, "The Thrill Of It All", is perhaps Roxy's finest opening song ever:

> "The sky is dark, the wind is cold
> The night is young before it's old and grey
> We will know
> The thrill of it all."

> (Words and music: Bryan Ferry, 1974)

Another Roxy rocker was the single from the album, "All I Want Is You", which narrowly missed the UK Top 10 that autumn. It's a song with a classic bridge:

> "Going out with other girls
> Was always such a bore
> But since I fell in love with you
> I need you more and more."

> (Words and music: Bryan Ferry, 1974)

The killer track, however, is "Out Of The Blue". Funnily enough, from Roxy Music through to Franz Ferdinand, art rock groups have always had great bass lines in their songs, and the bass line on "On Out Of The Blue" was one of the very finest. Johnny Gustafson remembers:

"Ninety-five percent of the bass playing was all my idea: they'd bang some chords out and I'd wait until something gelled and then I'd join in and develop it. But I stuck in a few things in the middle of that that I quite liked, some James Brown-y bits." "Out of The Blue" also deserves classic status for Ferry's wonderful vocal and gorgeous melody, as well as Eddie Jobson's electric violin solo at the end, which dissolves into brilliant cross-speaker phasing at the dénouement.

"Three And Nine", so named after the price of admission at the local cinema for the teenage Ferry, is slight but winsome and evocative, whilst the closing song, "Prairie Rose", is grand riff-rock on an epic scale. Then there's "Bitter Sweet", an astonishing piece of neo-Brechtian bombast:

> "These vintage years
> Lovers you consume,
> My friend
> As others their wine
>
> Nein, das is nicht
> Das Ende der Welt
> Gestrandet an Leben und Kunst
> Und das Spiel geht weiter
> Wie man weiss
> Noch viele schönste ... Wiedersehen."
>
> (Words and music: Bryan Ferry, 1974)

Ferry had created a truly articulate, pan-European lyricism, one in which he could switch from this strident, mock-operatic *Sprechgesang* to the doomy romanticism of "All I Want Is You":

> "If you ever change your mind
> I've a certain cure
> An old refrain, it lingers on
> L'amour, toujours, l'amour."

French, Latin, German – in the seventies, Ferry carried it all off without it ever sounding trite, misguided or foolish. It also bespeaks a great confidence to attempt a track such as "Triptych". To a haunting melody, evocative of medieval banqueting halls or Gothic cathedrals, Ferry's lyric depicts the crucifixion, poetically, without irony. Christ is "Nailed upon a wooden frame/twisted yet unbroken," before the conclusion: "Surely he will rise again".

On an album that shows Ferry growing as a songwriter, gaining in confidence, and revealing his brilliance at adopting new stances and new perspectives, "Casanova" is perhaps the most surprising track of all:

> "You – the hero
> So many times
> You've loved
> And didn't linger
>
> Now my finger
> Points at you
> Another loser."

Later, Ferry sings with contempt:

> "Now you're flirting
> With heroin
> Or is it cocaine?
>
> Casanova –
> Is that your name?
> Or do you live there?"

> (Words and music: Bryan Ferry, 1974)

For writer and Roxy fan Jon Savage, songs such as "Casanova" mapped the changing attitudes in the post-glam, pre-punk interregnum:

> Well, the idea of glam was divine decadence, *dahling* – even as far as the Sweet were concerned – and "Casanova" finds Bryan Ferry being rather short with the object of the song: that lyric about "heroin, or is it cocaine?" High glam never judged, did it? The lyrical concerns on *Country Life* move out from the nihilistic sheen of *For Your Pleasure* and *Stranded* into critique and optimism.

Country Life was released in November 1974. Although it failed to match the success of *Stranded*, it nevertheless managed to reach Number 3 in the UK album charts. For some longstanding Roxy fans, it's the album that has the perfect balance. Ashley Wright says: "My favourite Roxy album would, I think, be *Country Life,* which for me has everything that was good about Roxy, from the heavier stuff like 'The Thrill Of It All' and 'Out Of The Blue' to the smooth 'A Really Good Time' and the unusual 'Triptych'. Overall, it's a prime example of what was dubbed by the original fan club as the Roxy 'wall of sound'."

On its release, Nick Kent nailed the album in his *NME* review. Entitled "A Country Mile Ahead (Of Any Other Brand Of Poseur)", Kent's review points out how Ferry's songwriting had evolved:

"Three And Nine" … is whimsical in the finest tradition – like Ray Davies at his best, but without the obvious stylistic parallels. Mackay's melody may well be the strongest on the whole album while Ferry, lamenting the loss of innocence personified in the death of the grand celluloid fantasy and the coming of decimalisation (I know it sounds ridiculous here, but it actually works) is resolved at the same time to face oncoming changes … Without trying to sound overtly twee, the song does possess a warmth which is particularly heartening, simply because Ferry isn't trying as obviously hard as before. Instead of his work depreciating, it is instead starting to take on a charmed simplicity and directness.

And then there is "Casanova" which is possibly the best number here – full of bristling venom, utilising Ferry's taut approach to the fullest degree. Strained, leering vocals, a singularly eerie organ solo (by Ferry himself) and couched, prophetic lyrics which seem to almost gloat at the terminal condition of the classic reckless *nouveau romantic* gone awry. The approach here is incredibly powerful: a series of incisive three-line stanzas built up to portray the victim's predicament "Now you're nothing/But second-hand/In glove/With second-rate."

Country Life's caustic lyricism went against the public's perception of a man drifting into an early mid-life of comfortable elegance. It showed a new side to Ferry's writing, a "taut approach", an economy of style, and, more importantly, revealed Ferry more than ever before as a critic of the scene. Aloof, detached, never willing to be in the centre of things,

Ferry was emerging as a talented writer and diarist of the decadence of the mid-seventies' metropolitan lifestyle of white powder, fast cars, fast girls, quick thrills and, ultimately, meaningless hedonism.

While Ferry upped the ante lyrically, the controversial cover with its brazen depiction of full-frontal (if tastefully camouflaged) female nudity threw out a challenge to the rock world. Ferry likened the Roxy covers to a series or sequence. The first had been startling but playful, the work of a band intent on making the big time. The gold disc positioned next to model Kari-Ann was a fun piece of wishful thinking: there was a sort of naïvety about the image. However, two-and-a-half years down the line, Roxy's imagery seemed, like the barbed content of many of the lyrics, to have become much more confrontational and much less obviously ironic.

The cover was a confusion of conflicting images – tacky and down-market, it was at the same time obviously a spoof. Ferry admitted to admiring the more filmic beauty of Marilyn Monroe and Rita Hayworth, although he was equally in love with the Elsie Tanners and Bet Lynches of his imaginary world. "Money is important to me," said Ferry, in an unequivocal statement of intent that followed years of rock stars espousing hippy ways but living rich all the same. "I like tacky things and low life as much as high life," he added. In Britain the cover caused a bit of a stir, but in America, the album had to be sold in a plain wrapper. Some countries had alternative versions of the cover photo, showing only a close-up of the girls' faces, while others had the background foliage only.

The *Country Life* cover shows boobs and pubic hair, and features the banal, almost vacant expressions of two admittedly beautiful (if somewhat unconventionally so) women, Constanze Karoli and Eveline Grunwald (who were uncredited on the album sleeve). On one level, it's a more appealing image than the torn dress, post-coital glamour-puss shot of *Stranded*. Ferry's intent was to satirise a UK magazine, *Country Life*, with its depiction of other "wildlife": pheasant-shooting, welly-wearing toffs out on patrol amidst idyllic images of Albion. "The cover contrasts with the usual *Country Life* photography, where you normally have characters shooting ducks or jumping over fences in top hats," said Ferry in December 1974. "While I'm pleased with the controversy, I don't think the picture's depraved – a bit seedy perhaps, but you see far worse things than that." But those unschooled in post-modern irony missed the joke and merely saw it as another brazen attempt by Ferry to sell music with sex. Subsequent attempts to defend the cover have remained unconvincing. In 2001, Ferry told journalist Barbara Ellen: "[That cover] did not put down women. *No one* admires women more than me. I just like Hollywood glamour. Why else would we chose the name Roxy for the band?" It's the classic chauvinistic response, of course.

Ferry has always been obsessed (and it *is* an obsession) with glamour and beauty. This has led to some great art, but has also served to distance him from the lifestyles and experiences of the rest of us, for whom the imperfections of ourselves and our partners are just part of life. This doesn't apply to Ferry. From the age of thirty onwards he has seldom, if ever, dated same-age partners, always opting for younger and sleeker models. As a rock star, he is, of course, not alone in this. The late Robert Palmer, another northern lad made good and lover of beautiful "ladies" and cool sophistication, would also counter allegations of easy sexism in similar ways. Writer Tony Parsons deconstructed the Palmer image thusly:

> On record and in the toasted flesh, Robert Palmer is the ageing smoothie incarnate. Casual sexism and smug, menopausal good taste abound … Even more than Bryan Ferry in his capped teeth, white tux and gossip column period, even more than The World's Forgotten Lad Rod Stewart in his straw boater, art deco lamps and Swedish blow job phase, Robert Palmer has presented himself as the playboy of the western world, a smirking rake, a wolf in tropical weight clothing, frolicking as only a fancy man can by floodlit pools and on moonlit lawns. 'I'm a very private person,' he says, in his Yorkshire drawl."

Are there really any grounds for accusing Ferry of crudely using sex to sell music? Richard Williams thinks not: "It trod a very, very fine line. I think they were so ironic as to be utterly devoid of any possible sexist, misogynistic or anti-feminist intent. Of all the women I knew, I didn't know anybody that was upset by it." Perhaps a more accurate assessment of the *Country Life* cover would be that it is sexist by effect, not by intent, as record business veteran and longtime fan Paula Brown puts it: "Well, yes, I do think the covers are sexist, but I don't think that was the intent. In the same way the Tarzan movies enjoyed raising the leopard-clad lost tribe of Amazons to goddess status, so does Ferry elevate women."

In autumn 1974, Roxy Music were still major players in the UK. The music scene had changed: glam rock was essentially over, progressive rock was flourishing, and the disco offensive had started. Teen bands such as the Bay City Rollers were the new chart gods and, somewhere in Guildford, the Stranglers were beginning the slow metamorphosis from pub rockers to punk rockers that would gather such electric speed in the year ahead. But for Roxy, meanwhile, the *Country Life* tour was full of hedonistic fun.

Of course, Roxy were without a bass player for the tour. John Wetton takes up the story:

> I was managed by EG at the time. King Crimson had just broken up and I was kind of floating a bit. I didn't know what to do, and it was great fun to do a tour with Roxy Music and have knickers thrown at us! To come out of a group like King Crimson, which was predominantly beards and pullovers, into a group like Roxy, who were very much in the female genre – yeah, it was good fun! And the gig was really quite easy for me, on a musical level.
>
> I was part of the cross-fertilisation and germination of the EG camp at the time. I use the word "camp" very guardedly. I was playing on Bryan's albums and Phil's albums. Now you have to remember that we had the same management company: it was all one big family. The whole reason I slid into the job in the first place was that there used to be a pub across the road from EG in the Kings Road called the Markham. We were sitting there one summer afternoon, just chewing the cud with Mark Fenwick and Bryan over a half of lager, and Bryan said, "We need a bass player for the next tour and we need to go through the dreadful ordeal of auditioning people." And he said to me, "You wouldn't fancy coming down and vetting the auditionees would you?" It was at the Rainbow. And, I said, "Yeah, sure, course I will." We'd been friends for a long time before then. We used to live quite close to each other in Earls Court, so we'd go socialising and clubbing together. I went down to the Rainbow and watched a succession of very badly coiffured and even worse musical entities come across the stage. At the end of it, Bryan said to me, "Well, what do you think, then?" and I said, "Well, not much really". I didn't see anybody outstanding, and nobody with the sort of funk and the class that you're after. They all looked pretty shabby to me. And so he said, "Is there any chance that you would do it?" I said, "Actually, yeah, why not, why not?"
>
> The deal was to do thirty dates on a UK tour and that was it. It was to have a bit of fun and give the band a bit of beef. Actually, I always worked well with Paul Thompson. With this fairly nebulous front three, it gave them the kind of rock-solid foundation that they

needed. They couldn't exist without that, without a solid rhythm section. Thompson was rock-solid all the way through – that's what he's like as a person, that's what he's like as a musician too. I love him; I think he's great, as in "The Great Paul Thompson".

The *Country Life* tour was huge fun socially, as Roxy found themselves to be objects of desire for both sexes. "All I Want Is You" had entered the UK Top 20 and the band were booked to appear on *Top Of The Pops*. "We all used to go and ogle Pan's People [the show's all-female dancing troupe] while they were leaping about, and we'd make an enormous amount of noise, which was good fun," says Wetton with a smile:

Everyone in the band had their favourites [among Pan's People], and Bryan and I went out with a couple of them afterwards. The producer, the BBC bloke, he came up to me in the dressing room and he said, "I always love it when Roxy Music come on because you're so good-looking." Notoriously, the BBC producers were ninety percent gay, so they saw Roxy Music as sort of icons of availability! Roxy didn't mind having a gay following at all, although I can say that, within the fold, I never saw any trace of homosexuality, and I've been pretty close to most of them.

I would probably need a psychologist to get to the bottom of this question, regarding Bryan's and the band's rampant testosterone levels juxtaposed with being surrounded permanently with a posse of supermodels, whilst simultaneously being courted by a fierce gay lobby. I've got a feeling it's to do with the Phil Collins factor. Women feel safe because Ferry is the guy next door with feelings, and a great voice. Men feel safe because he's "no threat". Many beautiful women feel safe with gay men for that same reason, but Roxy were wolves in sheep's clothing. Maybe it wasn't as overt as, say, Whitesnake, and as the BBC producer commented, we were a nice-looking bunch – and charming, too. Not sweaty or smelly like the footballers, and definitely not monosyllabic.

However, critical reaction to the *Country Life* shows was often negative. In fact, 1974 would be the year that the music press turned on Bryan Ferry with a vengeance. The more they taunted, the more sensitive and defensive he became. Mean-spirited critics have always been identified by Ferry as the major bugbear of his life: "You can never trust a jour-

nalist," he told *Sounds* in 1974. The irony, of course, was that such criticism was nothing but friendly fire. The majority of Ferry's tormentors
were huge fans: it was simply that Ferry kept servicing them with
enough ammo to make the occasional cheap shot impossible to resist.

For the next two tours, to support *Country Life* and Roxy's fifth
album, *Siren*, Antony Price's stage designs were to set new standards for
the absurd within pop (and, ultimately, almost single-handedly invent
the New Romantics). Eddie Jobson recalls that the rest of the band was
foursquare behind Ferry's wild reinventions: "Well, the Hitler outfit and
the gaucho look received the most 'shock and awe'. But, hey, Bryan
was doing stuff that nobody else was doing, so we were all very
accepting of it." He adds:

> His style choices were "on the money" nine times out of ten. As for
> the *NME,* most of the people over there were socialist grubs: scruffy
> idiots with black leather pants, living in Camden. I don't think Bryan
> cared that much what they thought, because, at the end of the day,
> they would still give him the entire front page to himself.
>
> As I have gotten older, I have an even greater respect for some of
> music culture's more original characters, among them three I have
> worked with: Frank Zappa, Ian Anderson and Bryan Ferry. It's
> amazing that someone can come along and create, in themselves, an
> iconic personality and a character of such originality. These people
> deserve to be stars, because they take such personal risks. Let's face
> it, Bryan could have been laughed off the stage if he hadn't been so
> committed to seeing it all the way through.

The prime sartorial *faux pas* was the gaucho look worn by Ferry on that
autumn's *Country Life* tour, a look that was almost immediately torn to
shreds by the press. Ferry took to the stage in baggy velvet pantaloons
tied at the waist by a silk rope cord, a billowing shirt, a black sombrero
with a bull's-head toggle, and pantomime cream suede boots with
arabesque stitching. Ferry was supposed to possess the glamour of
Valentino but, to one critic, all he did was come over like "some refugee
from the Horse Of The Year Show". "Here he comes ... dressed as a
Spanish traffic warden," quipped *Sounds*. "I kind of lost faith in him
when he was dressed like an Argentinian cowboy," says Martyn Ware.
"It was camp, but in a very banal way."

The time was ripe for a critical backlash against Ferry and Roxy

Music, and it would be on the *Country Life* tour that the band endured their first real wave of public discontent. At the time Ferry thought the gaucho look was "blowsy, romantic, it fitted the songs", and that it was a successful piece of imaging. Now, he can see the other side, too. Was the look really a Spanish traffic warden outfit in all but name? "Well, fair comment really," said Ferry in the nineties, at pains to point out the prescience along with the silliness. "It was a very good idea, and it sort of predated the New Romantics ... by several years."

Ferry's other look for the *Country Life* tour wasn't so much amusing as alarming. "The Nazis had a great sense of visuals," Ferry told a journalist in the late seventies. "What we were doing with all that theatre was to create a style which matched the music." This led Ferry to overload the *Country Life* presentation with show-stopping visual set pieces, including a backdrop of velvet drapes emblazoned with the logo "RM" at the heart of a pair of eagle's wings. Ferry's Price-designed stage outfit reinforced these fascistic visual images. He took to the stage in riding breeches and what looked like jackboots, raven hair parted to the side.

To some extent, Ferry was doing nothing more than picking up on the Nazi chic of the mid-seventies, and there's no question of him ever being a Nazi sympathiser. Of course, he wasn't the only rocker with a taste for the decadent. Lou Reed's *Berlin* and Bowie's *Diamond Dogs* had painted future dystopian hells, and Iggy Pop, Viv Stanshall and Keith Moon played around "comically" with the swastika, paving the way for Siouxsie Sioux's appropriation of the symbol in 1976. Cultural critic Dick Hebdige, in his groundbreaking analysis, *Subculture: The Meaning Of Style*, probably correctly identified the appropriation of the swastika by punk as an empty symbol used only for its shock value, as an expression of the desire to be hated by the mainstream, rather than as a signal of a specific attachment to a Rightist political credo. Later, in 1980, Spandau Ballet, whose indebtedness to Ferry was transparent, also deployed pseudo "Strength Through Joy"-inspired fascistic imagery in their early artwork. Although since downplayed, critical reaction at the time to Ferry's role in this mining of Nazi style in the pre-punk years was incredulous and confused. It seemed to many yet another sign that Roxy Music shows were becoming triumphs of style over content.

However, it wasn't just the contrivance of the new imaging that grated with the press. It was also, so journalists would claim, Ferry's haughty, thin-skinned and humourless *mien*. Almost three years into Roxy's fame, the word at *NME* was that Ferry believed his own hype; that he had become a *bona fide* member of the jet set rather than a parodist of the scene. While the whimsical contrivance of the latter scenario was tolerated, the retaliation against the idea of Ferry as a coolly tuxedoed Bel Air rich kid *in actuality* was swift. It was also hinted that Ferry had sold out his working-class roots. Perhaps it would be fairer and more accurate to say that Ferry's music at the time articulated that sense of discomfort experienced when shedding one class skin only to don another. Perhaps the diffidence he presented to the press (though he was seldom so in private) was a by-product of the process of Ferry coming to terms with both artistic freedom and the bourgeoisification of his lifestyle. Ferry did not see the joke when, ridiculing what they perceived to be rock star pretension, the sharp-shooters at the *NME* began deliberately misspelling his name in newspaper copy, a development which ultimately led, on the appearance of the headline "How Gauche Can A Gaucho Get?", to Ferry pulling all the adverting for Roxy Music out of the *NME*. The friendly teasing had actually begun amongst his most ardent supporters in 1973, when Ian MacDonald wrote that Ferry was know in some quarters of the trade as "Biryani Ferret".

Ferry, a proud man with a genuine wish to produce and perform intelligent music with depth, found the taunting from former supporters in the media hurtful and distracting. "I'm the most sensitive person in the world, so I've had to develop a hard shell," he told *NME*'s Max Bell at the end of 1974. "I mean, criticism can be flattering, too, because you're being noticed. On the other hand, I tend to resent it because I'm very self-critical myself, so I usually know if it's valid."

Other taunts included "Bryan Ferrari'", "Brawn Fury", "Byron Ferrari", "Brown Fairy" and, later in the seventies, "Bryatollah Ferrani". Charles Shaar Murray, then a twenty-something hipster at the *NME*, remembers: "We despised the record industry, gave not even two hoots for the sensibilities of our publisher or the profits of their shareholders, and relentlessly satirised even favourite musicians like Bryan Ferry, whose ludicrous clothes and fragile ego inspired us to seek endlessly for new ways to misspell his name." A bloodthirsty press saw a wounded animal ready for the kill.

But was it taunting, or was it teasing? Surely, Ferry knew that behind the silly name-calling was possibly, in some cases, a grudging and back-handed statement of regard? Ferry did not help his own cause. In interviews, he was moody, standoff-ish, aloof: the "lone gaucho" mooching "restlessly" around (*NME*), a man possessed by "an overwhelming intensity" (*Playgirl*), whose photos were printed in the inkies above legends such as "MopealongaBry" (*NME* again). The reason for Ferry's wearied *mien* was simply that he disliked talking about both himself and his music, which he thought should explain itself and need no commentary from its author. What could he possibly add when the art itself had been so carefully crafted that, to the sensitive listener, it needed no explanation? So, basically, there was *no* agenda in a Bryan Ferry interview, which meant that the gaps had to be filled with pat answers and witty one-liners. Ferry could give good copy, but always in a literary or high-cultural world-weary way. The Wildean *bon mots* were hardly designed to appeal to the demotic aspirations of the pre-punk pack at the *NME*.

Ferry gave the impression that he suffered terribly for his art. And yet, irksome as this was to unsympathetic journalists, it was no charade. Ferry lived for and worried over his music. This work ethic led him to perform live as a solo artist in December 1974, immediately after the writing, recording and touring of *Country Life*. With two gold solo albums, Ferry regarded the concerts at the Royal Albert Hall as "test gigs". To faithfully reproduce the orchestrated sequences of these solo classic covers, Ferry would perform with 55 musicians.

This was one of the first manifestations of an attention to detail bordering on the obsessive. So consuming was his search for the right musical sound that Ferry was prepared to embark on a project that would almost certainly lose him money – and for what? Some rarefied, misguided concept of perfection. Ferry has always found it hard to accept that he lives in an imperfect world but this character trait would never leave him: his career has seen him make and lose millions, prepared as he is to self-finance months of recording in order to reach music nirvana. For Ferry it *has* to be right; the devil, as always, is in the detail.

After Christmas 1974, there would even be some better news for the band from the United States. Another tour won Roxy significant gains in America, as *Country Life* became the first Roxy Music album to crack the US Top 40. Then the tour moved on to Japan and Australia where, once again, Roxy's impact was far from stunning. John Wetton, later to become massively successful Stateside as part of super-group Asia, is of the opinion that Roxy's lack of a powerful musical image was a major reason for their frustrations:

The British are the most fickle nation on earth in terms of loyalty: they're into whoever's on the front of a magazine. In Japan, image is very important but what is more important is *musical* image and that's the reason Roxy never made in Japan. They see a guy in a dinner jacket singing covers, and they think, "Oh, it's a guy in a dinner jacket singing covers". They're not prone to the subtlety intended in Bryan's lounge lizard act. They just see what they get. The artists who have made it big in Japan, such as Queen, have a very strong image, and a very strong musical image as well. Roxy Music never had a very strong musical image. Bowie did well in Japan because he had both. He had a very identifiable musical style and was visually very identifiable, with no grey areas, and that's what they like over there. Unfortunately, Roxy Music never had that. They were always quite nebulous in terms of musical image.

But for Wetton, it wasn't the case that Roxy were too sophisticated for the American market; rather, it was their naïvety that did for them. Roxy simply lacked firepower:

Roxy always surrounded themselves with very good musicians, because I think there is an apparent weakness in the front three, the big three as it were, in that they're all pretty *floaty*. Very good arty ideas came out of them, and they had a very ample guitarist in Phil Manzanera, but if you look at them individually, there's not really one very strong force there. As for the vocalist, well, Ferry's not Robert Plant, is he? Not that he would ever try to be, to be fair. As far as Japan goes, if you get up in front of the microphone, you have to deliver. And as far as the Americans are concerned, it's the same kind of thing, really. Roxy never hitting it big in America was always one of the thorns in their side.

For the rest of the decade, his record company and his management would repeatedly tell Ferry that he had to extend his appeal beyond Europe. He felt pressured; unwilling to compromise artistically, he could, however, see the benefits of developing a sound, which would be globally accepted. Would he remain a cult star, or become a global brand name? The next three years would provide the answer.

STRIPPED BARE:
1975-1977

The male-dominated rock world loves to find a female scapegoat. Yoko killed the Beatles; Courtney, so some claim, "killed" Kurt. When women appear in rock history, which is seldom enough as it is, they're all too depressingly either Lady Macbeth figures – backseat drivers, daring and manipulating men to further their own foul ambitions – or good-for-nothing groupies and hangers-on, media whores riding on the coat-tails of their partners only to spill the beans with undignified haste when dropped. Sometimes, they are both.

Bryan Ferry's lyrics have tended to valorise the female form; seeking perfection, his lovelorn lyricism has, so often, depicted love lost and love unobtainable. Despite all his requests for privacy, and despite the singular path taken by him to avoid the traditional clichés of the rock world, Bryan Ferry's short relationship with Jerry Hall has provided tabloid editors and journalists with a comfortable entrance into the life and times of Bryan Ferry. It's not the wonderful songs, fantastic shows, or startling images that Ferry has provided for us that are the focus of attention, but rather the doomed relationship with the Texan girl who jilted him in favour of a member of the rock aristocracy.

Jerry Hall was born Jerry Faye on July 2, 1956, in Gonzales, Texas, one of five daughters. When she was two, she moved to the nearby working-class town of Mesquite. Her father, she has said, was a violent alcoholic: "He would come home and hit us and scream at us, and I lived in fear of him throughout most of my childhood." It was a home life Hall was keen to break out of. After spells modelling in Paris, the leggy, six-foot-tall model with the shoulder-length mane of cascading blond hair and the infectious, bright-eyed smile secured some plum assignments. The picture that caught Ferry's eye was Norman Parkinson's cover shot for the May 1975 issue of English *Vogue*. In powder blue swimsuit and swim cap, head tilted, speaking on the phone, Hall looks out cheekily from the cover. She was just 18 and clearly one of the most beautiful models of the age. "He [Ferry] picked me out and sent for me," says Hall:

> I was so impressed. He picked me up at Heathrow Airport in London in this big old Daimler limousine – you know, one of those old-fashioned cars the Queen has. They're so nice. And Bryan put me in a nice hotel and then took me out to dinner. He was charming. He was a real gentleman and handsome and beautifully dressed, and his hair was all black and shiny and slicked back and he smelled of Floris. I didn't have a boyfriend then and I really fancied him. I could see he liked me, too. The next day we took a train trip to Wales. I'd never been on a train like that – a beautiful old-fashioned train with leather seats. That was great. And we had Antony Price with us. He's a really good designer: he's still a friend of mine. So they started telling me the idea of the picture.

The shoot for the cover artwork for the fifth Roxy album was to take place in Wales. "I spotted the location on a TV film," says Ferry. "It was in Anglesey and the only other place in Britain where you'd get scenery like that would be in the north of Scotland, which is even further away. So on the hottest day of the summer about twenty of us went out to Anglesey and trooped down the cliff to do the cover." Hall would be transformed into a blue-painted mermaid, with comical results. Antony Price takes up the story:

> We went to look at the location the night before. It was still as anything. The sea had dropped thirty feet. Now the week I had gone before there was an incredibly rough sea, with massive waves, and it was all green. Everything was green so we decided [Hall's costume] would be green, then when we got there the week later, I said to Bryan, it's going to be blue, we've got to go blue. Luckily, I'd foreseen this horror and brought blue car paints with me and re-sprayed the whole bloody thing the night before to blue. Thank God.
>
> When we got there the next morning the whole thing was blue. Direct brilliant overhead sun. It was the hottest day. It reached 100 degrees. I had the glue from the costume welded into her fanny hairs.

It was unbelievable, the nails were coming off, everything was just melting: the make-up, everything.

What happened then? Well the famous story. She was covered in blue make-up. We immersed her into a bath full of make-up removing liquid [but] couldn't get it off her. We had to carry her stark naked, wrapped in towels, and we got on that train as it was, we literally ran and opened the door and shoved her on it, or we would have been stuck there for another 24 hours. The last Holyhead express to London, God, what a nightmare, and then they had her hanging out of the train taking pictures. I thought she was going to catch her hair in the mulberry bush in a moment and her head will be gone next. It was the most ghastly of nightmares.

There are photographs of Ferry (despite the blistering summer heat still wearing long trousers) smiling away and holding an umbrella to shade the visibly drooping mermaid. As if having to escort a semi-naked Jerry Hall round Wales wouldn't be enough to send most of the heterosexual male population giddy, it seemed that Ferry had, at last, found someone he wanted to spend time with on a rather more permanent basis. And Hall had found a dapper, attractive and famous man with whom to hang out. "I went to the bathroom on the train to try and towel it off but I couldn't get it all off," says Hall. "So when we got to London, Bryan asked me back to his place to take a bath. He had a nice house in Holland Park. And when I came out of the bathroom wearing a robe, he said, 'Why don't you just stay here? I have a guest room.' So, since it was late, I stayed there. And that's the night it began!"

When Hall returned to the States the new lovers kept in touch by letter but, in the meantime, Ferry had the fifth Roxy album to keep him company. In the UK, at least, the first six months of 1975 were the first time for three years that not much would be heard of either Roxy Music or Bryan Ferry. True, Ferry scored a minor hit that summer with his cover of the thirties standard "You Go To My Head" (it was later also recorded by Sinatra), but to all intents and purposes, both singer and band were off the radar. In fact, around the time he met Hall, Ferry was in the grip of one of his sporadic depressive episodes.

Like many creative people, Bryan Ferry has been frequently unhappy with his lot and wracked by self-doubt. For some rock stars, fame, money and adulation can never compensate for the stress and weight of expectation that stardom brings. And Ferry has been consistently prone, throughout his life, to moments of deep melancholy. An astonishingly hard-working man, he has always been a perfectionist and, like all perfectionists, is never quite satisfied with his lot, or with his work. Ferry had been completely taken by surprise at the great success of the first Roxy Music album, was thankful for it, and was gladdened that such a large audience existed for his work. Yet with each passing year, being a musician meant worry and more worry. Each record had to be different, better, a step forward. And Ferry was always concerned, perhaps more so than many other artists, with both critical acceptance and record sales. By the summer of 1975, he appeared to have reached something of a crisis point. He had become successful – but was he also happy? Most certainly not.

Caroline Coon of *Melody Maker* caught Ferry on an off-day when she interviewed him that summer. "I'm at a very low period, actually," Ferry cautioned. He had just moved to a Georgian house in Holland Park. "His new sitting-room is graciously spacious, uncluttered and calm," Coon reported: "The thick wall-to-wall carpeting absorbs the slightest sound in the house but, drifting through the huge bay windows, which overlook a garden where honeysuckle, roses and azaleas have been cultivated for years, float the sounds of birds singing and lawn mowers putting. It's an idyllic setting, as far removed from his working-class roots as his present financial success will allow. He probably changes for dinner."

Everywhere were symbols of status and of a rarefied concept of unobtainable beauty. Ferry judged himself not by the standards of the everyday, but against those icons whose brilliance he aspired to match: "He surrounds himself with the trappings of refinement: glossy fashion magazines, the Daimler, dancing at Annabelles, and he has a picture on the walls of those who made it – legendary figures like Monroe, Elvis and Kay Kendall. And it hurts. He's something of a masochist, living on the knife-edge of an identity crisis. He strains himself to the limit, turning his dilemmas and struggle into great music."

Ferry was recovering from the spring Roxy US tour and, having holidayed in Mustique, was meant to be writing tracks for the fifth Roxy album. But things just weren't flowing. Bursts of creativity tended to arrive in fits and starts, ideas for songs coming maybe once or twice a week. He found it difficult to write to order. With one or two exceptions (for example "Do The Strand"), Ferry also wrote his most resonate pieces when he was down: in the middle of the night, feeling unhappy and insecure. The eerie "Strictly Confidential" from *For Your Pleasure* had been written late at night. And now, in the early summer of 1975,

Ferry was in a vulnerable position. Roxy Music's relevance and impact appeared to be diminishing ever so slightly with each release and each year. They were by now an established band, but their initial art rock manifesto had been successfully delivered, and the two albums that followed, *Stranded* and *Country Life*, had, perhaps, taken them as far as they could go in terms of musicianship and craft. Where to next? *Siren*, Roxy's fifth album, was an attempt to recreate some of the sonic magic of the first album, but also to develop the themes of the second and third. Caught between action and reaction, it would be the first Roxy album to show slight signs of a lack of musical confidence.

But returning to Ferry the man: what was wrong with him back in 1975? Most things, it appeared:

> Well, you have to forfeit certain things if you're indulging in the sort of work that I do. You don't have time for domestic comforts – like being happily married. A domestic life is something I don't seem to be able to get together at the moment. It's a very fast life I lead. There's so much work I set myself to do. You see I feel that I started very late, and that I have to make up for lost time.

In what was one of the most revealing interviews in Ferry's career, Caroline Coon quizzed Ferry further about his melancholic disposition. "Sometimes I can be quite bright on occasions and full of high spirits," he said. "But I can get a certain amount of pleasure from my manic depression, too." Coon then bravely asked Ferry if his depression had ever led him to contemplate suicide. "I have in the past, but not for a long time," he revealed. "Not when I have something specific to get done. I'm not obsessed with suicide by any means, but the idea does interest me. I'm slightly overawed by it." He then added:

> I'm afraid to commit myself. I always tend to be the man on the outside, for some reason. That's why I tend to see a little of a lot of people rather than a lot of a few. I'm always careful not to see too much of someone in case I get bored with them – or they get bored with me. It's a selfish thing, and I'm a very selfish person. I love to like people. And I'm also very critical of people as well. If I get to know them well it spoils it.

It was into this emotional quagmire that Jerry Hall walked in the summer of 1975. Ferry was a man who possessed so many fine attributes: he was considerate, clever, stylish, good-looking and sensitive. Yet he also had many imperfections, most of which he freely admitted to. John Wetton, one of the Roxy touring team at the time and later part of the solo Ferry projects, became very fond of Bryan Ferry. He, too, could quite clearly see the demons within the man. At times, Ferry would be poleaxed by the dread incubus of self-doubt and self-pity. "I was with him at one point almost daily", says Wetton:

> I love him as a guy. We hit it off really well and went on holiday together. He had this ability to switch from being very high to very low. He was a paranoid schizophrenic, definitely, but they seem to make the best entertainers. He's got a wonderful sense of humour, yet there was something not quite right. There's a lot of stuff he has to let go of, but he will harbour that and let it rot inside. I think most people who exist in the public eye are emotionally constipated. They cannot allow themselves to be who they really are. It's not because God created him that way; it's because he doesn't want it to be.

Siren was the fifth Roxy Music album and, interestingly, the first since the debut to be largely worked out before recording began. "The only album we rehearsed was *Siren*," says John Gustafson:

> The other albums were largely done in the studio, as far as I can remember. Those were the days when you'd go in the studio, write the stuff in there, and waste bloody hours. In the seventies bands were famous for doing it: you couldn't do it now. We'd take two or three weeks to put the tracks down and then I'd go and they'd finish them off. *Siren* was rehearsed in the basement of a girls' dress shop called *Tarts And Bows* in Portland Road in Holland Park, London. We'd turn up there every day and do six hours. I don't know how they ran the shop with the noise down there.

For the song that would become Roxy's biggest hit single to date, "Love Is The Drug", Gustafson laid down one of the best bass lines in recording history:

> They'd start clanking away, or Bryan would start clanging away on his Fender keyboard. He was just banging away on D minor and I stood there to see what the rest of them would do. The drums joined in and

I waited for about five minutes thinking, and just hit it straight away. It was slightly different from the rhythm they were doing and it sort of jolted them out of it into this poppy funky thing, and we carried on like that. The rest of the songs were done in the same fashion.

For another newie, "Both Ends Burning", Gustafson said that his bass line was "straight from 'Dancing In The Street' by Martha and the Vandellas, actually."

The cover of *Siren*, as we have seen, was another Antony Price and Bryan Ferry collaboration. Blue was the new black, and there was lots of it. Blue-tinted and deeply beautiful, the sleeve depicted Hall as temptress and enchanter: the mermaid siren who would entice men to their death through their foolishness and her charms. Her hair cascaded like seaweed. Of the first four album covers, Caroline Coon remarked that, "The women he has on his album covers ... are as close to being men in drag as it's possible to get." Although there is still something harsh and predatory about Hall on the *Siren* cover, the picture as a whole lacks the obvious, brazen sexuality of the previous two sleeves. Yet, once again, it's a stereotypical image of a clichéd aspect of femininity as seen through the eyes of men: the archetype of womankind as the ruination of man.

However, although the cover was yet another well-executed promotional image, the music contained therein showed signs of the Roxy machine slowing down. There are splashes of colour and moments of brilliance and, for the very first time, music that would work in the disco, but overall it's not quite up to the standard of the first four albums. Five albums in three-and-a-half years, plus two solo records and half-a-dozen tours, was obviously too much for Ferry, and *Siren* simply lacked the magic of the previous four Roxy albums.

Not that it could be called bad. The first single, "Love Is The Drug", is quite clearly one of Roxy's best ever. Released in October 1975, it was only kept off the top spot by Bowie and his re-released "Space Oddity". Of the many positive reviews of the single, historically the most important must surely also be the most bizarre. Here is *Sounds* magazine's guest reviewer, TV star and light entertainer Bruce Forsyth:

Very, very good beat to the whole thing. Potential disco hit. This has got all the things that I think the kids want. It's not necessarily what I want. Think it's a great title. The lyrics are good. I could hear what he was singing about which is always a help, you know, especially for us older folk. We like to know what they are singing about and sometimes they are so incoherent that it makes it a bit difficult. I like it very much. It's the kind of thing that if I went out I would like to jig around to, and I love the line about when the lights go down and you can guess the rest. That was saucy. I think it deserves to do well, and good luck to Roxy Music.

Roxy were obviously not only playing the generation game by ensnaring old-timers into their ever-growing cohort of followers, but were also, as Forsyth mentions, heading for the disco in search of recruits. "I was always interested in dance records," says Ferry, looking back:

I spent a lot of time in clubs, I guess. It was really irritating that when we went out anywhere, there was never any of our music played in any clubs, because it wasn't really dance music. So I wanted to introduce something. I always wanted to do something where you'd see people actually getting up to dance, rather than sitting down when it came on. And to an extent, "Love Is The Drug" was good for that.

Producer Chris Thomas adds:

The song was written for a B-side, an Andy Mackay track that was heavy on the saxophone, and it didn't have any bearing on what was to follow. It was like, "OK, let's do one of Andy's songs now, here are the chords." It was a great tune for rowing to. We used to fool around in the studio and mime the Vikings rowing song across the sea, invading! It had no lyric and no one had any idea of what the song was going to be about. And then Bryan came in and put down the vocal, and we just couldn't believe it. The whole thing was completely transformed.

At the beginning of the song, Ferry, the loner out for some serious girl action, can be heard walking through a gravel car park, opening his door, and, in a Kraftwerk-aping moment, turning the key in the ignition. As the car revs up, so does Gustafson's famous bass line. A short, sexy lick from Mackay on the sax, and we're off: a groove to die for, an astonishingly taut drum sound from Thompson, and Ferry's tale of the thrill of the chase:

"Aggravated, spare for days
I troll downtown the red light place
Jump up bubble up, what's in store?
Love is the drug and I need to score."

(Words and music: Bryan Ferry and
Andy Mackay, 1975)

The title is really a bit of a misnomer. More than anything else, this is a song about the need for quick and obligation-free sex, rather than love in all its contradictions and depths of emotion.

Elsewhere on the album there are sly hints at Roxy's past. The fantastic squawking synth that announces the disco-driven second single, "Both Ends Burning", and the chill two-and-a-half minutes of avant-garde menace that begins the album's best song, the brilliant "Sentimental Fool", remind us of the original Roxy Music. Elsewhere, however, Roxy seem unsure of their sound. "She Sells", co-written with Eddie Jobson, is announced with a great piano figure, and there's a lightness of touch quite at odds with the darker themes explored in other Roxy songs, as well as switches in tempo, mood and focus. All the way through the album, the bass licks have been seriously funked-up as Roxy Music respond to the dance-oriented climate. "Whirlwind" is a storming slab of Roxy rock, "End Of The Line" and "Could It Happen To Me" are reflective and delightful and "Just Another High" is a great anthemic ending.

Overall, though, *Siren* lacks the gravitas of the previous four albums. Recorded on 16-track, it moves away from the denser textures of *Country Life* (recorded on 24-track). It was far and away the most mainstream Roxy offering to date. Well-crafted although slightly subdued, it lacks the helter-skelter twists and turns of the previous records. Nevertheless, in Britain, the album sold strongly, reaching Number 4. It met with almost blanket approval from the British press, the only exception being Angus MacKinnon, writing for *Street Life*, who was one of the few reviewers to detect that there was something amiss, although not even he knew what it was, as the ending of his review clearly shows: "*Siren* is static electricity, in suspension, with neither earthing nor starbound pulse." Er, come again?

The Roxy Music 1975 UK tour started at the Liverpool Empire on October 3. The support act was the Sadistic Mika band, managed by their very own Simon Puxley. Roxy were under-rehearsed, and the album release delayed. "The people who arrange these things always think they should take less time than they do," was Ferry's defensive response when asked by *NME* why *Siren* had yet to hit the shops, even though the tour had already started. "And when one is working on something that's of real importance, on something that you really want to do your best, then if it's a question of running a week over, that week has to be taken."

What was most interesting about the *Siren* shows was that, for the first time, the tour was promoted as featuring "Bryan Ferry and Roxy Music", purportedly "because the group's various solo projects have led to speculation about a split in Roxy". Indeed, by autumn 1975, Ferry wasn't the only one with a solo star profile. Outside interests meant that the rest of Roxy Music were in demand too. Mackay had recorded a solo album, *In Search Of Eddie Riff*, and had just released a single, "Wild Weekend". In addition to reforming his original band, Quiet Sun, to make the *Mainstream* album, Manzanera had also recorded a solo album, *Diamond Head*, and was much sought after as a session musician and collaborator.

Roxy's schedule for the autumn was a heavy one. Not only was a full UK tour booked, but also there would be dates in the United States and Canada to follow in short order. John Gustafson remembers one television appearance particularly vividly, and recalls that Phil Manzanera was not without his little rock-star foibles:

Oh yes, the TV show – *Supersonic*. We were in the dressing room about to go on and Phil Manzanera said, "I've forgotten my socks", and I said, "You've got socks on now, what's the matter with those?" He said, "They don't go with my shoes and my trousers, I need black socks." I had black socks under my cowboy boots, so he said, "can you lend me your socks?" And I said, all right, yeah, sure. Then I couldn't get my boots on without my socks, because cowboy boots have hard ledges inside, so he went on with my socks and I went on barefoot. I thought it was ridiculous. Because you couldn't see his socks, or his shoes for that matter.

Phil was also a bit funny about his guitars. I remember we were in Auckland Town Hall in New Zealand and he had all his guitars in their own room next door to the dressing room of the other people. I went in and started playing James Burton stuff, you know, sort of bendy things, and he didn't like that at all. He said, "I've just tuned all those", and I said, "Don't worry Phil, I know how to tune", and it was very odd. I actually never touched them again: he was very touchy about it.

On the *Siren* tour, Ferry would make as dramatic an entry as ever. The opener was "Sentimental Fool": Ferry, intoning the words of the first verse offstage, would make his theatrical flourish of an entry, walking in from the wings imploring, "How can I go on?" But the splendour and pomp of the previous two tours were gone: no palm trees, no thirty-foot eagle. What we got instead was Ferry in uniform, an update of the mildly fascistic attire of some of the *Country Life* performances, with a new, Americanised twist – a black tie tucked in above the third button, pale khaki shirt with long sleeves rolled up, lapels, a Roxy Music emblem on his epaulette, and slightly darker khaki trousers. The look was described by Ferry as "a kind of GI Joe". Two female backing singers in pale blue WRAF-style uniforms would be this year's Roxy "tottie". Another first would be the inclusion in the live set of various solo songs. Manzanera's "Diamond Head", Mackay's "Wild Weekend" and Ferry's "The 'In' Crowd" and "Hard Rain's" were featured, along with the debut live performance of "For Your Pleasure", a goodly chunk of *Siren* and Roxy classics such as "Street Life" and "Virginia Plain".

Perhaps the wildest night of the tour was in Glasgow. "If I had to attend a Roxy gig, I'd go to Glasgow," Ferry told *Sounds* in October '75. The atmosphere was always special, particularly for Andy Mackay, who was treated by the press like a returning hero even though he had been born and bred in London. "He'd never even been to Scotland before he joined Roxy," laughed his wife, Jane. *Sounds'* Jonh Ingham wrote:

> The band broke out of their studiousness, Mackay duck-walking and posing with Manzanera, the two girls gyrating and finger-popping. Their position at times seemed a bit superfluous, but during the last numbers a gaggle of girls assembled beneath them, copying every gesture, and their role between clear: surrogate audience.
>
> On the last night: a second encore. Reading from a page of lyrics, Ferry sang "A Hard Rain's …' … Already some of [the fans] had khaki shirts and a black tie neatly tucked between second and third buttons. During the last verse, Bryan ran out of paper and finished off in a display of "bom-boms", mumbles and scatting. A great moment."

"In Glasgow, there was a huge howling mob outside," recalls Gustafson. "It was difficult to get in and out." It was, however, in Glasgow that the gap between the permanent members of Roxy and the hired hand became quite clear to Gustafson. "It was quite a mercenary decision to join Roxy Music," he admits, "but I wasn't really encouraged, or made to feel part of the band. For example, at the Glasgow Apollo they broke the house record, and some guy came in at the end of the gig with awards to commemorate that, but only for them, not me. I thought it was quite rude that they didn't insist that I got whatever it was anyway. They didn't seem bothered by it either."

The two major concerts of the tour were at the Wembley Empire Pool on October 17 and 18, shows that were also filmed. Here, there was yet another minor sartorial hitch, remembers Gustafson: "I used to wear these jeans with a thousand patches on. The only time I did wear anything special was for the two Wembley concerts we did back-to-back. I had this short white zipper jacket and tight white trousers, and the second night I turned up in something else and they went crazy. They said, 'We're filming it!' So I had to go home and fetch this stuff, and it nearly delayed the gig."

In the New Year, Roxy once again headed for the United States, followed by Canada and selected gigs in Scandinavia. This time, however, it would be without John Gustafson. "They asked me to join the band after we recorded *Siren*, and I'd already done the photograph session for the album cover," says Gustafson:

Because I didn't agree to join them, they didn't put my picture on. Very petty, isn't it? The reason I didn't play with them any more was that my agent was asking outrageous money by then, and I was getting it. They were due for an American tour, and I remember Eddie Jobson coming up and asking, "Are you doing the American tour?" I said, "Nobody's asked me yet." And apparently there were negotiations going on between my agent and their agent, and my agent had gone over the top asking for outrageous money, and they called a halt to it and got somebody else.

From my point of view, Roxy was a bout of strangeness in between all my favourite types of music. It was a band I would never have formed or joined through choice, playing the kind of music I would never have played. It was more like fortune came up to me, knocked on my door, and said, come and play these tracks and then move on. And I moved on to the Ian Gillan Band, more or less without a break.

With Rick Wills recruited on bass and backing vocals, Roxy played to increasingly enthusiastic audiences in the United Sates. On one show, Ferry took the plunge and dedicated "Prairie Rose" to his new love, Jerry Hall. Ron Ross, writing for the *Phonograph Record*, argued that Roxy Music were beginning to close the gap between AM and FM radio. They were an intelligent rock act who had crossed over:

> The exciting aspect of Roxy's acceptance is that, despite the ever-calculated weirdness, they don't even seem to be controversial; "Love Is The Drug" is a hit on both CKLW (AM) in Detroit and KSAN-FM in San Francisco, and for all the right reasons. For the first time in years, album artists don't have to be afraid of a hit single, and AM stations aren't afraid of playing a hit single by a progressive artist.

For Ross, Roxy's success, like Bowie's the previous year, was the result of their image being de-glammed: out goes the glitter, in come the suits, and – hey presto! – America can't resist you. In the spring of 1976, "Love Is The Drug" reached Number 30 in the US charts, the highest position achieved by any Roxy or Ferry single. It was hardly the massive hit Ferry and Mark Fenwick must have longed for, but it was a start at least.

Then came the decision to end Roxy Music. On June 26, 1976, it was announced that Roxy Music were embarked on a "devolution"; their energies were henceforth to be channelled into non-Roxy projects. It was a bolt from the blue – or was it?

By the middle of 1976, Ferry was beginning to feel he had gone as far as he could go with Roxy Music. With his own solo career so important to him, he thought it was time to finish the group. Mackay and Manzanera were both increasingly involved in outside projects. Manzanera had by now branched out into production, working on the first album by New Zealand newcomers Split Enz, who supported Roxy on some of the *Siren* dates and who would later go on to great success in the early eighties before morphing into Crowded House. He was also in demand as a collaborator and guitarist on a variety of other projects, including work with John Cale and Nico.

Andy Mackay was busy working on *Rock Follies*, a new series for Thames TV. In the spring of 1975, Andy was put in touch with the New York playwright Howard Schumann, who had been commissioned to write a six-part drama about a female rock trio. The result would eventually be two series of the celebrated TV musical *Rock Follies* starring Charlotte Cornwell, Julie Covington, and Rula Lenska, as well as a Number 1 soundtrack album, a BAFTA Award for Best Television Drama and a 1977 hit single for its actress stars with "OK?" Mackay temporarily became arguably the most successful solo member of Roxy Music.

With Eddie Jobson also working on solo material, it seemed that the band were naturally – and almost inevitably – drifting apart. Manzanera was to explain it, rather obliquely, like this: "Well, I think we all got tired and there's so many other factors involved; complex situations with everyone's personal lives and wives and tours and money and publishing and lawyers and managers and all these things make it terribly complicated, the whole thing." "The awful thing was we weren't the sort of people who'd have a stand-up row about anything as a rule," reflected Ferry. "Everyone would go off and sulk."

There is no doubt there were also interpersonal problems too. There were reports that the rest of Roxy Music were sick to the back teeth of Ferry acting the star; reports of preferential treatment and hired limos for the singer whilst the band made do with less-than-luxurious treatment began to percolate out of the Roxy camp. "We never really broke up," claimed Ferry in 1977. "It was just really a case of being together for too long in one stretch. I think after playing with people for a long time you can feel a bit stifled. It's a very natural thing to want to have to change." "It just became obvious that the time had come for a natural break," he later added. "There were lots of reasons. There was a bit of bad feeling about my solo career being so successful. Nothing was said, but I could feel it."

There would be angry letters from fans, and general sadness that arguably the best group of their day had decided to split. At the time, it certainly felt as if Roxy Music had gone forever. Heeding the first signs of an artistic decline, some fans managed to applaud their bravery to bow out at the top. However, Eddie Jobson claims that the decision to end Roxy Music was taken with purely financial considerations in mind:

Roxy disbanded in 1976 as a way of getting out of debt and making a profit. The expense of maintaining a road crew, equipment, a major-domo, a publicist and the first-class-only road lifestyle was all removed by disbanding. They could sit at home and let the royalties pour in without the expenses. Of course, when the royalties started to run low, then they had to reform and make another album. They didn't bother telling me they were disbanding until the week that they did it. I had only a couple of weeks to find another job, which I did – with Frank Zappa.

Jobson went on to a successful career outside of the band. In the Roxy years he was already in-demand as a session musician and played on a variety of albums including Dana Gillespie's *Ain't Gonna Play No Second Fiddle* (1974), King Crimson's *U.S.A.* (1975) and John Entwistle's *Mad Dog* (1975). In addition, Jobson also appeared on Andy Mackay's *In Search of Eddie Riff* and *Rock Follies*, Manzanera's *Diamond Head* and *Listen Now*, and Ferry's *These Foolish Things* and *Let's Stick Together*. He also played with Zappa, formed UK with John Wetton, Bill Bruford and Allan Holdsworth, and later in the eighties found fame not only with numerous solo projects but also as a member of Jethro Tull and Yes. In fact, at one stage, his Stateside commercial successes and media profile was arguably higher than any of the other members of his former band.

What looked as if it would be the last-ever Roxy Music album, *Viva! Roxy Music* was released in the summer of 1976 and included just eight tracks recorded live on the previous three Roxy tours. When putting the album together, the band had listened to hours and hours of material taped between October 1973 and November 1975: a total of 39 songs recorded in 127 different versions. A double album had originally been planned, which, with hindsight, might have worked better, since there was no other Roxy compilation in the shops, and many of the band's well-known songs were absent from the line-up on *Viva!* The cover photos were taken at the Empire Pool, Wembley gig on the most recent tour. The tracks which were finally selected for the album were recorded at three different venues – Glasgow Apollo in November 1973, Newcastle City Hall in November 1974 and Wembley in October 1975 – although it was never confirmed which tracks came from which show.

As a demonstration of Roxy's live power, *Viva! Roxy Music* is an interesting period piece. However, overall it's a slightly flat, uninspired collection. None of the live versions actually improved on the original cuts, or redefined them in any significant way. And the fact that they were culled from different dates and venues meant that Roxy fans hoping for a memento of a particular tour, with songs appearing in the sequence in which they were played on the night, were bound to be disappointed. The album struggled to reach Number 20 in the UK charts in the summer of 1976.

Whilst Ferry was busying himself closing down the Roxy project, his old sparring partner Brian Eno was putting it about. Eighteen months after his car accident he was increasingly embracing the questionable delights of ambient music, and was to spend the next decade putting it into practice. Of course, he would do other things too, including occasionally appearing on stage, giving lectures, collaborating, writing more conventional pop songs and, of course, producing, but his big idea was the idea of music as space and environment: not as background music, but as music designed for specific locations. A succession of Eno recordings, starting with what is still his best album, 1975's *Another Green World*, and running through to perhaps the purest expression of ambient music, 1982's *Ambient 4: On Land*, secured his place in popular music history. None of these albums were instant successes, but the Eno catalogue has sold consistently over the decades and now probably runs into millions of units shifted. However, it was the importance, the cultural cachet and the influence these records had that was much more important, to Eno as well as to his supporters.

Eno's people were never backward in coming forward. Here's a snippet from one of their ludicrously hyperbolic press releases of the time:

> Brian Peter George St. John le Baptiste de la Salle Eno, now known simply as Brian Eno, is perhaps the most creative force in contemporary music today. A self-proclaimed "non-musician", he has been voted the fourth best instrumentalist in the world – in the miscellaneous category because Brian Eno definitely cannot be categorised. He is a modern "Renaissance Man": musician, poet, trained artist and consummate Technologist.

However, the PR guff in this case actually matched the quality of the music. *Another Green World* is as alive with futures as Roxy's first record. The utterly beguiling album spawned an instrumental title track which was later used for the *Arena* arts programme on BBC 2, and a succession of astonishing songs: beautiful, mysterious and delicate. With Robert Fripp's guitar and Phil Collins' drumming, it's an album as important as any made by the band he left. Later, 1977's *Before And*

After Science, confirmed Eno as one of rock's most important artists. Original Roxy fans were hopelessly hooked by the invention of it all. Here's writer and broadcaster Mark Radcliffe, bubbling over with the sort of enthusiasm many had for the Eno albums:

> Eno's never really been a solo artist in the sense that Bryan is. I mean, Bryan Ferry was the figurehead and everybody watched him, whereas Eno, to the general pop masses, has had more anonymity, there's probably less expected of him. But Brian Eno has made some fantastic pop albums and he more or less almost single-handedly invented the whole ambient scene, the ramifications of which are still with us now in many, many ways. I think Eno is also underestimated, I suspect by himself, as a maker of pop records. I really loved those first few Eno albums, I love *Taking Tiger Mountain By Strategy*: they do work as pop records because they're melodic, almost childish in some of their melodies, and yet they're full of little touches of weirdness and ambience and creative uses of the sound which just kind of twist them slightly. Then you've got *Another Green World*, with pop songs such as "I'll Come Running To Tie Your Shoe" – brilliant! And then you've got some more of the noodling, ambient things coming through. My favourite is probably *Before And After Science*: I think it's bloody marvellous. If I'm sitting at home and I'm trying to write something, I'll pull a record out and I'll quite often stick on "Here He Comes", because it's wonderful.

However, while Eno was three solo albums into one of the most thrilling solo careers in pop, Ferry appeared intent on branding himself as an entertainer. With the band brand name as a safety net, he could embark on ever more populist moves with a degree of confidence. Now that Roxy was finished, Ferry was in danger of simply being regarded as cultural irrelevance. He was now, perhaps for the first time in his life, a celebrity rather than a rock star.

Ferry's romance with Jerry Hall was continuing apace and, within six months, had led to a proposal of marriage. After the *Siren* cover shoot, the two had spent a couple of days together at Ferry's home before going their separate ways. Ferry had visited Hall in New York and Hall had spent Christmas 1975 *chez* Ferry in London. Then came a holiday in Mustique. In her biography, *Tall Tales*, Hall recalls the night Ferry popped the question:

I've never been a big drinker, you know. But this night was [an] exception. And I started telling everyone the story about how I'd been girls' champion leg wrestler back in Mesquite. Then I decided to give them a demonstration. And I'm doing this leg wrestlin' and being real loud mannered and, you know, hootin' and hollerin', and all these people are like eggin' me on. They thought it was so funny. Then I started telling Texas lines like, "Fatter than a hog on a fence", or "redder than a fox's ass in gooseberry time". And Bryan was really embarrassed. He thought I was making a fool of myself.

So when we got back to our room he was very upset with me, and I was crying and everything, because he said I'd embarrassed him in front of is friends with my leg wrestlin'. And I said, "You can't tell me what to do!" And then … all of a sudden, he said he wanted to marry me.

Hall decided to move from her model base with the Ford Agency in New York to live with Ferry in London. Hall, by her own admission, had two sides to her personality: the "ladylike" version of herself, which she got from her mother, and the "rowdy side" she got from being with cowboys and going to rodeos. Ferry, for his part, found it hard to cope with Hall. "Part of him liked that I was a model," she says. "He thought I was glamorous and funny. And then there was the other side of him that wanted a wholesome, aristocratic country life and wanted me to be a different kind of girl."

In London, Ferry introduced Hall to high culture. The combination of Ferry's extensive library and his frequent absences from home led Hall to discover Noel Coward, PG Wodehouse and Evelyn Waugh. Meanwhile, Hall was the hostess with the mostest, preparing dinner for guests and taking afternoon tea with smoked salmon and cucumber sandwiches on brown bread. Ferry introduced Hall to his circle of friends, including Charles Benson, a tipster, and his fiancée Caroline. "It was very grand and very social," recalled Hall in *Tall Tales*. "Once we even went together to stay with the Aga Khan in Sardinia. I loved that." But, according to Hall, it was her housewifely duties that brought Ferry pleasure: "Bryan would get excited about anything I did that was like a housewife. He loved it when I took up needlepoint."

In summer 1976, Ferry bought a large estate in west Sussex designed by William Clough Ellis, the architect of Portmerion. In a beautiful setting, it had its own stream, which dried up in the withering heat of that summer. "We were so excited by it," says Hall. "It was like kids exploring – we would go for walks in the woods and look at everything. And we dreamed about how we'd fix it up. That's where I started to feel this nesting thing. I loved going from room to room thinking how I'd do this and that. I wanted to have lots of kids to fill it up."

In the months before punk rock broke big in the national consciousness, Ferry began recording a succession of cover versions of modest ambition and mediocre artistry. One song, a re-working of Wilbert Harrison's "Let's Stick Together", would, paradoxically, provide him with by far his biggest solo hit. The song was a favourite from Ferry's days with the Gas Board. In early 1970, Canned Heat had reworked it into a Number 2 (as "Let's Work Together"), but Ferry's version went back to the source. John Wetton was once again called in to play on the record. To Wetton, Ferry's attention to detail, combined with a secrecy bordering on paranoia, was becoming increasingly evident:

I think Bryan puts a different hat on. He becomes Bryan the rock star, as opposed to Bryan the lothario. He's always tried to separate that, but, to me, it's inseparable: you are what you are. Your persona in the studio is the same persona you have outside of the studio. So I think it's a slice of schizophrenia going on there. I don't get it. When I go into a studio, I don't like 100 people in the booth, or in the control room: I like to keep it fairly clear, just me talking to one person who's hearing the same thing I'm hearing. Bryan won't have anybody in the control room, and he's got producers who are almost as paranoid as he is. Chris Thomas produced "Let's Stick Together" and we did 48 takes of the bass. He was as anal as Bryan was. It's not musical finesse that they're after: it's just paranoia that *they haven't got it yet*. Whereas any normal person would say, yeah, take three, we've got it – wrap it up. This kind of thing really starts to shake the foundations of who you are. I doubt whether Elvis was even bothered about how the bass sounded on his records.

Chris Thomas was anal but Bryan was just paranoid, even to the point of having to know who came to the studio on any given day. You're talking about a very strange person. If you're recording in central London, it's got your name on a bloody big board when you walk in, so people are going to know where you're recording including the music paper journalists, so you may as well accept that.

I have not the faintest idea why the guys in Roxy Music were, or are, so secretive. My attitude was, who cares what we did last night? Who's going to get a kick out of this? "Oh no, we shouldn't really say anything," was the answer from the people who surround them. Phil particularly was very secretive and paranoid about stuff getting out.

Despite the torture of the recording process, "Let's Stick Together" really did the trick for Ferry, and it continues to do so to this day. Go to any party populated by the over-forties and you can guarantee that, as the first bar of that blurting sax rings out, dozens of men in pullovers will get up for some serious "dad dancing".

Ferry seems to realise that he is to blame for this, one of the most harrowing aspects of the middle-aged party: "Funnily enough, the best dance song I did was 'Let's Stick Together'. It was the only record, really, where you'd see people jumping to their feet when it came on. It's got a bit of something about it." The video featured a slightly miserable-looking Chris Spedding in leather, Ferry in a suit, and the yelping sound of Jerry Hall in a leopard-skin dress.

In the summer of 1976, Ferry, sporting a new and rather anachronistic Errol Flynn moustache, would be photographed looking every inch the complacent and mildly irrelevant pop star he was in danger of becoming. He had just recorded some songs for the "Extended Play" EP of cover versions. The lead track was a cover of the Everly Brother's classic "The Price Of Love" and the EP also included covers of Jimmy Reed's "Shame Shame Shame", the Beatles' "It's Only Love" and a cover of Gallagher And Lyle's recent hit, "Heart On My Sleeve". John Wetton, for one, didn't get it: "Ferry doesn't capitalise on major brush strokes, which you can do, quite easily. To me, doing Everly Brothers covers at the time, I thought, why are you doing this? I though it was a mistake. It was a bit of a red herring. It was just something to satisfy the fans – the legions of women in the north of England who would have bought it."

"Let's Stick Together" was a Number 4 hit, lodging itself in the UK charts for ten weeks in the summer of 1976. Later that summer, the "Extended Play" EP would reach Number 7. In the autumn, an odds-and-sods collection of recent Ferry projects – the hit single, the hit EP, plus remakes of some classic Roxy songs such as "2HB" and "Chance Meeting" – charted in the UK under the name of *Let's Stick Together*. It appeared that Bryan Ferry's solo career was headed for unparalleled commercial success.

According to a 2004 report published by the New Economics Foundation think tank, 1976 was the best year on record as far as "quality of life" was concerned. Indeed, many look back at 1976 through the proverbial rose-tinted spectacles: it was the last year before economic crisis took hold and the country was plunged into biting recession. The summer was the driest since 1772. Plucky James Hunt was world motor-racing champion. There were plagues of biting ladybirds, but us resolute Brits didn't mind. Everything in the garden was, apparently, rosy. Except, of course, for the bloody music.

The apogee of extreme noise terror came during that summer of 1976. In fact, we can date it quite precisely to July 17, when Demis Roussos reached Number 1 in the UK singles charts with the "Roussos Phenomenon" EP, promoted by the wrist-slashing refrain of the song "Forever And Ever", which sounded like a man being turned into a eunuch. British pop culture could take no more.

By then, 1976 had already witnessed some of the worst Number 1's of all time: "Save Your Kisses For Me" by Brotherhood Of Man, "No Charge" by the catatonic JJ Barrie, "Combine Harvester" by the Wurzels. Even the kitsch "I Love To Love (But My Baby Loves To Dance)" by Tina Charles was completely terrible, as were the new Midge Ure-fronted teen idols, Slik, with their portentous "Forever And Ever". But the bearded, portly, and frankly unlistenable Roussos finally convinced us all that pop music had to change.

Punk – which had been fermenting since 1974 – fomented in 1976. Although yet to be signed, the Sex Pistols, Clash, Stranglers and Damned were already leading a violent fight-back in the pubs, clubs and universities where they hadn't already been banned by nervous local authorities who saw the beginning of a new youth rebellion. Ferry – with his model girlfriend, Chelsea pad, suits, moustache and cover versions – became outdated almost overnight. One of the sharpest observers of the intricacies and intrigues of the London scene, cultural commentator Peter York, gave a convincing explanation of why Ferry ran into trouble. York said that Ferry's fans stuck with him as he started to make real money and moved out of Earl's Court because, in the classic ghetto way, *he was doing it for them*:

Those spectacular girls, the stylisation, those magazine spreads with Jerry – that was what you *did* with hot new money. You patronised the new, the glamorous. The people never resent serious glamour – good luck to him, they say. And whatever he did, it was just a look ... So after [Ferry] had done Café Society from 1974 to 1977 he started on the real thing, rather in the manner of, say, Noël Coward or Fred Astaire. In an earlier age people would have said that he had found his own level. He was rich, handsome, well educated and well-mannered; why should he *not* knock around on the country-house circuit if he wished? In the late seventies, one would meet totally crusty people who said they had just met a *delightful* pop star in the country, not what they'd expected at all, so quiet and well-mannered. It was always Bryan. He had always defended it intelligently and quietly when challenged, saying that he believed in "social exploration" and that he was not, after all, public property except on stage – why should he be bound by the inverted snobbery of the plain and unadventurous? But it was against the temper of the times, against the clichés of the music business. And the exploration seemed very much one way. Difficult to swallow, difficult to follow, for the stylists could barely imagine a country house, let alone aspire to it. Trousers and attitude, Bryan, that's what counts on the club floor.

No longer an ironist, no longer playing at dressing up, Ferry was soaked to the skin in a deluge of upper-class toffery, style-culture buffoonery and high-cultural irrelevancy. In 1975, punk impresario and fashion designer Malcolm McLaren had couched his attack on the rock Establishment in suitably black-and-white sloganeering terms with his production of a new T-shirt for his *Sex* shop. Emblazoned with the words "You're Gonna Wake Up One Morning And *Know* What Side Of The Bed You've Been Lying On!", it divided life into "Hates" on the left and "Loves" on the right. McLaren's "verbal rap", as Clash manager Bernie Rhodes called it, positioned Mick Jagger, the Liberal Party, Yes, Melvyn Bragg and – of course – Bryan Ferry on the left, with Iggy Pop, Joe Orton and Eddie Cochran on the right.

Yet, paradoxically, at the very moment that Ferry began to be vilified and taunted, his influence on style culture was growing almost by the minute. Throughout 1975 and 1976, a shift in youth culture repositioned Ferry, and more particularly Roxy Music, at the centre of the cultural debate. Many of the movers and shakers in the incipient punk scene were also huge Roxy Music fans, and, although many were disappointed with the current product, one could hardly fail to notice that Roxy Music were a major influence. For some, Ferry was an even bigger influence than Bowie; the sense of detachment, the irony, the artistic intelligence, and the disorientating music of the first few records all formed a template that the arty punks knew mapped out a future for them. "You started to realise that it wasn't just you and your friends, that it was more than just music and clothes: it was what films you saw, and everything. It became a lifestyle. Roxy perpetrated that: seeing Eno have tea with Salvador Dali," says Simon Barker, one of that small, though influential group that fuelled the initial thrust of punk, the Bromley contingent. "Bowie had paved the way, but they took it a little further."

One of punk's most important bands, Siouxsie And The Banshees, actually formed at a Roxy Music concert at the Empire Pool, London in late 1975. "I was working as a temporary accounts clerk in the offices of RCA records just so I could get free Bowie/Reed/Ronson records as soon as they came out, but I had decided to leave and I pledged that I would never work for anyone again," says the band's Steven Severin today:

The evening of the day I left was the evening I met Siouxsie at Wembley. I went with my school friend, Simon Barker, and he had met Siouxsie through mutual acquaintances just a few days before, so he introduced me. I was in full Eddie Riff gear that night – drainpipes, blond quiff, red bomber jacket with zebra collar and shoes that had white crepe platforms and black patent uppers with two white diagonal stripes. My shoes were pretty unique and, because of the Adidas-style stripes, Siouxsie said to me with a wink, "You look very sporty."

Steven Severin had always been a huge Roxy Music fan:

By the turn of 1972, I was into Zappa, Beefheart, Can and Amon Düül II. T. Rex's "Metal Guru" and Bowie's "Starman" intrigued me, but I wasn't completely sold. I remember hearing "Virginia Plain" late one night on Radio Luxembourg and it completely blew me away. I think I'd read a live review previously in *Melody Maker* so I was aware of the name. I rushed out and bought it, and every subsequent release until they split. I saw them live several times, with and without Eno. They were always majestic. I liked Eno leaving! It gave us *Country Life* AND *Here Come The Warm Jets*.

Roxy were actually a bigger influence on me than Bowie. They were more inscrutable. I loved the photo of them having afternoon tea with Salvador Dali at the Pierre Hotel in New York. It looked like the most exciting, glamorous life imaginable. I used to pore over the gate-fold to *For Your Pleasure*. Bowie might have sung about aliens, but Roxy looked, and more significantly, sounded, like they really were extraterrestrials.

Severin was part of the Bromley contingent, the infamous gang of like-minded stylists, rock fans and would-be stars who would play a crucial role in establishing the broad intellectual trajectory of punk in the mid-seventies. Roxy were an important contemporary British influence on the scene. "Well, the Bromley contingent had its roots in a group of boys that went to either Bromley Tech, like myself and Hanif Kureishi, or Bromley Grammar, where Billy Idol went," says Severin:

> We had all grown our hair and gone to all the festivals during 1969-71, but the rise of "glam" caused a teenage schism! Everybody else went with it more for the fact that girls liked Bolan and Bowie rather than for love of the music. Simon, Billy and I would fracture off from the rest of this group via Sparks, the New York Dolls, and, finally, the Sex Pistols. Hanif was on the periphery of this group because he was a year older and into Dylan.

Severin recalls that Roxy Music, along with Bowie, began to make an impact on the disco-dominated club scene around 1975. It was an impact that affected both punk, and, a few years later, the New Romantic scene of the early eighties: "The club scene, such as it was, consisted basically of 'Love Is The Drug' wedged between KC & The Sunshine Band and Sister Sledge," says Severin. "The only time I heard Roxy records outside of my home was in late 1975, when they started doing Bowie nights down at a club called Crackers in Wardour Street, Soho. Up until then it was disco, disco, disco."

In terms of dressing up and street style, it would be Bowie that would initially make the biggest impact: "People tended to copy Bowie much, much more," recalls Severin. However, the *Siren* GI Joe look was the first Ferry image to be copied on a mass scale, and with not always great results. "The khaki period was when the poor unfortunates came off like extras from 'Sergeant Bilko'," says Severin. "It was never a good look. In fact, I thought Roxy split at completely the right time. The venues were getting too big, the audiences too homogenous and the "look" too simplistic. All that forties army stuff didn't do it for me. But *Siren* was a great swansong."

What Roxy Music did was not so much influence punk musically (although songs like "Editions Of You" and "Street Life" had always hinted at punk with their swagger and aggression) as in terms of attitude and approach. "What attracted me to Roxy and to the Velvets was the idea that you could mix, blend and borrow, not only from other pop music, but from other art forms too," is how Severin puts it. "John Cale had brought the avant-garde to the Velvets, and Ferry brought pop art to Roxy." There would be other high-profile Roxy casualties too. Paul Cook, the drummer with the Sex Pistols, revered Paul Thompson. His erstwhile chum, Steve Jones, might have famously nicked much of the PA when Bowie played Hammersmith Odeon in July 1973 but he also managed to walk out with a strobe tuner from Roxy Music at around the same time. Cook and Jones' band at the time was called the Strand.

However, it wasn't just the punk rockers that felt an affinity with the Roxy cause. Almost contemporaneous with the appearance of, as Dave Laing put it, one-chord wonder guitarists and gobbing and goading lead singers, came the statuesque one-finger-playing synth specialists. Around 1976, far from London's punk scene, doomy Northerners were perfecting their own brand of pop rebellion, and Roxy Music were a central inspiration. Phil Oakey of the Human League remembers the coming of Roxy Music as the final piece in the jigsaw:

We were arty. We were always at the film theatre at the library, which showed obscure European films. We were into Nic Roeg and Stanley Kubrick. We loved David Bowie. I think it was quite important that we didn't want to be macho. A world where heavy-metal guitarists, even though they were fiddly-diddly on guitar, were *real* men never really suited us. Music was big for us, and when Curved Air came out, we thought, oh, there might be some music that suits us. There was Cockney Rebel, there was Yes as well, but the key for us was Roxy Music. They played a free show at Sheffield University and really, that day, everything changed. We only went because of the instrumentation. There was a big buzz around Sheffield that here was a group who had both a synthesiser and a mellotron on stage at the same time. Those guys walked on in high heels, make-up and Lurex and our world changed that day.

Punk, new wave and electronica reclaimed the best bits of the Roxy oeuvre and secured the band's reputation at a time when many of the band's contemporaries saw their own reputations going down the pan. Yet Ferry's seemingly unstoppable drift towards more easily accessible repertoire continued throughout the mid-seventies. One reason, if only indirectly, was Ferry's continuing desire to become successful in the country that, in his eyes, set the standards for cultural excellence: America. His next two solo albums were quite conscious attempts to turn himself into a global superstar. John Wetton provides a fascinating insight into the workings of the Ferry camp at the time:

> I think Bryan would have cut off a limb to have a hit in America, but America wasn't having it. We were on tour somewhere when Boston's "More Than A Feeling" came on the radio, and Mark Fenwick turned to me and said, "Brilliant fuckin' record, isn't it? Brilliant." And I said, "Yes it is, it's a marvellous piece of music." And I could see in his eyes that all he wanted was to have one of those.

Punk was a perplexing time for many and not just for Bryan Ferry. Of the old school rockers, only David Bowie emerged with his reputation largely intact, and this was because he cleverly absented himself from the UK and began making very different sorts of music in Germany. Since so many of the original punks were also Bowie fans, it was unsurprising that Bowie would be the only British rocker to retain his enormous cultural cachet. At the end of 1977, *Melody Maker* chose *Heroes* – not debuts by the Stranglers, the Clash or the Pistols – as its album of the year. In the punk wars, if you were a millionaire rocker with a name like Rod, Eric or Elton, you were in for a rough ride. Rod Stewart's sales held up well and he even managed a UK Number 1 in the summer of 1977 with "I Don't Want To Talk About It", but Elton John's career went into commercial freefall.

Ferry's own position was ambiguous. Punks tended to like – indeed, love – the Eno-era Roxy Music and appreciated the sense of daring and style, but otherwise they regarded Ferry as a traitor to the cause. In 1976, when the Sex Pistols and the Clash began their urban warfare against the British Establishment and roots reggae and white punk began their astonishing mix, Ferry was photographed on a tennis court, wearing an Errol Flynn 'tache and beaming to camera to promote an album of cover versions. During the tension-filled summer of 1976, which erupted at the end of August during London's Notting Hill Carnival, Ferry was settling in at his huge estate in Sussex with his beautiful Texan girlfriend. His only care was whether the hydrangeas were getting enough water.

Retribution was swift. The press had targeted him in 1974: now, in early 1977, it was the turn of his public. *In Your Mind*, recorded in 1976 and released in the spring of 1977, was a lacklustre solo album with an out-of-character lousy cover. Bereft of the sonic weirdness that Mackay and Manzanera were wont to bring in Roxy, Ferry was treading musical water. It was the first Ferry album to contain only new material, but it was evident that he was missing Roxy badly. The first single, "This Is Tomorrow", was catchy but old hat all the same. The title looked back (once again) to his art school influences. As previously noted, the *This Is Tomorrow* exhibition at the Whitechapel Art Gallery, London had featured his old teacher Richard Hamilton's pop art classic, *Just What Is It That Makes Today's Homes So Different, So Appealing?* However, whereas it was obvious how the images and motifs of pop art had inspired classics such as "Virginia Plain" and "Do The Strand", it was hard to see how they were meant to relate to this likeable but defiantly mid-tempo Ferry rocker of 1977.

"This Is Tomorrow" would, however, keep Ferry in the UK charts, and actually climbed as high as Number 9 in the early spring of 1977. The follow-up, "Tokyo Joe", was also a Top 20 hit. However, with its dull melodies, soul-tinged backing and flat production, *In Your Mind* was by far the worst product ever to be released under the Bryan Ferry name. Even Ferry has little love for it. "[It is] my least successful album by a long chalk … it always sounds very square to me," he has admitted. "[But] there are some very nice top line things and songs which could have been really good, I think."

In Your Mind was recorded at Air Studios, London. George Martin was working in an adjoining studio on *The Beatles Live At The Hollywood Bowl*, but none of the fairy-dust magic of the Beatles classics permeated the studio walls to boost Ferry's material. Initially Chris Thomas was in the producer's chair, but, as Chris Spedding reveals, he didn't oversee the session for too long: "*In Your Mind* was produced by Chris Thomas, and half-way through, he left, and Bryan finished them with Steve Nye." The departure of Thomas was a major blow, particularly since his results with Ferry had hitherto been so good. "Whatever he produced always seemed to sound very good," says Spedding. "I never really figured out how or why. A lot of the times he'd leave the studio to have dinner and leave the engineer to work on something. I don't know what he told the engineer, but when we came back it always sounded fantastic. It seemed to be effortless on Chris's part – his results were always fantastic."

"*In Your Mind* was an attempt to break Ferry worldwide," says John Wetton:

And my take on that was that they booked the tour before they recorded the album, so it was actually in his mind that this would all happen, and of course it didn't. Australia was brilliant because he was coming on the back of "Let's Stick Together" but the rest of it didn't go well. In Japan and America they were almost twisting promoters' arms to put the shows on. Obviously the UK and Europe went well. I don't want to cast a cloak of doom over this whole thing, but I do think it demonstrates how easily the public are manipulated into thinking that something is great when it's not. I mean, to be a world-wide hit, you need a worldwide hit, and Roxy never, ever had that.

Australia was, indeed, one of the few territories where Ferry's popularity actually increased during this period. "He was not a struggling artist," says Chris Spedding. "I was in Australia with Bryan when 'God Save The Queen' was top of the charts, so we didn't get a sense of what was happening at all. He had already had his hit records so the punk thing didn't really affect him. It might have affected him later, but I had already stopped working with him by then."

As ever, while on tour Ferry maintained a certain distance between himself and his compadres. At a time when he might have benefited from fresh ideas musically, he was intent on writing and recording very much as a solo artist, says Wetton:

I remember having conversations with Chris Spedding in Australia. We were there for six weeks, and once we had done the initial set-up for the show, we were in each city for about a week. Chris and I discovered we had a common link in horse riding. We would get into the outback and get lost. We would do our best to ride out into the middle of nowhere. If we found our way back by four o'clock we'd be around for the soundcheck. We sort of paired up for the tour. It was great fun and I got the impression then that Bryan was using Chris as a kind of foil, but he would never allow him into the central fold.

In spring 1977, Ferry had toured medium-sized venues in the UK with a twelve-piece outfit that included Spedding on lead guitar as well as Manzanera and Thompson from Roxy. The set list was a smattering of Roxy Music (some unexpected, such as "Could It Happen To Me?" from *Siren*) and a swathe of solo cuts, including "You Go To My Head", "It's My Party", "The Price Of Love", "These Foolish Things" and the show-closing "Hard Rain's". But still to some, despite the magic and the power, Ferry was a gauche, awkward performer. "His stage movements would put Frankenstein in the Nureyev class," wrote a provincial journalist in February as the tour visited Leicester. The funny thing was that Ferry's straight-legged dancing and odd lurches *were* reminiscent of Boris Karloff's monster, and added yet another layer of artifice to the Ferry stage persona.

Some critics felt that Ferry rose to the occasion. Allan Jones at *Melody Maker* raved about the opening night at the Royal Albert Hall ("[Ferry] remains his own most inspired creation") although he heaped equal plaudits on Ferry's guitarist, Chris Spedding ("ridiculously brilliant … with his nonchalant pigeon-toed stance, the Hank B Marvin of the Blank Generation"). On vinyl, however, some found that Ferry was sticking to all-too-safe territory. For 17-year-old ex-Ferry supporter and *NME* writer and punk luminary Julie Burchill, Ferry was a fallen idol: "My heroes always disappoint me," wrote Burchill, in the wind-up-merchant mode that has remained with her for a quarter of a century:

> Joe Stalin, Indira Ghandi, Bryan Ferry – one by one they all blow it. Bryan Ferry blew his big chance by offering up the transcendental glory of Roxy Music to the altar of torch songs and the *Cilla Black Show*. He didn't just choose to pose in the middle of the road; he tied himself to the railway tracks and sacrificed himself to A Wider Audience. *In Your Mind* bears out this about-turn admirably. Catchy, cute and commercial, it comes over with all the conviction of an empty lipstick case when compared to the shimmering alien beauty of *For Your Pleasure*.

Later, writing with her future husband, Tony Parsons, at the height of the punk wars, it was Burchill who would provide Ferry's epitaph in their astonishingly vitriolic, though undeniably sharp, punk overview, *The Boy Looked At Johnny*: "Their first and second albums contain the only truly timeless rock music ever recorded, and were infinitely more convincing in their themes of alienation than Bowie playing Captain Kirk to his lead guitarist's Mr Spock. Roxy Music, alas, ended not with a bang but with a simper when Bryan Ferry subsequently joined the ... piss-pot parade [of less talented glam artists like Queen, Sweet and Wizzard]." In the punks' eyes, Ferry's crime was that age-old sin of selling out. At a time when his contemporary, David Bowie, was racing off in an astonishing new direction along with ex-Roxy-man Eno, Ferry appeared to have lost his nerve. He would soon lose his fiancée too.

The split with Jerry Hall is *the* aspect of Bryan Ferry's life that he feels must remain forever off-limits. However, journalists have plagued and bothered him for decades about the issue. It's well known that, having met Mick Jagger, Jerry dumped Ferry for the Rolling Stones singer. Forced into finally making a comment on the end of the relationship and on Hall herself, the most Ferry will reveal is to claim that Hall is "addicted to publicity". Hall's autobiography, *Tall Tales*, was offered to Ferry for pre-publication scrutiny, presumably to test the waters to see if he would sue or not. Ferry found Hall's account of their relationship biased and slightly fanciful, but not, in essence, inaccurate.

With hindsight, the Ferry/Hall liaison always looked improbable. There was simply too much separating them. Ferry was eleven years Hall's senior, and his experiences, tastes and entire deportment were very different to Hall's sometimes brash personal style. Ferry was a man of refinement and taste. Hall says in her biography that a visit to her parents in 1976 exposed the differences in personal style. Sitting down to dinner, a cockroach crawled across the wall. "Bryan sort of freaked out about it and everyone was embarrassed. Plus, I don't think he liked my mother's cooking too much – you know, real down-home cookin'. He made faces and picked at his food. He wasn't exactly what you'd call a good sport. And they were all sensitive enough to pick up on that."

Although Ferry's dry wit and courteous conduct were always charming, Hall found that he could be overly precious and self-centred. Mick Jagger, by stark contrast, was gregarious, boisterous, and, as Hall put it, "beyond one culture, really". Jerry first met Mick in London backstage after a Stones gig in the summer of 1976. Jagger was 33; Hall was 20. Jagger was then invited to Ferry's London home at Holland Park but, according to Hall, made a spectacle of himself by jumping on a table-tennis table. It was more than Ferry could stand, particularly when it became obvious that Jagger's interest in Hall went beyond the platonic. Jagger would call constantly, asking to meet up with Jerry and Ferry again, but the ex-Roxy man was having nothing of it.

Domestic life did not suit Jerry Hall, however. Having put her career on hold, she found herself playing the good housewife as Ferry went out to work. And, what was worse, Ferry was often on tour. The straw that broke the camel's back was when Ferry departed for Australia and Japan to promote *In Your Mind*. "I wanted to come with him but he said I couldn't go," says Hall. "He could be a bit tyrannical. Plus he said that he wouldn't call me for the whole two months because it was too expensive. I couldn't believe that. I mean – he's a rock star. So I decided to go back to New York and work for that period. And when I arrived I was like, 'Whew!'"

By the end of 1977 the relationship was over. Hall was with Jagger and Ferry was about to pour his misery into his next solo album, *The Bride Stripped Bare*. Publicly humiliated and exposed in the press, Ferry had, indeed, been stripped bare. His career was at its first real low, and his private life was miserable. "I behaved badly. No excuse," Hall would later freely admit. According to Simon Puxley, though, it was all for the best:

> I don't know that she wrecked anything, really. Or let's say that the boat that Bryan was on might have been something of a prison ship if it had continued. I mean I think he feels that in the end it was probably the best thing that ever happened that she met Mick Jagger, as far as he's concerned. He was upset at the time that she went running off with Mick but I think that he feels that it was a felicitous turn of events in the end.

"It was only a year out of a life," said Ferry in 1994. "It's like the Brian Eno thing – they do tend to take up too big an issue in your life and that makes you kind of … irritated." However, if Ferry had wanted to keep his private life private, he might have been better served by refusing press invitations to pose with Jerry Hall draped round him. He hardly kept his relationship with Hall under wraps: arguably, they were the Posh and Becks of their day. The media might not have been quite as intrusive and as it is today, and Ferry might not have been as global a brand name as the former Manchester United star and his former Spice Girl wife, but, nevertheless, for a while back in 1976, he and Hall were rock's biggest celebrity couple.

Hall would remain with Jagger for over twenty years and they would eventually have four children together. Jagger's wayward nature, however, was legendary, and the two would split, be reunited, and then split again until, in his mid-fifties, Jagger sired a child out of wedlock. Hall, still striking in her forties, has now developed a respected acting career and enrolled on an Open University course.

When Hall's marriage to Jagger finally ended in some acrimony in 1999, Ferry was one of the first to send her a message of support. Perhaps his own liaison with her was never meant to be: as many a journalist has said before, "Jerry Ferry" was too tabloid-perfect to ever become actuality. However, even today, at Ferry's London studio-cum-*pied-à-terre*, there's a daily reminder of his ex-fiancée. In 2002, one journalist was astounded to discover "in the loo, surprisingly, a gold-framed picture of Jerry Hall, who snapped Ferry's heart in two. It's an out-take from the *Siren* cover shoot, showing her on a rock, an eerie mermaid, hair vertical in the wind [with] six inch-long blue talons. Dangerous."

PART THREE

1978-2004

FORTRESS ROXY MUSIC:
1978-1981

Brand names are big business, in rock music as much as anywhere else. Mick Jagger solo albums shift a fraction of what the Rolling Stones do. Pete Townshend's solo records have fared little better, and few would seriously rate them as being on a par with his work in The Who. Bowie foundered critically when he became part of a band, Tin Machine. Brand names usually mean security, reliability, and an indicator of quality. At the height of the punk wars – when it appeared, if only very briefly, that the old would indeed be replaced forever by the new – Bryan Ferry saw his stock decline alarmingly. His recent music appeared instantly dated by comparison with the new wave, and the press had all the ammunition they needed in the fact that he had recently re-located to Los Angeles and Switzerland for months at a time. These were hard times for those who had it and who wanted, if not to flaunt it, then at least to spend it.

Melody Maker's Chris Brazier wrote of Ferry's 1978 summer single, "Sign Of The Times", that not only was it "the worst single Bryan Ferry has ever been involved with", but also that "anyone who spends £397 per night on an hotel room can neither expect nor deserve to say anything of value to the rest of humanity." Ferry himself, incidentally, was to rebut this accusation, indignantly denying spending such a (then) extravagant amount on hotel accommodation, and damning Brazier as a "cub reporter".

Yet Ferry's relationship to image was by now a huge handicap. Whereas in the early Roxy years critics had found Ferry's style-hopping fun, now they found him a society bore. With his rifle once again firmly pointed at his size tens, Ferry said this in one interview: "I mean, look, I know Nigel Dempster [a UK 'society' journalist]. If I see him at a party, I talk to him. But I don't invite him around to my place so that he'll write about me in his column. I just enjoy talking to him if I meet him. I'd rather talk to him than some kind of boring trade union official."

What made his plight worse was that, although he averred to be above it all, Ferry was obviously upset and damaged by the criticism and fought back, petulantly. "I've realised for a long time that I've been disliked," was how he opened up to long-time supporter Allan Jones at *Melody Maker*, in one of the most personal interviews of his career:

> But it's only lately that I've realized that I might actually be hated. If people hate me, fuck them. I don't need them. I'm sufficiently convinced of my own talent to be able to live without them. I'm as good as anyone else currently working in the field of rock music and better than most, I think. If some people don't realise that, they must be pretty fucking stupid, frankly … I'm the most severe critic of my work; no one is more critical of my work than I am myself. That's why I take so little notice of the so-called critics, who are mostly ill-informed and illiterate idiots. I know how good I am, and as long as I have faith in myself, I'll continue. And, as far as I'm concerned at the moment, everyone can just go and fuck themselves.

The sultan of suave needed his mouth washing out, but in his defence, Ferry was incensed by the failure of "Sign Of The Times". He also felt let down because he believed the new wave's attack on him was one-dimensional and overlooked the more energetic music he had made. "There were things I did with Roxy, like 'Street Life', that are probably more new wave than the new wave," is how he put it. However, he admitted that punk had been a bit of a shock to his system. "I was in America when it really happened," says Ferry. "It was after *In Your Mind*. Then I did a world tour after that, and I was living in LA. The punk records would sort of filter over. Some of them I liked a lot. It was a new generation, and it was a new audience."

Responding to charges that he was an upper-class squire *manqué*, Ferry scolded, "I'm a social explorer", before admitting: "To be casti-gated for that by the people I feel closest to is really hurtful. You see, I started off life with nothing. [I had] just a state education, you know. Nothing special. So there really [was] nowhere for me to go, except upwards. Socially, anyway. But that doesn't mean you lose touch or that you become a terrible snob."

While Ferry would be knocked off his feet by the punk tornado, Brian Eno positioned himself right in the eye of the whirlwind. In 1976, he had begun collaborating with David Bowie on a new album, originally entitled *New Music Night And Day*, and eventually released in January 1977 as *Low*. Half mechanoid pop, half moon-age instrumental, it completely reset the co-ordinates for modern rock music, and its influence is still being played out in the music of today. Five years into his career as a superstar, and Bowie was still breaking new ground. Ferry, the other major graduate from the class of '72, by contrast looked like an idol from another musical era altogether.

A second collaboration between Bowie and Eno, *Heroes*, recorded at Berlin's Hansa Studios, once again put Eno in the forefront of all that was modern and genuinely progressive in modern music. In 1978, he produced the debut album for new-wavers Devo, *Q: Are We Not Men? A: No, We Are Devo!* and Talking Heads' sophomore effort, *More Songs About Buildings And Food*, whilst also compiling and producing the *No New York* album, a snapshot of the "no wave" scene of the late seventies. Eno, in the centre of the cultural debate, was constantly drawn to the new, whereas Ferry, once again, appeared stranded in the past. But, interestingly, the animosity that had existed between the two in 1973 had by now disappeared. "Eno's a very clever man and deserves to do well. More strength to his arm," said a charitable Ferry in 1978. There was even talk of Eno playing on Ferry's *In Your Mind* album, a idea that sadly never came to fruition.

Ferry's response to the recent disappointments in his solo career was to build a fortress around his name by reactivating Roxy Music. In the late seventies, Roxy Music's status had not been severely damaged by the lukewarm critical response to Ferry's solo output. Punk was anti-Establishment and iconoclastic (often refusing to acknowledge the most blatant of influences), whereas the post-punk movement, artier and more image-conscious, was able to look back fondly at the glam rock/art rock era. Ferry could feel safer within the group format and less exposed to individual criticism. Besides, with only five Roxy Music studio albums recorded, there was some unfinished business to see to.

The fact that Ferry was single again, and had no family ties, made the decision to reactivate the band easier. He had been toying with the idea throughout 1977, but his new professional and personal circumstances meant that it all now made good sense. Single men and women feel more comfortable in touring bands, and it's probably not unrelated that Ferry's decision to opt out of the Roxy Music project came at a time when he was making a long-standing emotional commitment, and possibly needed the companionship that comes with being in a band less and less. By late 1977, Roxy's commercial standing was also rising. A *Greatest Hits* album released in late 1977 had gone Top 20 in the UK, and "Virginia Plain", re-issued to promote the retrospective, got to Number 11 in the UK charts five years after its first run.

Throughout 1978, Ferry had appeared lost. At 33, he was ten years or more older than most of the punk talent. Sporting, on occasions, an ill-advised stubbly beard, on promotional appearances he cut a mildly miserable figure. On *The Kenny Everett Video Show* on TV he poked fun at his own reluctance to open up by refusing to answer any of Everett's questions. In the spring of 1978, *Melody Maker* reported plans for a Ferry UK solo tour, but the tour would subsequently be cancelled. By any standards, Ferry's solo career – "Let's Stick Together" and a few other songs aside – had been a series of lowlights and commercial frustrations. In fact, a recent solo tour of the States in support of *In Your Mind* had been an unsettling and dispiriting experience. Atlantic did not hear a single off the album for US release and had asked Ferry to cancel his small-venue US tour. Ferry refused. Having lost a personal fortune on the tour, Ferry decamped for six months to Los Angeles to write *The Bride Stripped Bare*, but solo success continued to elude him. During his sojourn he befriended the writer Henry Edwards, then working on a screenplay for *Sgt Pepper*, and, through him, met Sixties counter-culture guru, Timothy Leary.

Ultimately, Ferry decided that LA was not the place for him: "I felt terribly alien there and the atmosphere made me, if it's possible, even more introspective than I've felt before." Ferry enjoyed the parties and took pleasure in his Bel Air estate, but he found so much that was distasteful. It was the longest time he had spent away from the UK, and he felt culturally alienated and slightly appalled at the greed of the place. "You get a lot of bad people; people who go there to make money," Ferry told *NME* in March 1978. "The whole Hollywood movie business stinks, it seems to me."

Atlantic Records had demanded that Ferry make "an American album", and although, as always, he made it a precondition that he would retain artistic control and not be at the whim of a big-name producer imposed by his record company, it was obvious even to Ferry that, if his career were to progress, he had to start selling records in the States. He was not, however, for wholesale change: "I'd like to be successful in America – no, I'd like my *music* to be successful in America, there's the rub," he said. Elton John, David Bowie and Rod Stewart had all by now had Number 1 singles in the US, and Ferry was failing to keep up with the competition. Of all the songs written during his time there, only "Can't Let Go", a live favourite to this day, captures the dazzle and the glitz of LA. Perhaps unintentionally, Ferry hardly endeared himself to the American public with statements such as "in America they do like albums to be background music: that seems to be the formula for success." However, Ferry obviously worried and fretted about why his music wasn't making the inroads he thought it should: "I do very emotional music, but in America they like to have their emotion smoothed down, with all the edges taken off."

The Bride Stripped Bare was recorded at Mountain Studios in Montreux, and later in New York, with Dr Simon Puxley, Ferry's media consultant, as co-producer. In Montreux, Ferry and his band had no distractions: "The only thing to do there was to make music. There were no distractions. It turned out to be the strangest album I've ever done … there was this band of musicians just stuck there. Like an Everest expedition or something. A real men-without-women number."

Ferry spent a lonely, dejected Christmas in Montreux in 1977. "There was a lot of pressure on me to use an American producer, to make an American-sounding record," he was to recall. "I can obviously see the commercial potential behind that. But at the same time, I didn't want to lose my own identity." He was, however, delighted to be working with some of the best session musicians that money could buy:

> I'd never worked with any American musicians at all, and there were lots that I'd always admired. When I was in LA, I met these characters, Waddy Wachtel [guitarist] and Rick Marotta [drummer], who were just brilliant players and I kind of hired their services. They were very bemused; they didn't know what to make of the hoops that I asked them to dance through, but, in the end, I think they really enjoyed it, especially since I brought some English musicians over as well that they'd never worked with.

The Bride Stripped Bare was originally planned as a double album. Tinkering around as ever, Ferry changed his mind about songs, altering the running order, recording new material for inclusion at the last moment, and remixing tracks. "Broken Wings", "Crazy Love", "Feel The Need", "He'll Have To Go" and "Four Letter Love" were all completed but left off the final version of the album (although all have been subsequently released in some shape or form). However, such indecision was indicative of Ferry's stalled self-consciousness. As his career progressed, Ferry's indecision would expand to a worrying degree – so many options, so many ways for the artist to go – and, as he got older, so too would his anxiety, and his difficulty in shaping the music in his own image. The project would also be produced by committee ("Wachtel, Marotta, Puxley/Nye/Ferry for EG Records" ran the sleeve credit), which also indicated the lack of a firm lead or the album.

An album made with the cream of America's session musicians (Wachtel at the time was playing with platinum-selling Linda Ronstadt), half of which was filled with cover versions, was never going to cut much ice with Ferry's original supporters. Martyn Ware, by then a recording artist in his own right, had this to say: "I stayed loyal to Roxy Music, but it was more a loyalty based on the hope that he would turn round and maybe loosen the creative reins a little and get some interesting people in. Whereas it just turned more and more into getting the best session players in. I detested *The Bride Stripped Bare*, the blandest album in the world at that time, but that's LA for you, that's what it does to you. Later, when I went to LA, I could totally understand why he would make an album like that."

"I can't fathom just why Ferry persists in covering vintage and veteran standards that have already been shriven and hallowed by singers infinitely more able than himself," wrote Angus MacKinnon in *NME*, echoing the sentiments of many who were baffled by Ferry's obsession with covering the repertoire of others when his own self-penned numbers were always more interesting:

> His taste may be reliably impeccable, but that's rarely enough to help any interpretative crooner through any night. Admittedly Ferry has sometimes transcended the severe limitation of his own singing by sheer sense of style and styling, but there's certainly no "Wonderful World" or "Smoke Gets In Your Eyes" on this luxury liner. Ferry's versions of Sam and Dave's "Hold On I'm Coming", Al Green's "Take Me To The River", itself the subject of a recent Talking Heads

cover, and Otis Redding's "That's How Strong My Love Is" are enjoyable, charming even, but ultimately both trivial and trivialising.

The decision to re-form Roxy Music came sometime in the summer of 1978, before the release of *The Bride Stripped Bare*, which failed to get higher than Number 13, staying in the UK charts for a grand total of just five weeks – by far the worst performance of any Roxy/Ferry studio album so far. Of the three singles from the project, the fine Velvet Underground cover, "What Goes On", missed the Top 50, the excellent Ferry composition, "Sign Of The Times", struggled to Number 37, whilst the genuinely moving version of "Carrickfergus", rearranged by Ferry and undoubtedly one of the highlights of his solo career, didn't even get into the Top 100. Asked about the failure of "Sign Of The Times", Ferry was to reply, "It's too tedious for words."

In actual fact, "Sign Of The Times", which was a surprise and very welcome addition to the *Frantic* tour set list in 2002, was a very fine single, riddled with a kind of fine existential angst:

> "We live, we die
> We laugh, we cry
> We know not why?"

Then Ferry sings:

> "Red is the bloody sign of the times
> The bride stripped bare
> Of all despair
> We're cut, but we don't care."

(Words and music: Bryan Ferry, 1978)

Here the biographical merges with the abstraction of Dadaist sloganeering. Was Ferry referring to recent harrowing episodes in his personal life? Or was he, with typical lightness of touch, simply attempting to recreate the sort of sloganeering style that fitted with the Duchamp-like references of the lyric – the futility of existence and the wretchedness of life? Probably both. Ferry rejected the original artwork for the picture sleeve for the single, saying it was "not punk enough":

I was shocked when *The Bride Stripped Bare* did so badly, because I felt it was the first grown-up record I'd ever made. But people didn't want grown-up. It's a shame, because one hit would have made all the difference. And "Sign Of The Times" actually referred to the whole snarling punk attitude, but the irony of a guy in a suit singing that song totally passed people by.

"Can't Let Go" detailed the emotional paralysis Ferry began to feel towards the end of his extended sojourn in LA. Indeed, although it contains only four Ferry originals, there is a deeply confessional tone to the album. Part angry, part disconsolate, part nothing more than a mirror held up to the blandness of LA culture, the album oozes a dispirited defeated air of the world-weary.

From this low point, Ferry began to resurrect his career and redefine his image. The latter involved the introduction of trendy narrow ties, a leather jacket and a sleeker look: the former, the regaining of his songwriting touch. Roxy reconvened to test the waters in the late summer of 1978. Eddie Jobson, however, was not to be part of Roxy Music Phase 3: "By the time they re-formed, I was leading [his band] UK and enjoying success in the U.S. and Japan playing my own music. They knew there was no way I would rejoin Roxy, and, wisely, they never asked me to." In September, Ferry told Radio One's *Rock On* programme that the band had been writing together and that "the separation period was obviously a very good thing," adding, "I've been playing bass, much to everyone's horror." He let slip that included in these tentative rehearsals were Alan Spenner on guitar and Paul Carrack on piano. A member of the group Ace, Carrack had secured a huge transatlantic hit with "How Long", a song much admired by Ferry.

The time was indeed ripe. All members of Roxy had recently completed work on solo projects. Mackay's album, *Resolving Contradictions*, was about to be released that autumn. The first reports of the new Roxy would come from Simon Puxley: "The music is very different to what they did before. It's not really the same kind of band." Later that autumn, as the new songs began to take shape, Roxy found their next bass player – the blond, cute, and eminently qualified Gary Tibbs, who had been playing with the seminal punk band the Vibrators. Anybody expecting sloppy, untutored playing, though, was in for a bit of a surprise. A superb technician, Tibbs added a new fluidity to the

Roxy sound. "I was introduced to them by Herbie Flowers, who was my 'bass guru' at the time," says Tibbs:

> He taught me a few things and was one of my inspirations for playing as a young lad. He was asked to do some session work by Bryan and wasn't available, so he recommended me. That's when I found out the band was re-forming and was asked to join. Bryan said I had the right haircut and tie, and I was only nineteen.
>
> I came from the grammar school Roxy/Bowie era. I was a bit shell-shocked at first, seeing all five of them in a room, after only having seen photographs. They were all really nice though; we had the same quirky sense of humour. Once we started playing it really clicked, so it just kept getting better.
>
> The album was already underway and was in very loose demo format. There were lots of bits and pieces of ideas lying around. Once we started playing, all live performance and then overdubbing, the songs just grew. Lyrics were left until everything was finished and the vocals done last, which I found fascinating. I found "Manifesto", "Trash" and "Spin Me Round" all really Roxy-sounding.

In early 1979, promotional shots for the new Roxy Music appeared. The tallest art rock group ever (Mackay, Manzanera and Ferry are all well over six feet tall) were back – moody, serious and more aggressively attired than of yore – to meet the new demands of the new wave. Thompson now had a short haircut, his long locks cruelly discarded just after Roxy disbanded in mid 1976. Manzanera, still only 28, still had a beard. Uncool in 1972, it looked positively antiquated in 1979. Mackay was a study of serious intent and schoolmasterly severity. Roxy were beginning to look their age.

The comeback initially went badly wrong. The first single, "Trash", was a slight, short, up-tempo number. Its new wave swagger was not enough to woo over a new audience, and after peaking at Number 40, it plummeted straight back out again. "It was worrying because it was so bad," says writer Mat Snow, bluntly. "It still doesn't sound any good to me. It just sounds like an attempt at a rave-up which doesn't come off." "You know, at first it looked like [the comeback] wasn't going to work," reflected Phil Manzanera. "There was a moment when the first single came out and it didn't do fantastically well. It was the time of the punk thing, and there was the thought that perhaps it wouldn't take off again."

However, there would be no need for any panic within the Roxy camp because the second single struck gold. In April 1979, "Dance Away" slowly climbed the charts until it lodged itself at Number 2, rivalling Roxy's previous chart best and confirming the group's comeback. With its slow, smoochy beat, torrid, lovelorn lyric, and classic Ferry vocal, it's remained a fan favourite ever since. Ferry himself later admitted that the song was one of his few blatant attempts to write a commercial hit single. Perhaps there is a tad too much of the cliché about the lyric, but seldom has the boy/girl, she loves me/she loves me not scenario been rendered so eloquently.

Like "Love Is The Drug", "Dance Away" opens with sound effects, in this case the striking of a match and a worried inhalation of smoke, over the sound of a simple drum machine pattern:

> "Yesterday – well it seemed so cool
> When I walked you home, kissed goodnight
> I said 'It's love', you said 'All right',
> It's funny how I could never cry
> Until last night and you pass by
> Hand in hand with another guy
> You're dressed to kill and guess who's dying?"

> (Words and music: Bryan Ferry, 1979)

The song actually had its roots in the sessions for *In Your Mind*. Ferry, ever the painter, had at that time turned the canvas to the wall and never finished the song. A year or so later, he had considered it for *The Bride Stripped Bare* but only ended up finishing it on Roxy's comeback album, *Manifesto*. Once it had been recorded, he took the tapes to New York for some overdubs and – *voila!* – Roxy's biggest hit to date. The single, remixed from the album cut, spent three weeks at Number 2, only kept off the Number 1 spot by Blondie's "Sunday Girl".

Yet the album's standout was undoubtedly the title track, which provided a real flavour of the dark intrigue of the original Roxy Music, but with a modernised and fresh sound. The opening cacophony of mantric noise is a moment of grand theatre: the slow, bass-driven beginning, the snippets of backing vocal, the foghorn blares of the sax, then the quickening pulse of the rhythm section and the lead guitar riff that prefigures Ferry's show-stealing opening – it's the album's highpoint

232

after just two-and-a-half minutes. The lyric itself, a superbly crafted agenda of intent reportedly inspired by a poem from the pop artist Clause Oldenburg, makes for compelling listening:

> "I am for a life around the corner
> That takes you by surprise
> That comes leaves all your need
> And more besides."

But the real meat of the manifesto comes with Ferry's claims:

> "I am for the revolution's coming
> I don't know where she's been
> For those who dare because it's there
> I know – I've seen."

(Words and music: Bryan Ferry/
Phil Manzanera, 1979)

Ferry had had the title of the new album in his mind for many months, even before the decision to reconvene and record was taken. The title song itself is a rallying call, not least, one suspects, to himself. After three years of aimless creative drift, Ferry the *artiste* was back.

Yet *Manifesto* is a schizophrenic album. Side One, dubbed the east side, was largely a success, with the big, bold, honking sax version of "Angel Eyes" (later re-mixed for an equally good disco version and a second Top 5 hit single in the summer of 1979) a standout. "Stronger Through The Years" carries a whiff of the art rock jiggery-pokery of the original band. "Still Falls The Rain", a song about schizophrenia, is a clever conceit; Ferry impersonates the reflective, melancholic Jekyll in pseudo-romantic verses, and the twisted, demonic Hyde in the furious stanzas that reply. The female backing singers copy the Stones' "Sympathy For The Devil" in a clever piece of cross-referencing. On stage, Ferry sang it with a showboating sense of theatre and fun, although it has not been played live for many years now.

Side Two, the west side, was where Roxy seemed slightly strained. While the east side dealt with Europeanisms, the west side was a rather awkward fumble towards blacker, American sounds. "Cry, Cry, Cry" was Stax-lite and a failure, while "Ain't That So" was a pleasant soul-inflected song that was rumoured to feature Luther Vandross, uncredited, on backing vocals. "My Little Girl" was a neat, pleasant trip, but rather lightweight. Only "Spin Me Round", the closing number, possessed that weird sense of disorientation that the old-style Roxy had had in superabundance. The closing sequence of the song, when the music fades to what sounds like the slow winding down of a music box, is a perfect touch, as the pirouetting ballerina slowly stops spinning.

Roxy Music had succeeded. The album spent a solid 34 weeks in the UK charts, and reached Number 7. Its sleeve broke with tradition, the cover girl series finally and unceremoniously brought to an end. But the *Manifesto* image was at least their equal. In the noughties, the press reported that Michael Jackson "lives with dummies": so isolated is he from the human race that he has mannequins for friends. Back in 1979, Ferry and Antony Price seemed to be ironically commenting on the bland march of the simulacra, the new post-modern world in which the make-believe and the replica were more authentic than the real. Roxy cover girls had always looked contrived, artificial and curiously like shop-window dummies. The cover for *Manifesto* would go the whole hog, depicting a party scene populated, it seemed, by mannequins. It worked perfectly.

Manifesto was greeted with mixed reviews. The *NME* announced, "Bryatollah Ferrani Returns – And It Ain't Half Tepid, Mum." Richard William's review in *Melody Maker* was much more on the money, praising the genuinely excellent tracks and seeing through the conceit of the weaker ones before sagely pronouncing: "Certainly it pulls some punches. But, reservations aside, this may be the first such return bout ever attempted with any degree of genuine success: a technical knockout against the odds."

Perhaps fearing stuttering ticket sales, Roxy Music cancelled plans to open the tour where they had ended the *Siren* tour, at London's Wembley Arena, electing instead to play smaller venues "because the big arenas are such bad places in terms of band/audience interaction", as one explanation had it. The set would include such oldies as "Ladytron", "Do The Strand" and "Editions Of You", plus half-a-dozen or so songs from *Manifesto*. In the wake of the new wave, it was hoped the lack of grandiosity might curry favour with punters and media alike. The band having rehearsed at Abba's studios, the tour began in Stockholm on February 24, 1979. *Melody Maker*'s Allan Jones was on hand for the scoop: "Ferry begins a curious little dance, his arse poking out between the hem of his jacket, his knees locked together. He remains an awkward, inelegant mover and reminds me suddenly of those occasional newsreels we see of Prince Charles attempting the Watusi with dusky maidens in grass skirts somewhere on the shores of Africa."

Terpsichorean disappointments notwithstanding, the show was a success: "My doubts about the pertinence of the Roxy reunion are already beginning to melt in the heat of the sheer enjoyment to be derived from the conspicuous thrill of the music." (So overwhelmed by the experience was Allan Jones that he admitted to getting hammered later that night and ending up in a club dancing with Agnetha Faltskog from Abba, without realising who she was). In Europe Roxy were supported by Wire, and in the UK by the Tourists. Journalist Mat Snow thought the new version of Roxy was a strong live prospect:

> I thought the live show actually was great and I thought they were better live in 1979 than they were in 1975. Live, they weren't the tightest band, which meant that the shows were never really much more than opportunities for the Roxy faithful to gather and preen and parade. You didn't get anything off the live act that you couldn't get off the record. And, to tell you the truth, the whole rock arena was not really what Roxy was about. Obviously they had to do it to promote the record and for an extra revenue stream. But I don't think they ever embraced playing live particularly enthusiastically. The shows them-selves lacked ambition. Basically, they'd set up and play, and it was all a bit *Rock Goes To College*.

As late as 1979, there were still hordes of Ferry look-alikes to be spotted at the reunion gigs, grateful for the chance to reactivate the glam stylings of yore. "Being from the older generation of fans, I've always modelled my dress sense on Ferry," says fan Ashley Wright. "The first Roxy concert I saw was in Liverpool in 1979. The number of Ferry look-alikes was amazing. You don't get that much now, probably because older Roxy fans are getting on a bit!" Ferry himself had always enjoyed the fun aspect of his fans dressing up. Back in 1977, he commented: "There have been some good ones. In LA we did one show that was full of them. I just wish they'd come up and stand in for me a couple of times, give me a chance to go and have a drink!"

Some fans, however, felt mildly betrayed that the band had reformed at all, perhaps suspecting that there was a certain amount of cynicism involved. Steven Severin recalls one particular moment with not a little embarrassment: "The Banshees recorded 'Happy House' and 'Christine' at Phil Manzanera's studio in Chertsey. He was so polite and gracious. Unfortunately the next time I met him was at the after-show party at the first Hammersmith reformation gig in 1979. I say 'unfortunately' because all the Banshees proceeded to get drunk, and I scolded Philip and Andy for daring to re-form! Highly embarrassing, thinking back now. I hope I was forgiven."

Television would play a big part in Roxy's comeback. In the three years since the last Roxy album, there had been a sea change in the way music was promoted, but Roxy were up to the challenge. More than ever before, it would be television that would decide whether a song was a hit or a stiff. At the time, Roxy had little problem getting their songs played on radio, but the transition to pop video was a move only some of the artists of the day were able to make with any élan. Roxy's promo for the remade "Angel Eyes" was ample proof that they would have no problem in making that transition. In fact, the new version of Roxy Music had begun a process of redefinition that would update their sound.

Dance music had always been a love of Ferry's, and the new version of Roxy Music would handle the contemporary styles of the day with a rare lightness of touch. The process had actually begun on *Siren*. Many of the bass lines contain funk elements: "Love Is The Drug" was a disco hit. In this regard, *Manifesto* was not so much a break with the past but a stylistic bridge from 1975 to even more daring dance experiments on subsequent works in the eighties. Roxy's re-recording of "Angel Eyes" was no misguided attempt by rock's gerontocracy to build some street cred into the music, but rather a totally convincing exercise in updating an already fluid and funky sound.

MTV was still two years away, but Roxy made sure that they got their share of television exposure. A gig at the Manchester Apollo was filmed by Granada Television and included a rare outing (for that tour at least) for "Virginia Plain". Their May *Top of The Pops* performance of "Dance Away", shown on the same programme as Bowie's video for "Boys Keep Swinging", would be a stark reminder to the 20-year-old Gary Numan of his musical forebears: he sang "Are Friends Electric?" with Tubeway Army on the same show. Roxy also filmed a TV special with Abba, shown over the Easter Bank Holiday weekend, on which they shared the bill with Boney M, Leo Sayer and Kate Bush. Gary Tibbs: "We did loads of TV all over the world, but the only one that stands out is one with Abba in a marquee on the side of a Swiss mountain, and me being obsessed with seeing Agnetha's ass through a small gap in her dressing room door!"

Around this time, *Record Mirror* ran one of those photos that should now be part of rock history, but sadly isn't: Bowie, Ferry and John Cale together in one frame. Here were two working-class lads, one from the north-east, one from south Wales, and a lower-middle-class boy from Brixton: between them, they had completely transformed British music. Cale was a relatively anonymous musician working on the fringes, but his work in the previous decade with the Velvet Underground had brought the avant-garde into the mainstream. Bowie was a global superstar, his work and stature unsurpassed. Ferry, as ever, was somewhere in-between: a crucial icon from earlier in the decade, it now seemed as if he was gaining a new relevance as the seventies drew to a close.

In May 1979, David Bowie took over as DJ for the day for a *Star Special* programme on Radio One. He played old King Crimson, Jeff Beck and Little Richard tracks, but what was noticeable was his emphasis on the new: the Mekons, Talking Heads, Blondie and New York no-wavers Mars all had their place in his pantheon of greats. However, he also chose two Roxy songs: "2HB" and "For Your Pleasure". "I saw them in concert the other week in New York – it was very good. Any of you see it?" Bowie asked the nation. "I'm quite pleased they re-formed. Their bass player is very good. He jumps very well. They've got a good jumping bass player you know, Roxy Music. Excellent. One of the best little jumpers I've seen."

"I met David a couple of times, even during the *Breaking Glass* movie sessions," remembers Tibbs. "He was a fan of my playing, I think. The jumping thing was to do with the fact that I cannot perform and stand still, coupled with sheer youthful energy. That whole tour was awesome [and is] still talked about now by fans. I used to particularly like 'In Every Dream Home A Heartache' and 'Mother of Pearl'."

With a successful tour and two big hit singles under their belts, Roxy began work on new material. *Manifesto* had reached Number 23 in the US and, finally, there was more than a glimmer of hope that the group might, even yet, find a mainstream US following. A cover of "In The Midnight Hour" was the first of the new songs to get a public airing, when the band appeared on the New Year's Eve edition of the UK's *Kenny Everett Video Show* along with David Bowie, who was reactivating

"Space Oddity". However, for the first time since 1973 there would be serious dissension in the Roxy ranks. The new album would be recorded without Paul Thompson. The third member of the original class of '72 would be gone.

On his official website, Thompson cites the hoary (and always deeply unconvincing) "musical differences" as the reason behind his disappearance from the Roxy Music line-up in 1980. It might very well have been the case that the groove-inspired music of the new band was less to Thompson's liking. Ferry, however, hinted at the time that Thompson had to leave because he was ill-equipped to play the more intricate syncopation of the new album, which would be entitled *Flesh + Blood*. It was rumoured that Thompson's departure followed a blazing, tie-severing row with Ferry. "This was a turning point for me," says Tibbs: "Paul was my friend, as well as a drummer I fitted perfectly with. We had chemistry as a rhythm section that I have found difficult to better to this day. We were both Zeppelin freaks and so we gave Roxy a 'heavy rock' platform that I think they always needed. I think he got fed up with not getting enough recognition from the others. Quite right."

Thompson was replaced by not one but a succession of new drummers, in the form of Andy Newmark (who was introduced by Paul Carrack), Allan Schwartzberg and Simon Phillips. It was the beginning of the emergence of a very different Roxy Music. With Thompson gone, Ferry felt free to experiment with different percussionists. The sound changed radically, from powerful rock to something much more Americanised, syncopated, funky and *muso*. In Ferry's decades-long quest for the Holy Grail of pop perfection, this was the very start of his addiction to session musicians.

Paul Thompson would go on to play with Gary Moore, Jonathon Perkins and the band Concrete Blonde, "with whom I had my first US gold album, something I never achieved with Roxy Music." In his Roxy days, Thompson's extra-musical interests included collecting old guns and ammunition. In the years ahead, he would take up parachuting and scuba-diving. He wouldn't be a member of Roxy Music again for another 21 years (and, even then, it is reported that he had to audition for his own part). The fact that "The Great Paul Thompson" left Roxy under a cloud, with no convincing explanation given to this day, has meant that Roxy fans have always felt that this most down-to-earth member of the band has never been fully appreciated. His huge popularity is, in part, a result of this.

Live, Roxy Music would suffer from the absence of Thompson. He was asked to play on the *Flesh + Blood* tour of 1980, even though he had, in effect, been removed from the band. At first he agreed, but then had to pull out after injuring himself in a motorcycle accident. The new Roxy were slinky and sexy in concert, but the pop-rock drumming of Thompson, which had anchored even the most extreme of Roxy's avant-garde musings in familiar territory, was replaced by a polyphony of drumming styles that moved the band away from rock and towards something more intricate, but ultimately less powerful.

Gone too was bassist Gary Tibbs, who went on to find fame for two years as part of Adam And The Ants. "I suppose this was the aftermath of Paul's departure, although I didn't know it at the time," is how Tibbs puts it today:

For some of *Flesh + Blood* I was away in the US doing another record [*Code Blue* – a one-off power-pop project] and I wasn't keen on a lot of the songs. It was all a bit MOR. Bryan had an obsession with breaking the US market at the time, and so chose a lot of songs for that purpose. It didn't sound like a Roxy album to me, more like a Ferry solo record. By the time I did "Jealous Guy" I was looking to move on, and just happened to get contacted by an old friend from north London saying that Adam, a massive Roxy fan, wanted me for the Ants. When I saw what they were doing, I thought in pop music terms it was way ahead of its time, so I wanted in.

Tibbs would be replaced, again, not by one bassist but by a succession of highly proficient session men over the next two years. Paul Carrack, who played piano on the *Flesh + Blood* tour, recalls, "Bryan seemed to be the most creative. Phil was very friendly and down-to-earth. I think Andy and Paul were a little wary of these other musos infiltrating their domain – probably quite rightly."

From May 1980 to January 1981, Roxy Music were almost permanently on the road, playing gigs mainly across Europe and later in the UK. Two concerts each in Spain and Portugal had to be cancelled when Ferry was struck down with a kidney infection, but that health scare aside, the *Flesh + Blood* tour would be a huge success. Performing in front of what can only be described as a massive pair of white Venetian blinds, the band drew heavily on new material, with the occasional dip into the past with a surprise return of "The Bogus Man".

Essentially, however, they were now a cool dance-rock act – brilliant songwriters, distinctive performers, but totally lacking the edge of their earlier incarnations.

Nevertheless, *Flesh + Blood* would be the biggest-selling record of their career to date. It was the first of their albums to reach Number 1 since *Stranded*, seven years earlier, and it would stay in the UK charts for 60 weeks. The cover, by Roxy standards, was strangely tame: three "Little Olympiad Nymphs", as the sleeve co-creator Antony Price called them, holding javelins. The brash postmodernism of the early sleeves was but a distant memory: the new Roxy Music was slickly packaged for the Saatchi & Saatchi generation. Roxy had finally entered the real mainstream of British popular music: their albums now competed with those of Abba, the Police, Bowie, Queen and Paul McCartney for the honour of the biggest-selling title of the year. Such was the popularity of *Flesh + Blood* that it would be Number 1 twice: for a single week at the beginning of June, then for three weeks in late August and early September.

Three big hit singles kept the parent album in the Top 10 for much of the second half of 1980, while "Over You", the first single, reached Number 5. A bouncy stab at fifties-inflected pop, it sounded neither retro nor trite, just another song in the dynasty of superb Roxy Music singles. Roxy fans knew that it was lightweight and a bit of a throwaway, but there was such fun in the grooves that nobody cared. The second single, however, was a more obvious and serious bid to win songwriting immortality. "Oh Yeah" (which would be covered by the Divine Comedy in 2001), with its gentle piano melody, shifting mood and storming chorus, was clearly Roxy at their very best. Released in the summer of 1980, it would eventually match "Over You" by reaching Number 5. The third single, "Same Old Scene", was the best of the three. Roxy's most perfect dance record, its unstoppable groove, funky, Chic-like base and blasts of sax made it another sizeable hit, reaching Number 12 late in 1980. That single, more than any other from the Roxy oeuvre, appeared to have been internalised by the incipient London club scene at the time. By 1981, the charts would be full of songs with a similar musical trajectory: rumbling disco bass, clipped, riffy guitar and a smooth vocal over the top.

By 1980, the influence of Bowie and Roxy on pop culture had reached its zenith. In 1979 and 1980, "the cult with no name", as it was first dubbed, had redefined youth culture along very different lines to

those of the initial punk explosion of 1975 and 1976. In a mighty, hedonistic brew of punk attitude but funk stylings, white men in costuming
which made the glam rock era look almost tame made the New
Romantics the first important youth subculture of the eighties.

The change had begun sometime around the end of 1978. As the
market wearied of the original impulse behind punk, new wave acts
such as Blondie, the Boomtown Rats and the Police added a photogenic
angle to the punk blueprint. A new twice-monthly magazine, *Smash
Hits*, had been launched which unashamedly treated the pop world in
tabloid fashion. With its star-related gossip and cheeky writing, it
reflected the views of a new community of record buyers who were tired
of the earnestness that punk had brought. And many musicians looked
to how Roxy invented themselves as glamorous style icons and
attempted a Roxy-esque coup of their own. "I never wanted to be a
musician. I just wanted to be a pop star," said John Taylor of Duran
Duran: "I just wanted to go on *Top Of The Pops*, really, and if being a
pop star meant you had to go up and down the M1 in the back of a
transit van for ten years, I didn't want to know. That's why I always liked
Roxy Music because they never ever did that. We never wanted to 'pay
our dues'. We had the spirit and the non-education of the punk bands
but we had the aspirations to be Roxy Music."

Just a year-and-a-half after their initial breakthrough, Duran
seemed to be on a self-conscious mission to redefine the pop world as
a glossy adjunct to the fashion business. With videos filmed in Sri
Lanka and a super-abundance of designer suits and leggy models,
they appeared on MTV as new tokens of eighties hedonism. Duran
looked to have soon outgrown their roots and were headed towards a
life of international jet-set pleasure. The link to Ferry appeared
obvious: "They've become very famous and very glamorous and they
suddenly find England a small area to work in," said Ferry of Duran.
"It's a natural thing. If you become a famous person, you become
intrigued with meeting other famous people, especially those whom
you might have admired before but never get the chance to meet." Yet
Duran had a teen-appeal and blatant pop sensibility that Ferry never
had. Although they took their craft seriously and, in Nick Rhodes,
possessed a *bone fide* link with the left-field, Duran were hardly in the
same heavyweight intellectual territory as Roxy.

Roxy had other disciples, too. ABC's *Lexicon Of Love* album defined
1982 and its stories of aspiration, glamour and success, imagined by

twenty-somethings from dour recession-destroyed Sheffield, seemed (even more than Duran) to have a link with Ferry's own rags-to-riches real-life story. More overtly ironic than Duran, ABC appeared in golden lamé: their singer, Martin Frye, was suitably bequiffed. By their second album, *Beauty Stab*, the sound had become more guitar-orientated and sax-dominated. While they could never be called Roxy copyists, their attitude carried something of the Roxy genetic code in their musical genome.

Cool, ironic, detached, stylish and danceable – these were the attitudes derived from Roxy, which lived on in the form of a new ideology for youth culture. Listening to these groups now, it is interesting that late-period Roxy Music appears to have just as big an influence on the scene as their earlier sonic experimentalism did. "Trash" may have been the poorest selling Roxy single but it was a turntable favourite at the Blitz Club in London. Duran Duran's initial sound had strong links to *Flesh + Blood*-era Roxy. Tony Hadley of Spandau Ballet also borrowed from the same period and, as Mark Radcliffe puts it, "Bryan Ferry seems to have single-handedly inspired David Sylvian to start singing." Radcliffe recalls, as a lad in Manchester, how Roxy infiltrated the mainstream of club culture: "I remember that there was a club in Manchester called Pips that used to have different rooms. One would be a punk room, one would be a soul room, and there was also a Roxy room, because they were so influential."

The list of artists influenced by Roxy also numbers Icehouse, whose catchy "Hey Little Girl" was a Roxy Music song in all but name. Later, it was obvious that Lloyd Cole and Tindersticks manifested some of Ferry's tortured, world-weary charm, whilst Morrissey's sharp, acrid songwriting and intensely camp, yet intensely literary writing are obviously linked to the work of Roxy Music.

There were other high-profile Bryan Ferry fans too, including those whose music seemed on the surface to bear little resemblance to his influence. Both Elvis Costello and Kevin Rowland were avid supporters. Yet, at the time, few musicians would admit to being influenced by Roxy. And, equally strangely, given the substantial body of work built up over the years, there are very few cover versions of Roxy songs, or at least very few successful and high profile ones. Perhaps there's something unique about Bryan Ferry that can't be copied, and that works against easy interpretation? If so, this is further evidence that Roxy and Ferry were musical one-offs, creating an idiolect all of their own. For it would be in terms of attitude, style, and ideology, rather than on the musical level itself, that Roxy would make their mark. Whereas Bowie copyists still abound, straight Roxy imitators have been comparatively few.

Ferry himself, if not wrong-footed by so many would-be's walking in his shadow, seemed perplexed by the appearance of all these Roxy clones in the New Romantic days. "There's not much I can do about it for a start, except be better and better, or try to be," he reasoned in 1983:

> But I think you have to make it very much a secondary issue, as much as you can. And just think about the quality of your work all the time: that you're doing the best you're capable of. And then what other people do shouldn't really matter to you. The only time it gets irritating ... depends how recent the plagiarism is. I mean, if it's a band that's influenced by what I did ten years ago then it's not so interesting, but if they're imitating what I did last year then it means I've got to work a little bit faster and run kind of a little more nimbly.

Shortly afterwards, he told *The Face*:

> I was always being asked what I thought of [New Romantics] and that was hard to deal with. Sometimes you felt they were a little too clone-like, and it would make me feel that maybe I had given away too much information. Not only in the music but interviews, where I'd named my heroes and particular tastes. I could recognise people writing songs in the same way, using those same reference points. It meant that I had to push ahead faster than I might have liked, leaving ground behind that I might have wanted to explore a little longer.

Flesh + Blood might have been a runaway success, but it also contained some very worrying portents for the band's future. In truth, half of the album could only be described using an adjective never before applied to a Roxy Music record: mediocre. It was even more worrying to hear Bryan Ferry extol the virtues of what is perhaps the blandest cut on the album: "Every album that you make seems to have a central song that the rest of the album kind of pivots around, and 'My Only Love' seems to be the central core of *Flesh + Blood* for me."

Yet it would also be a ballad that would bring Roxy Music their sole UK Number 1 to date, albeit in the most tragic of circumstances. The murder of John Lennon on December 8, 1980 was the biggest trauma that rock culture had ever undergone. More so even than the death of Elvis in 1977, the killing of a man so universally admired, loved and, by some, worshipped, shook rock culture to its very foundations. Ferry was deeply shocked: "Of all the English musicians and songwriters, he was my favourite. He was a Libra, like me, and I always respected his work very much. I was a great fan." Ferry had met Lennon just the once, in a Tokyo hotel, as he was on his way back from solo dates in Australia. "This guy came bounding across the lobby to say hello. I thought it was a fan, you know, and it was John Lennon. He was very pleasant, and it was a shame we didn't spend any more time together."

As news of John Lennon's murder flashed around a disbelieving world, Roxy, on the road at the time, decided to pay their respects in sound. "The week Lennon died we played one of the biggest shows we'd ever done, in Dortmund," says Ferry:

> It was a televised show, with a few other groups on the bill. And I thought it would be a very good idea to do a Lennon song as the last song in the show as a tribute to him. "Jealous Guy" happened to be a favourite song of his for me. And everybody liked it so much that they suggested that we put it out as a single. So the next week we recorded it.
>
> "Jealous Guy" was very much a sort of special one-off enterprise and it wasn't done in the same way that you would do a single as such. The three minutes of instrumental at the end were very important to me and made it so different from his original version for a start and threw a whole different light on the song, I think. And I wasn't going to cut it down for anybody.

Ferry realised that this was a high-risk move. There were bound to be accusations that the band were merely cashing in on the death of the most famous Beatle. Examining their motives before they committed the song to tape, they decided it seemed the right thing to do, by way of a tribute:

> It's a great responsibility doing someone else's song, especially if you really love the original, because you don't want to spoil it: that's the last thing you want to do. You want to do a different twist on it, perhaps a different angle. It's a kind of tribute thing, as well as being

interesting for yourself and for your career as well. I thought that most of his best work had been with the Beatles, but that was one song from his solo career that had a real edge to it.

Ferry was to also comment that he felt Lennon "would have liked" Roxy's version of his song.

Between the end of December 1980 and the close of February 1981, three Lennon songs got to Number 1 in the UK Charts. On March 14, 1981, Roxy's "Jealous Guy" made it four. The video that went with the song was simple but poetic: Ferry sang the song affectingly to camera. In an age when videos came with conceptual "non-linear" arty manifestos to support the visual trickery, Roxy Music's straight performance video was an attempt to bring out the emotion of the song, and "Jealous Guy" has been synonymous with the Ferry persona ever since. The long outro, as the music builds to a crescendo and Ferry whistles the final refrain, is as much a part of our perception of Ferry the entertainer as any of his self-penned songs.

The huge success of *Flesh + Blood* and "Jealous Guy" meant that, ten years into their career, Roxy Music were now at their commercial peak. Ferry recognised that the reason for this was that the music had been – well, not dumbed-down, but redesigned along less extreme lines. Of *Flesh + Blood* he said: "The music was more clearly defined and controlled as opposed to the earlier stuff, which was slightly more complex and not so easy on the ear. And I don't think it's necessarily a bad thing to make a record people can hear and like instantly."

On Easter Monday 1981, as *Chariots Of Fire* was stealing the cinema limelight and Britain "celebrated" Bucks Fizz's Eurovision Song Contest triumph, Ferry hosted Radio One's *Star Special* programme. Like Bowie two years earlier, he had been invited to play DJ for the afternoon. Ferry's selection was as revealing for what it left out as for what it contained. His running order was as follows:

"Road Runner" – Junior Walker and the All-Stars
"Be My Baby" – The Ronettes
"Pictures Of Lily" – The Who
"Don't Be Cruel" – Elvis Presley
"96 Tears" – ? And The Mysterians
"My Only Love" – Roxy Music
"Where Did Our Love Go?" – The Supremes

"Strangers In The Night" – Frank Sinatra
"River Deep, Mountain High" – Ike and Tina Turner
"A Day In The Life" – The Beatles
"Rock Your Baby" – George McCrae
"Will You Still Love Me Tomorrow?" – The Shirelles
"Ruby Tuesday" – Rolling Stones
"I Believe (When I Fall In Love It Will Be Forever)" – Stevie Wonder

The self-promoting Roxy song and "Rock Your Baby" aside, all of Ferry's choices were antiquated. He freely admitted that listening to new music was not a top priority, and that the contemporary music he heard failed to excite him in the way as the pop music of his youth. Ferry was, by 1981, a bit of a musical museum, with little real love for the new but a great deal of respect for the past. In fact, we can now draw a line under Ferry as a genuinely progressive artist. There would be moments of poetry and beauty in the future, that's for sure. But Ferry would never again sound as if he was fully engaging with the present.

No, from the early eighties onwards, save for one last brilliant parting shot from Roxy Music, Ferry seemed trapped by the past. Despite the enormous industry that marked all his future projects, his music began to repeat themes, ideas and ideologies. And what was even more damaging was that, for the first time, Ferry began to make errors of judgement in the recording studio and major miscalculations in terms of his career as a whole. We didn't know it then, but in 1981, the rot had set in. It would be twenty years before it would be successfully treated.

THE "CURSE" OF AVALON:
1981-1999

Roxy Music may have been at their commercial peak in 1981, but little else was rosy in their garden. When the band convened to record their eighth studio album, it was clear that they were a disintegrating unit. *Avalon* would eventually be hailed as classic rock album, and would stay in the British charts for over a year, making it their most successful studio album. Yet, it wasn't to be a happy time for those involved in making the record. There were professional and creative tensions, and also the sort of interpersonal problems that came from a dozen years of being together.

Things had, in fact, been difficult for some years. According to Andy Mackay, for the last three albums of the band's career, "There were a lot more drugs around as well, which was good and bad. It created a lot of paranoia, and lot of spaced-out stuff." "The time when I really knew Bryan was between 1972 and 1977," says photographer Mick Rock. "In those years, we all considered him straight, in terms of his chemical input. But I think that had changed."

The paranoia can be felt on *Avalon*. Behind its smooth contours and grand romance there is rigidity, and a real edginess, as if the striving for perfection had been taken to some secret absurd lengths. *Avalon* is that sound beyond slick: the sound of super-self-confidence and tortuous self-criticism. There are no flaws, nothing rough or discordant, everything is perfectly played: the whole is a dense fabric of sound in which mood and atmosphere overtakes songwriting and narrative. Every percussive beat, every bass note, every vocal phrasing appears to be exactly how Ferry and co. wanted it to be.

Avalon was one of the first albums ever to be released on CD, meaning that for the first time a Roxy album could be heard in almost exactly the same way as its creators had heard it in the studio. A new adult demographic was about to take the new, improved Roxy Music to their hearts. Although the band wouldn't be around later as recording artists to reap the massive commercial benefits, *Avalon* was in the vanguard of the new Adult Oriented Rock (AOR) formatting. By 1985, Dire Straits' *Brothers In Arms* would sell in its millions to the self-same audience that cherished *Avalon*. The Roxy album was to be a signature record of the new yuppie culture. In 2001, its title track would be Number 1 in a US magazine's "Greatest Make-Out Music Of All Time" list. Its effects were simultaneously damning and negative yet, as a record, it's a thing of sublime beauty. So just how was it made?

The band's eighth album would be fired by the singular artistic vision of its lead singer. Much of the material was written during a period when Ferry was based on the west coast of Ireland with his new girlfriend, Lucy Helmore. He had met Helmore at a New Year's Eve party in 1981, and the couple often made use of her parents' home near the Irish coast. While conceiving the album, Ferry would look out onto the very lake that was to feature on the original album cover artwork. His writing took a new turn: "I felt this was the most romantic, dreamlike album I'd ever done. It's very much a mood album, and the lyrics kind of appear here and there as little kinds of washes of colour. They're very vague, the lyrics on this album; for me in a nice way in a sense that they kind of colour the moods." The lyrics, and their performance, have an almost half-heard quality to them which is utterly beguiling: clusters of words which we strain to hear ululate, they scurry away before we can quite catch their meaning. *Avalon* is full of these moments: murmurs, sighs, and whispers. The overall mood is twilight: a romantic pool of deep mysticism: an incredible sonic experience.

Avalon, recorded at Compass Point in Nassau and The Power Station in New York, sounded different because Roxy worked on it in a different way. Phil Manzanera explains:

Avalon was very different to all the other albums in the sense that it was the first album done where we'd used the studio as an instrument.

We changed our method of working and virtually played in the control room. Things like a Linn drum, which was the first professional drum box, had just been invented, and I had that wired into the desk. I had a control room that was bigger than most recording areas and the keyboards in the control room. We were using the actual desk almost as an instrument. So because we'd changed our method of working, I think the method in which it was done created this incredible album.

It has been claimed that *Avalon* is a Bryan Ferry solo album in all but name. But how true is this? Neil Hubbard was brought in to play guitar while Fonzi Thornton sang backing vocals and Andy Newmark, who would become a good friend of Ferry's, became the band's permanent drummer. "I've heard that it's almost a Bryan Ferry solo album in that there's Neil Hubbard playing guitar, and various other people," suggests Peter Sinfield. "And Bryan only let Phil and Andy come in right towards the end to add touches, so that they could call it a Roxy album." "*Avalon* is very much a Bryan album," is how Phil Manzanera puts it. Although Manzanera can understand and appreciate the album, at the time he found it a problem to get a hold of: "[Bryan] was on a certain journey ... it very much reflects his mood at the time. That's why it was difficult. It wasn't necessarily the way I wanted to go, especially being a guitarist – you play through loud amps and you want a bit of angst in there."

For the title track, Ferry sprang a surprise on his band members. Recording in New York one Sunday, he noticed a group of Haitian singers by the coffee machine outside one of the studios. Eavesdropping on the incredible singing talent of Yanick Etienne, he knew instinctively that she could bring some magic to "Avalon", so he asked her to sing backing vocals. When Phil and Andy appeared at the studio to find that Ferry had unilaterally decided to add backing vocals to the track, they were not best pleased. Phil Manzanera: "When we came into the studio, she was already on the track. However, I do remember at the time, because one was so caught up with insecurity and stress, thinking, 'How dare you put something on without asking us?' But his instinct was totally right, and it was absolutely brilliant."

Avalon was a unique record: there was nothing else like it in 1982. Roxy had successfully overhauled their sound: it wasn't the sound of a band paring down, returning to first principles; but the sound of frustrated energy, clipped guitars, dreamy bass, sexy rhythms, and smooth, almost ambient soundscapes. More than any other Roxy album, it reaches for, and attains, sublime heights and moment of genuine, luxuriant beauty. There is the coda of "More Than This", when the music dies away to reveal one of the most lovely refrains in pop, the perfect neo-classical ending to that most stately of pop songs. And then there is "Avalon" itself, with its hypnotic charm, which attains an otherworldly state of consciousness. Avalon is the mystical final resting place where, defeated, King Arthur went to die. And "Tara", one of Andy Mackay's greatest moments: a haunting oboe refrain played over the distant echo of crashing waves. Or "True To Life", perhaps the signature song from *Avalon*:

> "Well it gets to seven
> And I think of nothing
> But living in darkness."

> (Words and music: Bryan Ferry, 1982)

Avalon creates its own unique, somnambulant world of befuddlement; the music entraps a sense of time slipping away, of yearning, as Ferry and the band approach their late thirties, and this is captured brilliantly in the fatalism of the first single off the album, "More Than This". It's the re-emergence of Ferry the wanderer, the loner, his melancholia reflected back by unending and ineffable nature:

> "I could feel at the time
> There was no way of knowing
> Fallen leaves in the night
> Who can say where they're blowing?"

Before the fatalistic chorus:

> "More than this – there is nothing."

> (Words and music: Bryan Ferry, 1982)

It is here that Ferry adopts a tactic he has frequently used on subsequent solo albums, namely the use of phrasing whereby the final word of a phrase or sentence, or maybe the final syllable, trails off into almost nothing. When he sings "more than this", the "this" is so quietly enunciated and so wearied and distracted that the final "s" is hardly pronounced at all. Perhaps this is an echo of Ferry's own distraction. He is, after all, a man who often drifts off in conversation, avoiding eye contact and seemingly having to kick start his quite fragile and hesitant conversation through a process of physical action (as previously remarked, it's not uncommon to witness a Ferry silence or pause punctuated by a sudden lurch round the room or a surprising jerk of an arm or leg).

Avalon's cover famously depicts the future Mrs Ferry, Lucy Helmore, dressed as a warrior queen, merlin on arm, looking out over a lake into the distance. The lake lay behind the lodge where much of *Avalon* was written. Antony Price gathered everyone together for the photo shoot at dawn: it was raining. Wanting an image of a mist-covered lake, Price had rockets launched over the water, which would explode and create hopefully just the right amount of fake mist. At dawn, the sky cleared, the sun shone, and Price got the shot he wanted. Just as well, because the very next rocket Price let off came back down vertically into the box of fireworks, blowing the whole lot up.

The lodge itself was burnt to the ground in 1997 and Lucy's father was tragically killed in the blaze. The report in the *Irish Times* of November 13, 1997 strangely referred to the Ferry marriage in the past tense:

Man (73) dies as blaze destroys lakeside lodge

A retired insurance broker living in Connemara died when fire engulfed his home, a lakeside fishing lodge, early yesterday morning.

Mr Patrick Helmore (73) had lived alone in the two-storey house, Crumlin Lodge, near Inverin. The blaze destroyed the building.

Mr Helmore had been a semi-invalid. His daughter Lucy was married to the singer Bryan Ferry, a regular visitor to the wooden lodge during the early 1980s.

Mr Ferry featured the lodge on the cover of his 1982 Avalon album, which reached number one in the British charts. He composed some of his music there and was a regular visitor to some of the local pubs during his visits to Connemara.

Released in May 1982, *Avalon* entered the UK Charts at Number 1 and would stay in the Top 75 for over a year – an astonishing achievement.

Worldwide sales of *Avalon* were the biggest of any Roxy album yet, and that for a band well into its eleventh year. "I think *Avalon* was a very elegant swansong," says Paul Du Noyer: "I love *Avalon* actually, but I love it in an entirely different way than the first two albums. They almost seem like to be the work of two entirely different acts. I wouldn't sit down and play them all in sequence, because they seem to belong to different parts of my brain almost, where I appreciate them in such fundamentally different ways."

Du Noyer is right. *Avalon* is the work of a band unrecognisable from their debut album released ten years earlier, and this would lead to a split within the ranks of the Roxy fans between those stout defenders of the early Roxy Music, especially the first two Eno-fired albums, and the newer fans who came on board around the time of *Avalon* or just before.

Ultimately, *Avalon* set just as many agendas as the first Roxy album. It is not Roxy's fault that the strains of music *Avalon* hinted at or reflected – ambient, new age, easy-listening, MOR – were later debauched by cruder and less inventive souls. What is undeniable, however, is that the astonishingly intricate music of *Avalon* would fixate Ferry for years to come. In effect, *Avalon* put a curse on Ferry. Feeling comfortable with the sound, he simply remodelled it for years and years to come, and finally stopped moving forward. In effect, *Avalon* put an end to Bryan Ferry as a major creative talent for the next twenty years.

Roxy launched a tour of Europe and the USA that began in 1982 and continued into the next year. Tickets for their Wembley gig would set you back a hefty £7.50. The tour was slick; too slick for some. In truth, the sound of Roxy Music in 1982 and 1983 was far closer to the one that Ferry would develop on his subsequent two albums than even the *Flesh + Blood*-era Roxy. Ferry, however, was thrilled with the technical ability of the new members of the touring and recording set-up. He said of Spenner, Newmark and Hubbard that they were "in danger of becoming a fixture": "They're all very good musicians. It's the biggest band and the most talented players. It's good to sing with a rhythm section that's as good as that. It feels like you are skating, gliding along."

The keyboard player on the tour was Guy Fletcher, the fresh-faced multi-instrumentalist who would later find fame with Dire Straits and the Notting Hillbillies: "I was asked to visit Phil [Manzanera]'s studio in Surrey, where Bryan was working on an album, which eventually turned out to be *Boys And Girls*. I showed up on the day with my Roland Jupiter 8 synth, set it up in the control room and Bryan asked me to jam over some tracks he was working on. A few turned out to be songs and takes, which ended up on the album. Very shortly after, I found myself rehearsing with the band for the *Avalon* tour."

Fletcher remembers Roxy Music with great affection:

> Bryan I always admired enormously as a singer, and my suspicions were confirmed when I had the opportunity to back him. Phil had always intrigued me greatly, and when I met him, he was absolutely charming and very accommodating. A tad loud on stage, but that's a "guitarist" thing, isn't it? Andy was always fun to be around and exhibited great showmanship on stage. The band itself was great, with Andy Newmark on drums, who really knew how to keep the groove simple, Jimmy Maelen, a brilliant percussionist who also played on *Brothers In Arms*, and Neil Hubbard, another one of the nicest guys around and a tremendously soulful guitarist.
>
> Alan Spenner on bass was my absolute hero. The funkiest white bass player ever, he was inspiring to me, as the bass was my first instrument. I understood a whole new chapter about bass playing from working with Alan. He was extremely funny to be around: one had to be on one's toes all the time or Alan would play some kind of prank. He had a remarkable habit of going off the deep end during after-show dinners, especially when there were record company executives present. He was always teetering on the verge of unemployment. Sadly, he had quite a self-destructive personality to say the least, and just about kept at bay a serious drug problem. He died in August 1991.

The *Avalon* tour didn't escape the odd hitch or two. In Berlin, the band almost didn't make it on stage at all. "I remember being stuck in a lift with the band on the way to the stage in Berlin … a real *Spinal Tap* moment," recalls Guy Fletcher: "It was quite a scary moment, mostly because it looked like Alan Spenner was about to throw up at any minute. It was at this show that he became so inebriated that one of the road crew had to crouch behind him whilst he was standing on stage, otherwise he would have collapsed in a drunken stupor. Amazingly, he played a note-perfect show."

Spenner was also a notorious wag on tour flights:

Alan also had a habit of playing in-flight pranks. One of his favourites was to go into the cockpit (in the days when it was allowed) and bribe the pilot into letting him borrow his jacket and hat. He would then add a pair of sunglasses and improvise a white stick and he'd burst out of the cockpit and fumble his way towards the rear of plane, dribbling out of his mouth all the way.

There were many incidents involving broken hotel room furniture, mostly from my room, and one particularly dangerous "large plant pot out of the window" incident, in New York of all places. Luckily, it crashed onto an empty street. Having said all that about Alan, I must stress that, when it came to it, he was always respectful and professional.

The heart-stopping show of the tour was the gig at Fréjus in the south of France on August 27, 1982, in a huge amphitheatre of a place. "The atmosphere in those venues really gets the blood racing," says Fletcher. The show was filmed and later released on album, and as a live concert video and DVD, *The High Road*. Here, Alan Spenner was up to his tricks again:

> We were ready to go on, waiting backstage. There was a countdown for the cameras, pyrotechnics etc, and just before we got the go-ahead Alan screamed, "It's no good, I can't take any more," and ran off into a field. Bryan's face was a picture. He looked at Mark [Fenwick] and Mark ran after him. When he reached him, 500 yards later, Alan said, "Just kidding". I think that really "threw" Bryan for most of the show. Watch the first couple of numbers on the video with this is mind!

By 1983, Roxy Music were back in America. "Life for me on the road on that tour was a real eye-opener," says Fletcher. "It was my first visit to America and my first proper tour. I was 21 and had bleached blond hair with a red streak, kind of like A Flock Of Seagulls. I recall stepping off a plane in Fresno, California and overhearing a local's comment: 'Hey, punk farmers!' It was a fantastic initiation into rock 'n' roll. I had a ball." By contrast, Ferry was quite candid to American journalists about his lack of enthusiasm for touring and his weariness with trying to break America: "We had kind of lost interest a bit, because we had much bigger audiences elsewhere in the rest of the world. And since we're not particularly fond of touring, and kind of limited the amount of touring we did, then obviously America would be the first to go. It was as simple as that really. Although the fans that we have had and still continue to have are a very true and loyal audience."

In fact, Ferry was tiring of touring altogether. One of the reasons for his increasing reluctance to play live was the fact that he was by now a married man. The news that would break a million girls' hearts had been announced in the *Times*. Ferry was no longer the most eligible bachelor in rock. At 37, after many years of playing the field, he had got hitched:

Mr B. Ferry and Miss L. Helmore

The marriage took place quietly on June 26, 1982 at the Church of St Anthony And St George, Duncton, Sussex, between Mr Bryan Ferry and Miss Lucy Helmore.

Ferry had met Lucy Helmore in 1981. She was the convent-educated daughter of a Lloyd's insurance broker, fifteen years his junior and, reportedly, had initially thought he was gay. Their home would be Ferry's Victorian house near Petworth in East Sussex. "The house holds an impressive collection of paintings, mainly by the Bloomsbury-set artists Duncan Grant and Vanessa Bell, along with a rare Clarice Cliff painted coffee table and some Keith Murray ceramics. Even the ping-pong table stands on an original William Morris rug," one journalist was to note. Ferry's elderly parents were by now also living with him, his father tending to the grounds.

Apart from being beautiful, Lucy was also good fun and well liked. Journalists found her "sparky and amusing", although it appeared to the media that Ferry became increasingly irritated by their fascination with her upper-middle-class background. Had Ferry married into a well-bred family to further his lifelong scheme to infiltrate the upper echelons? Ferry found such crass over-simplifications and assumptions hugely grating. He and his wife used the Surrey mansion as their base at weekends: Bryan was to buy his mother-in-law's house in Kensington for the working week.

Soon, Bryan and Lucy's first son would be born, named Charles Frederick Otis. "We call him Otis," said Ferry in 1983. "Hopefully it hasn't made me too serious or certainly too domesticated or any of those kind of terrors that you have," he continued:

I'm sure it's always a worry with a lot of artists that they'll lose their rough edge or be less cutting if they're married. Or maybe it's just I'm more worried about that. It's a very kind of self-centred business, as you can imagine, being your own product, and you can get very self-centred indeed. So I think it's a good thing for me to have some other responsibility – this strange clone creature – to think about other than myself. It adds another dimension to my life, really, which is good. I can't see anything negative about it, really. Obviously, it means that you live in a slightly different way, but you'd hope for that, really, after fifteen years of playing the field and running around in circles.

Ferry clearly felt that it was time to settle down. Post-Lucy, the rock 'n' roll lifestyle was no longer for him: "Just waking up and not remembering what you did last night. I never talk about drugs in interviews. There wasn't much time for the partying. I was so full of things I wanted to do, and no other commitments. No girlfriend. Lived on my own."

Bryan Ferry's domestic life might by now have been idyllic, but his musical future was less well-starred. In 1983, Roxy Music finally disintegrated completely. Ferry had already started planning the next record, and it became clear that he wanted to push off in his own direction: "There were too many conflicts, really. Not musical so much as personality conflicts. Before I did *Avalon* and while I was doing it, it felt to me that it had gone as far as it could go. It was no longer useful or stimulating to have that sort of conflict. I just wanted to work without that irritation. To keep [Roxy] together just as a business name didn't seem enough reason." Later he would say, "Splitting up Roxy just seemed like the right thing to do, the creative thing to do. I did a couple of weird things around that time. I think it comes under the heading of 'artistic indulgence'. Maybe I was wrong."

For Manzanera and Mackay, the decision came as no big surprise: "I got the impression they were not so much shocked as upset and angered by something which seemed inevitable," says Guy Fletcher, who continued to work with them on their post-Roxy project, the Explorers. Summing up the history of the reformed Roxy, Ferry said:

Some good things came out of it, thanks to some of the musicians who I picked up in the intervening years, like Alan Spenner, who was just the greatest English bass player, and Neil Hubbard: they became part of my repertory company, if you like. Andy and Phil were still part of it, of course, but they weren't really friends, which was a shame, really. And all because of money.

Although Ferry is being somewhat evasive here, it does seem to be the case that he felt a greater camaraderie with the newer "hired hands" than with the original nucleus of the band. What exactly could those money issues have been? Writer Mat Snow is the man in the know:

> I know there was some problem back in the early eighties with Andy Newmark. When Paul Thompson left, they got Andy Newmark, who had been the drummer with Sly and the Family Stone, and Ferry was a huge fan. But it caused gigantic ructions within the band, and I believe it was one of the reasons why the band split up, because Andy Newmark was actually getting more money than the rest of the band. And this caused huge, and indeed terminal, resentment.

At the time, the split was never intended to be as permanent as it turned out to be. It is one of the great disappointments in modern music that Roxy, to date, haven't recorded in the studio together since. "We really didn't say, 'We're going to split up', after *Avalon*," said Manzanera in 2001. "Bryan just went off and started doing his next solo album and said, 'Let's get together in a few years time.'"

The immediate future for Manzanera and Mackay involved the Explorers, formed with Liverpool-born singer James Wraith. Guy Fletcher liked the project: "I enjoyed making the album, mainly because I was intrigued by how it would evolve. I never thought much of the songs, though." To some ears, the band's first single, "Loreli", actually sounded more like Roxy Music than *Avalon* had. Yet this fine single, and three others, all failed to chart. The band toured in 1985 and appeared on the *Wogan* TV show but success, such as it was, was moderate. Their record company, Virgin, rejected a second album and the band folded in 1987.

Ferry's career would, however, match the commercial success of the last two Roxy records, at least initially. Bryan Ferry no longer saw himself primarily as a live performer. His family commitments, together with a genuine road-weariness, led him to reassess his new role in pop music as a studio musician only. In the next fifteen years, he would play only two major tours. What Ferry couldn't predict, however, was that, within that time, there would be only three albums of new material too.

The man who made three albums in just one year back in 1973 was seriously slowing down.

What caused this malaise? There were a number of factors which all contributed to Ferry's alarmingly slow productivity rate – managerial crises and personal problems all played their part – but the real problem was Ferry's working methods. In the Roxy Music days, the band would create the most suitable musical setting, very often out of Ferry's own musical ideas, then Ferry would go away and write a lyric and a melody over the top. What happened with *Avalon*, and the albums that followed, was that Ferry would be completely studio-bound. He would very often work with dozens of different musicians in an attempt to discover the perfect musical alchemy. Yet, after months of recording, all he would be left with would be atmospheres, textures and brilliantly played lines, but no melody, no lyrics and, therefore, no song.

The curse of *Avalon* would not be apparent for a while to come, but a curse it was. Ferry had begun the process of building up songs through grooves and licks and ambience, intricately layering these and then grafting on a melody and lyric, when appropriate, afterwards, in a painterly fashion. The background wash was pulsing and charged: Ferry would add the narrative detail of melody and words later. He perfected the technique on *Avalon*, but could never repeat the trick again to the same degree of success. So began years and years of work which all sounded like *Avalon* outtakes. With, some would argue, more money than sense, Ferry would now construct his music on such an absurdly intricate pattern that, as one journalist bluntly put it, "he refined himself out of existence". With so many spaces in a multi-track studio to fill up, and so many talented musicians to call on, Ferry would defer and demur, unsure which of the five fantastic solos should be fitted in at what stage.

For 1985's *Boys And Girls*, Ferry spent (or wasted) two years in the studio. Or, rather, in seven studios. In total, he used thirty musicians, including such luminaries as Dave Gilmour, Mark Knopfler, Nile Rodgers, Tony Levin and David Sanborn, as well as the "usual suspects" of Spenner, Newmark and Hubbard. At the time, Ferry referred to the album as his *meisterwerk*, but, with the benefit of nearly two decades' worth of hindsight, even he would not deny that he took his creativity to extraordinary lengths:

> I wanted to do an album of my own songs, and thought I'd done enough group albums. Now I wish I had done that, *Boys And Girls*,

with the group. It was a very painful record to make. I was very tired but also a glutton for punishment. I worked with far too many musicians and in the end it was a very expensive piece of tapestry, really.

Recording for *Boys And Girls* was to be interrupted by the sudden death of Ferry's father in 1984. Ferry, who had become increasingly close to both his parents, was devastated, and was to dedicate the album to Frederick Charles Ferry, a humble, unassuming man who Ferry fondly remembers as the sort of person who wouldn't be interested so much in the glamour or thrill of the pop world but in far more important things like what vegetables they sold abroad. "My dad just died like that [snapping his fingers]. It was a terrible blow to me," Ferry said in 1994. "And I … I kept blaming myself. That I hadn't … got enough help for him in the garden. It used to have six gardeners, and he was doing it nearly all when he died."

With so much time lost and so many deadlines missed, Ferry also blew what might have been the biggest chance of his career. He was offered a song by composer and movie-score producer Keith Forsey called "Don't You Forget About Me", to be recorded for the film *The Breakfast Club*. However, so overwhelmed was he by the making of *Boys And Girls* that he turned it down. Of course, it is impossible to tell whether a Ferry version of the song would have had the seismic impact on the US and British charts as the version recorded by Simple Minds, who gratefully took up Forsey's offer, but it is hard not see this missed opportunity as Ferry's last chance to make it big in the US.

Ferry himself later admitted that he had perhaps not been ready to make another solo album of his own material so soon after *Avalon* and the long world tour:

> I've made some stupid moves, I think … mainly in the eighties, when I basically thought I was more prolific than I was; at writing that is. After the *Avalon* album, I nearly did an old songs album, which I think would have been refreshing for me, and somehow I didn't. I'd like to shoot the person who advised me! I'm sure it was my own fault.

The first single off the new album was "Slave To Love" a mid-tempo pop song. It reheated the lugubrious style of *Avalon* musically, and covered old ground lyrically too, but without any of the tart epigrammatic wit of Ferry's bittersweet Roxy love songs. We get the same indistinct vocal phrasing as on *Avalon*, the same trademark sound effects of old (this time, an electrical storm in place of a revving motor-bike or speeding car). Yet the British public appeared happy with what they knew: the single reached the Top 10 in June 1985 and stayed in the Top 75 for a creditable nine weeks. However, to add insult to injury, Simple Minds' version of "Don't You (Forget About Me)" would simul-taneously be Number 1 in the USA and would eventually spend a total of 24 weeks in the British charts.

Boys And Girls all sounded impeccable, of course. The second single, "Don't Stop The Dance", co-written with Rhett Davies, was surprisingly only a moderate hit in the UK, reaching Number 21, but its sexy pulse and slinky sax made it a strong single. And lyrically, Ferry cleverly quotes from the old Arlen/Koehler standard, "Stormy Weather". Ferry sings:

> "Mama says it's only stormy weather
> Don't know why there's no sun in the sky."

> (Words and music: Bryan Ferry/Rhett Davies, 1985)

The album's focal point, though, was "Windswept", Ferry's favourite track in the collection: "That was just like a mood which just kind of intensified the more we worked on it. It just started off as a keyboard melody and Rhett [Davies] was very good at helping me find right the keyboard sound." In fact, Davies and Ferry would experiment throughout the album with a number of different rhythms, including, for the first time in Ferry's music, Latin styles: "I was always a big fan of *Come Dancing* on television," Ferry confessed. "I loved all those Latin American dances. So it was getting away from all the to and fro of rock drumming which I'd had it up to here with." "Windswept" contained the following lines:

> "Oh baby don't leave me there
> With a low whisper
> Windswept in the air."

> (Words and music: Bryan Ferry, 1985)

Here, Ferry captured the mood of the album in three taut lines of under-emoting. Overall, though, the album is hardly there at all. Like the non-particularised blocks of colour in the paintings of another arch depressive, Mark Rothko, *Boys and Girls* does as little as possible: one mood, one groove, one pace. It refers to nothing but itself. Journalist and Ferry fan Chris Roberts summed up the album perfectly when he wrote in *Melody Maker*: "With *Boys And Girls*, Ferry reached the zenith of his vagueness. It was the least eventful record of all time. As such, one could only pan it then, after cooling down, hold it up to the light and marvel at its perfect lack of any emoting. It was a muted sigh, not even a gasp ..."

Long-time Ferry fan Allan Jones saw through the album's central conceits in his *Melody Maker* review, headlined "A Sloane Square": "Over the nine songs here, Ferry presents himself in the familiar role of a soul in torment, buffered by the fates, confused by love and its demands, at the mercy of his own heightened sensations. Unfortunately, very little of any of this sounds very convincing. Brushed and scrubbed to within an inch of their lives, these performances actually have very little to say. Ferry surely knows his market, and no doubt *Boys And Girls* is perfectly pitched to its demands. Roxy Music's original fans may no longer be quite so young, but [are] very probably still upwardly mobile."

Although Ferry didn't tour the album, he really had no need to. Number 1 for two weeks in the summer of 1985, it hung around the UK album charts for ten months. A Roxy Music compilation album released the following year, *Street Life: 20 Great Hits*, was Number 1 for five weeks and clocked up 77 weeks in the charts, the best achievement of any Roxy or Ferry product. However, the only glimpse of Ferry live would be on July 13, 1985 at Wembley Stadium, when he played Live Aid. Ferry dithered about whether or not to appear, fretting about the logistics, and most of the efforts to secure his appearance were made between the event's organiser, Bob Geldof, and Lucy Ferry. Live Aid wasn't Ferry's finest hour. He played three songs from his new album: "Sensation", "Boys And Girls" and "Slave To Love". The pacing was slow and Ferry's positioning on the bill in late afternoon wasn't the best either, coming as it did just before the show-stealing sets by U2, Queen and Bowie, and after the dreary, mood-killing appearances by Sade, Sting, Phil Collins and Howard Jones. Ferry rescued his contribution somewhat with "Jealous Guy" but many thought that he had used his twenty-minute slot purely and simply to push new product, rather than entering into the spirit of the day with a more crowd-pleasing selection.

Of course, Live Aid as an event had its detractors, amongst them the Smiths, then easily the most important new band in Britain. Johnny Marr had this to say: "It should be pointed out that Bryan Ferry used the event for personal gain. He disappears for a few years and then comes back with a new record and shamelessly plugs it at Live Aid. The decent thing would have been to play at least one old song – but no."

In the spring of 1985, in a rare in-depth interview, Ferry spoke to James Truman of *The Face*. In 1975, *Melody Maker's* Caroline Coon had written a revealing exposé of Ferry as he was about to turn thirty. Despite his success, he was a depressive and unsure man. What strikes us about Truman's article a decade later is that so little had changed: Ferry's self-criticism and self-doubt seemed preserved in aspic. There would be the customary tight-lipped response to any question about his work: "I've always been reluctant to analyse what I do: it takes the pleasure out of it." Then there was the disdain for the mainstream pop business and the reluctance to give anything of himself: "I'm not in the public eye – I turn down everything that's offered. I'm really as much a recluse as it's possible to be in this business … as a rule, I've always been relieved when I haven't been recognised." Then there remained the same sensitivity to criticism, particularly comments about his alleged frivolous lifestyle: "Every record I've made I've suffered through. In a way that's why I've sometimes been a little self-righteous about it, especially when people were criticising me for apparently leading some frivolous jet-set life."

Ferry recognised his almost manic-depressive personality, caught between action and introspection: "I suppose there's a strange mixture in me, of on the one hand being moody, introspective, brooding, always thinking about work, and on the other hand dashing around madly, desperate to get hold of some new inspiration and excitement, of wanting to try everything." Finally, he admitted his own perennial alienation: "Having lived in various different places, and having known various groups of people, I've found that I don't really fit in with any of them." Ferry at forty was palpably as much the outsider as he had ever been.

Of his son, Otis, Ferry admitted: "I put him down for public school, but I'm not sure. I'd like him to go to the kind of grammar school I went to, but they don't seem to exist anymore. It's difficult to know what to do. People who go through the British public schools either come out as dreadful Hooray Henry types, or with that amazing self-confidence to do anything." Chided for his aristocratic manner and good taste, he felt compelled to remind interviewees of his work ethic. And mindful and proud of his working-class roots, he felt confused about his place in the social hierarchy and about the values wished for his own family. These insecurities mirrored those of many who felt that same sense of isolation and self-doubt that being "upwardly mobile" can bring.

In 1986, Ferry busied himself with a new studio album, but returned to the UK Top 40 with the song, "Is Your Love Strong Enough?" which he had recorded for the Ridley Scott fantasy film, *Legend*. The song was actually a Roxy Music number, having been demo-ed for *Avalon*, when it was known as "Circles". Asked to write something for the movie, Ferry finished it off in a six-week period. A video, featuring Ferry and Pink Floyd's Dave Gilmour and shots from the movie, helped push the single up to Number 22 in the UK.

If the *Boys And Girls* period was beset with problems, then 1987's *Bête Noire* and its aftermath era merely magnified Ferry's woes. Over the next five years, Ferry would be working in an unstable personal and professional situation. His manager of fifteen years' standing, Mark Fenwick, was removed following an acrimonious legal tussle, and was replaced by Dire Straits' manager, Ed Bicknell (who, like Fenwick, declined to be interviewed for this book). Certainly, Ferry is not the easiest person to manage. Considering himself to be an *artiste*, and having what seems like an infinite capacity for self-doubt, he would miss deadlines, make himself unavailable for interviews, and generally be, if not a loose canon, then certainly a driven man whose first loyalty was to himself and to his work.

On June 27, 1987, *Melody Maker* printed the following item about the split with EG Records, who were reported to be suing Ferry over his forthcoming album, *Bête Noire*:

Ferry claims his recording agreement with EG ended in March this year and is now in a position to sell his new album to any company. But EG say he is in breach of a 15-year contract which gives them exclusive rights to market the album in Canada and the United States. The action will be heard at the High Court in six months time.

In a preliminary hearing last Friday, the parties agreed that if the album is released before the main hearing, Ferry will pay a third of the royalties into a joint account with EG Records which they will receive if they win the case.

EG Records also agreed not to sue Warner Brothers, the company Ferry may take the album to, without first applying in the High Court. The EG Records logo will still appear on the album cover.

Bête Noire was eventually released in the late autumn of 1987 and was an obvious attempt to make a more radio-friendly record. There would be the usual cast of thousands on the record: three studios, three engineers, and a mere forty musicians. Much of the work had been done in LA and in Paris, where the Ferry family, now swelled to four with the birth of his second son Isaac, would live for a time. After the introversion of *Boys And Girls*, Ferry wanted to record outside of the UK, and to collaborate with new people. Patrick Leonard, Madonna's sometime producer, was brought in to add what it was hoped would be the necessarily happening production to give Ferry a hit, with Chester Kamen as co-producer. The brother of Nick Kamen, pop star of the Levis ads in the eighties, Chester Kamen has worked with musicians as disparate as Robbie Williams and Roger Waters, and had played with Ferry at Live Aid. He was to co-write one of the songs on the record, "Seven Deadly Sins".

Some of the songwriting was done during a four-month stay in LA. Two nannies were employed to look after Otis and Isaac. Mum Lucy was apparently concerned about encroaching Americanisation among her offspring when Otis came home from the Beverley Hills Montessori School and greeted them with "Hey, you guys." Dad Bryan, however, was more troubled by the ongoing crisis in his management. Although Ed Bicknell, who had taken over from Fenwick, had managed to place *Bête Noire* with Virgin Records, Fenwick himself was in a litigious mood. Chris Salewicz spent a year travelling around with the Ferry family during the writing and recording of the album and recounts the next stage in the managerial divorce:

After this spell in Los Angeles, Ferry moves to Paris to continue recording *Bête Noire*, dropping off in London on the way. As he steps out of the customs area into the main airport concourse, he is greeted with a writ that is thrust into his hands. It comes courtesy of the lawyer of his former manager, Mark Fenwick, who is somewhat concerned about being considered Bryan Ferry's former manager. Though such an action is by no means unexpected by Ferry, he finds the arch style of the announcement of the lawsuit to be rather unnecessary. To deal with this, various visits to London are required. Eventually Ferry and Fenwick meet, each accompanied by their lawyers: during the course of the five-hour meeting, during which a settlement is arrived at, they speak to each other only through their legal representatives. Ferry, who voices genuine affection for Fenwick, finds this distressing.

"I had a very painful business divorce from my managers at the time which dragged on for a couple of years and was very, very painful. It was my first experience of that," Ferry was to later reflect. "It seems to have happened to virtually every pop, rock and soul artist at some point or another in their careers, I think. So historically I was due for mine, and I got it in spades, I felt."

Ferry had put a huge amount of work into the album but the results were very mixed. *Bête Noire*'s sound was slightly dated, even by 1987's standards. "Day For Night" was similar in feel to Madonna's "Open Your Heart", released eighteen months earlier, while "The Name Of The Game" was a ringer for "Live To Tell". The clanging synths, busy percussion, slap bass and vaguely Latin feel had not worn well at all. The real problem, however, was the sharp decline in Ferry's own song-writing. The album attempts to move away slightly from the moods of *Avalon* and *Boys And Girls* but it never sets out a convincing enough new agenda, and ends up caught between pop blandishments and the old lovelorn romanticism of the past. None of the songs, with the possible exception of the second single, "Kiss And Tell", compares to anything recorded under the Roxy banner.

The public were somewhat indifferent. The first single was "The Right Stuff", co-written with Johnny Marr, who also guested on guitar and in the promotional video. Originally an instrumental written by Marr called "Money Changes Everything", it had been the B-side to the Smiths' single, "Big Mouth Strikes Again". Marr had sent the music to Ferry during the recording of the album, and Ferry wrote a lyric over the top. "The Right Stuff" struggled to Number 37 in the UK Charts in October, with *Bête Noire* reaching Number 9 the following month. Compared with *Avalon* and *Boys And Girls*, it was a commercial failure. And the critics were generally underwhelmed too. Anthony DeCurtis in *Rolling Stone* summed up the disappoint felt by so many:

Bête Noire is another step in Ferry's retreat from distinct songs into atmosphere and feel. The strategy can sometimes work wonderfully, as Ferry proved on the transcendent album *Avalon* from Roxy Music. But as his voice sinks more deeply into the murky layers of his music, as his lyrics are reduced to a Morse code of refined despair and his subjects recede into the mist, Ferry seems increasingly like Narcissus, enraptured by his own reflection in the pond – and the bottomless depth below.

Ferry's first tour in five years took place in 1988 and 1989. With Neil Hubbard and Andy Newmark retained from the late-period Roxy line-up, the strangely scheduled tour began almost a full year after the album had been released. "Casanova", "The Bogus Man" "In Every Dream Home A Heartache" and "Ladytron" represented the Roxy years, along with the obvious hits – "Jealous Guy" and "Love Is The Drug" – and a sizeable chunk of Ferry's recent solo material. As soon as the tour finished in early 1989, Ferry set about writing and recording what he hoped would be a quick follow-up to *Bête Noire*.

However, by the early nineties the first strains in the Ferry marriage were filtering through into articles and interviews. They would have two more sons, Tara and Merlin, born 11 months apart in 1990. However, Lucy was battling alcohol and drug addiction, and went public about her personal problems. She attended Alcoholics Anonymous and Narcotics Anonymous for two years before, in 1993, spending nine weeks at Farm Place in Ockley, Surrey, a £1,000-per-week clinic that tackled substance dependency via the twelve-step method. Ferry, meanwhile, talked to Louette Harding at *You* magazine about how Lucy came from a dysfunctional family, and how "she and her brothers suffered from that":

> She comes from a generation of people where they all went into the programme in their twenties or something, a particular sort of bad group of people … well, not bad, they're pretty sick – a lot of heroin and all that kind of thing. All those upper-crust kids are very spoilt. Thank God it's never been part of my life. When I was at university I saw a friend with heroin addiction ruin his brain. [It] put me off it for life.

The marriage would endure, despite increased media speculation about the prospects of the Ferrys remaining an item. "It's unbelievable the things they've written about her or us," Ferry told journalist Adam Sweeting in 1994. "The funniest thing was when she was a 'mayonnaise heiress'. Lucy's maiden name is Helmore. Helmore's mayonnaise! I'm a great subscriber to Hellmann's, actually. I use it a lot. I should get them to sponsor the tour."

Ferry, for his part, was to endure something of a mid-life crisis, becoming even more paralysed by the creative process than usual. It was not always so: in the first ten years of Ferry's success, he was one of the most productive men in pop. In the first rush of creativity, Roxy Music had produced five albums in three-and-a-half years. Between 1972 and 1982, there were a dozen Ferry and Roxy albums of original material. Yet there would be an astonishing seven-year gap between Ferry's *Bete Noire* and his next album of solo, self-penned songs, 1994's *Mamouna*. It might be that the dreamy textures of a Blue Nile album, the poetry of a Patti Smith, or the sophistication of a Ferry album simply requires longer to mature. But surely, eight years reflects not so much a honing of one's craft as ... indolence?

In fact, it doesn't. Ferry worked hard in the recording studio, labouring tirelessly for months and even years. The availability of digital recording, and 64-track at that, simultaneously inspired and entrapped him. It meant he could layer information, but it also meant that he could, once again, endlessly defer making a final judgement on what parts should fit where. Ferry hired dozens of expensive musicians to play on these new songs, and then found himself with too much information from which to choose. His brother in-law, the journalist Edward Helmore, put it like this: "It's unusual, because he actually writes in the studio. Instead of going in with complete songs ready for recording, he builds things up like a collage. Then he gets all these amazing session musicians to play their virtuoso pieces and he will rearrange them to fit the music. When he's singing he likes to create a bit of an atmosphere by having this huge incense burner, and he stands on a little Persian carpet in the vocal booth."

"For the last ten years I have had a dismal output of work," Ferry would confess to the *Times* in 1993. "It's because I got very self-conscious about bringing out a new album, conscious of what I was trying to beat and determined to write my masterpiece ... the first problem was that the technology got more and more sophisticated so my opportunities expanded and the possibilities became endless." The new album was originally to be called *Horoscope*, and initially Ferry was upbeat about the prospects of releasing it quite quickly after the relative failure of *Bête Noire*. But by 1992, he found himself without either a manager or a producer. And, with no one there to call a halt to

Ferry's increasingly grandiose designs, the recording sessions went on, and on, and on.

Ferry briefly linked up with the B52's manager, Martin Kirkup, in another short-lived experiment. However, the situation only stabilised when he hooked up again with his original manager, David Enthoven, who had come out of a ten-year retirement. According to Ferry, Enthoven was "tough enough and old enough to be able to kick me around." For his part, Enthoven would refer to his new client affectionately as "the old boy". Ferry was to make the following oblique comment about his management problems in 1993: "… after a two-year wrangle I settled out of court. I had reached a point where nothing seemed to be going right and everything was out of control."

Rumours had it that Ferry had financed the recording of the *Horoscope* album to the tune of £800,000. At one point it was costing him £2,000 per day to record the tracks, all financed solely from his own pocket. Although clearly no pauper, Ferry inevitably had cash flow issues. Such was the singer's relentless quest for perfection that, in 1993, he was forced to sell his home in New York to help balance the books as the recording of the new album went on, remorselessly, year after year.

Looking back at his *oeuvre*, Ferry was to admit in 1993 that he thought his music had "gotten more convoluted in some ways. Perhaps also less joyful, which is rather sad. I think the singing is better; the rhythm section is much better. Overall, certain aspects have improved; some have been lost. Nothing I should be too worried about … my big regret is that I haven't done as much in the last ten years as I'd have liked. So in the next ten years I want to do a lot more recording. And I mean ten years. I think I may have ten years left before my voice goes."

Personal and professional cares were understandably taking their toll on the singer. Listening to the tracks intended for *Horoscope*, Ferry and Enthoven, along with the record company, decided that, even after all the years of work, they were still not ready. Some reports claim that Virgin Records simply rejected the album out of hand, though this is rigorously denied by Ferry himself: "They seemed to like it, from what I remember. Warner Brothers in America didn't like it as much."

The main problem, the consensus ran, was the lack of anything commercial enough to be released as a single. The solution was to simply turn the canvas of *Horoscope* around to face the wall, and to return to the songs some time in the future, in true painterly fashion.

Some of the songs would ultimately be dropped, others reworked, and *Horoscope* would eventually be released in 1994 with the new title, *Mamouna*. This ill-fated album appeared to suffer from a conjunction of events that chimed all-too-well with the astrological import of the album title itself.

It was around this time that Ferry began taking Halcion sleeping tablets in an attempt to cure boughts of insomnia. Now unavailable in the UK, the drug has caused widespread controversy. According to the website HealthyPlace.com, "adverse reactions can include excessive daytime drowsiness, weakness dizziness and clumsiness and on occasion memory impairment, abnormal thinking/behaviour, confusion, anxiety and depression."

"He told me that he needed to have eight hours sleep, otherwise he'd be very cranky," said journalist Sylvie Simmons. In 1995, Ferry told Simmons: "I have taken Halcion – I wish had some now, ha! – but God no, I can't think of anything worse than taking Halcion during the day. It's just one of the sleeping pills that I've taken over the years, because I've always had problems sleeping. But I go for months without taking anything. Other drugs? I think it's hard to get through the music business without some nodding thing – but my lips are sealed."

It may of course be totally coincidental and an unrelated phenomenon, but in the 1990s, as Ferry by his own admission hit something of a midlife crisis and began seeking help in order to get a good night's sleep, his own music became ever more slumberous. The writer Mat Snow puts it like this: "Obviously, the whole creative metabolism does change, but with Ferry it seemed to be such a dramatic change. Also, all his music after the mid-eighties has got this ... people always talked about the languid lounge lizard, but if you listen to practically everything he did in the seventies, it's pretty upbeat and exciting. [There was] lots of energy – mental and, indeed, musical energy in there. But from the mid-eighties onwards, I guess it started with *Avalon*, you have this mood of reverie, which has settled entirely over his music. It just feels as if it's permanently exploring a dream state."

Another huge personal blow to Ferry was the death of his mother in 1991. It had been expected, but still, the shock of losing his mum to cancer was plain for all to see. Ferry was holding her hand when she passed away at their Sussex home. "Bryan was devastated when his parents died," said Antony Price. "The thing that made him most proud was being able to make his parents happy." Ferry was to reflect: "I was very close to my parents for the last fifteen years or so. It was great to have that sort of relationship, but when it goes, you miss it very much. But it's a strange thing – as the pain of the physical separation diminishes through time, so the spiritual bond that you had seems to grow stronger, so that's a good thing." "My great sadness is that three of my children never saw my dad," he was to add. "And they don't have my mother around: the best grandmother you could ever have. [My father] would have been great. I sort of carry him – the half of me that was him – to them. And I have to be my mother to them, nag them about school."

Around this time, Ferry also underwent some sort of therapy. "Once a week," he told a journalist in 1994. "And is it any good?" he was asked. "Yes, it is ... whether it's worth the money or not, I'm not so sure." No longer a smoker, Ferry's main vice by now appeared to be nothing more than a few glasses of wine after the sun had gone down over the yard-arm. Yet the perceived psychological trauma within the Ferry make-up, the air of distraction, and the melancholic episodes appeared to make him want to understand both his own problems, and those of his young wife.

In order to help him locate a muse that had given a good impression of having gone AWOL, Lucy Helmore suggested that Ferry throw himself into an interim project, a covers album, which would be recorded quickly, without fuss, using analogue equipment. Pre-production for the album was completed at Ferry's home recording unit, with the tracks cut at Matrix Studios in London. The result was *Taxi*, a stopgap album, arresting in places, but hardly essential Ferry. Robin Trower, who co-produced it with Ferry, encouraged him to take a much more direct approach: "I think I brought a more black-and-white outlook on music – especially the performances," is how Trower puts it:

> The idea we had going into *Taxi* was that it would be made quickly so that it still felt fresh at the finish. Bryan decided to work on a 24-track machine only, to limit himself and thereby make a "simpler" album. My particular favourite was "I Put A Spell On You". We tried to inject as much "live" performance into *Taxi* as possible – bass and drums

went on very early in the process. Some of the vocals were the "demo" vocals – full of energy and freshness.

Ferry has always enjoyed interpreting the work of his favourite singers, and at that stage it had been almost two decades since he had last released an album of covers. He had always admired Sinatra and Elvis for their ability to base a whole career on their interpretative powers, and *Taxi* reawakened his interest in this side of his creativity. One of the most successful covers on the album was a ghostly, melancholic rendering of the Shirelles' 1961 classic, "Will You Still Love Me Tomorrow", a song that he loved, and that had actually been slated for *These Foolish Things*. The original Brill Building Goffin and King classic, which reached Number 4 in the UK, is upbeat, if bittersweet. However, Ferry teases out the self-doubt in the original lyric and bases the whole mood of the song on this new twist.

According to Ferry, the key to a successful cover is not the ability to match the original slavishly, but to take the song somewhere else and to stamp one's own individuality on it: "An old song is a point of departure," he told the BBC's Johnnie Walker. "Instead of having a blank canvas, you're starting with something there, some information which you can then take from it what you want. Obviously you use the basic lyric – you might want to change a few lines to make it work better for you – you might even change the melody."

Taxi took Ferry back into the UK charts, reaching Number 2. The first single, "I Put A Spell On You", put him back into the Top 20 and gave him an appearance on *Top Of The Pops*. Ferry's live vocal take of the song over a backing track, on which he accompanied himself on piano, would be pre-recorded for the show.

Despite this success, the rest of the album once again appeared mildly lethargic and one-paced. Ferry's choices seemed to be drawn from an MOR repertoire that would please the over-forties but that would have problems convincing any new fans of his relevance. The individual songs chosen were open to question too. "I Put A Spell On You", apparently the only song on the album to have been suggested to Ferry by an outsider, had already been covered many times over: by 1986, a total of 28 versions were known to have been recorded. The definitive version was made by Screaming Jay Hawkins way back as 1955, but Nina Simone, Creedence Clearwater, Arthur Brown, Them, Audience, John Mayall, Alan Price, Manfred Mann and Nick Cave had all had a bash too.

"Answer Me", featuring Ferry on "organ and witch" (which sounds uncannily like a theremin), was a mildly creepy cover of another oft covered song. Frankie Laine had had the earliest hit with it back in 1953, while Nat "King" Cole would also interpret it, and Barbra Dickson would take it to Number 9 in 1976. The rest of *Taxi* could be filed under "mildly diverting"; the only real error of judgement was the reading of "Amazing Grace", which fell flat on its face. With a backing track that sounded as if it had been lifted from Madonna's "Justify My Love", it truly tested the limits of how far a song could be reconstructed to make it work. Overall, the overriding response to *Taxi* could only be one of mild incredulity. Could the man who wrote "In Every Dream Home A Heartache" and "Out Of The Blue", the star who was revered for his own brilliant songwriting, really be the same person as the one who strolled through this rather staid and obvious collection of covers?

During the promotional chores for *Taxi*, Ferry revealed that he had met up with Brian Eno again and had lunch: "We talked about the horrors of 48-track recording. We got on very well." Pressed by a journalist about the possibility of a full-scale Roxy reunion, Ferry appeared far more open to the idea than might have been expected. "I'd quite like to make another record with them one day – whoever 'they' are, there's about twenty people who've been in it at some point," he said, before adding, "I can certainly see myself working with him [Eno] again, with him as co-producer. Not sole producer – he's not musical enough. But he's a very good producer of a certain type – an agent provocateur, and a very good editor of ideas."

Ferry could still cut a somewhat mournful figure. He told Mat Snow that the thought of playing live filled him with "dread": "I'm not very healthy. I used to have tonsillitis all the time and now I don't have tonsils; I cough instead. That's why I stopped smoking four years ago. Every winter I was in such pain I had to stop." Snow asked him, "What happened to the playful mood of yore?" to which Ferry replied sadly, "It's not playful any more. You go through dark periods and sometimes they can be really long. I'd like to think I've come out of it, and turned the corner with this new record. I really do hope so."

As it turns out, the worst was indeed over. *Horoscope* had finally been finished and released under the new title of *Mamouna*, with the help of Robin Trower, as co-producer. To the excitement of original Roxy Music fans, the album featured the reappearance of Brian Eno, who was credited with "sonic awareness", "sonic ambience", "sonic emphasis", "swoop treatments", "sonic distress" and just plain "sonics". It was clear that, in the intervening 21 years since he had last figured, the last thing Eno had bothered to do was to learn how to play an instrument.

One track, "Wildcat Days", was a Ferry/Eno composition; the first time Eno had gained a co-songwriting credit with his former Roxy colleague. With the presence of Manzanera and Mackay on the album too, fans were hopeful of a full-scale Roxy studio reunion. However, it was not to be. There were still too many issues to resolve. Mackay and Ferry were willing to discuss the idea; Phil Manzanera was the one resisting. He had enjoyed playing on *Mamouna* ("I had a great day there. I played on several tracks, though I can't hear myself on any of them"), but poured cold water on any idea of a full-scale reunion:

> I saw one of [Ferry's] Hammersmith shows. He sang very well, but everyone around him was wrong, and he's surrounded by so much baggage. At that point, I thought I could never see the Roxy thing ever happening again. There would be no point doing it unless the music sounded great. A lot would have to change before it was a serious consideration.

"Mamouna" – which means "good luck" in Arabic – was the title of a new song Ferry had composed after the *Taxi* sessions. According to writer Adam Sweeting, Ferry had "draped the walls with an Arab tent-hanging he'd bought in Marrakech ten years earlier, and something about its minaret shape and faded Saharan colour scheme whispered in his ear as he plonked away at the keyboard."

Ultimately, though, the *Horoscope/Mamouna* album was a *folie de grandeur*. Six years of recording, utilising an astonishing 112 musicians – even by Ferry's standards, this was simply silly. "I had a sort of mid-life crisis,' he said frankly in a *Guardian* interview in 2002. "Certainly concerning the creative process, I was hiding myself more and more. I listened to *Mamouna* the other day and thought, 'Wow, really interesting, but I can't hear the vocal. Where am I?'" Some of the album's material had been worked and reworked for years. One song, "The Only Face", was actually begun in demo form as long ago as 1976. Fan and webmaster John O'Brien has this to say: "Some of his music would be overworked, and by the time he finished it, the music had missed the boat and the original idea was contemporary when first started but dated by completion."

"I think *Horoscope* got bogged down purely because Bryan had kept working on the tracks but (in many cases) did not have lyrics for them," is producer Robin Trower's take on the situation:

> Plus he was trying to paint his "masterpiece", but maybe had too many colours in his palette and not a well enough defined subject. Bryan is an artist – very creative, very intuitive – and he does not work to a formula. My job was to keep an eye on the practicalities of what he was doing. There are some tracks on *Mamouna* that show Bryan at his very best – "Which Way To Turn", for example. The whole album is a beautiful piece of work. When we returned to *Mamouna* after *Taxi*, we had great fun finishing it off. Things learned from *Taxi* were applied – [the] same bass and drums, [and] also a couple of new songs added.

Despite the elegant mix, dense textures, brilliant playing, and occasional wonderful song ('Which Way To Turn' is, indeed, the highlight), *Mamouna* is still an album marked by Ferry's near absence. Sonically closer to *Boys And Girls* than *Bête Noire*, it's actually a more reclusive record than that masterpiece of demurral. "Your Painted Smile" was chosen for the first single, but it failed to register with the public, reaching only Number 52. The second single, the title track itself, fared no better, stalling at Number 57. The album itself, released in September 1994, was commercially possibly the least successful Ferry studio album: it was in and out of the charts in just a month, and reached only Number 11. Like *Avalon*, one mood prevailed throughout the ten songs, but unlike *Avalon*, there were hardly any memorable melodies, not even on repeated listening. Those in need of a late-night fix of intriguing self-analysis, trippy beats and *chanteuse* vulnerability would turn to the likes of Portishead's *Dummy* and a dozen other albums rather than to Ferry's *Mamouna*, which seemed to have been recorded in a different era altogether. In fact, it had. Five years in the making, it sounded dated before it was even released.

Ferry decided to tour the album nevertheless, embarking on a world tour and his first concerts for six years. More than ever before, the emphasis would be on his balladry. Ferry's now mostly middle-aged audience greeted "Put A Spell On You", "Slave To Love", "Windswept", "Mamouna", "Carrickfergus", "Avalon" and the obligatory "Jealous Guy" enthusiastically. However, unlike established artists such as David

Bowie and Neil Young, he had stopped appealing to a younger audience almost completely. The rows of sensibly attired, middle-class patrons were Ferry's fan base now and, on the *Mamouna* tour, Ferry played to the gallery rather than looking to win any new supporters.

Ferry too was now middle-aged and was finally living the life his youthful version had merely aspired to (and had, indeed, sent up). He was a kind of country gent, weekending with Lucy and his four sons. In fact, according to Alice Thompson of *The Times*, who visited him at around that time, "he now has four children, three homes, a maid, a secretary, a couple of nannies and a gardener. He has put his children down for public schools, including Eton, because this is where his wife's family went, but says he would have been equally happy to send them to his old school, Washington Grammar. He makes his children speak Geordie for part of each day ... beside his bed he has a John Osborne biography, the *Spectator* and the *Literary Review*." As ever, Ferry professed himself completely uninterested in modern music: "I don't admire Seattle grunge at all, and most dance music now is so awful and conventionalised." No, it was not music, but style that continued to fascinate him:

> Once you develop an eye it never stops. You are fussy about every-
> thing, whether it's clothes, wallpaper, buildings or car design. Not to
> be an old queen about it, but if you're going to have something why
> not get something you like the look of? I think the one thing that sums
> me up is what I wear every day. It's a rough black suit from *Comme
> des Garcons*. It has a slightly left-bank intellectual look and I like to
> think Baudelaire could have worn it.

And, once again, class, or rather Ferry's continued upwardly mobile trajectory, caused instant irritation when mentioned by any journalist keen to find out just why the man had, as far as the rest of us were concerned, all but joined the aristocracy: "The British are obsessed by keeping their artists suffering in the gutter. They never allow you to move: it's very smothering. Why can't I fly in someone's private jet if I want to, walk with the dogs or take up fishing? I like new experiences ..."

Simon Mills, commissioned to write a piece on Ferry in 1994, received this piece of good advice from a fellow journalist: "If you ask him a direct question, you won't get much out of him. If you generate light conversation you'll get a lot more." Interview-mode Ferry is indeed an odd mixture – very keen on a bit of gossip, fun, personable, yet also simultaneously evasive and diffident when asked any blunt or probing questions. Twenty years on, and, to all intents and purposes, a Ferry interview was the rock journalistic equivalent of Bill Murray's *Groundhog Day*. It seemed as if he just didn't change, year in, year out, decade in, decade out: his likes and dislikes, his twitchy defensives and evasions, were unchanging. The journalistic agenda never changed either – the fascination with someone who had skipped the middle classes and had seemingly joined the aristocracy was a constant theme.

Writer Sylvie Simmons, who met him in 1995 and again in 1999, noted Ferry's routine and industry:

> His house is in Kensington, quite near Earl's Courts, at the far end of Kensington High Street. It's a big old house and the downstairs basement area is where he works on his music. And he goes there every day. He was living in the countryside at weekends with his wife and family. He told me he worked every day from 11am to 7pm, except weekends. He had his artwork upstairs and his music down here. His basement studio has old sofas draped in Moroccan rugs, a grand piano, synthesisers, state-of-the-art computers, shelves stuffed with reel-to-reel tapes. I went digging through the tapes, being a music fiend, and there were some demos of "Virginia Plain" in there.
>
> It looked like a great place to hang out. It was very unlike the place I would expect him to be in. I expected something debonair and lounge lizard-y. It was very much a kind of rich hippy look, with lots of records lying around, or rather, put neatly on the walls, him being a Libra. He struck me as a guy who was very much into routine. He seemed to have almost this need to make it look like a job. Maybe that comes from his northern working-class background, where it was a bit shameful not to have a job to go to.

In addition to work on his own solo music, Ferry was also at that time involved with the re-mastering of the original Roxy Music albums. A four-CD box set, *The Thrill of It All*, a collection of album tracks, B-sides and remixes, had been produced in 1995, and now all eight of the original albums, together with his solo work, were due for reactivation in 1999. Simmons says:

> He told me, "I have been working on the catalogue which they had been re-mastering and I slightly redesigned some of the stuff. Some

of them are pretty good, gatefolds, so they look like mini-albums." He added, "I've also been struggling to set up this internet thing, a website, which is apparently what you have to do these days. Not that I'm very computer-friendly: I still write on paper, I don't use, what are they called? ... word processors." I said, "Your kids should help you with that." And he said, "Yeah they're totally into it. That's the other thing I do. At the weekends I see my children. I have four boys. It's not very family-friendly being in this business but some people tend to manage it quite well." He noticed at the end of this discussion that he had children, which is quite sort of a scary thing really! It must be a very odd marriage if you're just spending two days a week with your wife and kids.

In the meantime, Ferry had begun work on another album, to be called *Alphaville*. However, as if in some existential nightmare, he went on to repeat the mistakes of the *Horoscope* project. After *Mamouna* he had disappeared to write and record new songs and, once again, it had gone wrong. Sometime in 1998, he decided, just as he had done during the recording of *Horoscope*, to stop his new studio album, and begin work on another covers album. This time he would look even further back into the mists of time, to the thirties and the songs of his parents' youth. At the same time, he was worrying about his future. In early 1999, he said:

> I would like to get on the road again. I'm getting rather anxious about that – it's been much too long. I sort of finish a tour full of energy, and then I say, right, I've got to make an album, and then I get bogged down. And the record company didn't like the album I did. And it's all been rather disastrous, really. It's all geared now towards Take That, and the Spice Girls, and Radio One, and MTV.

Rich though not super-rich, famous but not super-famous, Ferry, now in his mid-fifties, was much admired, much loved, yet slightly adrift. Whereas Eno's career had exceeded its early promise with a welter of kudos and big name productions (his work on U2's *Achtung Baby* reinvented the world's most famous rock band, and for the better) and radical records, Ferry appeared in need of new challenge, a new goal, a new relevance. Fortunately for him, critical and commercial salvation was just around the corner.

NO GRAND EXIT:
1999-2004

"The grand exit is very appealing, isn't it? It's really more down to how you devise it, though. The motorcycle accident and the plane crashes have all been done ... I'm quite in favour of the 'pile of clothes on the beach' one myself. That hasn't been done in rock yet, has it?"

Bryan Ferry, 1976

On Friday 29 December 2000, on flight BA 2069 from Heathrow to Nairobi, Bryan Ferry came within seconds of losing his life. At 35,000 feet, Paul Mukonyi, a 27-year-old man with a history of mental health problems, attacked the cockpit crew. Attempting to grab hold of the flight controls, he accidentally disabled the autopilot and the aircraft took what seemed to be an unstoppable dive towards the ground. The plane plummeted steeply, before banking left at a sharp angle and continuing its downward trajectory. A few extra metres of tilt, and it would have been upside-down in mid-air and impossible to control. Lights out, oxygen masks dangling from the overhead compartment, engines shrieking, the plane shuddering, three downward plunges in quick succession: it was the stuff of nightmares.

Ferry was on board with his wife, Lucy, and their three younger sons, Isaac, Tara and Merlin, on their way to a New Year's holiday in Zanzibar. They were seated towards the front of the plane in the upper section right next to the cockpit and so had a perfect view of the incident. There is a priceless photo of a slightly crumpled-looking Ferry standing bleary-eyed as the cabin crew wrestle the attacker to the ground. Also on board the flight were Lady Annabel Goldsmith, widow of the late Sir James Goldsmith, their son, Benjamin, and daughter,

Jemima, wife of the famous Pakistani all-rounder Imran Khan, with her two sons.

In the overall panic of praying, screaming, swearing, weeping and vomiting, Ferry simply looked as if he'd incorrectly plumped for "true" on "Call My Bluff". "The plane was going to crash. We were all going to die. I just thought, 'Oh no, I've got an album to finish. Could we reschedule?" laughed Ferry to journalist Barbara Ellen a few weeks later. What did he now think of his brush with death? "It was *marvellous*. A real buzz. I'd do it again."

"He was holding a prayer book. He seemed to be delirious, talking away to himself," was Isaac Ferry's description of the man who had almost brought down a British Airways jumbo jet carrying 398 passengers. "He walked up the aisle towards the cockpit and was hanging around the toilets." Reportedly (and with his tongue, doubtless, wedged firmly in his cheek), Ferry was just as upset by both the foul language emanating from his understandably terrified son, the then 15-year-old Isaac, and the would-be hijacker's socks ("they were pretty awful stripes") as he was by the fact that they were within a few brief moments of almost certain death. "Everyone was freaking out everywhere," said Isaac. "Except Dad, who told me to stop swearing. The co-pilot and the pilot were involved in a struggle with the man. Then two people broke into the cockpit and dragged him out. It looked as though they had gouged his eye and they secured him with seatbelts ... He wasn't trying to hijack the plane, it was a suicidal [sic] attack. He wanted the plane to crash."

Eventually, with the assailant sedated, blindfolded and restrained, the plane's captain, Captain Hagan, announced, "Ladies and gentlemen, it is all under control now, but a madman has just tried to crash the plane." The physical injuries suffered were relatively light: a flight attendant had broken her ankle, and the assailant had bitten the pilot's finger and ear. Captain Hagan had managed to drag him into club class, where passengers helped to restrain him. Phil Watson, the co-pilot, managed to right the plane and pull it out of its dive. According to one source, Isaac Ferry managed to video some of the disturbance.

"The crew were wonderful, so brave," said Benjamin Goldsmith. "They must have been as terrified as all of us, yet the stewardesses were going up and down reassuring everyone. They gave hot tea to people, and vodka ... the pilot came on later and said five or six seconds more and the plane would have tilted on to its back and blown up." On his arrival at Nairobi Airport, Ferry, ever the master of understatement, told a waiting reporter, "I'm relieved to get here in one piece."

Ferry's brush with death came twelve months after the demise of one of his closest personal friends, Simon Puxley, his own "sixth Beatle". In all matters of creativity, Puxley had been the singer's sounding board. "We did everything together," said Ferry. "So even before the plane thing I'd already been thinking, 'God, Simon's dead … I must get my act together'." The loss of the man who was his publicist, confidant and kindred spirit was a huge blow to the singer. Despite this, by the end of the nineties there were already signs that he was getting his career back on track.

In fact, 1999 had witnessed a mini-revival in Bryan Ferry's fortunes. *As Time Goes By*, a collection of oldies but goodies, was released that autumn and reached Number 16 in the UK charts, selling strongly for many months throughout some European territories. The idea of recording a full album's worth of material had come when Ferry worked with the arranger and performer Colin Good on two songs, "Sweet And Lovely" and "If I Didn't Care", for the soundtrack for the film *Richard The Third*. Now in his mid-fifties, Ferry allowed himself the luxury of recording music from an era so bygone that only pensioners would remember when the songs were first popular. He liked the idea of re-creating a world in which well-crafted songs were the norm, and well-grounded men lived lives of urbane charm. "People often expect artists of any sort to live extremely, but some of the best are, or were, very bourgeois and need a solid grounding to indulge their fantasies," he reminded us.

Ferry used his home studio for rehearsals, but did the actual recording at Lansdowne Road Studios in London, which specialise in jazz and orchestral work. "It's an old-fashioned studio, with wonderful old microphones and a big live room," he enthused. "It was ideal for the job at hand. We found ourselves tending to mike things from a distance, to try to get the sound of the band, rather than close-miking." The basic tracks would be recorded live.

There were fifteen songs in all on the album. Ferry's vocal, infirmities and all, was pushed right to the front of the mix for the first time in years. Rhett Davies, who had been away from the music business for ten years and had last been seen on a Ferry record back in 1984, returned to co-produce the album with Ferry, whilst Robin Trower also co-produced two of the songs, "When Somebody Thinks You're

Wonderful" and "You Do Something To Me". "I made sure Bryan selected a song that suited him and got the key right for his voice, which is very important for Bryan," he says. "And I worked along with Bryan and Colin Good on arrangement, and oversaw recording."

As with every other Ferry covers album, there are moments of rare charm – "Where Or When" for example, and "Sweet And Lovely" (where Ferry brings out his dormant Northern accent to almost comedic effect on the last word of the title – *luv*ely!) – as well as some pretty, diverting songs. No one could doubt Ferry's sincerity, or commitment to authenticity. With tinkling pianos, weird ondes martenots (a keyboards synthesiser very like a theremin, which was used in avant-garde performances in Paris in the thirties), harps and violas, this was a very careful sonic recreation of the pop music of the day. The only time Ferry steps into the present is on "I'm In The Mood For Love", where he allows Phil Manzanera to plug in his guitar and Colin Good to switch on the synth.

At first, Ferry's record company were less than enthused by the project. "The publishers wouldn't have it at first," said Ferry in 1999. "Virgin UK said no and it was brought out by Virgin in Germany. The fact that it's so successful is great, but it wasn't planned as a big commercial thing. I just love the songs – beautiful melodies, intelligent lyrics."

As Time Goes By was a quietly gentrified collection of songs for Ferry's post-*Avalon* fans and is as disconnected from the world of rock as is possible to imagine. The cover art depicts a forlorn Ferry, greying quiff, standing in front of pen-and-ink drawings of thirties cool dudes. A series of slim, beautify-coiffured men in sharp suits and women in elegant lingerie peer lifelessly from the CD booklet. This was an era of good brandies, fine cigars, tiffin, the National Programme on the radio and nannies and housemaids to perform unseemly domestic duties: in fact, not unlike the life of certain rock stars today.

It was difficult to foretell who would actually buy the music: probably not rock fans, and possibly not aficionados of Roxy Music either. Perhaps the music might appeal to the generation of aging part-time music listeners for whom Radio 2 was too happening, and who had long since gravitated towards that prison of the middle-aged – classical music. It was as far removed from the cutting edge as Ferry had ever been. Not that that worried him unduly. Rigorously opposed to style-hopping simply in order to remain relevant, Ferry appeared to be a genre all of his own.

Ferry toured *As Time Goes By* with one of the most technically gifted bands of his career. Musical director Colin Good had studied music at Queen's College, Oxford, and was from the jazz scene. Enrico Tomasso on trumpet had played with Louis Armstrong, whilst Alan Barnes, another veteran, had played with Van Morrison. The beautiful Royal College Of Music-trained harpist Julia Thornton opened the gigs with "Chanson Dans La Nuit", whilst violinist Lucy Wilkins would be a powerful and mildly cheeky stage presence throughout the tour. On bass for the vast majority of the gigs would be New Yorker Zev Katz, a man whose CV included work with the Eurythmics, Dr John, Aretha Franklin, Billy Joel, Elton John and Pavarotti.

The tour was a meld of acoustic thirties music and the rock stylings of the Ferry and Roxy material that formed the second half of the show, explains Zev Katz:

I enjoyed playing half the night on acoustic bass and being part of a large ensemble with horns, strings and harp. Colin Good's arrangements were beautiful, and the musicians were all experts at the thirties' style of playing. I hadn't had much experience with that musical era and those players taught me a lot about how to play it authentically. Then there was the "rock" half of the gig, during which I played electric bass in a style with which I was very familiar and very comfortable, but still the presence of horns and strings took it out of the ordinary. On top of all that, I must not forget to add that Bryan's singing was great. He really nailed the thirties' music, which was very impressive; it was dripping with character.

The critics loved the tour. "Lots of bands have DJs nowadays," ran the strap-line in the *Observer*. "No one apart from Bryan Ferry still wears one." Veteran Ferry-watcher Caroline Boucher heaped on the praise:

Ferry's latest album *As Time Goes By* is a collection of thirties songs and the stage set reflected this; black backdrop pinpricked with tiny stars, a suspended revolving silver ballroom ball and raised bandstand reminiscent of the big band era when musicians stood to take a solo and then settled back again. All very Stork Club. But then presentation has always been at the forefront of the Ferry agenda ...

The band highlighted Ferry's strengths, his melancholic voice, and the curious key-changes of his compositions that can end a song on a relative fourth. Diehard fans might worry at the prospect of "Love Is The Drug" or "Jealous Guy" played by a 13-piece backing band, but the songs took on a whole new slant while still bringing the audience to its feet and down to (and on to) the stage.

The choice of venues served only to confirm Ferry's quasi-aristocratic leanings, including a home gig at Petworth Park in Sussex, as well as Tatton Hall in Cheshire and Elton Hall in Northants. The tour ended in September 2000 at the Kremlin Palace in Moscow. Of the country house concerts, Ferry said, "They are big venues, but not soulless stadiums." They were certainly as far from the 100 Club as you could imagine. That said, Ferry was simultaneously admitting, perhaps for the first time ever, to liking some contemporary music. Beck, Radiohead, Missy Elliot, Macy Gray, Massive Attack, Tricky and Red Hot Chilli Peppers were all mentioned in interviews, along with Atomic Kitten ("I like them – they're kind of kitsch"), before he threw in the inevitable caveat: "But I don't hear much that blows me away." Another thing that he had realised he didn't hear much of on the radio were Roxy Music songs.

Ferry had noticed how well the older Roxy material was being received on the tour and this, along with some hard cash from a promoter, appears to have been the main reason for the shock announcement in January 2001 that, eighteen years and several inches on the waistline after they first appeared, Roxy Music would be re-forming for a world tour. A press conference was held at The Lancaster Room in the Savoy Hotel – a suitably upper crust establishment – and there they were: Ferry, Manzanera and Mackay. Their combined age was 158 and combined income, one would guess, tens of millions of pounds. Combined, they would once again be Roxy Music.

Save for a few songs, Roxy Music's back catalogue was largely dormant: seldom played on the radio, it was only performed on stage on Ferry's occasional live outings. Yet recent pop history had shown that Roxy Music were a constant, if understated, influence. Pulp's art-school conceits appeared to owe something to Ferry's seventies' blueprint. Blur's sonic experiments on their 2001 album *13*, particu-larly on songs such as "1992", appeared to draw upon the intensity and weirdness of the first couple of Roxy albums. One particular electro-pop group went one better, naming themselves "Ladytron" after Roxy's 1972 track. Radiohead and Moby were fans. Moloko had wittily parodied an early Roxy Music performance in the video for their single, "Pure Pleasure Seeker". Todd Haynes' 1998 film *Velvet Goldmine* had also put Roxy back in the media spotlight, if only indirectly. The soundtrack featured remakes of Roxy classics such as "Ladytron" and "Bitter Sweet" played by The Venus In Furs, an indie supergroup featuring Bernard Butler, Clune, Paul Kimble, Thom Yorke, Jon Greenwood and an original Roxy man, Andy Mackay. And in 2002, parts of Coldplay's "God Put A Smile Upon Your Face" were to bear more than a passing resemblance to "Out Of The Blue".

Yet if you had asked anyone under twenty about Roxy Music or Bryan Ferry, there was a good chance that they would not have heard a single song by them, such was the band's total lack of teen appeal. Old-timers such as Bowie, Iggy Pop, Lou Reed, and even Neil Young had retained the interest of youth by either collaborating with happening artists, playing the festivals, being openly cited by younger bands as prime influences, or simply by making good, headline-grabbing new music. Roxy, however, were largely a completely unknown phenomenon for many younger music fans, at most just a name they might know – something very definitely from their parents' generation. In order to sell out the very large venues, the Roxy reunion tour therefore had the dual task of getting enough of the original fans in as well as appealing to a younger demographic. In the UK, where Roxy had always been big, this was no problem. In the likes of Germany, however, Roxy would take to the stage in front of houses that were only two-thirds full.

There had been at least two other attempts to reunite Roxy Music before the band agreed to pow-wow in earnest in 2000. "One insider once told me that Roxy had come to within hours of re-forming in about 1995/6, with a drummer who used to be with Prince, but Ferry pulled out of that," reveals Roxy fan Ashley Wright. Now, though, for the first time in eighteen years there were no scheduling conflicts, no major musical difficulties and no massive interpersonal problems. But, just who *were* Roxy Music, 2001 style? The idea of a five-piece bashing out some songs had been dropped after the *Manifesto* tour in 1979. Later incarnations of the band had seen an augmented line-up with several specialist players brought in, and this was adopted as the template for 2001.

There would be a return for veteran Chris Spedding on guitar. Spedding was delighted to be back:

I got a call from Rhett Davies to be second guitar on the Roxy tour. I shared guitar parts with Phil Manzanera – both rhythm and lead – to make it sound like the records. I don't know many of the records, I just learn what I have to learn and play it, and sometimes I learn the wrong part. I'll assume that Phil will play a certain lead part and then I'd find out later that Phil didn't play that part on the record and I'm supposed to play it, so I've been listening to the record at home and I've played the wrong part.

Colin Good would be the pianist and musical director for the tour, and one of his first tasks was to find a drummer. According to one source, Paul Thompson had to audition for his own role in Roxy Music. Having spent the last decade largely away from the rigours of touring and from recording too, it was, to some, an open question whether Thompson could still cut it. There was, of course, nothing wrong with him. Having endured years of being under-appreciated, it can hardly have come as a surprise to Thompson that he would be obliged to prove himself yet again.

"Paul Thomson? I've always been a big fan of his ever since the early days and, if it's possible, he's actually improved over the years," is Chris Spedding's assessment:

> He is very conscientious, very hard-working, and you can have a lot of fun around him. He's a very impressive musician. I think people underrate him a lot, because for the Roxy tour he was able to take all those different feels from all those different Roxy drummers from after he left and he was able to play them perfectly, so that's pretty impressive. He didn't just play the Paul Thomson style; he played everyone else's style as well.

Sarah Brown was hired on backing vocals, along with Julia Thornton on percussion and keyboards, and Lucy Wilkins, who would play the Eno role on synths and Jobson's parts on violin. "Lucy's really vibrant," says Roxy fan and webmaster John O'Brien. "A friend of mine who's seen Ferry since 1972 said Lucy looks like a fan who's escaped onto the stage and is going to make the most of it until the roadies catch her. She's a very vibrant person, fun person, and you can see that onstage."

It appears that Brian Eno was never officially asked to join the tour and, in truth, why should he have been? As a player, he had been involved in only one-quarter of their recorded output. He had not played with the band since 1973 and had not appeared on stage himself since 1995, and then only for a one-off, one-song performance in Modena as part of U2 offshoot the Passengers. Eddie Jobson, who was in Roxy for longer and at least has a co-writing credit (something Eno never managed), would have had far stronger claims to have been asked to join a reformed line-up. Yet, in the public and media perception of the group, Eno's place in its history had assumed colossal importance. "To tell you the truth, we didn't actually ask him, but we thought about it. Then we found ourselves at the press launch with people saying, 'Is Eno doing it?' and we looked at each other and said, 'Oh shit! I thought *you* were going to ask him,'" said a mildly unconvincing Manzanera. "We all wondered if perhaps he hated the later stuff that he wasn't part of. We were all a bit afraid to ring him, I think. It's a bit embarrassing for all of us because we would love him to be part of it. He's not really the kind of person to go out on a big tour any more, as Bryan asked him a couple of year ago to do something and he said, 'No, I'm a studio animal these days. I don't do live.' But if he'd only turn up and go on with us somewhere, we would love it and the audience would love it."

Eno was reported as saying that the idea of Roxy reactivated was mildly pointless: it could only have been for the wrong reasons. It was unlikely that the original line-up had all simultaneously awoken one morning with a burning desire to play together again. And it was to play a well-established (though inactive) repertoire rather than to create anything new. The idea apparently left "a bitter taste". According to Ferry, though, Eno was misquoted: "Brian was incredibly embarrassed and tried to get it retracted. He thought the tour was quite good. He wouldn't have expected to have been asked to join us, and he wasn't."

For Eno, though, the whole deal smelt of reaction and nostalgia. Asked by writer Paul Morley about the difference between returning to work with U2 (which he was doing) and the Roxy tour (which he most certainly was not), he explained:

It's the difference between making something that you hope is going to be new, and remaking something you know isn't. Of course, these might not turn out to be true assessments of the future. I've never liked the idea of touring old music – I just couldn't face it. I don't want to put them down for doing the tour. If they want to do it, that's fine. But where's the pleasure? I was never actually asked directly. It

Avalon-era cool: Ferry in 1982.

On stage at Live Aid, 13 July 1985.

Ferry takes the crowd's applause,
Live Aid, 1985.

Ferry in Marrakesh, 1994.

Andy Mackay, Bryan Ferry,
Gray Tibbs and Phil Manzanera
in the *Flesh + Blood* era.

It's alive! The Roxy regeneration, 2001.

Singer and dancer Katie Turner..

'Vulgarity, I think, is quite amusing. There was always an element of that in Roxy –
vulgarity mixed with sophistication.' Ferry on stage, 2001.

Brian Eno today.

Bryan Ferry on stage (with Colin Good and Chris Spedding behind). At nearly 60, and still the epitome of style.

was known that I'd say no from the start to any such idea. Not only does touring make me slightly nauseous, but just talking about touring makes me slightly nauseous.

Fans would have loved some new material, to be sure. However, any worries that the band would take the stage and tarnish forever the gilded legacy of Britain's greatest art rock experiment were assuaged once the first night in Dublin was underway. The shows themselves did anything but a disservice to the idea of Roxy Music. In fact, while the *Avalon* tour had been smooth and functional, the 2001 Roxy reunion gigs crackled with energy and cackled at the idea of being a nostalgia trip. Playing with a surprising ferocity and commitment, Roxy took the stage to "Re-Make/Re-Model', with Ferry seated at the piano stool and a collage of early Roxy images showing as a back-projection. By the second number, "Ladytron", and Phil Manzanera's astonishing guitar solo at the song's ending, it was apparent that, for some of the audience at least, this was not going to be an easy ride. In fact, a cognisance of a fair proportion of Roxy album tracks was needed to enjoy the show. Those who, confusing the Roxy and Ferry products, expected to hear "Let's Stick Together" or "Smoke Gets In Your Eyes" were in for a rude awakening.

Although Ferry may disagree, Mackay, Manzanera, and Paul Thompson gave his aesthetic musings the sort of visceral kick that is missing from virtually all his solo appearances, both live and in the studio. Although "Do The Strand" and "Virginia Plain" were traditionally placed near the end of the set, Roxy would close with the arch melodrama of the album track "For Your Pleasure", each band member waving to the hall as they left after soloing. There were no encores.

Interestingly, Roxy favoured their earlier work for the gigs. "I always like a heavier sound ... songs like 'In Every Dream Home A Heartache', 'Mother Of Pearl', 'Ladytron' [and] 'Out Of The Blue'," said Manzanera. "You slot them in today next to Radiohead or the White Stripes or something and they don't sound cheesy or seventies or dated. They retain a core. We always said we were inspired amateurs back then, and were learning to play. By the time we got to *Avalon*, it was a lot smoother. We only just decided we'd play ['Avalon'] ... that speaks volumes." The astonishing visual excess was gone, true enough, but the sheer sense of style and theatre that Roxy brought to those 2001 shows made them compare favourably to the mundane nature of the vast majority of today's live rock experiences. Ferry's gold glitter jacket, at least, was a graphic reminder of a more daring musical era.

Overall, fans and critics found the remade, remodelled Roxy a joy. The absence of Eno was regarded as the one negative that kept the whole experience from being as truly thrilling as it might have been. "On that last tour it would have been great to have seen Eno patching up his old synths with a telephone exchange at the side of the stage," is Mark Ratcliffe's opinion. "They did do some of his solos exactly burble for burble. I could have lived without the Moulin Rouge dancers. We could have done without them, but evidently Bryan couldn't, so, fair enough, it's up to him." Another mild gripe was the set-list, which hardly varied throughout the tour, with a maximum of twenty numbers being played each night from a repertoire of just twenty-two. Compared with Bowie's shows between 2002 and 2004, which were not only much longer but had an ever-changing repertoire of songs both old and new, Roxy seemed to slightly short-change their fans, particularly at £34 per ticket for some UK shows.

However, the majority of diehard fans were over the moon, Bryan. "I was 41 years old and have never been so excited by anything in my life before," says Colette Robertson, a Roxy fan since 1972, of the June 2001 Glasgow gig. "Roxy Music had not played together for eighteen years and it was a sight we thought we would never see again. The feeling when the lights went down and the familiar party noise and clinking glasses drifted over the SECC was amazing. When the opening bars of 'Re-Make/Re-Model' started and the curtains pulled back I thought my heart was going to jump right up out of my mouth it was beating so fast. I will never forget that feeling."

The tour was followed by the *Best Of Roxy Music* album, which was a clever and unusually sequenced retrospective. Arse-about-face, it started with the drifty "More Than This" from *Avalon*, and stepped back in time with each track before arriving at 1972's "Re-Make/Re-Model". The journey served to re-emphasise one fact: just how dotty early Roxy Music were. The smooth, slumberous, beguiling rhythms of late-period Roxy are cool and affecting, but the sonic trickery found at the end of the CD is as barking mad as anything that has ever graced the charts. Other Roxy Music and Bryan Ferry compilations had stressed the smooch factor, but this new compilation made us look back to a moment of pop dottiness every bit as weird and wonderful as the much-vaunted *Kid A* era of today's pop avant-garde.

The compilation, however, was a moderate success only. Since the mid-seventies, Ferry had been subjected to an unremitting "death by anthology". It would be easy to lose count of the exact number of compilations and best-ofs that had been put out since the seventies. There was *Roxy Music's Greatest Hits* in 1977, *The Atlantic Years*, a collection of late-period Roxy, then *Street Life* in 1986, followed, illogically, in 1988 by *The Ultimate Collection*. In the nineties and noughties we've had *The Thrill Of It All*, a four-CD anthology, and *Slave To Love*, a collection of love songs and ballads, and so it goes on. Astonishingly, though, not one compilation actually does what it says on the tin: put all Ferry's and Roxy's Top 40 hits on two CDs in chronological order. Until June 2004, that is, when the *Platinum Collection*, a 45-track three-CD box set did just that.

What fans wanted, of course, was a new Roxy Music studio album. As the years roll by, it appears an ever less likely prospect. Fan Ashley Wright's view is typical: "The Roxy tour in 2001 was also great, as many people had given up on seeing them in one place again. But what they need to do is move on from there and do some new stuff and get Eno involved. They are in danger now of overdoing the touring and should get round to doing something new."

With Roxy deactivated for 2002, Ferry's new solo album, which had been largely completed before the tour, was quickly finished off in some busy recording sessions. Most of the work on the album had been done with Dave Stewart of Eurythmics' fame as Ferry's songwriting partner, and many of the songs from this abandoned project made it onto the record in either re-mixed or re-recorded form. Other tunes were recorded with the 2000 *As Time Goes By* touring band, including Colin Good, Zev Katz and the string section, whilst some songs were again re-recorded with members of the Roxy Music touring entourage of 2001, including Paul Thompson. The name of the album had now changed from *Alphaville* to *Frantic* to reflect a mad rush to meet its deadline – somewhat ironic, after seven years of work on the record.

Expectations for the new Ferry album, the first for eight years with any new material, were low. *Mamouna* had been mildly disappointing, *Bête Noire* possibly his most unconvincing work, whilst *Boys And Girls* was a generation ago. How pleasant, then, the surprise when *Frantic* turned out to be by far and away Ferry's most successfully realised solo album. The sound was punchy, the singing wonderful, the playing powerful, the melodies memorable without being derivative and, for the first time since *Avalon*, Ferry had penned some classic material. Although none of the singles charted, the album reached Number 6 in the UK, the highest for a Bryan Ferry solo album since *Boys And Girls*. One of the standouts was "Goddess Of Love", a love song for Marilyn Monroe:

> "Marilyn says I got nothing to wear tonight
> Only a pair of diamond earrings that catch the light
> Platinum blonde – is it true that you have more fun?
> Siberia – now I'm sad and all alone"

Then the chorus swooped in to admit:

> "Nobody cares like I do – what can I do?"

> (Words and music: Bryan Ferry
> and Dave Stewart, 2002)

"I've always loved female glamour," said Ferry, rather stating the obvious. "I suppose it comes from a fascination with screen stars and chorus girls." "Goddess Of Love" may be an old theme, yet it's Ferry's new openness that strikes the listener. In *Frantic*, writer and long-time Ferry fan Paula Brown saw a psychological shift within Ferry:

One of the subjects that I have been interested in and can only piece together through articles is how his writing habits changed. As most people acknowledge, there was a fracture of sorts in his writing and music post-Jerry Hall. Before, we saw prolific lyrics, an outpouring of almost visual abstractions coupled with the most sincere love songs and longing. Afterwards, bearing in mind the time lag between writing and release, we see him begin to bury himself in layers of orchestration, beginning on *Avalon* and going forward, until *Frantic,* which saw him coming out again.

I think he went through a very long period of depression or a sort of half-life suppression during which he couldn't really reach into himself and pull it out intact. I think he's slowly getting it back, but in recent interviews he still says the music comes easy but he has trouble writing lyrics. Imagine the man who wrote "Mother of Pearl" having trouble writing lyrics! There must be a reason, and I think the reason is that he is not willing to jump back into the breakwater of hell that is passion.

Elsewhere on the album, Ferry ups the tempo to break out of the near-catatonic pace of so much of the post-*Avalon* period. "Cruel", partly inspired by a Native American poem, is another moment when the patina of milky melancholy dissolves to reveal Ferry rediscovering the sureness of touch we thought he'd lost for good. The first third of the song looks at the plight of the Native Americans, their way of life destroyed:

> "Yes I know what it is to be free
> To run as far as the eye can see
> The long knife come – buffalo gone
> Like blades of grass they cut us all down."

Then Ferry turns his attention to the here and now, and, in a novel twist, shows fellow-feeling with the emotionally dispossessed in his own society. Ferry, writing about ordinary people? This was most odd. Did it mark a new awareness in Ferry's worldview?

> "Here is a girl who's working in a factory
> Spends all her time there thinking what she wants to be
> She got no boyfriend – she got no window
> She just a lonely heart – it's tearing me apart."

> (Words and music, Bryan Ferry/Dave Stewart, 2002)

Songs such as "Cruel" and the cover of Dylan's "It's All Over Now, Baby Blue" swing with a new vitality. Zev Katz played on the sessions and recalls how the dynamic music was put together:

I was very pleasantly surprised, when we first rehearsed for those sessions, to find Bobby Irwin was the drummer. I had seen Bobby in New York with Nick Lowe, of whom I'm a great fan, and loved his playing. The engineer was Neil Brockbank, who also worked a lot with Nick and Bobby on some records I really love. Mick Green was also there, and he was clearly a real gritty rock 'n' roller who wasn't afraid to play simple. So what came next was not a surprise. Bryan wanted to make a loose, roots-y kind of record, and I felt that was right up my alley. We went through the rhythm tracks quickly and with greater attention to feeling than to detail. I thought that was great, and that Bryan's vocal performances and his harmonica playing were outstanding.

Ferry himself put it like this: "It was a big thing for me to rediscover the audience. I don't care if there's a note wrong, as long as the feeling's strong ... I just wanted a focused sound, very different from the previous album. I thought plenty of electric guitars, which is a big change."

It would be unreasonable, perhaps, to expect everything on *Frantic* to be as good as "Cruel" and "Goddess of Love". "Goin' Down" recorded by JJ Cale amongst others, was dull, while covers of Leadbelly's "Goodnight Irene" (left over from *Taxi* and reshaped for this album), and a second Dylan song, "Don't Think Twice, It's Alright", unfortunately lessen the overall impact of the album. It was Ferry's *own* songs we needed, not remakes. It is, indeed, a sad irony that Ferry, who so loves to record the works of others, hardly ever has the compliment returned.

Just before he died, Johnny Cash recorded several quite stunning covers from contemporary acts such as Nine Inch Nails and Depeche Mode, reinventing them so completely that they sounded like Cash originals rather than covers. Cash's "Hurt" teased a deep melancholy out of the paranoia of the original, and totally reinvented the song. Seldom in recent years has Ferry come close to matching such excellence with his own cover versions, and it would be unimaginable that he would look to today's music scene for inspiration: he seems perennially intent on researching the past.

There are, however, two other gems towards the end of the set. Just when we thought we would never hear the likes of the creepy electronic melancholy of the *For Your Pleasure* years again, up pops "San Simeon", a sepulchral recitation and a chill moment of supreme power. Against a dense weave of strings, piano, whispers, giggles, and Alison Goldfrapp in the backing vocals, this was how we all wanted Ferry to sound – plain weird as opposed to just plain. So it came as no surprise to learn that the lyric had originally been written in 1973 for "In Every Dream Home A Heartache", but had been left out of the final version. Ferry took these half-forgotten rushes, and reshaped them into a tale of times gone by, set in newspaper tycoon William Randolf Hearst's "paradise" fairytale castle, San Simeon, the inspiration for Xanadu in *Citizen Kane*. "It's a good idea for a song when you wander into this ghostly castle which has all the memories of a glamorous past," says Ferry, adding that

"San Simeon" was "like finding a vintage unworn suit that still fits." The other gem is "I Thought", the sort of wonderful song you would expect a reunited Roxy Music to be able to fashion at will. Co-written with Eno (who also features on backing vocals), it's simply the best song on the album, a slow sing-along reminiscent of Eno's early solo work:

> "I thought I'd be your streetcar named desire
> Your man – the one you'd seek
> I thought I'd take you deep within myself
> Subtitles when we speak."

> (Words and music: Bryan Ferry/Brian Eno, 2002)

However, while *Frantic* marked a return to form in Ferry's professional life, his personal life was once more in turmoil. In the summer of 2002, his marriage to Lucy Helmore, which had long rumoured to be heading for the rocks, finally foundered. In interviews in the nineties, Ferry had remained tight-lipped, mentioning only that the marriage was "turbulent" and describing Lucy as "a Virgo ... not easy" and "Garbo-esque".

The relationship equivalent of "musical differences" is surely "we have drifted apart", and "we have drifted apart" is what the *Mirror* reported Lucy Helmore to have said in Italy, where she was staying with friends. The same newspaper gleefully reminded the nation that they had snapped Ferry kissing TV girl Mariella Frostrup in a London club almost two years earlier. Lucy herself had admitted to adultery, Ferry having suspected an affair for over two years: in fact, Bryan and Lucy had been apart for far longer than the media had thought.

On tour in the late summer of 2002, Ferry was photographed by the paparazzi in the company of Katie Turner, a dancer and singer in his tour ensemble, and thirty-five years his junior. She was just two years older than Ferry's oldest son, as the papers delighted in telling us. "She is being a tremendous support to Bryan at this difficult time, as he heads to the divorce courts," one "friend" told the *Sun*. At 21, Katie Turner was a striking 5' 10" model. The duo were photographed shopping in Munich, and peering at the jewellery and watches in Cartier and Tiffany. Journalists opined that Katie resembled the young Lucy Helmore.

The *Sun* went to town, diligently researching and revealing the relationship. It soon transpired that "leggy brunette" Katie had attended Lutterworth Grammar School in Leicestershire, although "staff remember her as a blonde". According to the same report, Bryan had set Katie up in a flat near his west London recording studios and the two could be seen in Ferry's favourite restaurant, "a discreet Italian called Cibo". "But mainly the romance has blossomed behind closed doors," explained a helpful "friend".

However, as photographers clicked and journos speculated on the romance, Ferry was working as hard as ever. As far as his touring band were concerned, Ferry's love interest had no impact at all. According to them, it was business as normal with Ferry, who acted, as ever, as the model professional. "Those in the band would learn about Bryan's emotional turmoil from the papers, not from anything that happened on the road," says Chris Spedding. "That was our method of learning – from the tabloids. We wouldn't have known anything about it if we hadn't read them."

In 2002, Ferry also garnered some unwelcome adverse publicity as a result of the arrest of one of his sons, and the suspension from school of a second. Nineteen-year-old Otis, who had left Marlborough College to become an amateur "whipper-in" for the Middleton Hunt in Yorkshire, was caught attempting to put up posters for the Countryside Alliance on the walls of Prime Minister Tony Blair's constituency home in Sedgefield, County Durham. Otis Ferry was challenged by two officers after passing through the security gates at 4am, and arrested when he refused to give his personal details. No charges were pressed. *BBC News* reported that a spokesman for the Countryside Alliance had said: "Obviously we would not condone anyone breaking the law, but that was not the case here. Otis had no intention of doing any harm or causing damage to property. I'm glad we have people like Otis on our side." Otis later became joint master of the South Shropshire hunt, where he claimed that, "Hunting is a hell of an adventure and a real adrenaline ride. Every day of the season has a certain brilliance about it."

Meanwhile, Otis' younger bother Isaac was suspended from school after sending an abusive e-mail to Simon Wild, of the East Sussex Wildlife Protection Group. It read: "You are a fucking looser [*sic*]. Why don't you stop waisting [*sic*] your time and get a real job/hobby, you cunt?" According to the ever-controversial Julie Burchill, Ferry may have been more dismayed by the spelling mistakes in his privately educated son's e-mail than its contents. In the *Guardian*, Burchill commented:

There are the usual theories about why they [Bryan and Lucy] have split up: her past fondness for drink, Bryan's timeless affair with himself ... But myself, I think there may have been a more unusual reason for it. What if Bryan Ferry – thought by many people to have been, at his peak, the finest English writer of love poetry since John Donne – was so ashamed of producing an offspring who, at the age of 16 and with an eye-wateringly expensive Eton education behind him, could still not write properly in his mother tongue, that he felt the desperate need to distance himself from his co-spawner?

However, the adverse publicity centering on Isaac and Otis confirmed Ferry/the Ferrys in the public imagination as at best traditionalists, and at worst reactionaries. Long since regarded by the left as an acid test of a society's inherent decency and humanity, fox hunting is an emotive issue. For some, it's a natural form of pest control; for others, it's emblematic of a sick mindset. In the same *Guardian* article, Julie Burchill wrote:

> It seems a good time, for those of us who believe that killing animals in pursuit of sexual satisfaction is a bit sick, to consider the enemy ... If hunters had one brain cell and half a sense of humour between them, they would see that it's partly the sheer mob-handed bullying angle of hunting that strikes most fair-minded people as both comic and grotesque; two dozen people on two dozen horses with two dozen hounds chasing one titchy fox! I mean, why not get the Red Arrows in while you're at it!

The first indication of Ferry Senior's views on the matter came in February 2001, on the eve of the Roxy Music reunion tour, when it was reported that he decided against attending a pro-hunting demonstration organised by the Countryside Alliance. The official reason was that hunt saboteurs had targeted him, but in reality he possibly may have felt that the ensuing bad publicity in the press might be bad for ticket sales. A group which campaigned to protect what they regarded as the rights and liberties of country folk, much of the support for the Countryside Alliance came from the new landed interests, big businessmen and women who had bought their way in and formed a new squirearchy. Their message was simple – only us landed people know about the coun- tryside; the rest of you, particularly all you concerned, woolly-minded liberal townies, should simply stay off our land. Hunting and shooting, they claimed, were effective means of controlling unsustainable natural growth in the animal population.

It was a hard case to defend. In 2002, an estimated 36 million pheasants were reared and released purely for Britain's fastest growing "sport": "[They are] bred for £10, shot for £30, and worth absolutely nothing," said the *Guardian*'s John Vidal. "Only a third are likely to be shot and fewer than half that number may be eaten. The rest will be taken by predators, catch diseases and die, or may be quietly buried in pits by shoots which can barely give away the birds." The hunting, shooting and fishing brigade found some celebrity support: TV racing presenter John McCririck, chef Lady Clarissa Dickson Wright and ex-footballer turned hard-man actor Vinnie Jones were at the forefront of the Barbour jacket brigade. The heart sank at the thought of Bryan Ferry in the same motley crew: many would have preferred it if he had joined the real Mötley Crüe. Ferry's politics dismayed some fans, although for others, at least it could be said that he was being true to his convictions. Mark Radcliffe opines: "It's always somewhat difficult, isn't it, when someone who you've idolised, like Bryan Ferry, has views that are markedly different to your own. You'd want to think that, on the major issues, he thought like you think; and, of course, there's no reason at all why he should."

He sent his four children to Eton. He professed to be "on the right" politically. Was he a Tory? "I'm not telling you. Voting is secret," he told one reporter:

> My mother was a staunch Labour Party worker. They had a women's Labour Party in our village in the north and she was the treasurer, and very good with figures. They would go on trips out to Whitley Bay, which was the St Tropez of the north. I was born in a place that had a 23,000 Labour majority and one Tory voter with his little sad blue sticker in the window. I don't quite know where I stand really, though I tend to be more on the right wing than the left, I must confess.

However, in interviews, Ferry appeared as un-reconstituted as they come: "Abolishing the House of Lords was such a mistake. Keep them, even if it's just for amusement value. Who wants a bunch of political cronies instead? Likewise, I would not want to ban bull fighting in Spain. It's part of their culture: even if it's barbarous, it's also fabulous," he informed society bible the *Tatler*.

The trajectory of Ferry's social ambition – upwards and onwards, away from his working-class roots and into the cultured classes – was the reverse of many of those who wrote about him, reflects Jon Savage: "Most of the people in the music press are white, male, middle-class, and heterosexual, and many try to shave off a class notch or two in their accents and attitudes. You know, all that polytechnic snivelling by Cambridge graduates." In the mid-nineties in Britain, it was cool to be a boozing, girl- and football-obsessed unreconstructed male: it was a climate in which it was OK to admit that you liked the Faces. In Britpop, a middle-class coup if ever there was one, it was *de rigueur* to deny one's roots and to be a geezer.

Bryan Ferry is not a geezer. He is particular. In 2002 the *Tatler* discovered that he likes his sandwiches to be made from brown bread, mayonnaise instead of butter, tuna or prawns, no tomatoes. His coffee has to be Taylor's of Harrogate's Italian Blend. By day, he drinks carrot juice or mineral water (Evian or San Pellegrino). He collects paintings from the Bloomsbury group, including some Duncan Grant oils. The Stubbs on the cover of *Mamouna* comes from his own collection. Away from home, the Ferry tour rider must be one of the most debonair in the rock business. The *Herald Sun* in Australia revealed that Ferry demands a full-length mirror, an iron and ironing board, bottles of Dom Perignon champagne on ice, "high quality" French wines and fresh flowers. His hotel suites cost £700 per night and more, while the rest of the band "slum it" in more modest settings. He is a rich man with taste and style. What else did we expect?

"You may find him being entertained by the Marches beneath their famous Canalettos in the small, round dining-room at Goodwood, or dropping in for a drink at the Bamfords' villa in Barbados," wrote the *Tatler* in April 2002. "A good buddy is 'Johnson' Somerset. He shoots pheasants with the Earl of Arundel or, in New York, quietly slips into his regular suite in the Carlyle. Jasper Johns embraced him there by personally cooking him a dinner of wild mushrooms, hand-picked from his upstate New York estate." "I eat meat. I shoot birds. I play snooker and tennis," said Ferry. "To be a rock star, you don't have to wear an anorak and a horrible pair of trainers. You can put on elegant leather shoes and a Homburg."

Yet despite all these high-cultural mannerisms, the perennial paradox remains. Ferry is ultimately still very attached to his roots; very proud to be called a northerner. "I love the north," he has said. "I took my boys to an FA Cup Final to see our boys [Newcastle United] getting thrashed by Manchester United. I'm not ashamed of my background. I'm really privileged to have had so much variety and contrast in my life, which, being a Libran, you might understand. Librans tend to like to have extremes of good and evil."

Although Ferry was now once again a legitimate bachelor, he had in fact been living the bachelor life for many years. He had been working and staying in London from Monday to Friday every week for years. However, on the *Frantic* tour he seemed to be completely taken with Katie Turner and, the *Sun* reported, even introduced himself to the girl's family.

The *Frantic* tour itself was mildly disappointing. It was simply the case that, despite the excellent songs and standard of musicianship, Ferry solo just didn't possess the repertoire or the power of the reunited Roxy Music. The arrangements sounded slightly lightweight and square. But that didn't stop him gaining new fans. A seven-year-old newcomer, Penny O'Brien, contributed this review to a fan website:

> I was bored during "Out Of The Blue" until Lucy played the violin. I just stared at her because she was fantastic. All the band went off stage for a cup of tea during "Don't Think Twice" and left Bryan and the piano man who was very good. All the crowd seemed to like "Both Ends Burning." I heard one of the guitar men made a mistake but it was OK. … At first I didn't want to go to the concert but I am glad I did because Bryan was really good. But I think he should get his hair cut. My special bit was when I met Lucy the violin girl. She was really nice. I got my photo with her and her autograph and I really liked her trainers, they were cool.

Bryan Ferry
by
Penny O'Brien

After the *Frantic* tour was over, 2003 saw no new Ferry material, but several attempts to reaffirm his live credibility. Roxy Music were reactivated for a handful of concerts in America and one each in Portugal and Germany, the planned headlining concert in July in Hyde Park, however, being cancelled when the promoters, Triple A, went into receivership. There was also product of sorts to promote in the form of *Roxy Music Live*, released that June. A 22-song-strong collection, it was culled from a variety of sources and sequenced as if it were a real concert. It had great playing and wonderful songs, but, as live albums tend to be these days, was totally overlooked by the public. There are certainly sound financial reason for keeping Roxy rolling, as Chris Spedding points out: "I think the fact that Roxy play bigger venues than Bryan Ferry must demonstrate that to him. It is a fact of life: he's playing huge venues with Roxy Music, and earning a lot more money. The gates must be ten times bigger; they must be, when you look at the number of people we're playing to, compared with Bryan Ferry."

On March 21, 2003, Bryan and Lucy Ferry were granted a decree nisi by District Judge Berry at the High Court Family Division in central London. In divorce papers before the court, Ferry said that "the respondent [Lucy] has admitted to adultery" but had not named the other man. Ferry said that he had first suspected his wife of infidelity in May 2000, and the adultery was ongoing when they separated. The decree was granted in a mere 55 seconds; neither party was in court.

Unsurprisingly, Ferry found his divorce – after twenty years of marriage – deeply troubling. "It is a very unpleasant business. It takes up a lot of your head-space', he told Marianne MacDonald of the *Evening Standard*:

I think my wife was ill-advised to call Dempster [the *Daily Mail*'s former gossip columnist] to tell him we were separating. And then everyone goes, "Woo! What's going on here?" And it's embarrassing to be having to do interviews and being obliged to discuss it … It has got me down. All this kind of – the legal thing and all the stuff you have to go through – it's rather scary. It's very hard for everyone who gets involved in it. All one's friends – I think you give a hard time to everybody around you when you have such a thing going on in your life.

It was reported that Lucy's demands in the Ferry's divorce settlement were to keep their £6m home and to receive an annual income of

£250,000 from Ferry – only "fair and just" after twenty years of marriage, according to Lucy. A "friend" of Ferry's told gossip magazine *Hello*: "He wants to be as fair as possible, but he thinks Lucy's claim is over the top." In actual fact, Lucy's settlement was one of the largest on record in the UK. Reportedly, she was to receive around a third of Ferry's total fortune: a cool £10m.

Bryan Ferry was hardly strapped for cash, but the sudden disappearance of a third of his wealth obviously gave him cause for concern. Earlier in 2003, an attempt at Sotheby's to sell a Victorian oil painting from his collection, by Edward Arthur Walton, which was valued at between £80,000 and £120,000, had failed. And, in what may or may not be a totally unconnected move, Ferry had begun taking on corporate gigs. The former art school superstar was contemplating life as a single man with a whacking big divorce settlement to fund, and so accepted gigs such as appearances at a corporate function at Selfridges and, perhaps even tackier, 2003's Miss World Competition in China (won, incidentally, by the daughter of Chris De Burgh). Miss World, long-since removed from British network television for reasons too obvious to restate, was now targeted at that minority of the viewing public whose sexual politics were still rooted in the reactionary wing of the seventies. Sadly, it seemed Ferry chose to ignore such glaring reasons not to attend. We were reminded of Ferry's jokey answer to the first question in *Q* magazine's Questionnaire in 1993: What's the first thing that you do when you wake up in the morning? "Count my money!" answered Ferry. At the end of 2003, Ferry even played the Vatican, a venue possibly lacking the rock 'n' roll cool of Shea Stadium or Glastonbury.

Ferry's financial status has always bothered him. Perennially inquisitive about how other rock stars have made their fortunes, in 1999 he complained to me that, "I've never made money out of touring." His absurdly long studio sojourns in the eighties and nineties were, of course, largely self-funded. Were his advisers simply too afraid to stand up to Ferry and tell him that his endless deferral about what should, or should not, be considered a worthy fifth guitar part on a track was not only stifling creatively, but made no sense financially as endless recording sessions, and an orchestra of musicians all came and went? Some of this material has never even been used. Rich, talented, good-looking, healthy and, if only he'd see, adored by many, on paper Bryan Ferry should not be bitter about his relatively impecunious state compared with Bowie, Jagger, Elton and – perhaps more appositely – presumably Brian Eno. But dissatisfied he is, and, increasingly, it seems that making money on catch-up is a top priority. In the same *Q* questionnaire he was asked, "What is the biggest myth about fame?" His predictable answer was, "That it brings eternal happiness".

By October 2003, Ferry's relationship with Ms Turner had come to an end "amid accusations that he was too possessive and told her to turn down modelling jobs," claimed the *Mirror*. It was hard to see how it would ever have worked. When fans had heard that Ferry had been hospitalised after falling off a mountain bike whilst on holiday in Spain with Katie, the thought naturally suggested itself that here was a man going through the male menopause. The paparazzi had been tipped off to the final split, and, rather cruelly, photographs of Katie clearing out her stuff from the flat Ferry had bought her in London were published in early 2004, showing Turner humping a heavy box of her possessions whilst Ferry looked on impassively, refusing to help. Allegedly, when he saw some headphones in one box he plucked them out claiming they were his.

The two-year relationship with Katie Turner at an end, within weeks it was reported in the press that Ferry had a new romance. Thirty-year-old Rita Konig was already the successful author of two makeover books, *Rita's Tips For Domestic Bliss* and *Domestic Bliss: How To Live*. Konig was very much part of the "scene". In August 2002, she had been Number 19 in *The Tatler's* "Top Thirty Most Invited" dinner party guests, below Bryan and Lucy at Number 4 and Hugh Grant at 13, but – perhaps surprisingly – above Charles Saatchi and the Hon. Nigella Lawson. "Bryan and Rita are being very secretive about their relationship," said one "insider". "They have known each other for a while due to the circles that they move in. They're both really keen on each other but want to keep it quiet for now. Bryan was surprised at how much interest there was in his relationship with Katie and doesn't want a repeat performance." However, Katie Turner and Ferry remain friends. In April 2004, Ferry told the *Daily Express* "she's a good friend of mine. She came with me to the ballet last week. We worked together, and that creates quite a bond."

It seems, as ever, that Ferry remains drawn to beauty and to younger partners. Inside, he says, he still feels exactly the same as he did when he was a young man. It's a saga that, one suspects, is set to run and run. "What can I say?" says Ferry. "Women are impossible to understand.

But you can't live with them, can't live without them. I really need to look inside the mystery of women. I mean, why can't they be as transparent and straight as us blokes?"

Far more interesting is the future for Bryan Ferry as a singer and an entertainer. The promise of *Frantic* suggests that he will be one of those rock stars who will be able to produce the goods into his sixties. A commitment to live work is a feature of the past five years: "Ironically, the place I'm least shy is on stage," he reflected in 2002.

And chances are he will be accompanied in his later-life musical journey by drummer Paul Thompson, who can always be guaranteed the sort of reception normally meted out to the star singer. "An incident in Stockholm was fun," says fan Peter Ingvarsson:

> I had talked to all my friends, ten of us, before the concert. And during the minutes before the show started, I talked to all the people in the seats around me, telling them to salute Paul the best they could. When it was time for Paul's introduction I was shouting around to get them all going. So, about twenty to thirty people were screaming their balls out when Bryan introduced Paul. We could see a very broad smile on Paul's face, but a more disturbed face from Bryan – like, what is going on?

One of the most dramatic moments ever at a Bryan Ferry gig occurred in Auckland in February 2004, when 62-year-old guitarist Mick Green collapsed on stage. Band member Julia Thornton recounts in her web diary the upsetting scenes:

> He froze in a spasm, then collapsed and hit the stage, knocking his music stand over, still holding his guitar. It seemed like a lifetime before five crew members appeared and carried him from the stage, to the horror of every one of us. Some members of the audience screamed. We followed Bryan's lead, which was to carry on, and continued with the set. Over the next few numbers, those of us that could see watched three doctors (who luckily had come to the show – thank God Bryan attracts an older and therefore professional concert-goer!) as they performed CPR on Mick, lying on the floor stage left. It was horrific. They were working on him for nearly 20 minutes. We just had to keep playing whilst watching the whole thing and trying to keep going ...

Towards the very end of the show, just before we come off to go back on for the encores, I caught our production manager's eye, and he mouthed distinctly at me; "He's OK." Then we came off and were told that he was conscious, talking, and on his way to hospital.

Ferry's commitment to touring is ongoing. What's more, Christian Wainwright, his wardrobe guy, is still with him after more than thirty years, and is still keeping Ferry's suits in good order. Despite this, Ferry appears totally at odds with the rock world, consciously targeting a more genteel clientele. It's almost as if he has bought into his own myth. "I think it's a shame that a lot of people think of him as some sort of Radio Two crooner. They don't know the early work, why should they?" is how Mark Radcliffe puts it:

I suppose if they're new to Ferry then they have to judge him on his last record, which, in the case of *Frantic* is not too damning really. But he just seems, in my opinion, to have been badly advised. He seemed to go down a blind alley, really, making ever more smooth records, taking ever longer over them, getting writer's block, doing the *Taxi* thing. I do think there were some lost years there and I do think it was a shame that he hadn't had the confidence of just doing what he did really, which was to just write songs, bang 'em out. He probably did think that he was Mr Smooth and that everything had to be ultra-sophisticated, so that all the kind of spiky bits about Roxy Music got left behind and it became an ever-decreasing circle. I think he's woken up from that now. I hesitate to get into personal matters, but I wonder whether the new record and the break-up of the marriage are two sides of the same coin. There were signs there, with some of the music and collaborating with Eno, of him awakening from a type of musical slumber. The ending of the marriage and going out with a younger woman is a classic mid-life crisis kind of thing, but that can be a positive thing.

At the time of writing, the only new Ferry product was a duet with Jane Birkin on "In Every Dream Home A Heartache" on her 2004 album *Rendez-Vous*: hardly a punishing release schedule. Since Ferry's last solo album, David Bowie has released two studio albums. It's yet another reminder of the tortuous pace that Bryan Ferry seems to feel eternally obliged to proceed at.

Yet Ferry's career is full of paradoxes, and that's what makes it so interesting, and the man himself such an attractive personality. He is a working-class lad with gentrified tastes; a shy man whose job it is to entertain in the spotlight in front of thousands of people. And now the original British avant-garde rocker (and, initially, self-proclaimed non-musician) has become a crooner – of sorts, says Mark Radcliffe:

> I love his voice, but he's quite often flat, which makes it very interesting. In some ways, it's testimony to his individuality and style that technically, I don't think anyone can describe Bryan Ferry as a great singer, so it's extraordinary that not so long ago he was doing a crooning tour. He played in Tatton Park in the open air with an orchestra and you think, *why*? But it's a testimony to his style and presence that the very thing that he doubts about himself seems to carry it through. Because he's certainly not a great torch singer. No way. Yet there are other people who can get away with that particular sense of style. If you think about Nick Cave, as a vocalist he is ill-equipped for doing ballads, but the imperfections of the voice almost add to it. That's the enduring appeal of Ferry; all the imperfections, and the struggle for him to try and get it together have still created this hugely glamorous individual, but I still think, probably, these imperfections give him this human edge and have kept him a very warm character.

One factor that might dissuade Ferry, however, from taking on such a relatively heavy live schedule is that, as he grows older, he is increasingly falling prey to throat problems. In 2003, he revealed, "I recently got some sort of throat problem and my voice packed up. I had to postpone some shows, which was a drag. It's been very worrying; briefly, I thought my days were numbered. I'm seeing three different doctors: one is a singing expert, one is a voice therapist, and the other's a sort of neck physiotherapist who massages your larynx. I was astonished at how specialised that whole world is. Sticking their fingers up your nose, little torches … it's like sci-fi."

One area where Ferry has been slow off the mark is the internet. With the launch of Bowienet in 1998, Ferry's contemporary David Bowie was one of the first acts in the world to recognise the creative potential of the web, and most major acts now have excellent and informative websites. Not so Bryan Ferry: his official site can be slow at delivering news and has minimal content. However, Ferry has been well-served by unofficial sources, who have been quicker at carrying new stories and have proved effective in getting tour schedules and ticket information to the fans. John O'Brien has waged a one-man crusade to get information out on his excellent site, *Vivaroxymusic*: detailed and knowledgeable, it's a superb "virtual museum". *Roxyrama*, run by Chris Turner, is another excellent Roxy and Ferry site, whilst Phil Manzanera's official site contains – as work in progress – a complete history of the band. Elsewhere, the Avalon discussion group allows fans to swap ideas and information, while Paul Thompson's site has a lively message board, on which Paul often appears in person. As ever with these sorts of networks, sometimes it's abused and used to bitch and smear other fans, an unfortunate aspect of net fan culture, but it demonstrates that Ferry and Roxy still have a lively and, overall, extremely articulate fan base (details of all of these websites can be found in the bibliography).

After several years with the Riverman management company, from late 2003 Ferry has been helped out in a managerial capacity by the ex-Squeeze front man Chris Difford (who, incidentally, worked on some unreleased songs with the Roxy singer a few years back). A real barrier to taking Ferry's career forward, however, is the lack of airplay that all artists of his vintage receive on national radio. BBC Radio 2 has long been the natural home for artists like Ferry, yet his slowness in producing new material (and unwillingness to record again with Roxy to date) has seriously compromised his cultural and commercial standing. Over the last couple of years, however, there have been sporadic signs that the chances of a Roxy reunion *in the studio* are becoming increasingly likely. Commercially and creatively, it's the logical next step. Let's hope Ferry takes it soon.

NOW THE PARTY'S OVER?

Bryan Ferry will be sixty on September 26, 2005. At thirty, he was one of the biggest pop stars in Britain. At sixty, he's an *artiste*, a possessor of a certain faded filmic cool. *The Thrill Of It All* has attempted to speak for those of us who remember just what a star Bryan Ferry was, and who are dismayed that, in the annals of pop history, he's been reduced to something of a footnote. It has also attempted to relive the excitement and danger in the career of Bryan Ferry and Roxy Music, and to recapture the fun, the intellectual vigour and the sheer scale of the Roxy Music project.

So what, finally, is Bryan Ferry's legacy? "If nothing else, he rescued an entire nation from the necessity of dressing like Joe Cocker," said Paul Du Noyer in *Q* magazine back in the eighties, and for this we should all be grateful. What is certain is that Bryan Ferry and Roxy Music changed our perception of what rock bands could be. A band containing (initially at least) not one, but *two* untrained musicians – or, as Eno put it at the time, "non-musicians" – was something quite new. They arrived on the scene without a fanfare, with no history and having made no attempt to build a career in any meaningful way. From his first gig, it took David Bowie eight years to become a star. It took Roxy Music just eight months. They changed our idea of a rock band in another important way too. Roxy Music may have included, in Brian Eno, one of the – allegedly – most promiscuous men in pop, but, in general, their demeanour was resolutely un-rock 'n' roll. They were the anti-Oasis of their day.

Fundamentally, Ferry's view of his music, and its place within popular music, has not altered. In the seventies, he did not see himself as being in competition with other glam rock acts. His brief was not to make popular music, but music that was artistically valid and true to itself. Back in 1978, Ferry said of his then new album, *The Bride Stripped Bare*, that it was "connoisseurs' music": "There's a lot of great work that's been done that hasn't been a popular success. Standards, often, aren't terribly high: the commonplace is often accepted too easily." From the very beginning, Roxy Music were an elitist band, and, one suspects, quite proud of the fact. You had to be clever enough to get their references: if you weren't, tough shit. Ferry also consistently maintained the view that an artist's work, its meaning and value, should be self-evident to like-minded, discerning critics and fans. "An entertainer cares more about the audience than the work he's doing and the reverse is true of an artist," he said in 1982. "An artist is interested in the audience's reaction, but he won't compromise to get it." Writer Sylvie Simmons sums up Roxy's influence thus:

> I find it interesting that a band with such a strong conceptual basis – Bryan Ferry's whole Duchamp thing, the sound-collage and the avant-garde electronics – and whose music was so manifestly intelligent could be considered as having a greater rock historical significance for their visual style, although visual style, in the dark ages when Roxy Music emerged, had a very different connotation than it had in the MTV eighties or the glossy magazine nineties. There was something gravely funny and anarchically serious about Roxy Music and their car-crash of musical/visual styles, and, when it came out, "Virginia Plain" was a template: highly distinctive.

Perhaps Ferry's biggest achievement lay in the way he sent the whole pop culture up so brilliantly with Roxy Music. The injection of artifice and parody, and the gentle mocking of the music business and the counter-cultural values of the times, paved the way not just for glam but also for punk, and for the ironists of the early eighties too. In 1993, Bryan Ferry told *Details* magazine that the biggest crime a musician could commit was "being too earnest ... it inflicts a deep embarrassment upon the audience."

Roxy Music were, in their own words, "inspired amateurs". It was perhaps because of, rather than despite, the many weaknesses in their actual musicality that they made such an impact. Mackay and Manzanera were good, not great, musicians. Thompson developed into a fine and versatile drummer, but he was no supreme, muso technician. And Ferry could never in a million years be regarded, technically at least, as a wonderful singer. One critic memorably described his vocal as "like Edith Piaf cycling over cobbles." Which is all part of the charm, of course. It's the imperfections that make his voice so beguiling.

Like all the truly great singers, Ferry, for all his rough edges, has created an unmistakable sound. His personality, his idiolect, is unique. From the first bar of the vocal we know exactly who it is. The timbre, the forced vibrato, the ululating vocal: it's inspirational, it's him, it could not be anyone else. Likewise, his dancing gave us all hope. Legs stiff, suit clinging and quiff matted in sweat, Ferry lurches around the stage, and we love him for it.

And for all his surface languor, Ferry is obsessive about his music. His ex-wife Lucy once commented, "Bryan's music is the only thing that really matters to him, but I'm not jealous." He's also, of course, obsessive about his image, one of those people who always looks elegant, no matter what hour of the day. "Bryan is an enormously attractive person," says John Wetton:

He has the looks; he's a clothes-horse. Everything he puts on seems to look good on him, much to my consternation when we went on holiday together. He just puts on a T-shirt and a pair of shorts and looks brilliant. I mean, I just look like a shambles, so that's really annoying! I've seen quotes from Jerry Hall saying that he's the most handsome person she's been out with.

Photographer Mick Rock, who worked with so many of the great icons from the seventies, knew immediately that Bryan Ferry was a very different kind of rock star – he was an old-style gentleman:

I liked Bryan. He wasn't somebody who anybody knew that well, apart from those in the band, because he was not fucked out of his brains, he was not a rampant sex fiend; he was a man of style and obviously a very fine artist. I don't think he was deliberately aloof. I used to think he was aloof until I got to talk to him, when I realised he was simply quite shy. Once he started talking, he was actually quite friendly and open. When we did pictures, he wasn't a big gossip, not like Freddie Mercury and David Bowie – both of them loved to have a good gossip. Bryan wasn't like that at all; he was quite reserved. If you went to his house, it was very civilised by comparison to some of the other characters on the scene. It had a big sense of order and style and integration to it. In that sense he was more sophisticated, at an earlier age, than any of us.

However, it is clear that Ferry is not a man without imperfections. On occasion, his thorough commitment to style crosses the boundary between healthy self-grooming and vanity of the comedic sort.

A possibly apocryphal music business tale, involving an ex-roadie coming to collect Ferry from his home, that often emerges when the brandies and cigars are being passed around tells the tale of Ferry about to embark on a US tour. "All packed up and ready to go?" said the aide. "Yep," came the reply. "Got your passport?" "No, I haven't got my passport." Where is it?" "I've thrown it away." "Bryan, but you can't go to America without your passport." Bryan sulked for a while and eventually revealed that he had thrown his passport in the bin. Ferry's aide had to rummage through all the old food to retrieve the passport, which had, apparently, been mutilated and stamped upon. The reason being, as Ferry eventually admitted, that he simply didn't like the picture of himself in it."

Former manager Ed Bicknell has regaled music industry conferences with anecdotes about Ferry's multiple idiosyncrasies, including the occasion that the distressed singer woke him with a phone call at 1.30am with the news that his son's budgie had died. "He will be so upset when he wakes up," Ferry said. "Maybe if I get a replacement he won't notice. Can you find out where I can buy a budgie at this time of night?" "I suggested that he nail the dead one to its perch," says Bicknell. "So Bryan put the phone down on me."

Roxy Music was undoubtedly Ferry's baby. From the outset, it was clear that it was he who had the vision for the band. "I think most of the best bands have been benign dictatorships, but dictatorships none the less. You only had to look at Phil Manzanera to discover that the vision wasn't his," opines Mark Radcliffe. "You only had to look at him to realise that this was a man who wasn't entirely happy with being put in the clothes he was put in, and he refused to go the whole hog: he still had a rocker's hairdo."

Some of those who have worked with Ferry feel that, at times, he has been unhappy or unwilling to give credit to others. Indeed, some feel that the Ferry/Manzanera/Mackay trio have taken great care to protect their vested interests in the Roxy brand name. Eddie Jobson has this to say:

It has been offensive to me that Bryan, Andy and Phil have chosen to completely downplay my significance and contribution to Roxy over the years. They have even released Best Of albums with my name listed in alphabetical order among a long list of insignificant session players. They have done similar things to Paul Thompson. "Historic" albums have been released and gone gold without my even knowing they existed: I get no royalties, no gold album, and often no mention. I think Brian Eno's and Bryan Ferry's successes are both well deserved. However, it has just been a sad reflection on the remaining three's lack of generosity that they were so unwilling to give credit, or royalties, to anyone else.

But it should be said that the media representation of Bryan Ferry as an austere, unsmiling, pompous control freak is false. The first thing you encounter, and have to overcome, is his shyness. Ferry speaks to you hesitantly, making eye contact only when sure of you. He manifests unease at talking about himself or being branded a pop star. He'll make sure that even any mildly critical comment made about any of his peers is kept very much off the record, and has a rich line in self-depre-cation. With a good memory for faces, he'll make a point of greeting someone he has not seen in years. A man with great personal charm, he is polite, courteous and happy to pose for photos or to reminisce with fans about triumphs past. "Depending on the day and the circum-stance, you could meet any one of three Bryan Ferrys," said journalist James Truman. "The off-duty Ferry is light-hearted, buoyant, gossipy and very funny. The one who's spent the best part of two years making an album is the reverse: nervous, fretful and prone to monumental bouts of self-doubt and irritation with himself. The third Bryan Ferry is the icily polite, non-committal, slightly wooden figure that often emerges in interviews."

What drives Bryan Ferry on? There's obviously still an audience for his music, a fact that, in the mid-nineties, even he must have been unsure of. However, what would really, one suspects, secure a sizeable chunk of media coverage, and, of course, increased sales, would be a Roxy reunion in the studio. If their elegant recent live dates are anything to go by, theirs could be one of those rare comeback albums that adds something to the oeuvre rather than tarnishes the memory.

Overall, though, it's plain that, despite the fantastic records, Roxy (and Bryan Ferry) never quite became the huge act hinted at by their early promise. "They supported Bowie at the Astoria, and have done ever since," says their first producer, Peter Sinfield:

Which is a bit cruel [laughs]. David is more open to using a team than Bryan. One of the things that Andy and Phil did when they tried to get their songs on an album was that they pushed Bryan to higher standards of writing, just by their presence, and made him work much harder. You often find this in groups. There are a couple of people who make you think, what on earth are they doing there? But what they do is make the leader of the group keep proving he's the leader. That's why Bryan's solo albums, in my opinion, sometimes aren't as good as the ones with the band.

"Ferry's never had a *Heroes*, has he?' states Mark Radcliffe. "*Station To Station*, *Low* and *Heroes* were amazing albums. Everybody looked at those albums and thought, 'Fuckin' hell, look what he's doing!' Bowie changed the whole landscape of major league popular music rock albums, and I don't think even the most ardent fans of Ferry, of which I am one, could claim that he had that sort of effect."

There is, in the final analysis, a sense though that Bryan Ferry could, and should, have been a much bigger star. He has never quite become the musical or cultural icon his muse has deserved. On a purely commercial level, one can easily see his reluctance to court mainstream America as a pivotal factor, whether via his distaste for committing to long and arduous tours, or his commercially fatal decision to pass on recording more radio-friendly music in the eighties. There have been too many lost opportunities, too many failures, and too many wrong decisions by Ferry for that dream to come true. John Wetton reflects, "I think it's a shame that he never really cracked it, because he had everything else going for him, you know. He could have been another Elvis." "I think Roxy, as much as I love them, are one of the greatest missed opportunities, because, looking at what Eno went on to do, what would it have been like if he had stayed in cahoots with Ferry?" asks Mark Radcliffe:

I think for most of us, Bryan Ferry's solo career has been a series of mild disappointments, whereas Eno's has been a series of wonderful discoveries. So if you could have taken this fantastic sonic voyage that Eno has taken, and bolted on what Ferry undoubtedly has, that pure pop sensibility, they might have created something beyond what either of them have achieved individually. I think they would certainly have achieved something beyond what Ferry has achieved. Which is not to decry or denigrate him – I just think that, when Eno left, they were still a wonderful band, but you got the feeling that Ferry had got rid of the thorn in his side to an extent, and had full control of the band. Even though they still made wonderful, wonderful records, they'd lost that kind of spirit of adventure. You got the impression that the rest of them would make a song and finish it, whereas Eno was the one who would unravel it, and throw it into the unknown.

The enduring sadness is that Ferry and Eno couldn't find a way together, because you do suspect that Eno would have kept that spiky, adventurous and experimental edge to what Ferry went on to do. If they could have both found a way of getting what they wanted out of Roxy, I think it could have been probably one of the best and most important bands there has ever been, whereas as it is, their early albums are crucial and seminal works, and then after that, for Ferry, possibly, there's always a tinge of *what if*.

For writer Paul Du Noyer, it's plain that what Ferry needs are others to bounce ideas off. Drawing a parallel between Ferry and Morrissey, he says:

Again, there's a sense that both men worked at their best when they were part of a coherent musical unit, and once cut adrift from that, and forced to assume the responsibilities of leading their own band and shaping their own records, I think both were found wanting. A lot of people might find that a harsh judgement on Morrissey but I don't, actually. Conventional as it is, I think he needed Johnny Marr, and has floundered a bit since.

Unlike the brilliant wordsmith Morrissey, Ferry has always been an unwilling interviewee. Given the fact that virtually all the major rock icons of the past forty years have been, if not willing, then at least comfortable with feeding the press printable stories, Ferry's reluctance to play ball, and his obvious discomfort at being under the media spot-light, have diminished his impact. "I was on a trip with a journalist who was full of tales of woe regarding Ferry, whom he found the least co-operative subject," reflects Du Noyer. "When Bryan Ferry finally bestirred himself to talk, he was a 'cypher', the writer said: 'hardly there at all'."

Sometimes journalists have gone to almost absurd lengths to elicit a response from Ferry. Whereas Bowie, or Lennon would seem to instinc-tively know what the press would love to print, Ferry was simply unable to connect to a wider public through the print media. "How does it feel to know women look at your picture and masturbate?" writer Diane Robbens asked him in 1975. Eventually, Ferry replied, "Actually, I'm very flattered." "Never has such a sexy question received such a cold answer," Robbens told him. "I'm a Libra," said Ferry. "I don't give anything away."

Inevitably, writers and journalists have been fixated on the very topics that Ferry would much rather avoid. The departure of Eno is one, Jerry Hall another, and the third is undoubtedly the whole issue of class. There's something peculiarly British, or more precisely, English, about both Ferry's self-betterment, and the media's fascination with a man's social climbing. Mark Radcliffe says:

> Bryan Ferry may have working-class roots, but he will have been rich now for longer than he was ever poor, so, you know, what should he be doing? Should he be drinking in a pub in south Tyneside with some welders from the docks? We all have the capacity to change. He's spent all his life hanging round with musicians, some of whom were working-class and some of whom probably weren't. His wife was fairly aristocratic and landed, shall we say, and he's chosen to live the life he wants. I'm sure that the people closest to him, and the members of his family who are still around, would say that he's the same guy. But when you've made several million pounds and you've travelled the world thirty times, and lived in the best hotels and had the best designers and the most fantastic houses, it's pretty unrealistic for people to expect you to be exactly the same. In fact, I think it would be kind of sad if you'd had all those experiences and had not assimilated any of them. Also, Roxy Music weren't six working-class lads off the pit face, were they? Brian Eno and his thirteen names – this was not a plumber's mate in the making, was it? Bryan Ferry threw himself into that art school crowd. Without rejecting his roots, he probably thought, "Well, that's great, I've nothing against that, but there's a world out there."

Perhaps the reason why Ferry is such a relatively poor interlocutor is his fundamental shyness. He's equally idiosyncratic when it comes to collaborations and ideas. Ferry has to originate the idea, or at least feel as if he has done so. Anyone wanting something out of him directly and who tries to impose their own agenda is certain to come away without Ferry's backing. More than defensiveness, more than shyness even, there's also a real sadness in Bryan Ferry, a deep-rooted melancholy, as Sylvie Simmons so accurately describes:

> There's a real sadness about him in his eyes. Actually, he seemed not to want to catch my eye at all. He always looked down. And if he did look at you, he always seemed to be in a permanent state of bewilderment; like, just what am I doing here? He seemed incredibly shy, slightly bewildered about everything, and very sad. But I think that at the same time the sadness in his eyes has always been part of the glamour – that kind of ruined aristocratic glamour that he somehow manages to give off.

So, despite his mistakes, miscalculations, and long periods of absence, Ferry is more, much more than a footnote in English post-Beatles pop. In the early seventies, Ferry and Roxy Music were the bridge between modernism and postmodernism. He remains an eccentric, immediately recognisable vocalist, with an astonishing vocal register that teeters on the edge of self-destruction, his warbling vibrato straining, at times, to even remain in tune. It's at once contrived, yet somehow enormously human and likeable, just like the man himself – a shy, polite, moody, but surprisingly warm and self-deprecating man.

Thirty years ago, in "The Thrill Of It All", Bryan Ferry sang

> "All the pleasure that's surrounding you
> Should compensate for what you're going through."

Yet all these years later, he still seems unhappy with what life has brought him, lurching from one personal crisis to the next, from one professional triumph to the next harrowing defeat. In all of this, he seems oddly human, and just like the rest of us after all. Yet he is also at the same time one of the most important icons in modern music, and his work, in all its subtleties of language, mood and unquenchable desire, speaks to us all.

NOTES

The following is a brief summary of the main sources used in the writing of each chapter. For a full list of all the secondary sources and exclusive interview material quoted in this biography, please consult the bibliography and the credits.

Preface

I interviewed Bryan Ferry in February 1999 for a book I was writing on David Bowie (*Strange Fascination: David Bowie – The Definitive Story*, Virgin Books, 1999). Although the majority of the quotes from Ferry are from previously published sources, some of the most candid revelations and most interesting perspectives came from this exclusive lengthy interview, during which Bryan spoke not just about Bowie, but also his own career in general. Apart from this first-hand material from Ferry, the quote from Peter Sinfield is from my extensive interview with him. Touching on a variety of topics, a transcription of the interview can be found on Peter's website, http://www.songsouponsea.com/buckley.htm. Other quotes are from *NME*, *Sounds* and a number of other printed and audio sources

Introduction

The title is meant to be an affectionate reference to Bryan's low profile in the late nineties, and actually comes from one of his own comments to the media. "It's that taxi driver thing: 'Still in the music business, mate? 'I work every day!' 'Oh, what do you do nowadays then? You used to be Bryan Ferry, didn't you?'"

Chapter 1: Washington Blues: 1945-1964

By far the biggest source of material for this chapter was an e-mail correspondence with one of Bryan's ex-schoolfriends, Audrey Fletcher. Her recollections, written specifically for this book, were an invaluable source. Audrey herself is another famous Washingtonian. She writes, "I am the person who not only discovered the lost constellation of the Ancient Egyptians, the celestial sphinx, but also that a sky chart dating back to 14,000 BC (complete with celestial River Nile, celestial Sphinx and three celestial pyramids) is the blueprint for the ground plan at Giza. My website is at http://ancientegypt.hypermart.net/." Audrey's website on Bryan, A Washington Lad (http://www.geocities.com/pictorialwashingtonuk/BryanFerry.html) is rich in information about the early years of the future "sultan of suave". Chapter 1 also draws on the personal recollections of Bryan, an interview with one of his fellow students at Newcastle University, Michael Brick, and my interviews with the writers Mat Snow and Paul Du Noyer, and with ex-Roxy member Eddie Jobson. Another helpful source here was the Channel 4 documentary "This Is Tomorrow", which looked at Hamilton and pop art and included an interview with Bryan Ferry (thank you to Colin Fallows for suggesting this, and to John O'Brien for copying the tape for me). Other quotes were sourced from *Arena, Mail On Sunday,* the *Guardian, The Face,* the *NME, Financial Times* and other print media. An excellent audio source is *The Bryan Ferry Story,* an in-depth history of Bryan and Roxy Music, which was broadcast on BBC Radio One in 1994.

Chapter 2: So Different, So Appealing: 1968–1971

I was very lucky to be able to speak to the journalist Richard Williams for this chapter. Williams was one of Roxy's staunchest supporters from the very early days, and he provided me with a fascinating insight into their early years. Roger Bunn, Roxy's original lead guitarist, and David O'List, his replacement, were also interviewed for the book. The rest of the chapter draws on a variety of secondary sources in the print media, particularly *Melody Maker* columns by Richard Williams, and later articles by Tim De Lisle, Robert Sandall and others.

Chapter 3: The Sixties End Today: 1972

Roxy Music's first album remains the author's personal favourite, so it was a particular pleasure to be able to interview its producer, Peter Sinfield, who spoke intelligently and charmingly on the making of the record. Other first-hand interview material came from David O'List, photographer Mick Rock and *Melody Maker* journalist Chris Charlesworth. The John Peel quote is sourced from my book on Bowie, *Strange Fascination*. Also invaluable is the history of the band to be found on Phil Manzanera's official site, www.manzanera.com. Allan F. Moore's analysis of Roxy Music comes from his book, *Rock: The Primary Text*. I am also indebted to the Roxy biographies by Johnny Rogan and Paul Stump (details in the bibliography), as well as to a variety of contemporary print sources, including *Sounds* and *Disc*.

Chapter 4: Make The Big Time: 1972–73

I was very fortunate in this chapter to have access to first-hand testimony from Richard Williams, Peter Sinfield, Mick Rock, Michael Brick and, of course, Bryan Ferry himself. Martyn Ware, later of the Human League and Heaven 17, recounts the impact of the live Roxy, as do writers Paul Du Noyer and Mark Paytress, and broadcaster and writer Mark Radcliffe. Fans Richard Mills and John O'Brien also provided material for this section. During 1972 and 1973, Roxy Music were seldom out of the music press, and Ian MacDonald at the *NME*, Caroline Boucher, Richard Williams again, Nick Kent and Robin Denselow are just some of the writers who provided valuable insights. For more information, see the documents section. The idea that innovation in pop is connected with a rejection of the Beatles' legacy was suggested to me by the writer Geoff Ward.

Chapter 5: Ta-Ra: 1973

The exoskeleton of this chapter was formed by the excellent Radio One documentary, *The Bryan Ferry Story*, with help from Johnny Rogan's slight but informative *Roxy Music – Style With Substance*, and the Phil Manzanera web history of the band. First-hand interviews were conducted with Mick Rock, Chris Spedding, Chris Charlesworth, Martyn Ware, and Mark Radcliffe, whilst Bryan Ferry himself commented candidly on his jealousy concerning Eno's incredible success with the ladies. Secondary sources included Steve Peacock at *Sounds*, and Ian MacDonald and Nick Kent at the *NME*, the *Mojo Collection*'s review of *For Your Pleasure*, and Dave Simpson's 2002 profile of Ferry in the *Guardian*. The quote from Phil Oakey was from an interview I conducted with *Mojo* with the Human League. Thanks to *Mojo* and Phil for use of the quote.

Chapter 6: Roxy Music, Phase 2: 1973

For this chapter I received invaluable information from Eno's replacement in Roxy Music, Eddie Jobson. John Gustafson, who was Roxy's bassist for three albums, also agreed to be interviewed. He and John Wetton, who played with Roxy Music in 1974 and 1975, together paint a fascinating picture of the mid-period Roxy Music. Other interviewees include Mick Rock, Mat Snow, Chris Charlesworth, and Ian Burden (ex-Human League), who provides some great information on Ferry's compositional technique. Two radio shows, Brian Matthew's *My Top 10* from 1974, and Paul Gambaccini's 1975 interview with Ferry for BBC Radio One's *Insight*, were very useful. Finally, Ferry's own words on the *These Foolish Things* album come mainly from my interview with Bryan in 1999.

Chapter 7: The Thrill Of It All: 1974–1975

John Wetton, a member of Roxy music between 1974 and 1975, was perhaps the most important interviewee for this chapter, along with fellow band member Eddie Jobson. Paula Brown and Ashley Wright provided two pieces of fan testimony. Perhaps the most revealing quote came from Bryan Ferry himself, in my 1999 interview with him, when he talked about why Roxy Music didn't find more success than they did in America. Other pieces of exclusive material were provided by writer and academic Geoff Ward, Mat Snow, Martyn Ware from Heaven 17, Chris Charlesworth, and Jon Savage. I also referred, as ever, to a wide variety of printed sources. Perhaps the most important were *Melody Maker* (where Allan Jones was always a true Roxy supporter and provided lively copy), and the *NME*, where Nick Kent, in particular, had many persuasive things to say about the band. The Tony Parsons section on the late Robert Palmer is from his scurrilous, though excellent article, "Ageing Smoothy", which can be found in Dylan Jones' *Meaty Beaty, Big And Bouncy!*

Chapter 8: Stripped Bare: 1975–1977

Jerry Hall declined to be interviewed for this book, so her voice is reconstructed from the pages of *Tall Tales*, her autobiography. *The Bryan Ferry Story* (Radio One, 1994) was once again an invaluable source of material. Peter York, one of the keenest observers of the nuances of London style culture, wrote a perceptive piece on Ferry's fascination with style for *Harper's & Queen* in 1983. Entitled "Bryan's Interior", this article was influential in my reading of Ferry's social "progress". Other secondary sources included the UK music press (I was particularly tickled to find Bruce Forsyth's review of "Love Is The Drug") and Jon Savage's classic study of punk, *England's Dreaming*. First-hand interviews were conducted with John Wetton and John Gustafson, who played with Ferry during this time, while fans such as Steven Severin (Siouxsie and the Banshees) and Philip Oakey from the Human League also contributed.

Chapter 9: Fortress Roxy Music: 1978–1981

The most important sources for this chapter were new interviews with Gary Tibbs, Roxy's bassist, and Paul Carrack, who played with the re-formed line-up. Although the departure of Paul Thompson remains shrouded in a certain mystery, some new light has been shed on the circumstances of his departure. Two Radio One *Star Specials*, the first hosted by David Bowie and the second, in 1981, by Ferry himself, showed how very different their musical tastes were. The Chris Brazier quote on the "Sign of The Times" single is from *Melody Maker* in August 1978, whilst Ferry's petulant attack on his critics is quoted from an Allan Jones feature that appeared in the same newspaper later in the year. As ever, I based this chapter on dozens of secondary sources. Special mention should, however, be made of Paul Rambali's 1978 article for the *NME*, "Bryan Ferry: The Prisoner", which gives an interesting insight into Ferry's uncomfortable solo years.

Chapter 10: The "Curse" Of Avalon: 1981–1999

The *Avalon* album was given the five-star treatment by Radio 2 in 1999 when it was featured in their classic albums series, and my analysis of the album was greatly helped by this programme. The Andy Mackay quote about drug use is to be found in Rob Chapman's 1995 *Mojo* article on Roxy, whilst the assertion that Ferry had a cocaine habit in the late seventies comes from Siobhan Synnot's 2002 article in *Scotland On Sunday*. This assertion is substantiated by my interview with Mick Rock. Writer Mat Snow was a great help in building a picture of Ferry's mid-life ennui, and also very helpful in suggesting reasons for the demise of the band. Guy Fletcher, who was part of the late-period Roxy line-up, also gave me some excellent material. Several quotes from Ferry were sourced from the *Inside Track* radio interview from 1983. Chris Roberts' assessment of *Boys And Girls* is from his 1987 review of *Bête Noire*, which appeared in *Melody Maker*. The quote from Johnny Marr about Ferry at Live Aid is from Johnny Rogan's *The Severed Alliance*. Chris Salewicz spent a year with Ferry during the recording of *Bête Noire* and his 1988 *Q* article was a great source of information. Robin Trower, who worked as co-producer on a series of Ferry records, also contributed his thoughts on *Taxi* and *Mamouna*. The Edward Helmore quote on Ferry's working practices is from Richard Mill's article, "L'uomo Vague", whilst Alice Thompson's "Ferry Across The Decades" in the *Times* was also of great help. Finally, *The Bryan Ferry Story* radio documentary helped piece together Ferry's musical mid-life crisis.

Chapter 11: No Grand Exit: 1999–2004

The description of Ferry's brush with death on flight BA 2069 to Nairobi is based on several accounts in the *Observer, Mail On Sunday, Daily Telegraph* and *Guardian*. Chris Spedding and Zev Katz provided valuable information on Ferry's work in the noughties. John O'Brien, Paula Brown and Peter Ingvarsson gave the fans' point of view of the re-formed Roxy. Eno's comments on the repackaged Roxy are from an interview with Paul Morley in *Uncut*. The text of Isaac Ferry's abusive e-mail to Simon Wild was sourced from the *Daily Telegraph*. Julie Burchill's response to the Ferry divorce and much more features in her article "The Killing Fields" in the *Guardian*, August 2002. Writer Sylvie Simmons provided a fascinating portrait of Ferry the man, while Mark Radcliffe's career-spanning assessment of Ferry is also from an exclusive interview.

Chapter 12: Now The Party's Over?

This career-spanning review of Bryan Ferry was written with the help of those who worked with him – Mick Rock, Eddie Jobson, Pete Sinfield and Gary Tibbs – and made further use of first-hand interviews with writers and fans Sylvie Simmons, Paul Du Noyer and Mark Radcliffe.

BIBLIOGRAPHY

Despite a thirty-year career, four Number 1 albums in the UK and dozens of Top 40 entries all over the world, there are very few biographies of Bryan Ferry or Roxy Music.

In 1976, publicist and band adviser Simon Puxley penned *The Bryan Ferry Story*. Written under the pseudonym of Rex Balfour, this slight book (a mere 128 pages in all, around a third of which are given over to photographic material) is quite strange. Massively partisan to the Ferry cause (the account of Eno's departure is wince-inducing, and Mackay and Manzanera are hardly mentioned at all), and deferential to his master's voice, it nevertheless contains nuggets of highly perceptive and well-written analysis.

This was followed in 1981 by Johnny Rogan's *Roxy Music: The First Ten Years, Style With Substance*. An unofficial but highly readable short history of the band, like *The Bryan Ferry Story* it is long since out of print. Apart from that, there's only Paul Stump's confusingly titled *Roxy Music Unknown Pleasures: A Cultural Biography Of Roxy Music* (confusing because the title references a Joy Division track!), which makes a number of useful connections, discussing British pop art, dada, high fashion and the origins of eighties style culture along the way.

At the time of writing, two other Roxy books are in the pipeline: *Both Ends Burning: The Complete Roxy Music* by Jonathan Rigby (Reynolds & Hearn), and *Roxyism* by novelist and critic Michael Bracewell (Flamingo).

Below is a list of books, articles, audio and Internet sources consulted during the research and writing of this book.

i) Books

Balfour, Rex: *The Bryan Ferry Story* (Michael Dempsey, 1976).

Bracewell, Michael: *England Is Mine: Pop Life In Albion from Wilde To Goldie* (Flamingo, 1997).

Burchill, Julie and Tony Parsons: *"The Boy Looked At Johnny": The Obituary Of Rock 'n' Roll* (Pluto Press, 1978).

Chambers, Iain: *Urban Rhythms: Pop Music And Popular Culture* (Macmillan, 1985).

Cunningham, Mark: *Good Vibrations: A History of Record Production* (Sanctuary, 1996).

De Lisle, Tim: *Lives Of The Great Songs* (Pavilion, 1994).

De Rogatis, Jim: *Let It Blurt: The Life And Times of Lester Bangs* (Bloomsbury, 2000).

Eno, Brian: *A Year With Swollen Appendices: Brian Eno's Diary* (Faber, 1996).

Goodwin, Andrew: *Dancing In The Distraction Factory: Music Television and Popular Culture* (Routledge, 1993).

Eddy, Chuck: *The Accidental Evolution Of Rock 'n' Roll* (Da Capo, 1997).

Geldof, Bob with Paul Vallely: *Is That It?* (Penguin, 1996).

Frith, Simon and Howard Horne: *Art Into Pop* (Methuen, 1987).

Gorman, Paul: *The Look: Adventures In Pop & Rock Fashion*. Foreword by Malcolm McLaren (Sanctuary, 2001).

Gorman, Paul: *In Their Own Right: Adventures In The Music Press* (Sanctuary, 2001).

Hall, Jerry with Christopher Hemphill: *Tall Tales* (Elm Tree Books, 1985).

Hoskyns, Barney: *Glam! Bowie, Bolan and the Glitter Rock Revolution* (Faber, 1998).

Hunt, Leon: *British Low Culture: From Safari Suits to Sexploitation* (Routledge, 1998).

Irvin, Jim (ed): *The Mojo Collection: The Greatest Albums Of All Time* (Mojo Books, 2000).

Kuresihi, Hanif and Jon Savage (eds): *The Faber Book Of Pop* (Faber, 1995).

Mackay, Andy: *Electronic Music: The Instruments, The Music And The Musicians* (Phaidon, 1981).

Marwick, Arthur: *The Sixties: Cultural Revolution in Britain, France, Italy, and the United States, c.1958-c.1974* (Oxford University Press, 1999).

Moore, Allan F: *Rock: The Primary Text: Developing a Musicology of Rock* (Open University Press, 1993).

Moore-Gilbert, Bart (ed): *The Arts In The 1970s: Cultural Closure?* (Routledge, 1994).

Napier-Bell, Simon: *Black Vinyl, White Powder* (Ebury Press, 2002).

Rogan, Johnny: *Roxy Music: Style With Substance – Roxy's First Ten Years* (Star, 1982).

Rogan, Johnny: *Morrissey and Marr: The Severed Alliance* (Omnibus, 1993).

Rimmer, Dave: *Like Punk Never Happened: Culture Club And The New Pop* (Faber & Faber, 1985).

Rimmer, Dave: *New Romantics: The Look* (Omnibus, 2003).

Savage, Jon: *England's Dreaming: Sex Pistols And Punk Rock* (Faber & Faber, 1991).

Shaar Murray, Charles: *Shots From The Hip* (Penguin, 1991).

Shepherd, John *et al* (eds): *The Continuum Encyclopaedia of Popular Music Of The World* (Continuum, 2003).

Sinclair, David: *Rock On CD: The Essential Guide* (Kyle Cathie, 1993).

Slabin, Roger (ed): *Punk Rock: So What?* (Routledge, 1999).

Street, John: *Rebel Rock: the Politics of Popular Music* (Basil Blackwell, 1986).

Stump, Paul: *Unknown Pleasures: A Cultural Biography of Roxy Music* (Quartet, 1998).

York, Peter and Charles Jennings: *Peter York's Eighties* (BBC Books, 1995).

ii) Articles

Aizlewood, John: "Ferry: A Slave To Self-Love", *Evening Standard*, October 8, 2002.

Anon (uncredited): "The Roxy Music File", *Melody Maker*, October 14, 1972.

Anon (uncredited): 'Witty, Polished, Puzzling Roxy", *Sounds*, November 10, 1973.

Anon (uncredited): "Roxy: An Air Of Lush Decay", *Melody Maker*, November 10, 1973.

Anon (uncredited): "Ferry, Roxy – Big Tour", *Melody Maker*, August 30, 1975.

Anon (uncredited): "Ferry's Tour, Mackay's Solo", *Melody Maker*, April 15, 1978.

Anon (uncredited): "Roxy: All Systems Go", *Melody Maker*, February 10, 1979.

Anon (uncredited): "Roxy Roll!", *Melody Maker*, February 24, 1979.

Anon (uncredited): "Phil Manzanera Interview", *Record Collector*, June 1995.

Anon (uncredited): "Roxy Music Face Anti-Hunt Protestors", dotmusic.com, February 16, 2001.

Anon (uncredited). ©1996-1998. Amanda Lear Biography. www.eurodance-hits.com

Anon (uncredited): "Roxy Music – Re-Make/Re-Model", *Uncut*, March 2001.

Anon (uncredited). "Teenage Models From Eton And Brixton', *Daily Telegraph*, July 26, 2001.

Anon (uncredited): "Vancouver: Bowie Fans Like Roxy Too", August 3, 2001.

Anon (uncredited): "Eno Blasts Roxy Reunion", February 23, 2002.

Anon (uncredited): "Bryan Ferry's Son Suspended From Eton", ananova.com, March 21, 2002.

Anon (uncredited): "Ferry's Son Arrested At Blair Home', bbc.co.uk, August 5, 2002.

Anon (uncredited): "Better Than Bowie, Cooler Than Sinatra", *Times Boston*, 12 November, 2002

Anon (uncredited): "Bryan Ferry Biog", bryanferry.com, 2002.

Anon (uncredited): "Bryan Ferry faces £10m Divorce Claim", *Hello*, March 13, 2003.

Atterborn, Daniel: "15 Minutes With Bryan Ferry", March 18, 2002.

Baker, Lindsay: "The Guy Can't Help It", *Daily Mail and Guardian South Africa*, April 14, 2002.

Barrell, Tony: "Stand Out In A Crowd", *Times*, June 1, 2001.

Bell, Max: "Bryan Ferry Interviewed", *NME*, December 21, 1974.

Bell, Max: "Bryatollah Ferrani Returns – And It Ain't Half Tepid, Mum", *NME*, 1979.

Bonyata, Tony: "Ferry Seduces Chicago", concertlivewlire.com, November 23, 2002.

Boucher, Caroline: "Roxy – Glamorous Paupers (Or Virginia Might Be Plain But She's Expensive)", *Disc*, September 16, 1972.

Boucher, Caroline: "The Real Mackay", *Disc*, February 17, 1973.

Boucher, Caroline: "Ferry Interesting: Bryan Ferry On The New Album And Roxy Music in General", *Disc*, March 24, 1973.

Boucher, Caroline: "Bryan The Cole Miner", *Observer*, December 19, 1999.

Bracewell, Michael: "Look Back In Languor", *Guardian*, June 14, 1997.

Bracewell, Michael: "Pop Is Dead, Long Live Pop", *Times Review*, September 13, 2003.

Brazier, Chris: "Cremation Corner", *Melody Maker*, August 5, 1978.

Brown, Glyn: "Bryan Ferry: Behind The Suave Façade', *Independent*, April 26, 2002.

Burchill, Julie: "Artiste In Search Of A Wider Audience', *NME*, 1977.

Burchill, Julie: "The Killing Fields", *Guardian*, August 24, 2002.

Callan, Jessica, Eva Simpson and Niki Waldegrave: "Very Very Ferry", *Mirror*, December 11, 2003.

Catchpole, Zoe and Dan Newling: news report on Ferry's split from Katie Turner, *This Is London*, 2004.

Chapman, Rob: "They Came From Planet Bacofoil", *Mojo*, December 1995.

Charlesworth: Chris. "Roxy: We're Not Killing Ourselves In America", *Melody Maker*, May 18, 1974.

Charlesworth, Chris: "Roxy Step Up The Ladder", *Melody Maker*, June 15, 1974.

Clarke, Steve: "Birmingham – Roxy Music/Sharks" [live review] *NME*, March 24, 1973

Coon, Caroline: "Bryan Ferry: Putting On The Style", *Melody Maker*, July 12, 1975.

Coon, Caroline: "The Brian Eno Interview", *Ritz*, 1977.

Cooper, Tim: "Roxy Are Dancing Away Again 18 Years On", *Evening Standard*, February 12, 2001.

Cushman, Robert: "These Foolish Things", in Tim De Lisle (ed): *Lives Of The Great Songs*, Pavilion, 1994.

Dalton, Stephen and Chris Roberts: "Scary Monsters, Super Freaks", *Uncut*, October 1998.

Davies, Caroline and Sean O'Neill: "Battle For Life At 35,000 Feet", *Daily Telegraph*, December 30, 2000.

Deans, Jason: "Goldsmith Slams 'Insensitive' BBC', *Guardian Unlimited*, January 26, 2001.

DeCurtis, Anthony: *Bête Noire* review, *Rolling Stone*, 1987.

Denselow, Robin: "Roxy Music Profile", *Guardian*, October 9, 1972.

De Lisle, Tim: "Re-Make-Re-Model", *Sunday Times Review*, March 7, 1993.

De Lisle, Tim: "50 Eno Moments", *Independent On Sunday*, May 10, 1998.

De Lisle, Tim: "Ferry Knows How To Keep Us Under His Influence", *Mail On Sunday*, April 21, 2002.

DeRogatis, Jim: "The Boys Are Back", *Chicago Sun Times*, July 27, 2001.

Dillon, Barry: Roxy interview, *Sounds*, April 28, 1973.

Dodd, Vikram: "Training Tells As Pilots Face The Unexpected', *Guardian*, December 30, 2000.

Dwyer, Michael. "Rock Of Ages", *Melbourne Age*, 2001.

Edmands, Bob: "Roxy Doxies Fail To Please", *NME*, October 27, 1973.

Edmonds, Ben: "Roxy Music: Siren", *Phonograph Record*, December 1975.

Edwards, Mark: "Frantic Review", *Sunday Times*, April 2002.

Elliot, Valerie: "Anti-Hunt Protesters May Aim At Ferry", *Times*, February 17, 2001.

Ellen, Barbara: "The Life Of Bryan", *Observer*, May 13, 2001.

Eno, Brian and Peter Schmidt: *Oblique Strategies: Over One Hundred Worthwhile Dilemmas*, 1979.

Fallows, Colin: "Art And Art Schools", in *The Continuum Encyclopaedia of Popular Music Of The World* (Continuum 2003).

Ferry, Bryan: "Whatever Turns You On: Bryan Ferry's Musical Influences", *NME*, December 1972.

Fortnam, Ian: "Roxy Music", *Other*, April 2000.

Forsyth, Bruce: "Love Is The Drug" [review] *Sounds*, October 4, 1975.

Fowler, Alice and Polly Borland: "A Close Shave", *The Mail On Sunday*, May 13, 2003.

Frith, Simon: "Roxy Music's Picture Palace", *Let It Rock*, May 1974.

Fox-Cummings, Ray: "Solo Ferry Sets Sail", *Disc*, June 23, 1973.

Fox-Cummings, Ray: "For Your Very Real Pleasure – Roxy Music", *Record Mirror*, October 18, 1975.

Fox-Cummings, Ray: "So Ferry Stylish ...", *Record Mirror*, October 25, 1975.

Galloway, Simon: "Roxy Music – The BBC Sessions", *www.roxyrama.com*

Gannon, Louise: "A Very British Pin-Up", *Daily Express*, October 1, 2000.

Gill, Andy: "Towards An Understanding Of Pop Past And Present", *Q*, November 1993.

Gill, Andy: "Brian Eno", *Mojo*, June 1995.

Gill, Andy: "Brian Eno: To Infinity and Beyond", *Mojo*, June 1998.

Gill, Andy: *Frantic* album review, *Independent*, April 26, 2002.

Gittins, Ian: *Best Of Roxy Music* review, amazon.co.uk, June 2001.

Goldman, Vivien: "Eno: Extra Natty Orations", *Sounds*, February 5, 1977.

Goldman, Vivien: "Brian Eno: Before And After Science", *Sounds*, December 10, 1977.

Grant, Linda: "Pinned To The Myths By Punk", *Guardian*, February 10, 1998.

Grealis, Tom: *Frantic* review, *RTE Interactive*, May 1, 2002.

Greig, Geordie: "On The Road Again", *Tatler*, April 14, 2002.

Grun, Jonathan: Bryan Ferry concert review, *South Wales Argus*, 1977.

Guarino, Mark: "More Than This – Roxy Music Make A Sudden Return", *Chicago Daily Herald*, July 2001.

Hamer, Rupert: "Star Bryan's Got My Stolen Picture', *Mirror*, March 7, 1999.

Harding, Louette: "Bryan's Long-Distance Race To Perfection", *You*, August 21, 1994.

Harron, Mary: "Interview With Brian Eno", *Punk*, summer 1977.

Hayman, Martin: "Roxy On A Pilgrimage To Wonderland", *Sounds*, December 30, 1972.

Hayman, Martin: "The Very Physical Mr Ferry", *Sounds*, June 9, 1973.

Hayman, Martin: "Phil Looks To Roxy's Phase 2", *Sounds*, October 13, 1973.

Hayman, Martin: "Stylish Doyens Of Rock", *Sounds*, June 8, 1974.

Hebdige, Dick: "Style As Homology And Signifying Practice" in Simon Frith and Andrew Goodwin (eds): *On Record: Rock, Pop and the Written Word* (Routledge 1990).

Hedblade, Jay: "Roxy Music Timeless Style", *Illinois Entertainer*, February 1, 2001.

Hoggard, Liz: "Ferry's Return Trip", *Mail On Sunday*, April 14, 2002.

Hollingsworth, Roy: "For Your Pleasure ... is the Title of Roxy Music's Sensational Second Album", *Melody Maker*, March 17, 1973.

Howarth, Stephen: "Time Goes By For The Voice Of Glam Rock", *Financial Times*. April 2000.

Hoskyns, Barney: "Bryan Ferry: Melancholic Of Glam", *Independent*, June 16, 2001.

Huddlestone, Paul: Live review, Leicester De Montfort Hall, *Leicester Mercury*, February 4, 1977.

Hynde, Chrissie: "Everything You'd Rather Not Have Known About Brian Eno", *NME*, February 2, 1974.

Ingram, Jonh: "The Roxy Music Story', *Sounds*, October 4, 1975.

Ingram, Jonh: Live review, Glasgow, *Sounds*, October 18, 1975.

Jackson, Blair: "Producer Chris Thomas: Three Decades On The Cutting Edge And The Charts", *Mix*, January, 1999.

Jenkins, Mark: "Bryan Ferry's Standards and Practices", *Washington Post*, October 29, 1999.

Jones, Allan: "The Heavy Side Of Ferry", *Melody Maker*, July 6, 1974.

Jones, Allan: "Rockin' On The Road", *Melody Maker*, July 3, 1976.

Jones, Allan: "Caught In the Act: Ferry – Coolly Superb", *Melody Maker*, February 12, 1977.

Jones, Allan: "Ferry Gets Into Your Mind", *Melody Maker*, February 19, 1977.

Jones, Allan: "Darkness Falls: Ferry In The Confessional", *Melody Maker*, September 15, 1978.

Jones, Allan: "Roxy's Swedish Love Night", *Melody Maker*, March 3, 1979.

Jones, Allan: "A Sloane Square", *Melody Maker*, June 8, 1985.

Kelly, Nick: "Roxy Music Returns", thetimes.co.uk, June 11, 2001.

Kent, Nick: Live review, Newcastle, *NME*, November 18, 1972.

Kent, Nick: "All This and Eno Too: How Can They Fail?", *NME*, December 18, 1972.

Kent, Nick: "A Flight Of Fantasy: Nick Kent Explores the Bizarre Domain of Roxy's Synthesiser Kid", *NME*, February 3, 1973.

Kent, Nick: "Last Tango In Amsterdam", *NME*, June 9, 1973.

Kent, Nick: "Of Launderettes and Lizard Girls", *NME*, July 28, 1973.

Kent, Nick: "Tonight Southport, Tomorrow The … Errh … World …", *NME*, April 20, 1974.

Kent, Nick: "Snake-Eyed Lothario Goes Pan-Tonic", *NME*, August 24, 1974.

Kent, Nick: "A Country Mile Ahead (Of Any Other Brand Of Poseur)", *NME*, November 9, 1974.

Kent, Nick: "Still Raining, Still Posing', *NME*, May 19, 1979.

Kent, Nick: "Life Of Bryan", *Melody Maker*, April 19, 1986.

Kirkup, Martin: "New Look Roxy Twice As Tough", *Sounds*, March 24, 1973.

Lake, Steve: "Keeping Roxy Fresh", *Sounds*, August 3, 1974.

Logan, Nick: "GI Blues (How To Get Them, How To Lose Them)', *NME*, October 11, 1975.

Lubow, Arthur: "Brian Eno", *People*, October 1983.

MacDonald, Ian: "Foxy Roxy – A Menace To Society", *NME*, August 12, 1972.

MacDonald, Ian: "Ferry Interesting Roxy", *NME*, October 14, 1972.

MacDonald, Ian, Charles Shaar Murray and Nick Kent: "The Man Who Put Sequins Into Middle Eights", *NME*, January 20, 1973.

MacDonald, Ian: "Under the Influence [Brian Eno]", *NME*, March 10, 1973.

MacDonald, Ian: "Under The Influence [Phil Manzanera]", *NME*, April 1973.

MacDonald, Ian: "Roxy: The Kind Of Example We Wish To Set Our Parents?", *NME*, September 23, 1973.

MacDonald, Ian: "A Pearl Beyond Price", *NME*, November 10, 1973.

MacDonald, Ian: "Before And After Science", *NME*, November 26, 1977.

MacDonald, Marianne: "Ferry Was Close To the End", *Evening Standard*, March 3, 2003.

McKay, Neil: "70s Is Roxy Music to the Ears of Many" *Newcastle Journal*, May 7, 2001.

McKay, Neil: "The Sultan of Suave Comes Home", *Newcastle Journal*, October 23, 2002.

McKinnon, Angus: "Roxy: Static Electricity", *Street Life*, November 1, 1975.

McKinnon, Angus: "The Poignant And The Pointless – Ferry Takes The Plunge", *NME*, September 16, 1978.

Makowski, Pete: "The Two Sides Of Mr Manzanera", *Sounds*, August 24, 1974.

McInnes, Gavin: Live review, New York, *NME*, July 23, 2001.

Mahoney, Elizabeth: "Bryan Ferry, Catwalk King", *Guardian Unlimited*, June 13, 2001.

Mahoney, Elizabeth: Live Review, Prince Street Gardens, *Guardian Unlimited*, June 3, 2002.

Miles: "Eno ... As Thin And Serious People Gather To Make Music", *NME*, November 27, 1976.

Miller, Jim: *Country Life* review, *Rolling Stone*, February 27, 1975.

Miller, Kathy: "Eno Creates New Frictions", *Creem*, 1973.

Mills, Simon: "L'uomo Vague", 1994.

Moon, Tom: "Empty Seats Greet Roxy Music At Tweeter", *Philadelphia Inquirer Review*, July 19, 2001.

Moore, Malcolm: "Eton Suspends Singer's Son Over Email", *Telegraph.co.uk*, March 22, 2002.

Morley, Paul: "The Man Who ...", *Uncut*, August 2001.

Nouaree, Andisheh: "Atlanta: Love Is The Drug", *Creative Loafing*, July 26, 2001.

Oakes, Philip: "Doing It In Style", *Goings On*, 1977.

O'Brien, Glen: "Eno At the Edge Of Rock", *Interview*, June 1978.

O'Brien, Penny: Live review in Edinburgh, vivaroxymusic.com, June 1, 2002.

Obrist, Hans-Ulrich: "Pop Daddy", *Tate Magazine* issue 4, 2003.

Palmer, Tony: "Shock Tactics From The Roxy", *Observer*, April 15, 1973.

Parade, Nicky: "Another Time, Another Place: Bryan Ferry Relives The Early Roxy Years", *Rock's Back Pages*, June 2001.

Parnes, Djuana: "Another Glam World: Brian Eno's Adventures In Roxy Music", *Rock's Back Pages*, June 2001.

Parsons, Tony: "Bitter Triumph Of A Pop Catalyst" in *Dispatches From The Front Line Of Popular Culture* (Virgin 1994).

Parsons, Tony: "Ageing Smoothie: Robert Palmer", reprinted in Dylan Jones (ed): *Meaty Beaty Big And Bouncy! Classic Rock And Pop Writing From Elvis To Oasis* (Hodder and Stoughton, 1996).

Payne, John: "For Your Pleasure: Bryan Ferry Twists The Love Song Again", *L.A. Weekly*, November 22-28, 2002.

Peacock, Steve: "Roxy: A Nice Touch", *Sounds*, 1972.

Peacock, Steve: "Eno: The Sounds Talk In", *Sounds*, 1972.

Peacock, Steve: "Roxy: What Next – A Marching Band?' *Sounds*, January 27, 1973.

Peacock, Steve: "Unease Of The Bogus Man", *Sounds*, March 10, 1973.

Peacock, Steve: "The Case Of The Vanishing Image", *Sounds*, July 1, 1973.

Penman, Ian: "The Shattered Glass: Notes On Bryan Ferry" in Angela McRobbie (ed): *Zoot Suits And Second-Hand Dresses* (Macmillan, 1989).

Reynolds, Simon: "Roxy Music: The Thrill Of It All", *Uncut*, September 1999.

Reynolds, Mark and Neil Sears: "Ferry's Young Love', *Daily Mail*, September 4, 2002.

Rambali, Paul: "Bryan Ferry: The Prisoner", *NME*, March 4, 1978.

Reesman, Bryan: *Frantic* review, *Mix*, March 1, 2003.

Rimmer, Dave: "Ennui", *Q*, December 1987.

Robbens, Diane: "Playgirl Interview", *Playgirl*, 1975.

Robbins, Ira: "Roxy Music: Anarch-O-Rock In Motion", *Other*, September 1976.

Robbins, Ira: "Manifesto Destiny: The Return Of Roxy Music", *Trouser Press*, 1979.

Robinson, Lisa: "God Bless America", *Disc*, 1972.

Roberts, Chris: "Chanel Ferry", *Melody Maker*, November 7, 1987.

Roberts, Chris: "Slave To Love", *Melody Maker*, November 12, 1988.

Roberts, Chris: "Re-Make/Re-Model", *Uncut*, July 2001.

Roberts, Chris: *Roxy Music Live* review, *Uncut*, July 2003.

Robertson, Peter: "Ferry Sexy", *She*, May 2002.

Rodger, Jennifer: "Interrogation: Call Yourself Cool?", *M Celebs*, 2002.

Rodgers, Sheila: Live review, *Rolling Stone*, 1988.

Rose, Cynthia: "Oblique Strategies", *Harpers & Queen*, 1979.

Rose, Cynthia: "Brian Eno", *NME*, July 26, 1980.

Ross, Ron: "Roxy Music: 'Love Is The Drug' in Bi-centennial Year!", *Phonograph Record*, March 1976.

Salewicz, Chris: "Bryan Ferry: In Every Dream Home A Heartache", *Q*, January 1988.

Sandall, Robert: "Back To the Future: Brian Eno", *Q*, November 1990.

Savage, Jon: "Blitz Culture", *The Face*, April 1981.

Savage, Jon: "Humpty Dumpty And The New Authenticity", *The Face*, July 1985.

Savage, Jon: "Tainted Love: The Influence Of Male Homosexuality And Sexual Divergence On Pop Music And Culture Since The War" in Alan Tomlinson (ed): *Consumption, Identity And Style* (Routledge, 1990).

Savage, Jon: "Keeping Busy?", *Mojo*, October, 1994.

Savage, Jon: "Androgyny: Confused Chromosomes And Camp Followers", in *Time Travel: Pop, Media And Sexuality 1976-96* (Chatto & Windus, 1996).

Scott, James: "Love Split Heartache For Ferry", *Daily Record*, August 14, 2002.

Scott, James and Sara Nuwar: "Bryan Ferry Splits From Wife", mirror.co.uk, August 14, 2002.

Seely, Peter. B: "Roxy Music And The Counter-Culture Of Art Glam", unpublished paper presented at American Culture Association Conference, New Orleans, 1993.

Sinclair, David: "Once More For Your Pleasure", thetimes.co.uk, 2001.

Shaar Murray, Charles: "Pleasure Indeed – Roxy Are Staggeringly Fine", *NME*, March 24, 1973.

Shaar Murray, Charles: "Glam Rock Remembered", in *Shots From The Hip* (Penguin, 1991).

Shaar Murray, Charles: "Roxy Music – For Your Pleasure Once Again", *Daily Telegraph*, February 17, 2001.

Simmons, Sylvie. 1995: "Bryan Ferry", *Rolling Stone*, October 1995.

Simpson, Dave: "Mmm. We Seem To Be Zooming Down To Earth At A Colossal Rate Of Knots", *The Guardian*, April 19, 2002.

Snow, Mat: "Bryan Ferry: My Indecision Is Final ..." *Q*, February 1993.

Soghomonian, Talia: "An Interview With Bryan Ferry", *New York Rock*, December 2002.

Stuart, Liz: "I Could See The Ground. It Was Very, Very Close", guardian.co.uk, December 2000.

Stephens, Jessica: "Ferry's Son Hunting For A Career", *Birmingham Post*, March 22, 2004.

Sullivan, Jim: "On His New Album, Bryan Ferry Is More About Beauty Than Bang", *Boston Globe*, November 10, 2002.

Sullivan, Jim: "Bryan Ferry Surrenders The Depths Of His Soul", *Boston Globe Review*, November 13, 2002.

Sutherland, Steve: "Roxy Give Blood", *Melody Maker*, August 9, 1980.

Sutherland, Steve: "Roxy Music: The Atlantic Years 1973-1980", *Melody Maker*, November 5, 1983.

Stone, Carol: "Ferry Sad", *The Mirror*, February 20, 2002.

Sweeting, Adam: "Zealous Guy", *Vox*, October 1994.

Synnot, Siobhan: "Fading Life Of Bryan", *Scotland On Sunday*, September 8, 2002.

Tannenbaum, Rob: "Steadfast In Style", *Village Voice*, August 28, 2002.

Te Koha, Nui: "Ferry's Pitch For Nic', *Sunday Tasmanian*, February 3, 2004.

The Seth Man: "Roxy Music – First Album Review", heritage.co.uk, June 23, 2001.

Thomson, Alice: "Ferry Across The Decades", *Times*, 1993.

Truman, James: "Editions Of Roxy", *Melody Maker*, May 26, 1979.

Truman, James: "Bryan Ferry: The *Face* Interview", The *Face*, April 1985.

Truman, James: Interview, *Details*, May 1, 1993.

Turner, Steve: "Roxy Music", *Beat Instrumental*, October 1972.

Tyler, Tony: "Roxy Music – The Answer To A Maiden's Prayer Or To Anyone Else's", *NME*, July 1, 1972.

Valentine, Penny: "The Bride Wore Black", *Melody Maker*, September 16, 1978.

Vasager, Jeevan, Vikram Dodd and Liz Stuart: "Two-Minute Fight For BA2069", guardian.co.uk, December 30, 2000.

Vidal, John: "Fat, Sluggish And Just Waiting To Be Killed', *Guardian*, October 7, 2002.

Warner, Simon: "Out Of His Pen: The Words Of Richard Williams", rock-critics.com, 2002.

Weiner, Matthew: *Frantic* review, *Stylus Magazine*, June 2, 2002.

Whitaker, Thomas: "Ferry And Kate Shop For Gems", thesun.co.uk, August 2002.

Whitaker, Thomas: "Bryan Dated Before He Split", thesun.co.uk, 2002.

Williams, Richard: "Roxy In The Rock Stakes", *Melody Maker*, August 7, 1971.

Williams, Richard: "Roxy Music", *Melody Maker*, February 12, 1972.

Williams, Richard: "Roxy: They've Only Just Begun", *Melody Maker*, June 24, 1972

Williams, Richard: "Roxy Music: The Sound Of Surprise", *Melody Maker*, July 1, 1972.

Williams, Richard: "Roxy Music", *Melody Maker*, July 29, 1972.

Williams, Richard: "If You Think Roxy Music Are A Hype, You Should Have Been At The Hardcore Last Week," *Melody Maker*, November 18, 1972.

Williams, Richard: "Roxy In Paris: In Which Our Heroes Dally With Dali", *Melody Maker*, May 12, 1973.

Williams, Richard: *Manifesto* album review, *Melody Maker*, February 14, 1979.

Womack, Sarah: "Remember 1976? Britain's Best Ever Year," telegraph.co.uk, 17 March, 2004.

Wonfer, Sam: "The Return Of The Sultan Of Suave", *Newcastle Journal*, October 22, 2002.

York, Peter: "Bryan's Interior", *Harper's And Queen*, January 1983.

Zahora, George: "Roxy Music: Chance Meeting", *Splendid*, 2003.

iii) Audio Sources

A huge thank you to Simon Galloway for helping me with these audio sources:

"My Top 10", BBC Radio One, April 21, 1974

Canadian radio interview, Bryan Ferry, July 20, 1974

"Nightbird & Co" (US radio) – Andy Mackay, August 18, 1974

"Insight" BBC Radio One, 1975

"Nightbird & Co" (US radio) – Bryan Ferry, March 7, 1976

2MS (Australian radio) – Bryan Ferry, 1977

"Radio One Road Show", Mallory Park – Bryan Ferry, July 30, 1978

"Rock On", BBC Radio One – Bryan Ferry, September 23, 1978

"What's It All About?", US radio – Phil Manzanera, July 1979

"Rock On", BBC Radio One – Bryan Ferry, May 24, 1980

"Star Special", BBC Radio One – Bryan Ferry, April 20, 1981

Earth News Radio (USA) – Bryan Ferry, September 1983

"Inside Track" (USA) – Bryan Ferry, 12 September 1983

BBC "Rock Profile" Radio One – Bryan Ferry, 1985.

"The Island Records Story", BBC Radio One, 1987

The Johnny Walker Show, BBC Radio One – Bryan Ferry, 1993

"The Bryan Ferry Story", BBC Radio One, 1994

"The Bryan Ferry Story", BBC Radio One, July 1999

Jools Holland, BBC Radio Two – Bryan Ferry, 1999

Nicky Campbell, BBC Radio Five Live – Roxy Music interview, 2001

iv) Internet Sources

These six websites are excellent sources of old articles and information about tours and releases:

These Vintage Years: www.vivaroxymusic.com John O'Brien's excellent virtual Roxy Music museum is one of the most important resource on the net.

Roxyrama: www.roxyrama.com Chris Turner's essential Roxy site

Rock's Backpages: www.rocksbackpages.com Superb research tool.

Phil Manzanera's official website: www.manzanera.com. A superbly detailed history of the band can be found at: www.manzanera.com/RoxyArchive/RMarchive1.htm

A Washington Lad: www.geocities.com/pictorialwashingtonuk/BryanFerry.html Audrey Fletcher details the story of Ferry's pre-fame years

Enoweb, music.hyperreal.org/artists/brian_eno An unofficial, though essential, Brian Eno website

The following sites are also worth a visit:

Roger Bunn	www.212.net/mihra/roger.html
Paul Carrack	www.carrack-uk.com
Bryan Ferry	www.bryanFerry.com
Guy Fletcher	www.guyfletcher.co.uk
Eddie Jobson	www.eddiejobson.com
Zev Katz	www.zevkatz.com
Andy Mackay	www.sierrabravo.co.uk
David O'List	home.ix.netcom.com/~dfirmin/olist.html
Roxy Music Central	home.ix.netcom.com/~dfirmin/amlinks.html
Peter Sinfield	www.songsouponsea.com
Chris Spedding	www.chrisspedding.com
Eric Tamm	www.erictamm.com/index.html
Paul Thompson	www.pauldrum.com
Julia Thornton	www.juliathornton.com
John Wetton	www.johnwetton.co.uk

DISCOGRAPHY

A special thank you to John O'Brien for constructing this excellent discography

Albums

Title	*Roxy Music*
Catalogue No.	Island ILPS 9200
Release Date	June 1972
UK chart position	10
Tracks	"Re-Make/Re-Model" *(Ferry)* 5.12
	"Ladytron" *(Ferry)* 4.20
	"If There Is Something" *(Ferry)* 6.30
	"Virginia Plain" *(Ferry)* 2.58 [CD bonus track]
	"2HB" *(Ferry)* 4.27
	"The Bob (Medley)" *(Ferry)* 5.48
	"Chance Meeting" *(Ferry)* 2.55
	"Would You Believe?" *(Ferry)* 3.47
	"Sea Breezes" *(Ferry)* 7.02
	"Bitters End" *(Ferry)* 2.02

Title	*For Your Pleasure*
Catalogue No.	Island ILPS 9232
Release Date	March 1973
UK chart position	4
Tracks	"Do The Strand" *(Ferry)* 4.00
	"Beauty Queen" *(Ferry)* 4.36
	"Strictly Confidential" *(Ferry)* 3.44
	"Editions Of You" *(Ferry)* 3.45
	"In Every Dream Home A Heartache" *(Ferry)* 5.23
	"The Bogus Man" *(Ferry)* 9.19
	"Grey Lagoons" *(Ferry)* 4.11
	"For Your Pleasure" *(Ferry)* 6.53

Title   *Stranded*
Catalogue No.   Island ILPS 9252
Release Date   November 1973
UK chart position   1
Tracks   "Street Life" *(Ferry)* 3.28
      "Just Like You" *(Ferry)* 3.32
      "Amazona" *(Ferry/Manzanera)* 4.14
      "Psalm" *(Ferry)* 8.04
      "Serenade" *(Ferry)* 2.55
      "A Song For Europe" *(Ferry/Mackay)* 5.43
      "Mother Of Pearl" *(Ferry)* 6.52
      "Sunset" *(Ferry)* 6.01

Title   *Country Life*
Catalogue No.   Island ILPS 9303
Release Date   November 1974
UK chart position   3
Tracks   "The Thrill Of It All" *(Ferry)* 6.22
      "Three And Nine" *(Ferry/Mackay)* 4.01
      "All I Want Is You" *(Ferry)* 2.58
      "Out Of The Blue" *(Ferry/Manzanera)* 4.43
      "If It Takes All Night" *(Ferry)* 3.09
      "Bitter Sweet" *(Ferry/Mackay)* 4.49
      "Triptych" *(Ferry)* 3.09
      "Casanova" *(Ferry)* 3.23
      "A Really Good Time" *(Ferry)* 3.43
      "Prairie Rose" *(Ferry/Manzanera)* 5.07

Title   *Siren*
Catalogue No.   Island ILPS 9344
Release Date   October 1975
UK chart position   4
Tracks   "Love Is The Drug" *(Ferry/Mackay)* 4.05
      "End Of The Line" *(Ferry)* 5.14
      "Sentimental Fool" 6.12 *(Ferry/Mackay)*
      "Whirlwind" *(Ferry)* 3.34
      "She Sells" *(Ferry/Jobson)* 3.45
      "Could It Happen To Me?" *(Ferry)* 3.33

"Both Ends Burning" *(Ferry)* 5.12
"Nightingale" *(Ferry)* 4.05
"Just Another High" *(Ferry)* 6.06

Title	*Manifesto*
Catalogue No.	Polydor POLH 001
Release Date	March 1979
UK chart position	7
Tracks	"Manifesto" *(Ferry/Manzanera)* 5.30
	"Trash" *(Ferry/Manzanera)* 2.13
	"Angel Eyes" *(Ferry/Mackay)* 3.32
	"Still Falls The Rain" 4.13 *(Ferry/Manzanera)* 4.13
	"Stronger Through the Years" *(Ferry)* 6.13
	"Ain't That So" *(Ferry)* 5.39
	"My Little Girl" 3.13 *(Ferry/Manzanera)*
	"Dance Away" *(Ferry)* 4.18
	"Cry, Cry, Cry" *(Ferry)* 2.56
	"Spin Me Round" *(Ferry)* 5.14

Title	*Flesh + Blood*
Catalogue No.	Polydor POLH 002
Release Date	May 1980
UK chart position	1
Tracks	"In The Midnight Hour" (Cropper/Picket) 3.09
	"Oh Yeah" *(Ferry)* 4.51
	"Same Old Scene" *(Ferry)* 3.57
	"Flesh And Blood" *(Ferry)* 3.08
	"My Only Love" *(Ferry)* 5.16
	"Over You" *(Ferry/Manzanera)* 3.27
	"Eight Miles High" *(Clark/Crosby/McGuinn)* 4.55
	"Rain Rain Rain" *(Ferry)* 3.20
	"No Strange Delight" *(Ferry/Manzanera)* 4.44
	"Running Wild" *(Ferry/Manzanera)* 5.03

Title	*Avalon*
Catalogue No.	Polydor EGHP
Release Date	June 1982
UK chart position	1

Tracks "More Than This" *(Ferry)* 4.30
"The Space Between" *(Ferry)* 4.30
"Avalon" *(Ferry)* 4.17
"India" *(Ferry)* 1.45
"While My Heart Is Still Beating" 3.25 *(Ferry/Mackay)*
"The Main Thing" *(Ferry)* 3.53
"Take A Chance With Me" 4.42 *(Ferry/Manzanera)*
"To Turn You On" *(Ferry)* 4.15
"True To Life" *(Ferry)* 4.25
"Tara" *(Ferry/Mackay)* 1.32

Roxy Music Compilation Albums

Title *Greatest Hits*
Catalogue No. Polydor 2001 739
Release Date October 1977
UK chart position 20
Tracks "Virginia Plain" *(Ferry)* 2.58
"Do The Strand" *(Ferry)* 4.00
"All I Want Is You" *(Ferry)* 2.58
"Out Of The Blue" *(Ferry/Manzanera)* 4.43
"Pyjamarama" *(Ferry)* 2.52
"Editions Of You" *(Ferry)* 3.45
"Love Is The Drug" *(Ferry/Mackay)* 4.05
"Mother Of Pearl" *(Ferry)* 6.52
"A Song For Europe" *(Ferry/Mackay)* 5.43
"The Thrill Of It All" 4.20 *(Ferry)* (Edit)
"Street Life" *(Ferry)* 3.28

Title *The Atlantic Years*
Catalogue No. Polydor EGLP 54
Release Date October 1983
UK chart position 23
Tracks "Dance Away" *(Ferry)* 3.45
"Angel Eyes" *(Ferry/Mackay)* 3.32
"Over You" *(Ferry/Manzanera)* 3.27
"Love Is The Drug" *(Ferry/Mackay)* 4.05
"Oh Yeah" *(Ferry)* 4.51

"Ain't That So" *(Ferry)* 5.39
"My Only Love" *(Ferry)* 5.16
"In The Midnight Hour" 3.09
"Still Falls The Rain" *(Ferry/Manzanera)* 4.13
"Do The Strand" *(Ferry)* 4.00

Title	*The Thrill Of It All* (4 CD Box Set)
Catalogue No.	Virgin CDBOX 5
Release Date	October 1995
Disc 1	"Re-Make/Re-Model *(Ferry)*" 5.12

"Ladytron" *(Ferry)* 4.20
"If There Is Something" *(Ferry)* 6.30
"2HB *(Ferry)*" 4.27
"Chance Meeting" *(Ferry)* 2.55
"Sea Breezes" *(Ferry)* 7.02
"Do The Strand" *(Ferry)* 4.00
"Beauty Queen" *(Ferry)* 4.36
"Strictly Confidential" *(Ferry)* 3.44
"Editions Of You" *(Ferry)* 3.45
"In Every Dream Home A Heartache" *(Ferry)* 5.23
"The Bogus Man" *(Ferry)* 9.19
"For Your Pleasure" *(Ferry)* 6.53
"Street Life" *(Ferry)* 3.28
"Just Like You" *(Ferry)* 3.32
"Amazona" *(Ferry/Manzanera)* 4.14

Disc 2   "A Song For Europe" *(Ferry/MacKay)* 5.43
"Mother Of Pearl" *(Ferry)* 6.52
"Sunset" *(Ferry)* 6.01
"The Thrill If It All" *(Ferry)* 6.22
"Three And Nine" *(Ferry)* 4.01
"All I Want Is You" *(Ferry)* 2.58
"Out Of The Blue" *(Ferry/Manzanera)* 4.43
"Bittersweet" *(Ferry)* 4.49
"Casanova" *(Ferry)* 3.23
"A Really Good Time" *(Ferry)* 3.43
"Prairie Rose" *(Ferry/Manzanera)* 5.07
"Love Is The Drug" *(Ferry/MacKay)* 4.05
"Sentimental Fool" *(Ferry/MacKay)* 6.12

"Could It Happen To Me?" *(Ferry)* 3.33
"Both Ends Burning" *(Ferry)* 5.14
"Just Another High" *(Ferry)* 6.06

Disc 3

"Manifesto" *(Ferry/Manzanera)* 5.30
"Trash" *(Ferry/Manzanera)* 2.13
"Angel Eyes" *(Ferry/MacKay)* 3.32 (Original Version)
"Stronger Through The Years" 6.13
"Ain't That So" *(Ferry)* 5.39
"Dance Away" *(Ferry)* 4.18 (Original Version)
"Oh Yeah" *(Ferry)* 4.51
"Same Old Scene" *(Ferry)* 3.57
"Flesh And Blood" *(Ferry)* 3.08
"My Only Love" *(Ferry)* 5.16
"Over You" *(Ferry/Manzanera)* 3.27
"No Strange Delight" *(Ferry/Manzanera)* 4.44
"More Than This" *(Ferry)* 4.30
"Avalon *(Ferry)*" 4.17
"While My Heart Is Still Beating" *(Ferry/MacKay)* 3.25
"Take A Chance With Me" *(Ferry/Manzanera)* 4.42
"To Turn You On *(Ferry)*" 4.15
"Tara *(Ferry/MacKay)*" 1.32

Disc 4

"Virginia Plain" *(Ferry)* 2.58
"The Numberer" *(MacKay)* 3.30
"Pyjamarama" *(Ferry)* 2.52
"The Pride And The Pain" *(MacKay)* 4.12
"Manifesto (Remake)" *(Ferry/Manzanera)* 4.00
"Hula Kula" *(Manzanera)* 2.32
"Trash 2" *(Ferry/Manzanera)* (3.09)
"Your Application's Failed" *(Thompson)* 4.45
"Lover" *(Ferry/Manzanera)* 4.29
"Sultanesque" *(Ferry)* 5.24
"Dance Away (Extended Remix)" *(Ferry)* 6.33
"South Downs" *(Ferry)* 5.08
"Angel Eyes" (Extended Remix) *(Ferry/MacKay)* 6.39
"Always Unknowing" *(Ferry)* 5.25
"The Main Thing (Extended Remix)" *(Ferry)* 7.43
"India *(Ferry)*" 1.45
"Jealous Guy" *(Lennon)* 6.10

Title	*The Early Years*
Catalogue No.	Virgin CDV 2919
Release Date	August 2000
Tracks	"Re-Make/Re-Model" *(Ferry)* 5.12
	"Ladytron" *(Ferry)* 4.20
	"If There Is Something" *(Ferry)* 6.33
	"2HB" *(Ferry)* 4.30
	"Chance Meeting" *(Ferry)* 3.00
	"Virginia Plain" *(Ferry)* 2.56
	"Pyjamarama" *(Ferry)* 2.52
	"Do The Strand" *(Ferry)* 4.00
	"Beauty Queen" *(Ferry)* 4.35
	"Editions Of You" *(Ferry)* 3.40
	"In Every Dream Home A Heartache" *(Ferry)* 5.25
	"The Bogus Man" *(Ferry)* 9.22
	"Street Life" *(Ferry)* 3.27
	"A Song For Europe" *(Ferry/Mackay)* 5.44
	"Mother Of Pearl" *(Ferry)* 6.53
	"Sunset" *(Ferry)* 6.00

Title	*The Best Of Roxy Music*
Catalogue No.	Virgin CDV 2939
Release Date	June 2001
Tracks	"Avalon" *(Ferry)* 4.16
	"More Than This" *(Ferry)* 4.14
	"Jealous Guy" *(Lennon)* 4.56
	"Over You" *(Ferry/Manzanera)* 3.26
	"Same Old Scene" *(Ferry)* 3.57
	"Oh Yeah" *(Ferry)* 4.51
	"Angel Eyes" *(Ferry/Mackay)* 2.51
	"Dance Away" *(Ferry)* 3.46
	"Both Ends Burning" *(Ferry)* 5.14
	"Love Is The Drug" *(Ferry/Mackay)* 4.08
	"Out Of The Blue" *(Ferry/Manzanera)* 4.44
	"All I Want Is You" *(Ferry)* 2.52
	"Mother Of Pearl" *(Ferry)* 6.34
	"Street Life" *(Ferry)* 3.28
	"Do The Strand" *(Ferry)* 4.01

"Pyjamarama" *(Ferry)* 2.51
"Virginia Plain" *(Ferry)* 2.56
"Re-Make/Re-Model" *(Ferry)* 4.52

Roxy Music Live Albums

Title	*Viva! Roxy Music*
Catalogue No.	Island ILPS 9400
Release Date	June 1976
UK chart position	6
Tracks	"Out Of The Blue" *(Ferry Manzanera)* 4:40
	"Pyjamarama" *(Ferry)* 3:27
	"The Bogus Man" *(Ferry)* 7:05
	"Chance Meeting" *(Ferry)* 3:01
	"Both Ends Burning" *(Ferry)* 4:54
	"If There Is Something" *(Ferry)* 10:29
	"In Every Dream Home A Heartache" *(Ferry)* 8:10
	"Do The Strand" *(Ferry)* 3:55

Title	*The High Road* (live EP)
Catalogue No.	Polydor EGMLP 1
Release Date	March 1983
UK chart position	26
Tracks	"Can't Let Go" *(Ferry)* 4:29
	"My Only Love" *(Ferry)* 7:52
	"Like A Hurricane" *(Young)* 7:48
	"Jealous Guy" *(Lennon)* 6:40

Title	*Heart Still Beating*
Catalogue No.	EG EGCD 77
Release Date	October 1990
Tracks	"India" *(Ferry)*
	"Can't Let Go" *(Ferry)*
	"While My Heart Is Still Beating" *(Ferry/MacKay)*
	"Out Of The Blue" *(Ferry/Manzanera)*
	"Dance Away" *(Ferry)*
	"Impossible Guitar" *(Manzanera)*

"A Song For Europe" *(Ferry/MacKay)*
"Love Is the Drug" *(Ferry/MacKay)*
"Like a Hurricane" *(Young)*
"My Only Love" *(Ferry)*
"Both Ends Burning" *(Ferry)*
"Avalon" *(Ferry)*
"Editions Of You" *(Ferry)*
"Jealous Guy" *(Lennon)*

Title	*Roxy Music Live*
Catalogue No.	Eagle Rock EDGCD 250
Release Date	June 2003
Tracks	"Re-Make/Re-Model" *(Ferry)*

"Street Life" *(Ferry)*
"Ladytron" *(Ferry)*
"While My Heart Is Still Beating" *(Ferry/MacKay)*
"Out Of The Blue" *(Ferry/Manzanera)*
"A Song For Europe" *(Ferry/MacKay)*
"My Only Love" *(Ferry)*
"In Every Dream Home A Heartache" *(Ferry)*
"Oh Yeah" *(Ferry)*
"Both Ends Burning" *(Ferry)*
"Tara" *(Ferry/MacKay)*

"More Than This" *(Ferry)*
"If There Is Something" *(Ferry)*
"Mother of Pearl" *(Ferry)*
"Avalon" *(Ferry)*
"Dance Away" *(Ferry)*
"Jealous Guy" *(Ferry)*
"Editions of You" *(Ferry)*
"Virginia Plain" *(Ferry)*
"Love Is the Drug" *(Ferry/MacKay)*
"Do the Strand" *(Ferry)*
"For Your Pleasure" *(Ferry)*

Roxy Music Singles

7" single

Tracks "Virginia Plain" *(Ferry)* 2.58 c/w "The Numberer" *(Mackay)* 3.30
Catalogue No. Island WIP 6144
Release Date August 1972
UK chart position 4

7" single

Tracks "Pyjamarama" *(Ferry)* 2.52 c/w "The Pride And The Pain" 4.12 *(Mackay)*
Catalogue No. Island WIP 6159
Release Date March 1973
UK chart position 10

7" single

Tracks "Do The Strand" *(Ferry)* 4.00 c/w "Editions Of You" *(Ferry)* 3.45
Catalogue No. Island 12713 AT (Europe, Japan and US)

7" single

Tracks "Street Life" *(Ferry)* 3.28 c/w "Hula Kula" *(Manzanera)* 2.32
Catalogue No. Island WIP 6173
Release Date November 1973
UK chart position 9

7" single

Tracks "All I Want Is You" *(Ferry)* 2.58 c/w "Your Application's Failed" *(Thompson)* 4.45
Catalogue No. Island WIP 6208
Release Date October 1974
UK chart position 12

7" single

Tracks "The Thrill Of It All" *(Ferry)* 3.20 c/w "Your Application's Failed" *(Thompson)* 4.45
Catalogue No. ATCO45-7018 (USA)
Release Date October 1974

7" single

Tracks	"Love Is The Drug" *(Ferry/Mackay)* 4.05 c/w "Sultanesque" *(Ferry)* 5.24
Catalogue No.	Island WIP 6248
Release Date	October 1975
UK chart position	2

7" single

Tracks	"Both Ends Burning" *(Ferry)* 3.55 c/w "For Your Pleasure (Live)" *(Ferry)* 5.00
Catalogue No.	Island, WIP 6262
Release Date	December 1975
UK chart position	25

7" single

Tracks	"Virginia Plain" *(Ferry)* 2.58 c/w "Pyjamarama" *(Ferry)* 2.52
Catalogue No.	Polydor 2001 739
Release Date	October 1977
UK chart position	11

7" single

Tracks	"Do The Strand" *(Ferry)* 4.00 c/w "Editions Of You" *(Ferry)* 3.45
Catalogue No.	Polydor 2001 756
Release Date	January 1978

12" single

Tracks	"Do The Strand" *(Ferry)* 4.00 c/w "Editions Of You" *(Ferry)* 3.45
Catalogue No.	Polydor 2001 756
Release Date	January 1978

7" single

Tracks	"Trash" *(Ferry/Manzanera)* 2.13 c/w "Trash 2" *(Ferry/Manzanera)* 3.09
Catalogue No.	Polydor POSP 32
Release Date	March 1979
UK chart position	40

7" single

Tracks	"Dance Away" *(Ferry)* 3.45 c/w "Cry, Cry, Cry" *(Ferry)* 2.56
Catalogue No.	Polydor, POSP 44
Release Date	April 1979
UK chart position	2

12" single

Tracks	"Dance Away (Extended Remix)" *(Ferry)* 6.33 c/w "Trash 2" *(Ferry)*
Catalogue No.	ATCO DDK 7504 (Canada)

7" single

Tracks	"Angel Eyes" *(Ferry/ Mackay)* 3.06 c/w "My Little Girl" *(Ferry/Manzanera)* 3.13
Catalogue No.	Polydor POSP 67
Release Date	August 1979
UK chart position	4

12" single

Tracks	"Angel Eyes (Extended Remix)" *(Ferry/ Mackay)* 6.39 c/w "My Little Girl" *(Ferry/Manzanera)*
Catalogue No.	Polydor POSPX 67
Release Date	August 1979

7" single

Tracks	"Over You" *(Ferry/Manzanera)* 3.27 c/w "Manifesto (Remake)" *(Ferry/Manzanera)* 4.00
Catalogue No.	Polydor POSP 93
Release Date	May 1980
UK chart position	5

7" single

Tracks	"Oh Yeah (on the radio)" *(Ferry)* c/w "South Downs" *(Ferry)* 5.08
Catalogue No.	Polydor 2001 972
Release Date	July 1980
UK chart position	5

7" single

Tracks   "The Same Old Scene" *(Ferry)* 3.57 c/w "Lover"
(Ferry/Manzanera) 4.29
Catalogue No. Polydor ROXY 1
Release Date November 1980
UK chart position 12

7" single

Tracks   "In The Midnight Hour" *(Cropper/Picket)* c/w "Flesh
And Blood" *(Ferry)*
Catalogue No. ATCO ST-80C-38517 (US and Portugal)

7" single

Tracks   "Jealous Guy" *(Lennon)* 6.10 c/w "To Turn You On"
(Ferry)
Catalogue No. EG ROXY 2
Release Date February 1981
UK chart position 1

7" single

Tracks   "More Than This" *(Ferry)* 4.10 c/w "India" *(Ferry)*
1.45
Catalogue No. EG ROXY 3
Release Date March 1982
UK chart position 6

7" Single

Tracks   "Avalon" *(Ferry)* 4.17 c/w "Always Unknowing"
(Ferry) 5.25
Catalogue No. EG ROXY 4
Release Date June 1982
UK chart position 13

7" single

Tracks   "Take A Chance With Me" *(Ferry/Manzanera)* 3:45
c/w "The Main Thing (Remix)" *(Ferry)* 3:45
Catalogue No. EG ROXY 5
Release Date September 1982
UK chart position 26

12" single

Tracks "Take A Chance With Me" 3:45 *(Ferry/Manzanera)* c/w "The Main Thing (Extended Remix)" *(Ferry)* 7.43

Catalogue No. EG ROXY X5

7" single

Tracks "Love Is The Drug (Live)" *(Ferry/ Mackay)* 3:41 c/w "Editions Of You (Live)" *(Ferry)* 3:58

Catalogue No. EGO 55

Release Date September 1990

12" single

Tracks "Love Is The Drug (Live)" *(Ferry/ Mackay)* 3:41 c/w "Editions Of You (Live)" *(Ferry) 3:58* "Do The Strand (Live)" *(Ferry)* 3:52

Catalogue No. EGOX 55

Release Date September 1990

CD single

Tracks "Love Is The Drug (Live)" *(Ferry/Mackay)* 3:41 "Editions Of You (Live)" *(Ferry)* 3:58 "Do The Strand (Live)" *(Ferry)* 3:52

Catalogue No. EGOCD 55

Release Date September 1990

Cassette single

Tracks "Love Is The Drug (Live)" *(Ferry/Mackay)* 3:41 c/w "Editions Of You (Live)" *(Ferry)* 3:58

Catalogue No. EGOC 55

Release Date September 1990

12" single

Tracks "Love Is The Drug (Rollo & Sister Bliss remix)" (Ferry/Mackay)

Catalogue No. EG VSCDT 1580

Release Date April 1996

UK chart position 33

12" single

Tracks   "Love Is The Drug Monster Mix" 8:41 c/w "Love Is
                      the Drug Deep Mix" 6:42
Catalogue No.   Virgin VST 1580
Release Date   April 1996

Cassette single

Tracks   "Love Is the Drug Monster Mix Edit" 4:13 "Love Is
                      the Drug Monster Mix" 8:41
                      "Love Is the Drug Original Mix" 3:59 "Love Is the
                      Drug Deep Mix" 6:42
Catalogue No.   Virgin VSC 1580
Release Date   April 1996

CD single

Tracks   "Love Is the Drug Monster Mix Edit" 4:13 "Love Is
                      the Drug Monster Mix" 8:41 "Love Is the Drug
                      Original Mix" 3:59 "Love Is the Drug Deep Mix"
                      6:42
Catalogue No.   Virgin VSCD 1580
Release Date   April 1996

Bryan Ferry Albums

Title   *These Foolish Things*
Catalogue No.   Island ILPS 9249
Release Date   October 1973
UK chart position   5
Tracks   "A Hard Rain's A-Gonna Fall" *(Dylan)* 5.20
                          "River Of Salt" *(Brown/J & B Zackery)* 1.48
                          "Don't Ever Change" *(Goffin/King)* 2.15
                          "Piece Of My Heart" *(Berns/Ragovoy)* 3.06
                          "Baby I Don't Care" *(Lieber/Stoller)* 1.52
                          "It's My Party" *(Wiener/Gold/Gluck Jr)* 1.58
                          "Don't Worry Baby" *(Wilson/Christian)* 4.13
                          "Sympathy For The Devil" *(Jagger/Richards)* 5.51
                          "Tracks Of My Tears" *(Robinson/Tarplin/Moore)* 3.05
                          "You Won't See Me" *(Lennon/McCartney)* 2.32
                          "I Love How You Love Me" *(Kolber/Mann)* 3.02

"Loving You Is Sweeter Than Ever" *(Hunter/Wonder)* 3.06

"These Foolish Things" *(Maschwitz/Strackey)* 5.42

Title	*Another Time Another Place*
Catalogue No.	Island ILPS 9284
Release Date	June 1974
UK chart position	4
Tracks	"The 'In' Crowd" *(Page)* 4.35

"Smoke Gets In Your Eyes" *(Kern/Harbach)* 2.53

"Walk A Mile In My Shoes" *(South)* 4.44

"Funny How Time Slips Away" *(Nelson)* 3.30

"You Are My Sunshine" *(Davis/Mitchell)* 6.48

"(What A) Wonderful World" *(Cook/Alpert/Adler/ Campbell)* 2.54

"It Ain't Me Babe" *(Dylan)* 3.53

"Finger-poppin'" *(Turner)* 3.34

"Help Me Make It Through The Night" *(Kristofferson)* 4.16

"Another Time, Another Place" *(Ferry)* 4.46

Title	*Let's Stick Together*
Catalogue No.	Island ILPS 9452
Release Date	June 1976
UK chart position	19
Tracks	"Let's Stick Together" *(Harrison)* 3.00

"Casanova" *(Ferry)* 2.45

"Sea Breezes" *(Ferry)* 6.10

"Shame, Shame, Shame" *(Reed)* 3.15

"2 HB" *(Ferry)* 3.50

"Price Of Love" *(Everly/Everly)* 3.25

"Chance Meeting" *(Ferry)* 3.35

"It's Only Love" *(Lennon/McCartney)* 3.45

"You Go to My Head" *(Gillespie/Coots)* 2.50

"Re-Make/Re-Model" *(Ferry)* 2.40

"Heart On My Sleeve" *(Gullagher/Lyle)* 3.30

Title	*In Your Mind*
Catalogue No.	Polydor 2302 055
Release Date	April 1977
UK chart position	5
Tracks	"This Is Tomorrow" *(Ferry)* 3.40
	"All Night Operator" *(Ferry)* 3.10
	"One Kiss" *(Ferry)* 3.36
	"Love Me Madly Again" *(Ferry)* 7.28
	"Tokyo Joe" *(Ferry)* 3.54
	"Party Doll" *(Ferry)* 4.33
	"Rock Of Ages" *(Ferry/Thomas)* 4.31
	"In Your Mind" *(Ferry)* 5.19

Title	*The Bride Stripped Bare*
Catalogue No.	Polydor POLD 5003
Release Date	September 1978
UK chart position	13
Tracks	"Sign Of The Times" *(Ferry)* 2.28
	"Can't Let Go" *(Ferry)* 5.14
	"Hold On I'm Coming" *(Hayes/Porter)* 3.37
	"Same Old Blues" *(Cale)* 3.21
	"When She Walks In The Room" *(Ferry)* 6.28
	"Take Me To The River" *(Green/Hodges* 4.29
	"What Goes On" *(Reed)* 4.11
	"Carrickfergus" *(Traditional: Arranged by Ferry)* 3.46
	"That's How Strong My Love" *(Jamison)* Is 3.17
	"This Island Earth" *(Ferry)* 5.06

Title	*Boys And Girls*
Catalogue No.	Polydor/EG EGCD 62
Release Date	June 1985
UK chart position	1
Tracks	"Sensation" *(Ferry)* 5.04
	"Slave To Love" *(Ferry)* 4.25
	"Don't Stop The Dance" *(Ferry/Davies)* 4.19
	"A Wasteland" *(Ferry)* 1.00
	"Windswept" *(Ferry)* 4.31
	"The Chosen One" *(Ferry)* 4.51
	"Valentine" *(Ferry)* 3.46

"Stone Woman" *(Ferry)* 4.56
"Boys And Girls" *(Ferry)* 5.23

Title	*Bête Noire*
Catalogue No.	Virgin CDV 2474
Release Date	November 1987
UK chart position	9
Tracks	"Limbo" *(Ferry/Leonard)* 4.59

"Kiss And Tell" *(Ferry)* 4.52
"New Town" *(Ferry)* 5.02
"Day For Night" *(Ferry/Leonard)* 5.38
"Zamba" *(Ferry/Leonard)* 3.01
"The Right Stuff" *(Ferry/Marr)* 4.22
"Seven Deadly Sins" *(Ferry/Kamen/Pratt)* 5.11
"The Name Of The Game" *(Ferry/Leonard)* 5.29
"Bête Noire" *(Ferry/Leonard)* 4.59

Title	*Taxi*
Catalogue No.	Virgin CDV 2700
Release Date	March 1993
UK chart position	2
Tracks	"I Put A Spell On You" *(Hawkins)* 5.27

"Will You Love Me Tomorrow" *(Goffin/King)* 4.16
"Answer Me" *(Winkler/Rauch/Sigman)* 2.46
"Just One Look" *(Doris/Gregory)* 3.32
"Rescue Me" *(Miner/Smith)* 3.40
"All Tomorrow's Parties" *(Reed)* 5.32
"Girl Of My Best Friend" *(Ross/Bobrick)* 3.24
"Amazing Grace" *(Traditional arranged by Ferry)* 4.01
"Taxi" *(Banks)* 5.30
"Because You're Mine" *(Ferry)* 1.44

Title	*Mamouna*
Catalogue No.	Virgin CDV 2751
Release Date	September 1994
UK chart position	11
Tracks	"Don't Want To Know" *(Ferry)* 4.06

"N.Y.C." *(Ferry)* 4.05

"Your Painted Smile" *(Ferry)* 3.19
"Mamouna" *(Ferry)* 5.11
"The Only Face" *(Ferry)* 4.40
"The 39 Steps" *(Ferry)* 5.01
"Which Way To Turn" *(Ferry)* 5.44
"Wildcat Days" *(Ferry/Eno)* 4.34
"Gemini Moon" *(Ferry)* 3.47
"Chain Reaction" *(Ferry)* 5.09

Title	*As Time Goes By*
Catalogue No.	Virgin 8482702/CDVIR89
Release Date	September 1999
UK chart position	16
Tracks	"As Time Goes By" *(Hupfield)* 2.35

"The Way You Look Tonight" *(Fields/Kern)* 3.33
"Easy Living *(Robin/Ranger)*" 2.14
"I'm In The Mood For Love" *(Wilmot/McHugh/Fields)* 4.20
"Where Or When" *(Rogers/Hart)* 3.20
"When Somebody Thinks You're Wonderful" *(Woods/Dunn)* 3.00
"Sweet And Lovely" *(Arnheim/Tobias/Lamare)* 3.10
"Miss Otis Regrets" *(Porter)* 2.44
"Time On My Hands" *(Adamson/Gordon/Youmans/Connelly)* 3.01
"Lover Come Back To Me" *(Romberg/Hammerstein)* 2.51
"Falling In Love Again" *(Hollander/Connelly)* 2.27
"Love Me Or Leave Me" *(Kahn/Donaldson)* 2.42
"You Do Something To Me" *(Porter)* 2.46
"Just One Of Those Things" *(Porter)* 2.44
"September Song" *(Anderson/Weill)* 3.00

Title	*Frantic*
Catalogue No.	Virgin 811984-2/CDVIR167
Release Date	April 2002
UK chart position	6
Tracks	"It's All Over Now, Baby Blue" *(Dylan)* 4.05

"Cruel" *(Ferry/Stewart)* 3.55

"Goin' Down" *(Nix)* 3.40
"Goddess Of Love" *(Ferry/Stewart)* 3.32
"Don't Think Twice, It's Alright" *(Dylan)* 4.05
"Nobody Loves Me" *(Ferry/Stewart)* 3.21
"Ja Nun Hons Pris" *(Richard Coeur de Lion)* 0.36
"A Fool For Love" *(Ferry)* 4.43
"Goodnight Irene" *(Ledbetter/Lomax)* 3.20
"Hiroshima ..." *(Ferry)* 3.14
"San Simeon" *(Ferry/Stewart)* 4.34
"One Way Love" *(Russell/Meade)* 3.05
"I Thought" *(Ferry/Eno)* 5.40

Bryan Ferry & Roxy Music Compilation Albums

Title	*Street Life 20 Great Hits*
Catalogue No.	Polydor/EG EGTV1
Release Date	April 1986
UK chart position	1
Tracks	"Virginia Plain" *(Ferry)* 2.59

"A Hard Rain's A-Gonna Fall" (Dylan) 4.15 (Edit)
"Pyjamarama" *(Ferry)* 2.52
"Do The Strand" *(Ferry)* 3.46 (Edit)
"These Foolish Things" *(Maschwitz/Strackey)* 4.49 (Edit)
"Street Life" *(Ferry)* 3.29
"Let's Stick Together" (Harrison) 2.59
"Smoke Gets In Your Eyes" *(Kern/Harbach)* 2.53
"Love Is The Drug" *(Ferry/Mackay)* 4.04
"Sign Of The Times" *(Ferry)* 2.27
"Dance Away" *(Ferry)* 3.44
"Angel Eyes" *(Ferry/Mackay)* 2.51
"Oh Yeah" *(Ferry)* 4.36 (Edit)
"Over You" *(Ferry/Manzanera)* 3.26
"Same Old Scene" *(Ferry)* 3.58
"In The Midnight Hour" *(Cropper/Picket)* 3.08
"More Than This" *(Ferry)* 4.10
"Avalon" *(Ferry)* 4.16
"Slave To Love" *(Ferry)* 4.17
"Jealous Guy" *(Lennon)* 4.56 (Edit)

Title	*The Ultimate Collection*
Catalogue No.	EG EGTV2
Release Date	November 1988
UK chart position	6
Tracks	"Let's Stick Together" ('88 Remix) *(Harrison)* 2.54

"The 'In' Crowd" *(Page)* 4.33
"Dance Away" *(Ferry)* 3.44
"Angel Eyes" *(Ferry/Mackay)* 3.04
"He'll Have To Go" *(J&A Allison)* 4.02
"Tokyo Joe" *(Ferry)* 3.54
"All I Want Is You" *(Ferry)* 2.50
"Jealous Guy" *(Lennon)* 6.11
"The Price Of Love" *(P&D Everly)* 3.23
"Don't Stop The Dance" *(Ferry/Davies)* 4.20
"Love Is The Drug" *(Ferry/Mackay)* 4.02
"This Is Tomorrow" *(Ferry)* 3.35
"Slave To Love" *(Ferry)* 4.26
"Help Me" *(Ferry/Rodgers)* 4.36
"Avalon" *(Ferry)* 4.13

Title	*More Than This*
Catalogue No.	Virgin CDV 2791
Release Date	October 1995
UK chart position	15
Tracks	"Virginia Plain" *(Ferry)* 2.56

"A Hard Rain's A-Gonna Fall" *(Dylan)* 4.15 (Edit)
"Street Life" *(Ferry)* 3.29
"These Foolish Things" *(Maschwitz/Strackey)* 4.49 (Edit)
"Love Is The Drug" *(Ferry/Mackay)* 4.07
"Smoke Gets In Your Eyes" *(Kern/Harbach)* 2.53
"Dance Away" *(Ferry)* 3.44
"Let's Stick Together" 2.59
"Angel Eyes" *(Ferry/Mackay)* 2.51
"Slave To Love" *(Ferry)* 4.17
"Oh Yeah" *(Ferry)* 4.36 (Edit)
"Don't Stop The Dance" *(Ferry/Davies)* 4.20
"Same Old Scene" *(Ferry)* 3.58
"Is Your Love Strong Enough?" *(Ferry)* 4.56

"Jealous Guy" *(Lennon)* 4.56 (Edit)
"Kiss And Tell" *(Ferry)* 3.59 (Edit)
"More Than This" *(Ferry)* 4.10
"I Put A Spell On You" *(Hawkins)* 3.55 (Edit)
"Avalon" *(Ferry)* 4.16
"Your Painted Smile" *(Ferry)* 3.13

Title	*Slave To Love: The Best Of The Ballads*
Catalogue No.	Virgin 7243 8 49585 2 7
Release Date	July 2002
UK chart position	11
Tracks	"Slave To Love" *(Ferry)* 4.17

"Jealous Guy" *(Lennon)* 4.56
"This Love" *(Armstrong/Burns)* 4.39
"More Than This" *(Ferry)* 4.10
"Falling In Love Again" *(Hollander/Connelly)* 2.27
"Smoke Gets in Your Eyes" *(Kern/Harbach)* 2.53
"Will You Still Love Me Tomorrow" *(Goffin/King)* 4.17
"Oh Yeah" *(Ferry)* 4.36 (Edit)
"Is Your Love Strong Enough?" *(Ferry)* 4.56
"Zamba" *(Ferry)* 3.00
"These Foolish Things" *(Maschwitz/Strackey)* 4.49
(Edit)
"Crazy Love" *(V. Morrison)* 4.30
"Sonnet 18" *(Shakespeare/Kamen)* 2.52
"Avalon" *(Ferry)* 4.16
"Where Or When" *(Rogers/Hart)* 3.20
"To Turn You On" *(Ferry)* 4.15
"Windswept" *(Ferry)* 4.23
"My Only Love" *(Ferry)* 5.16

Bryan Ferry Singles

7" single

Tracks	"A Hard Rain's A-Gonna Fall" (Dylan) 5.20 c/w "2 HB" *(Ferry)*
Catalogue No.	Island WIP 6170
Release Date	September 1973
UK chart position	10

7" single

Tracks   "I Love How You Love Me" c/w "2HB" *(Ferry)*

Catalogue No.   Island 6138 035 (France)

7" single

Tracks   "The 'In' Crowd" *(Page)* c/w "Chance Meeting"
                     (Ferry)

Catalogue No.   Island WIP 6196

Release Date   May 1974

UK chart position 13

7" single

Tracks   "Smoke Gets In Your Eyes" *(Kern/Harbach)* c/w
                     "Another Time, Another Place" *(Ferry)*

Catalogue No.   Island WIP 6205

Release Date   August 1974

UK chart position 17

7" single

Tracks   "You Go To My Head" *(Gillespie/Coots)* 2.47 c/w
                     "Re-Make/Re-Model" 2.42 *(Ferry)*

Catalogue No.   Island WIP 6234

Release Date   June 1975

UK chart position 33

7" single

Tracks   "Let's Stick Together" *(Harrison)* c/w "Sea Breezes"
                     (Ferry)

Catalogue No.   Island WIP 6307

Release Date   June 1976

UK chart position 4

"Extended Play" EP

Tracks   "The Price Of Love" *(Everly/Everly)* "Shame Shame
                     Shame" *(Reed)* c/w "It's Only Love" *(Lennon/
                     McCartney)* "Heart On My Sleeve" *(Gallagher/Lyle)*

Catalogue No.   Island 1EP1

Release Date   August 1976

UK chart position 7

7" single

Tracks   "The Price Of Love" *(Everly/Everly)* c/w "Another Time Another Place" *(Ferry)*

Catalogue No.   Island 17309 AT (Germany)

7" single

Tracks   "Heart On My Sleeve" *(Gallagher/Lyle)* c/w "Re-Make/Re-Model" *(Ferry)*

Catalogue No.   Atlantic 45-3364 (USA)

7" single

Tracks   "This Is Tomorrow" *(Ferry)* c/w "As The World Turns" *(Ferry/Jobson)*

Catalogue No.   Polydor 2001 704

Release Date   February 1977

UK chart position 9

7" single

Tracks   "Tokyo Joe" *(Ferry)* c/w " She's Leaving Home" *(Lennon/McCartney)*

Catalogue No.   Polydor 2001 711

Release Date   May 1977

UK chart position 15

7" single

Tracks   "What Goes On" *(Reed)* c/w "Casanova" *(Ferry)*

Catalogue No.   Polydor POSP 3

Release Date   May 1978

UK chart position 67

7" single

Tracks   "Sign Of The Times" *(Ferry)* c/w "Four Letter Love" *(Ferry)*

Catalogue No.   Polydor 2001 798

Release Date   August 1978

UK chart position 37

7" single

Tracks   "Carrickfergus" *(Trad: Arranged by Ferry)* c/w "When She Walks In The Room" *(Ferry)*

Catalogue No.   Polydor/EG 2001 834

Release Date   October 1978

7" single

Tracks   "Slave To Love" *(Ferry)* 3.59 c/w "Valentine (Instrumental)" *(Ferry)* 4.09

Catalogue No.   EG FERRY 1

Release Date   April 1985

UK chart position 10

12" single

Tracks   "Slave To Love (Extended)" *(Ferry)* 5.48 c/w "Valentine (Instrumental)" *(Ferry)* 4.09 "Slave To Love (Instrumental)" *(Ferry)* 4.17

Catalogue No.   FERRYX 1

Release Date   April 1985

7" single

Tracks   "Don't Stop The Dance" (Ferry/Davies) 3.57 c/w "Nocturne" *(Ferry)* 4.42

Catalogue No.   EG FERRY 2

Release Date   August 1985

UK chart position 21

12" single

Tracks   "Don't Stop The Dance (Extended)" 5.45 *(Ferry/Davies)* c/w "Nocturne" *(Ferry)* 4.42 "Don't Stop The Dance (Instrumental)" 4.20

Catalogue No.   EG FERRX 2

Release Date   August 1985

7" single

Tracks   "Windswept" *(Ferry)* 4.34 c/w "Crazy Love" *(Morrison)* 4.31

Catalogue No.   EG FERRY 3

Release Date   November 1985

UK chart position 46

Tracks

7" EP

"Windswept" *(Ferry)* 4.34 "Crazy Love" *(Morrison)* 4.31 c/w "Feel The Need" *(Tilman)* 4.33 "Broken Wings" *(Ferry) 3.02*

Catalogue No. EG FEREP 3

Release Date November 1985

Tracks

12" single

"Windswept" *(Ferry)* 4.34 "Crazy Love" *(Morrison)* 4.31 c/w "Feel The Need" *(Tilman)* 4.33 "Broken Wings" *(Ferry) 3.02*

Catalogue No. EG FERRX 3

Release Date November 1985

Tracks

7" single

"Is Your Love Strong Enough?" *(Ferry)* 4.55 c/w "Windswept (Instrumental)" *(Ferry)* 4.30

Catalogue No. EG FERRY 4

Release Date March 1986

UK chart position 22

Tracks

12" single

"Is Your Love Strong Enough? (Extended)" *(Ferry)* 7.06 c/w "Windswept (Instrumental)" *(Ferry)* 4.30 "Is Your Love Strong Enough?" *(Ferry)* 4.55

Catalogue No. EG FERRX 4

Release Date March 1986

Tracks

7" single

"Help Me" *(Ferry/Rodgers)* 4.36 c/w "Broken Wings" *(Ferry)* 3.00

Catalogue No. Warner/EG 28582-7 (USA)

Tracks

7" single

"The Right Stuff" *(Ferry/Marr)* 4.22 c/w "The Right Stuff (Brooklyn Mix)" *(Ferry/Marr)* 4.25

Catalogue No. Virgin VS 940

Release Date September 1987

UK chart position 37

12" single

Tracks "The Right Stuff (Extended)" *(Ferry/Marr)* c/w "The Right Stuff (Dub Mix)" "The Right Stuff (Album Mix)" *(Ferry/Marr)*

Catalogue No. Virgin VS 940 12

Release Date September 1987

CD single

Tracks "The Right Stuff" *(Ferry/Marr)* 4.22 "The Right Stuff" 6.33 (Long Version) *(Ferry/Marr)* "The Right Stuff (Dub Mix)" *(Ferry/Marr)* 6.06

Catalogue No. Virgin CDEP 8

Cassette single

Tracks "The Right Stuff" *(Ferry/Marr)* 4.22 "The Right Stuff" 6.33 (Long Version) *(Ferry/Marr)* "The Right Stuff (Dub Mix)" *(Ferry/Marr)* 6.06

Catalogue No. Virgin VSC 940 12

7" single

Tracks "Kiss And Tell" *(Ferry)* 4.04 c/w "Zamba" *(Ferry/Leonard)* 3.00

Catalogue No. Virgin VS 1034

Release Date February 1988

UK chart position 41

12" single

Tracks "Kiss And Tell (Dance Mix)" c/w "Kiss And Tell (Dub Mix)" "Zamba" *(Ferry/Leonard)*

Catalogue No. Virgin VST 1034

Release Date February 1988

CD single

Tracks "Kiss And Tell" *(Ferry)* 4.04 "Kiss And Tell (Dub Mix)" *(Ferry)* 5.37 "Zamba" *(Ferry/Leonard)* 3.00 "Kiss And Tell (Dance Mix)" *(Ferry)* 7.02

Catalogue No. Virgin CDEP 19

Release Date February 1988

7" single

Tracks   "Limbo (Latin Mix)" *(Ferry/Leonard)* 4.05 c/w
"Limbo (Brooklyn Mix)" *(Ferry/Leonard)* 3.56

Catalogue No.   Virgin VS 1066

Release Date   June 1988

UK chart position   96

12" single

Tracks   "Limbo (Latin Mix)" *(Ferry/Leonard)* c/w "Bête
Noire (Instrumental)" *(Ferry/Leonard)* "Limbo
(Brooklyn Dub Mix)" *(Ferry/Leonard)*

Catalogue No.   Virgin VST 1006

Release Date   June 1988

CD single

Tracks   "Limbo (Latin Version) (Extended)" *(Ferry/Leonard)*
6.38 "Bête Noire (Instrumental)" *(Ferry/Leonard)*
5.01 "Limbo (Brooklyn Dub Mix)" *(Ferry/Leonard)*
8.19

Catalogue No.   Virgin VSCD 1066

Release Date   June 1988

7" single

Tracks   "Let's Stick Together (Westside '88 Remix)"
(Harrison) 2.54 c/w "Trash" *(Ferry/Manzanera)* 2.10

Catalogue No.   EG EGO 44

Release Date   October 1988

UK chart position   12

12" single

Tracks   "Let's Stick Together (Westside '88 Remix
Extended)" (Harrison) 5.12 "Trash"
(Ferry/Manzanera) 2.10 c/w "Shame Shame Shame"
(Reed) 3.15 "Angel Eyes (Extended)"
(Ferry/Mackay) 6.37

Catalogue No.   Virgin EGOX 44

Release Date   October 1988

CD single

Tracks "Let's Stick Together (Westside '88 Remix)" (Harrison) "Trash" *(Ferry/Manzanera)* 2.10 "Sign Of The Times" *(Ferry)* 2.27 "Casanova" *(Ferry)* 2.45

Catalogue No. Virgin EGOCD 44

Release Date October 1988

7" single

Tracks "The Price Of Love (R&B '89 Remix)" (Everly/Everly) c/w "Lover" *(Ferry/Manzanera)* 4.25

Catalogue No. EG EGO 46

Release Date January 1989

UK chart position 49

CD single

Tracks "The Price Of Love" (R&B '89 Remix) (Everly/Everly) 3.25 "Don't Stop The Dance (Extended)" *(Ferry/Davies)* 5.45 "Slave To Love (Extended)" *(Ferry)* 5.48 "Lover" *(Ferry/Manzanera)* 4.25

Catalogue No. EG EGO 46CD

Release Date January 1989

12" single

Tracks "The Price Of Love (R&B '89 Remix Extended)" 5.21 "Lover" *(Ferry/Manzanera)* 4.25 c/w "Don't Stop The Dance (Extended)" 5.45 *(Ferry/Davies)* "Nocturne"

Catalogue No. EG EGOX 46

Release Date January 1989

7" single

Tracks "He'll Have To Go" (Allison/Allison) 4.01 c/w "Carrickfergus" *(Trad: Arranged by Ferry)* 3.44

Catalogue No. EG EGO 48

Release Date April 1989

UK chart position 63

12" single

Tracks   "He'll Have To Go" (Allison/Allison) 4.01
"Carrickfergus" 3.44 c/w "Windswept" *(Ferry)* 4:34
"Is Your Love Strong Enough?" *(Ferry)* 4:55

Catalogue No.   EGOX 48

Release Date   April 1989

CD single

Tracks   "He'll Have To Go" (Allison/Allison) 4.01 "Take Me
To the River" *(Green/Hodges)* 4.26 "Broken Wings"
(Ferry) 3.00 "Carrickfergus" 3.44

Catalogue No.   EGOCD 48

Release Date   April 1989

7" single

Tracks   "I Put A Spell On You" *(Hawkins)* 3.55 c/w "These
Foolish Things" *(Maschwitz/Strackey)* 5:41

Catalogue No.   Virgin VS 1400

Release Date   February 1993

UK chart position   18

Cassette single

Tracks   "I Put A Spell On You" *(Hawkins)* 3.55 c/w "These
Foolish Things" *(Maschwitz/Strackey)* 5:41

Catalogue No.   Virgin VSX 1400

Release Date   February 1993

CD single

Tracks   "I Put A Spell On You (Single Mix)" *(Hawkins)* 3.55
(remixed by Bob Clearmountain) "I Put A Spell On
You (Yage Mix)" 5.17 (remixed by Future Sound of
London) "I Put A Spell On You (Haunted House
Mix)" 7.25 (remixed by Sven Taits) "I Put A Spell On
You (Yage Mix Long Version)" 10.00 (remixed by
Future Sound of London) "I Put A Spell On You
(Council House Mix)" 5.50 (remixed by Richard
Norris/Sven Taits)

Catalogue No.   VSCDG 1400

Release Date   February 1993

Tracks

CD Single 2 (disc 1 of The Archive And Live Collection)
"I Put A Spell On You (Single Mix Long Version)"
(Hawkins) 5.09 (remixed by Bob Clearmountain)
"These Foolish Things" (Maschwitz/Strackey) 5.41
"Ladytron (Live)" (Ferry) 7.23 "While My Heart Is
Still Beating" (Live) (Ferry/Mackay) 5.18

Catalogue No. VSCDX 1400

7" single

Tracks "Will You Love Me Tomorrow (Single Mix)"
(Goffin/King) 4.08 c/w "A Hard Rain's A-Gonna
Fall" (Dylan) 5.19

Catalogue No. VS 1455
Release Date May 1993
UK chart position 23

Cassette single

Tracks "Will You Love Me Tomorrow (Single Mix)"
(Goffin/King) 4.08 c/w "A Hard Rain's A-Gonna
Fall" (Dylan) 5.19

Catalogue No. VSC 1455
Release Date May 1993

CD single 1

Tracks "Will You Love Me Tomorrow (Single Mix)"
(Goffin/King) 4.08 "Crazy Love (Morrison) 4.31 "Feel
the Need" (Tilman) 4.29 "A Hard Rain's A-Gonna
Fall" (Dylan) 5.19

Catalogue No. VSCDG 1455

CD Single 2 (Disc 2 of The Archive And Live
Collection)

Tracks "Will You Love Me Tomorrow (Single Mix Long
Version)" (Goffin/King) 6.05 "A Hard Rain's A-
Gonna Fall" (Dylan) 5.19 "A Waste Land (Live)"
(Ferry) 0.53 "Windswept" (Live) (Ferry) 5:02

Catalogue No. VSCDT 1455

7" single

Tracks	"Girl Of My Best Friend" *(Ross/Bobrick)* 3.24 c/w "Are You Lonesome Tonight?" *(Turk/Handman)* 5.08
Catalogue No.	VS 1468
Release Date	September 1993
UK chart position	57

Cassette single

Tracks	"Girl Of My Best Friend" *(Ross/Bobrick)* 3.24 c/w "Are You Lonesome Tonight?" *(Turk/Handman)* 5.08
Catalogue No.	VSC 1468
Release Date	September 1993

CD single 1

Tracks	"Girl Of My Best Friend" *(Ross/Bobrick)* 3.24 "Nocturne *(Ferry)* 4.42 "Are You Lonesome Tonight?" 5.08 "Valentine (Instrumental)" *(Ferry)* 4.09
Catalogue No.	VSCDG 1468
Release Date	September 1993

CD single 2

Tracks	"Girl Of My Best Friend" *(Ross/Bobrick)* 3.24 "Let's Stick Together" *(Harrison)* 2.57 "Boys And Girls (Live)" *(Ferry)* 7.02 "The Bogus Man (Live)" *(Ferry)* 5.01
Catalogue No.	VSCDT 1468
Release Date	September 1993

7" single

Tracks	"Your Painted Smile" *(Ferry)* 3.13 c/w "Don't Stop The Dance (Live)" *(Ferry/Davies)* 4:07
Catalogue No.	Virgin VS 1508
Release Date	October 1994
UK chart position	52

Cassette single

Tracks	"Your Painted Smile" *(Ferry)* 3.13 c/w "Don't Stop The Dance (Live)" *(Ferry/Davies)* 4:07
Catalogue No.	Virgin VSC 1508
Release Date	October 1994

CD single

Tracks   "Your Painted Smile" *(Ferry)* 3.13 "Don't Stop The Dance (Live) *(Ferry/Davies) 4:07* "In Every Dream Home A Heartache (Live)" *(Ferry)* 7:27 "Bête Noire" (Live)" *(Ferry)* 3:57

Catalogue No.   Virgin VSCDG 1508

Release Date   October 1994

CD single

Tracks   "Mamouna (single edit)" *(Ferry)* 3.44 "Jealous Guy (Live) *(Lennon)* 5:20 "Slave To Love (Live)" *(Ferry)* 4:37 "The 39 Steps (Brian Eno Mix)" *(Ferry)* 5.48

Catalogue No.   Virgin VSCDG 1528

Release Date   January 1995

UK chart position 57

Cassette single

Tracks   "Mamouna (single edit)" *(Ferry)* 3.44 c/w "The 39 Steps (Brian Eno Mix)" *(Ferry)* 5.48

Catalogue No.   Virgin VSC 1528

Release Date   January 1995

CD single

Tracks   "As Time Goes By" *(Hupfield)* 2.35 "Falling In Love Again" *(Hollander/Connelly)* 2.27 "If I Didn't Care" *(Lawrence)* 2.54

Catalogue No.   Virgin 8962522

Release Date   October 1999

UK chart position 108

CD single

Tracks   "Goddess Of Love" *(Ferry/Stewart)* 3.32 "Which Way To Turn" *(Ferry)* 5.44 "Smoke Dreams Of You" *(Gibsone/De Granville)* 2.52

Catalogue No.   Virgin DINSD238

Release Date   May 2002

UK chart position 82

CD single

Tracks   "A Fool For Love" *(Ferry) 4:43* "One Way Love" *(Russell/Meade)* 3:05

Catalogue No.   Virgin DINSDJ254
Release Date   December 2002

Videography

Title   *The High Road* – Roxy Music (video/laser disc/DVD/video CD)
Release Date   1983
Catalogue No.   PolyGram/4Front 083 576 3
Catalogue No.   Channel 5 CFV 00012
Running Time   75 minutes
Recorded at Frejus, France on August 27, 1982.
Tracks   "The Main Thing"
"Out Of The Blue"
"Both Ends Burning"
"A Song For Europe"
"Can't Let Go"
"While My Heart Is Still Beating"
"Avalon"
"Dance Away"
"Love Is The Drug"
"My Only Love"
"Like A Hurricane"
"Editions Of You"
"Do The Strand"
"Jealous Guy"

Title   *New Town* – Bryan Ferry (video)
Release Date   1990
Catalogue No.   Virgin Video VVD 609
Running Time   88 minutes
New Town – the European leg of Bryan Ferry's 1988/89 World Tour (was filmed over several shows).
Tracks   "Nimrod"
"Limbo"
"The Chosen One"
"Casanova"

"Slave To Love"
"The Bogus Man"
"Ladytron"
"While My Heart Is Still Beating"
"Don't Stop The Dance"
"A Waste Land"
"Windswept"
"In Every Dream Home A Heartache"
"New Town"
"Boys And Girls"
"Kiss And Tell"
"Love Is The Drug"
"Avalon"
"Do The Strand"

Title	*Total Recall* – Roxy Music (video/laser disc)
Release Date	1990
Catalogue No.	Virgin Video VVD 649
Running Time	90 minutes
	Total Recall is a collection of excerpts from performances from TV, live shows and promotional videos. Some tracks have a custom-made visual created from images from the album sleeve artwork and unreleased artwork.
Tracks	"Re-Make/Re-Model"

"The Bob (Medley)"
"Ladytron"
"If There Is Something"
"Virginia Plain"
"Would You Believe?"
"For Your Pleasure"
"In Every Dream Home A Heartache"
"Do The Strand"
"Editions Of You"
"These Foolish Things"
"The Paw Paw Negro Blowtorch"
"Wild Weekend"
"A Hard Rain's A-Gonna Fall"
"Street Life"
"A Song For Europe"

"Smoke Gets In Your Eyes"
"It Ain't Me Babe"
"A Really Good Time"
"All I Want Is You"
"Diamond Head"
"You Go To My Head"
"Whirlwind"
"Love Is The Drug"
"Both Ends Burning"
"Let's Stick Together"
"Baby's On Fire"
"The Price Of Love"
"In Your Mind"
"Trash"
"Dance Away"
"Angel Eyes"
"Ain't That So"
"Same Old Scene"
"Oh Yeah"
"Jealous Guy"
"Avalon"
"The Main Thing"
"Can't Let Go"
"Slave To Love"

Title	*On The Road* – Roxy Music (video/laser disc/DVD)
Release Date	1992
Running Time	60 minutes
	Recorded at the Manchester Apollo by Granada TV in 1979.
Tracks	"Manifesto"
	"Song For Europe"
	"Still Falls The Rain"
	"Mother Of Pearl"
	"In Every Dream Home A Heartache"
	"Ain't That So"
	"Love Is The Drug"
	"Editions Of You"
	"Re-Make/Re-Model"
	"Virginia Plain"

Title	*Bryan Ferry & Roxy Music: The Video Collection* (video/DVD)
Release Date	1995
Catalogue No.	Virgin Video VID 2791
Running Time	98 minutes
	A collection of promotional videos by both Bryan Ferry and Roxy Music.
Tracks	"Your Painted Smile"
	"Same Old Scene"
	"Limbo"
	"These Foolish Things"
	"Re-Make/Re-Model"
	"Will You Love Me Tomorrow"
	"Let's Stick Together"
	"Windswept"
	"A Hard Rain's A-Gonna Fall"
	"Slave To Love"
	"The Right Stuff"
	"What Goes On"
	"Is Your Love Strong Enough?"
	"The Price Of Love"
	"Angel Eyes"
	"Don't Stop The Dance"
	"You Go To My Head"
	"I Put A Spell On You"
	"The Main Thing"
	"Girl Of My Best Friend"
	"Kiss And Tell"
	"Don't Want To Know"
	"Mamouna"

Title	*Psalm* (video/CD)
Release Date	1997
	Double CD CD1 Audio CD2 Video (for use on PC) This CD is an audio/video recording from the German TV show *Musikladen* in 1973-1974.
Tracks	"A Hard Rain's A-Gonna Fall"
	"If It Takes All Night"
	"Out Of The Blue"

"Psalm"
"Street Life"
"Virginia Plain"

Title	*Valentine* (video/CD)
Release Date	2000
	This Video CD (for PC) released by the Burning Airlines label features tracks filmed on German TV's *Musikladen* in the seventies.
Tracks	"Do The Strand"
	"Street Life"
	"In Every Dream Home A Heartache"
	"Re-Make/Re-Model"
	"All I Want Is You"
	"Virginia Plain"

Title	*Live In Paris At The Grand Rex* – Bryan Ferry (DVD)
Release Date	2001
Catalogue No.	Virgin DVD 7243 492466 9 0
	Bryan Ferry recorded on March 9, 2000 on his *As Time Goes By* tour.
Tracks	"The Way You Look Tonight"
	"Love Me Or Leave Me"
	"Smoke Gets In Your Eyes"
	"Chance Meeting"
	"Casanova"
	"Where Or When"
	"Bittersweet"
	"Out Of The Blue"
	"The Only Face"
	"Oh Yeah"
	"You Do Something To Me"
	"Just One Of Those Things"
	"Avalon"
	"Jealous Guy"
	"Let's Stick Together"
	"Love Is The Drug"

Title	*Vintage* (video/CD)
Release Date	2001

This is a compilation Roxy Music album of five songs recorded live in Bremen in 1973-4. It includes videos of all the performances.

Tracks
"Out Of The Blue"
"Psalm"
"If It Takes All Night"
"Editions Of You"
"A Hard Rain's A-Gonna Fall"

Title	*Roxy Music Live At The Apollo* (video/DVD)
Release Date	2002

Roxy Music's final 2001 show at the Hammersmith Apollo, London. The DVD has a bonus documentary featuring interviews with Bryan Ferry, Phil Manzanera, Andy MacKay, Paul Thompson and Chris Spedding, and footage from backstage and at rehearsals for the tour.

Tracks
"Re-Make/Re-Model"
"Street Life"
"Ladytron"
"While My Heart Is Still Beating"
"Out Of The Blue"
"A Song For Europe"
"My Only Love"
"In Every Dream Home A Heartache"
"Oh Yeah"
"Both Ends Burning"
"Tara"
"Mother Of Pearl"
"Avalon"
"Dance Away"
"Jealous Guy"
"Editions Of You"
"Virginia Plain"
"Love Is The Drug"
"Do The Strand"
"For Your Pleasure"

INDEX